Sex, Politics and Society

Themes in British Social History

edited by Dr J. Stevenson

Sex, Politics and Society

The regulation of sexuality since 1800

Jeffrey Weeks

Longman
London and New York

Longman Group Limited
Longman House
Burnt Mill, Harlow, Essex, UK

Published in the United States of America
by Longman Inc., New York

© Longman Group Limited 1981

First published 1981

British Library Cataloguing in Publication Data

Weeks, Jeffrey
  Sex, politics and society. − (Themes in British
  social history).
  1. Sex customs − Great Britain − History
  I. Title II. Series
  301.41′7941   HQ18.G7   80−40862

  ISBN 0−582−48333−6
  ISBN 0−582−48334−4 Pbk

Printed in Singapore by Kyodo Shing Loong Printing Industries Pte Ltd

For my Mother,
And in memory of my Father

Contents

Preface

This book has had a long gestation, and is intended to sum up a great deal of original research and a wide reading in secondary material. But as the Belgian historian, Henri Pirenne, noted, every work of synthesis inspires a new crop of specialised research, and I am clearly aware of the provisional nature of this work, and the host of fresh questions it raises.

It should be said, however, that this book was never intended as a detailed or exhaustive account of all the multifarious patterns of sexual behaviour. It is in essence, as the title and subtitle imply, a discussion of the forces that have organised and regulated sexuality within a particular historical period (roughly the period of industrial capitalism) in a particular geographical and political area (Great Britain, and chiefly that part south of Scotland). But I hope that some of the conclusions suggested will have a wider resonance. Its working premise, set out in some detail in Chapter 1, is that 'sexuality' is not an unproblematic natural given, which the 'social' works upon to control, but is, on the contrary, an *historical* unity which has been shaped and determined by a multiplicity of forces, and which has undergone complex historical transformations.

In order to account for some of the changes that have taken place, the book, while largely chronological in form, avoids a simple narrative structure. It revolves around three broad issues: the meaning given to sexuality in Victorian society; the construction of sexuality as an area of social concern, scientific investigation and reforming endeavour in the late nineteenth and early twentieth centuries; and the place of sexuality in twentieth-century consciousness and social policy. In tackling these questions I am aware that I have ignored other domains of interest, and have bypassed other questions that might fruitfully have been discussed. My excuse is that my aim has been a modest, but I believe vitally important, one: to delineate the forces, ideas and social practices that have elevated sexuality into a prime focus of social concern over the past two hundred years.

Acknowledgements

I owe an enormous debt to a large number of people, though it goes without saying that no one apart from myself can be held responsible for the final shape of the book.

For encouragement, stimulation, moral support, intellectual sustenance and/or practical assistance I have to thank: Sally Alexander, Victor Bailey, Michèle Barrett, Gregg Blachford, Keith Birch, Sue Bruley, Colin Buckle, Bob Cant, Jane Caplan, Emmanuel Cooper, Ros Coward, Leonore Davidoff, Anna Davin, Barry Davis, Philip Derbyshire, Françoise Ducrocq, Annabel Faraday, Andy Fay, Kim Gale, Philip Jones, Jean L'Esperance, Jane Lewis, John Marshall, David Morgan, Frank Mort, Janet Parkin, Michael Rodgers, Sheila Rowbotham, Helen Rugen, Raphael Samuel, Ann Scott, Jo Sinclair, Lawrence Taylor, Lloyd Trott, Randolph Trumbach, Don Tylor, Judy Walkowitz, Simon Watney, Elizabeth Wilson, Roy Wolfe, Peter Wood, Nigel Young. Chris Cook provided the initial stimulus.

I owe a special debt to Mary McIntosh and Ken Plummer who gave me great encouragement and intellectual stimulation as colleagues and friends.

I have to thank all the librarians and archivists who assisted me, with especial thanks to the Departmental Record officer at the Home office who gave me access to hitherto unavailable files.

The Social Science Research Council provided generous financial support for research projects which usefully employed me for a number of years. By suddenly ending such support at a crucial time they also gave me the space to finish this book. I therefore owe them a double debt.

I have to thank John Stevenson, editor of this series, and the publishers, for their immense patience and support for a project which grew longer and took longer as the years went by.

Micky Burbidge and Angus Suttie lived with the enterprise from start to finish. I can simply thank them.

My greatest debt is to the dedicatees, who made the whole thing possible.

Chapter One

Sexuality and the historian

Histories of sex

Sex in history, an American historian remarked in the early 1970s, is a 'virgin field'. 'Historians have been reluctant', he went on, 'exceedingly reluctant, to deal with such a delicate topic.'[1] Since that was written much has changed. The new 'social history' has challenged our ignorance of the subject. Family reconstitution and literary archaeology have revealed a mountain of more or less valuable information. Simultaneously the sexual radical movements of the 1970s have undermined our preconception of the 'naturalness' and inevitability of contemporary gender roles and sexual attitudes. So (to continue the metaphor) the territory now has flourishing settlements; there is a healthy interest in exploration. But what is still lacking is any general survey of the terrain. That, in part, is the purpose of this book.

Historical explorations of sexuality are not of course new. Specialised studies of sex as a social experience have been appearing for almost a hundred years, since at least the time of the great pioneering sexologists and anthropologists of the late nineteenth century; and what appeared then were works which have been profoundly influential, not only in describing but in constructing and delineating the areas to be discussed. The aim of this chapter is to question the subject matter that they so confidently explored, for it is by no means clear what we mean when we raise the prospect of 'a history of sexuality'. The usual assumption is that sex is a definable and universal experience, like the desire for food, with the minority or unorthodox forms filtering off into distributaries, which may, or more usually may not, be navigated by the conscientious explorer. I want to suggest that it is the centrality given to this concept of sexuality that constitutes a problem for historians, for it ignores the great variety of cultural patterns that history reveals, and the very different meanings given to what we blithely label as 'sexual activity'.

In most historical works on the topic of sex there have been two broad approaches, though they are not mutually exclusive, and there has, in practice, been a considerable overlap between the two.[2] The first I would label the 'naturalist' approach, and the classic British example is the highly influential work of Havelock Ellis, especially his majestic *Studies in the Psychology of Sex*. This is a vast and still very valuable chronicle of sexual behaviour and beliefs, essentially descriptive in form, ostensibly classifying and categorising sexual forms that exist 'in nature'. Most works since, whether detailed monographs, or general cross-cultural surveys, have taken for granted the merits of such an approach, and the result had been an extremely important garnering of sexual knowledge. What it has not been able to do is provide a coherent explanation of the variations it often describes, nor account for changes in *mores* and consciousness.

The second broad approach is what Kenneth Plummer has labelled the 'meta-theoretical',[3] and usually derives from a psychodynamic or neo- (or even would-be) Freudian theory. Psycho-history no doubt has its value, and can often provide valuable insights, but its major difficulty (the opposite of the naturalistic problem) is that by and large theoretical constructs take precedence over empirical evidence. The dangers of such an approach can be seen at its most extreme in Gordon Rattray Taylor's neo-Freudian interpretation of *Sex in History*: 'The history of civilisation is the history of a long warfare between the dangerous and powerful drives and the systems of taboos and inhibitions which man has erected to control them'.[4] He develops a theory which accounts for changing attitudes in terms of largely unexplained swings between 'matrist' and 'patrist' cultures, leaving us with a grandiloquent but unsubstantiated cyclical theory of social change. Such an approach has been influential even amongst professional historians, so that Lawrence Stone, for example, hints at such a cyclical explanation in his own work on *The Family, Sex and Marriage*: 'In terms of both sexual attitudes and power relationships, one can dimly begin to discern huge, mysterious, secular swings from repression to permissiveness and back again.'[5] Even such a sensitive cultural critic as Steven Marcus in *The Other Victorians* relies on a Freudian explanation, which by and large distorts rather than clarifies. In a prefatory motto for the book he quotes from Freud to the effect that 'perhaps we must make up our minds to the idea that altogether it is not possible for the claims of the sexual instincts to be reconciled with the demands of culture.'[6] So Marcus's explanation of nineteenth-century pornography, for instance, is in terms of this conflict between the overpowering demands of the sexual drive and a social fabric disrupted by massive change.

What we have in both the approaches is an 'essentialist' view of sexuality; sex conceptualised as an overpowering force in the individual that shapes not only the personal but the social life as well. It is seen as a driving, instinctual force, whose characteristics are built into the biology of the human animal, which shapes human institutions and whose will must force its way out, either in the form of direct sexual expression or, if blocked, in the form of perversion or neuroses. Krafft-Ebing expressed the orthodox view in the late nineteenth century when he described sex as a 'natural instinct' which 'with all conquering force and might demands fulfilment'. It is, we might note, a basically male drive. It is also a firmly heterosexual drive. William McDougall in the 1920s spoke representatively of the 'innate direction of the sex impulse towards the opposite sex'.[7] Few have risked challenging this.

What we have then, is a clear notion of a 'basic biological mandate' that presses on, and so must be firmly controlled by the cultural and social matrix. Such an approach has the merits of appearing commonsensical, according with our own intimate experiences. And it has largely been unquestioned until recently in the work of most theorists of sex, from naturalists and Freudians to taxonomists like Alfred Kinsey (in his concept of 'sexual outlet') and the research clinicians such as William Masters and Virginia Johnson (in their descriptions of physiological responses). Moreover, the instinctual (or 'drive reduction') model has been embraced by all shades of opinion, from the conservative moralist anxious to control this unruly force to the Freudian left (Wilhelm Reich, Herbert Marcuse, Erich Fromm) wanting to 'liberate' sexuality from its capitalist and patriarchal constraints.

Against this, J.H. Gagnon and William Simon have argued in their book *Sexual Conduct* that sexuality is subject to 'socio-cultural moulding to a degree surpassed by few other forms of human behaviour',[8] and in so arguing they are building both on a century of sex research and on a century of questioning the notion of 'natural man'. Over the past few decades, in particular, in structuralist anthropology, psychoanalysis, and Marxist theory, there has been a major theoretical effort to challenge the naturalness of the 'unitary subject' in social theory, to see the individual as a product of social forces, an 'ensemble of social relations', rather than as a simple natural unity. 'Sexuality' has in many ways been most resistant to this challenge, precisely because its power seems to derive from our biological being, but there have recently been several sustained challenges to sexual essentialism, from quite different theoretical approaches: the interactionist (associated particularly with the work of Gagnon and Simon, and in Britain Kenneth Plummer); the psychoanalytic (associated with the reinterpretation of Freud initiated by Jacques Lacan, and taken up by feminist writers such as Juliet Mitchell); and the discursive, taking as its starting point the work of Michel Foucault.[9] Between them they have posed formidable challenges to our received notions of sexuality, challenges which historians are duty bound to confront and respond to.

Despite their different approaches, and in the end different aims, their work converges on several important issues. Firstly, they all reject sex as an autonomous realm, a natural force with specific effects, a 'rebellious energy' which the 'social' controls. In the work of Gagnon and Simon, it seems to be suggested that nothing is intrinsically sexual, or rather that anything can be sexualised (though what creates the notion of 'sexuality' itself is never answered). In Jacques Lacan's reinterpretation of Freud, sexuality, or rather sexual desire, is constituted in language: it is the law of the Father, the castration fear, and the pained entry of the child into the 'symbolic order', that is the world of language and meaning, at the Oedipal moment, which instigates 'desire'.

In Foucault's work 'sexuality' is seen as an historical apparatus, and 'sex' is a 'complex idea that was formed within the deployment of sexuality': '*Sexuality* must not be thought of as a kind of natural given which power tries to hold in check, or as an obscure domain which knowledge gradually tries to uncover. It is the name that can be given to a historical construct.'[10]

It is not fully clear what are the elements on which these social constructs of sexuality play. In the psychoanalytic school, there is the notion of the 'component instincts' which are unified in the complex process of acculturation, though the issue is complicated by a transhistorical concept of the Oedipus complex which, it is argued, is basic to all culture, or in Juliet Mitchell's version, patriarchal culture. Gagnon and Simon (and Plummer) seem to accept the existence of bodily potentialities on which 'sexuality' draws, and in this they do not seem far removed from Foucault's version that what 'sexuality' plays upon are 'bodies, organs, somatic localisations, functions, anatamo-physiological systems, sensations, and pleasures', which have no intrinsic unity or 'laws' of their own.[11] In other words, they are unified only through ideological constructs ('scripts' in the terms of Gagnon and Simon), and it is these that constitute 'sexuality'.

Secondly, then, what links the anti-essentialist critique is a recognition of the social and historical sources of sexual definitions. In the feminist appropriation of Lacan this can be seen as a result of patriarchal structures, and the differential entry into the world of language of the human male and female. But this as I have suggested poses massive theoretical problems, particularly in the attempt at a materialist position which would locate variations within changing social relations. The problem here is that the *transhistorical* account of the Oedipal crisis and the consequent focusing on the eternal problems of the shaping of sex and gender already presupposes the existence of basic drives which are outside culture. On the other hand, both the interactionists and Foucault make clear the historical specificity of Western concepts of sexuality. Gagnon and Simon suggest that: 'To earlier societies it may not have been a need to constrain severely the powerful sexual impulse in order to maintain social stability or limit inherently anti-social force, *but rather a matter of having to invent an importance for sexuality*'.[12] The mechanisms of this 'invention' are not specified but the stress is important. Foucault makes a much clearer, though controversial, historical specification and locates the rise of the 'sexuality apparatus' in the eighteenth century, linked with identifiable historical processes.

As a consequence of this concept of an historical construction of sexuality, a third point of contact lies in the rejection, both by the interactionists and Foucault, of the notion that the history of sexuality – especially in the nineteenth century – can fruitfully be seen in terms of 'repression'. Foucault is most explicit on this, arguing that what he terms the 'repressive hypothesis' regarding Victorian sexuality is misleading: because it points to too narrow an interpretation of the family; because it avoids class differentiation; and because it is based on a negative rather than positive concept of power. Gagnon and Simon have been less historically specific, but both interactionists and Foucault tend to the view that sexual behaviour is organised not through mechanisms of 'repression' but through powers of 'incitement', definition and regulation. More specifically, both approaches stress the central organising role of sexual categorisation and the various social practices that sustain the categories. So, for instance, the definitions of 'normality' and 'abnormality' are clearly social definitions but so are such descriptions as 'homosexual', 'paedophile', 'transvestite', and so on, and these can act as mechanisms of control. Though neither the interactionists nor Foucault make much of the point (the first leaning towards an essentialist view of gender, the latter showing little theoretical interest in the issue), this also points to the importance of categorisation along lines of gender; the construction, in other words, of categories of masculinity and femininity, building on obvious biological differences, but reinforcing these through ideology and various social practices. In the case of Gagnon and Simon and those influenced by them (such as Kenneth Plummer), the theoretical framework derives from Meadean social psychology, which sees the individual as having a developing personality which is created in an interaction with others; and from labelling theories of deviance, which concentrate on the public processes of stigmatisation. In the case of Foucault, it derives from his belief that it is through 'discourses', ensembles of beliefs, concepts, organising ideas, that our relation to reality is organised. The significance of both approaches is the challenge they gave to the 'naturalness' of what appear as basic divisions.

Fourthly, however, in all three tendencies there is a curious relationship to history which makes their easy assimilation into historical research difficult. Symbolic interactionism, by stressing the subjective and the impact of particular labelling events, has almost invariably displayed an ahistorical bias. The psychoanalytical school, almost by definition has based itself on supra-historical assumptions which have been almost valueless in detailed analyses. Foucault, and those influenced by him, have displayed a great scepticism about the possibilities of a conventional history: Foucault stresses that his work is basically aimed at constructing a 'genealogy', the locating of the 'traces' of the present rather than reconstructing the past. It is basically a 'history of the present', a concept which poses problems of its own.[13]

Each of the approaches has nevertheless proved stimulating to historians. The interactionist approach has, for instance, been very important in explorations of 'deviant' or unorthodox sexuality, particularly directing researchers to the significance of labelling events and the importance of subcultural responses.[14] Its strengths – the stress on the subjective and the significance of individual meanings – have however been the obverse of its weakness, which is precisely the absence of any wider historical theory. The neo-psychoanalytic approach has offered a most important emphasis on psychological structuring in the creation of historically specific forms of 'masculinity' and 'femininity' and has encouraged a break away from discussions in terms of social 'roles', with all that concept's inherent functionalism. But its full deployment demands – and to some extent is now getting – a greater historical specification than many devotees of psychoanalysis would regard as altogether orthodox or proper.

Foucault's work also offers a series of difficulties, in part relating to his lack of concern with those issues that precisely engage the other approaches: individual meanings and psychological structuring. But despite this, Foucault's essay on *The History of Sexuality* does offer a most stimulating challenge to traditional historical accounts, partly because of its undermining of conventional approaches, partly because it is an aspect of a much wider intellectual effort, whose implications are likely to be of major importance. Foucault's approach and analyses have also to some degree informed this work and for that reason alone deserve a critical appraisal. The following section therefore explores some of the implications of Foucault's work.

Sexuality and power

Michel Foucault is not the first to say many of the things he argues. His conclusions often overlap with those produced by other theoretical approaches, including, amongst others, the interactionist and labelling theories. His historical conclusions also articulate closely with the empirical research of recent social historians, particularly those influenced by feminism and the radical sexual movements. But his speculation – so far only seen in outline, in a methodological (and often polemical) essay rather than in a series of detailed studies – point to what I believe to be the correct questions even if he does not provide all the right answers. And the central point is the one captured in the English title of his work: *The History of Sexuality*. The definite article is important, for what it suggests is that the modern notion of sexuality – both the importance we assign to it, and the theoretical unification it implies – is an historical construct of the past few hundred years. The fundamental question, as posed by Foucault, is how is it that in our society sex is seen not just as a means of biological reproduction nor a source of harmless pleasure, but, on the contrary, has come to be seen as the central part of our being, the privileged site in which the truth of ourselves is to be found.

Foucault's recent work has been dominated by an explicit preoccupation with 'power', and in his *History* he argues that the apparatus of sexuality is of central importance in the modern play of power. His work at the same time marks a break with conventional theorisations of power. Power is not unitary, it does not reside in the state, it cannot be reduced to class relations; it is not something to hold or use. Power is, on the contrary, omnipresent, it is the intangible but forceful reality of social existence and of all social relations. Foucault is not interested in a grand theory of power, but in the 'concrete mechanisms and practices through which power is exercised'.[15] Power, that is to say, is not a single thing: it is relational, it is created in the relationships which sustain it.

Although he is unwilling to specify in advance any privileged source of power, there nevertheless underlies his work what has been described as a 'philosophical monism', a conception of a 'will to power' forever expanding and bursting forth in the form of a will to know. What Foucault is interested in is the complex of 'power–knowledge', the way in which power operates through the construction of particular knowledges. The French title of the first volume of his *History* sums up his preoccupation: *La Volonté de Savoir*, 'The will to know'.

It is through 'discourse' that power–knowledge is realised. Foucault is not interested, that is to say, in the history of mind but in the history of discourse. What he is suggesting is that the relationship between symbol and symbolised is not only referential, does not simply describe, but is productive, that is it creates. The history of sexuality becomes, therefore, a history of our discourses about sexuality. And the Western experience of sex, he argues, is not the inhibition of discourse, is not describable as a regime of silence, but is rather a constant, and historically changing, deployment of discourses on sex, and this ever-expanding discursive explosion is part of a complex growth of control over individuals through the apparatus of sexuality.

But behind the vast explosion of discourses on sexuality since the eighteenth century there is no single unifying strategy, valid for the whole of society. And in particular, breaking with what has become an orthodox Marxist problematic, he denies that the recent history of sexuality can be simply interpreted in terms of the 'reproduction' of capitalist social relations and labour power. In the *Introduction* to his *History of Sexuality* Foucault suggests four strategic unities, linking together a host of practices and techniques of power, which formed specific mechanics of knowledge and power centring on sex: a hysterisation of women's bodies; a pedagogisation of children's sex; a socialisation of procreative behaviour; a psychiatrisation of perverse pleasures. And four figures emerged from this preoccupation with sex, four objects of knowledge, four types of human subjects, subjected; targets of and anchorages for the categories which were being simultaneously investigated and regulated: the hysterical woman, the masturbating child, the Malthusian couple, and the perverse adult. The thrust of these discursive creations is control; control not through denial or prohibition, but through 'production', through imposing a grid of definition on the possibilities of the body. 'The deployment of sexuality has its reasons for

being, not in reproducing itself, but in proliferating, innovating, annex-
ing, creating, and penetrating bodies in an increasingly detailed way,
and in controlling populations in an increasingly comprehensive way.'[16]

This is obviously related to Foucault's analysis of the genealogy of
the disciplinary society, a society of surveillance and control, which he
sets out in his book *Discipline and Punish*, and to his argument that
power proceeds not in the traditional model of sovereignty (that is neg-
atively, 'thou shalt not') but through administering and fostering life
(that is positively, 'you must').[17] In the emergence of 'bio-power', Foucault's characteristic term for 'modern' social forms, sexuality becomes
a key element. For sex, argues Foucault, is the pivot of two axes along
which the whole technology of life developed: it was the point of entry
to the body, to the harnessing, identification and distribution of forces
over the body; and it was the entry to control and regulation of populations. 'Sex was a means of access both to the life of the body and the life
of the species.'[18] As a result, sex became a crucial target of power organised around the management of life rather than the sovereign threat
of death.

There are several problems in this approach. In the first place there
are difficulties with Foucault's view of power which, as one critic put it,
'remains almost as a process, without specification within different
instances'.[19] A notion of power which goes beyond, say, class re-
ductionism is obviously useful in attempting to grasp the history of the
subordination of women, or the regulation of unorthodox sexualities,
but if power is everywhere it is difficult to understand how it can be resisted or broken out of. 'Where there is power, there is resistance', Foucault argues, but nevertheless, because of this, 'resistance is never in a
position of exteriority in relation to power'.[20] Indeed, the very existence
of power relies on a multiplicity of points of resistance which play the
role of 'adversary, target, support or handle in power relations'. It is
difficult to resist the conclusion – which Foucault actually denies[21] –
that the techniques of discipline and surveillance, of individuation, and
the strategies of power–knowledge that subject us, leave us always
trapped. His emphasis on the growing importance of the 'norm' since
the eighteenth century is one index of the problem. He notes that
'Another consequence of this development of bio-power was the growing importance assumed by the action of the norm at the expense of the
juridical system of the law.'[22] In stressing the importance of the norm,
Foucault is pinpointing a vital aspect of social regulation, though his
comments are not new. On the one hand they have clear antecedents in
the more mundane observations of liberal historians that the development of an individualistic society in the nineteenth century led to an increase of conventionality. On the other hand, it is not far distant from
the theories developed by the Frankfurt School of Marxists in the 1930s
(and Foucault acknowledges his debt to them) about the internalisation
of bourgeois values. But in emphasising the role of the norm he is quite
consciously diminishing the role of the state – at least as expressed in its

legal apparatus – and in doing so he underplays its role in constructing attitudes to sexuality, through marriage laws, the regulation of deviance, the judiciary, the police, as well as, more generally, the education system, the welfare system, and so on. Regulation is exercised both through 'the norm' and through political power. Foucault would not, of course, deny this, but in stressing the 'norm' over the law there is a danger of ignoring important political transformations.

Secondly, there are difficulties with some of the assumptions in Foucault's challenge to the 'repressive hypothesis'. This has been invaluable in challenging simplicities about, say, the 'repression' of sexuality in nineteenth-century Europe, and in questioning the teleological view which sees a gradual climb towards permissiveness from Victorian darkness. His approach is particularly important in helping us to grasp that control is not just negative, and might in fact be just as tight today despite an ostensible 'liberalisation', that power over sexuality is not in the simple form of censorship and denial but in regulation and organisation, and that this takes many forms. But Foucault's formulation of the 'repressive hypothesis' seems to slide between the two usages.[23] On the one hand he is clearly, and correctly I think, rejecting a theory based on 'drive reduction' theories, where repression (as in the psychoanalytical usage) is the blocking or re-directing of sexual energy (the hydraulic model). But on the other hand, in doing this he is in danger of passing over altogether the notion of social 'repression'. It seems clear that at certain times some political and social regimes are more 'repressive', both ideologically and physically (as in the case of Nazi Germany) than others. The polemical rejection of the repression hypothesis obscures the very real formal controls that can be exercised, and were often implemented in nineteenth-century Europe.

Thirdly, there is, as has already been implied, a latent functionalism in Foucault's work. On the most general level Foucault's society of normalisation is in danger of being as rigidly functional, tending towards a necessary social equilbrium, as Talcott Parsons', particularly as both the resistances and the individual internalisations are not specified: social control seems to be absolute. Moreover, in the stress on the pluralism of institutions and practices that organise sexuality, he goes further towards a neo-functionalism, and Foucault at times seems in danger of meeting up, as Nicos Poulantzas has put it, 'with an old traditional of Anglo-Saxon sociology and political science, running from functionalism to institutionalism – from Parsons, to Merton, Dahl, Lasswell, and Etzioni – a tradition in which the centre of analysis is shifted from the state towards the "pluralism of micropowers".' Poulantzas goes on to say that it is ignorance of these writers, and the provincialism of the French intellectual arena, 'which allows these most hackneyed of ideas to be presented as something new.'[24] This is too harsh, but points to an important ambiguity in Foucault's work: the neologisms and allusive argument conceal an approximation to older theoretical traditions.

Finally, there is a latent essentialism in his work, and this comes out in his use of 'the body' as a final court of appeal, as that which is irreducible to power even as power invests it. For the implication of his theory of power is that if we break out of the regime of sexuality then power will play through a new series of discourses. And yet simultaneously there is the assumption that 'the body and its pleasures' will transcend this control.[25] It is difficult to see why the 'body' should have a 'reality' denied other social phenomena.

Despite these difficulties, Foucault's work has been of considerable influence in recent explorations of sexuality, and there are two areas which seem of particular significance. Firstly, despite the functionalist tendencies already mentioned, *The History of Sexuality* does offer an alternative view of seeing the relationship between sexuality and wider social forces to the traditional functionalism of many (particularly) left interpretations, which tend to see a direct relationship between the nuclear family and organisation of sexuality, either in the interests of capitalism or as directly responsive to the urges of 'modernisation'.[26] Foucault points out several factors which fundamentally challenge this: the fact, for instance that the sexual apparatus and the nuclear family were produced by the bourgeoisie as an aspect of its own self-affirmation, not as a means of controlling the working class; that there are class sexualities (and different gender sexualities); that indeed there are sexualities, not a single uniform sexuality. Sexuality is not a given that has to be controlled. It is an historical construct that has historical conditions of existence.

Secondly, again despite the qualifications mentioned earlier, Foucault's emphasis on the emergence of discourses and practice which both produce and regulate the objects of knowledge, does direct us correctly to investigate the role of particular apparatuses, such as the medical, psychiatric, social welfare, charity and legal institutions, in shaping sexualities. He indicates, for instance, the importance of the medical institutions in the nineteenth century in organising definitions of female sexuality, or the close interconnections between medicine and law in the emergence of the homosexual category in the late nineteenth and early twentieth centuries. But simultaneously the emergence of categorisations of formal controls, of localised interventions to organise 'sexuality' produce points of opposition, of challenge, of contestation. What is ultimately of most significance in Foucault's work is this recognition of the constant struggles within the definitions of sexuality. It is here that we can see the power of his rejection of the concept of 'liberation'. It is not the release of a hidden or blocked essence that should be the target of sexual radicalism, he suggests, but conscious intervention at the level of the definition of appropriate sexual behaviour.[27] But to historicise this recognition effectively we need to understand that discourses and practices do not arbitrarily emerge from the flux of possibilities; nor are discourses the only contact with the real; they have their conditions of existence and their effects in concrete historical, social, economic and ideological situations.

The making of 'modern' sexuality

This book covers a period of some two hundred years. They are the years, roughly, of British industrialisation and urbanisation, so this work is in broad terms an examination of various aspects of the regulation of sexuality within the period of industrial capitalism. No simple causative relationship between industrialisation and the organisation of sexuality is suggested. The directing principle of this work is that over the past few centuries sexuality has assumed major symbolic importance as a target of social intervention and organisation, to a degree that differentiates this period from those preceding it. There was, obviously, no simple starting point for the developments we shall examine, nor any pre-ordained culmination. The dates are to that extent arbitrary. Nevertheless, this roughly delineated period did see major transformations in the role of sexuality, and the book, as a whole, traces some of the major shifts in this process. But before looking in more detail at these developments we must clarify the focus of our argument. Robert Padgug has recently written that 'Biological sexuality is the necessary precondition for human sexuality. But biological sexuality is only a precondition, a set of potentialities, which is never unmediated by human reality.'[28] That sums up a fundamental assumption of this work. We are increasingly accustomed to questioning the eternal validity of social roles, and we now recognise that the way in which we define masculinity and femininity, 'motherhood' and 'fatherhood', even 'childhood', are culturally specific and often bear little relationship to the expected or ascribed roles in other cultures, nor are they, of course, simple products of biology.[29] We have been more wary of challenging the transcultural verity of sexual categories, but in reality a minimum awareness of the evidence should alert us to the fact that though various cultures share general sexual forms, this does not mean that their content, inner structures and meanings are identical. The sexual potentialities of the body have been integrated into a vast range of different social contexts: from pedagogic relations and puberty rites, to fertility cults and religious ceremonial. Some cultures have seen no connection between sexual intercourse and conception; others have seen the only justification for sex in reproduction. Some cultures have made little distinction between heterosexual and homosexual forms, concentrating rather on the age or class of the partner; our culture has made the distinction of prime social significance. In some societies, sex is a simple source of pleasure, a key to the glorification of the erotic arts; in others it is a source of danger and taboo, of mortification of the flesh.

In our society sex has become the supreme secret ('the mystery of sex') and the general substratum of our existence. Since the nineteenth century it has been seen as the cause and 'truth' of our being. It defines us socially and morally; its release or proper functioning can be a factor in health, energy, activity; its frustration is a cause of ill health, social unorthodoxy, even madness.

There are two further characteristics which separate our conception of sexuality from other notions. Firstly, it is seen as a supremely *private* experience. It is not (at least ostensibly) an element in religion, in the rites of passage from youth to adulthood, there are no obvious fertility rites: it is the supreme act of self-expression between partners.[30] It is also seen as the archetypally 'natural' act. Since at least the time of Rousseau it has been the assertion of self against the preternaturally distorting effects of modern, and later industrial civilisation; sex, that is to say, is the essence of our individual being which asserts itself against the demands of culture, and this has had a profound resonance in our thinking. Secondly, it is seen as a unified domain. It is not just a series of acts, not a collection of bodies which can be eroticised, but a thing in itself, with its general causations and specified effects. 'Sexuality' has become a continent of knowledge, with its own rules of exploration and its own expert geographers. And strikingly, the world of 'sexuality' developed more or less contemporaneously with the domain of the 'economy' and of the 'social' itself. Social life was being demarcated into distinct areas of knowledge, each with their own hierophants and esoteric mysteries.

Against the historical unification we would stress that sex is relational,[31] is shaped in social interaction, and can only be understood in its historical context, in terms of the cultural meanings assigned to it, and in terms of the internal, subjective meanings of the sexed individuals that emerge. This in turn demands an exploration of a variety of forces that have shaped and constructed 'modern sexuality', and these range from the familial and extra-familial forces that shape sexual and gender orientation at the level of the individual, to the social and industrial transformations that have altered class relations.[32] What follows is not an exhaustive list of factors but a series of guidelines that have shaped the contents of this work.

1. Kinship and family system

We need to be aware of changes in patterns of kinship and in the organisation of the family and household. Changes in the organisation of inheritance, the importance assigned to primogeniture, shifts in the rules of exogamy and in the permitted degrees of marriages, in the construction of family forms in ideology and in welfare practices, the class differences in family and household patterns, the shaping of sex and gender divisions: all have to be taken into account in the organisation of sexuality.

Within this context we must also be aware of the changing effects of these family and kinship relations on the actual construction of sexed individuals, that is individuals whose biological differences and personal proclivities are given cultural meaning. Juliet Mitchell in her work *Psychoanalysis and Feminism* has pointed to the significance of this task, but the problem, as suggested above, has been that most analyses have not been sufficiently historically specific to make them usable.[33] Some recent work, however, particularly in attempting to historicise the insights of Freud, and to demonstrate the specificity of his categories (that is, showing how they refer to a particular cultural milieu) has opened up new possibilities. A recent reinterpretation of Freud's analysis of 'Little Hans' has, for instance, demonstrated clearly the ways in which the process of psychoanalysis itself acts to install culturally and class-specific prescriptions of correct sexual and gender attitudes.[34] Such work, though still exploratory, may transform our ways of understanding the historical creation of 'sexed individuals'.

2. Economic and social changes

Changes in family and kinship patterns have to be seen in the context of long-term social transformations, leading to new class alignments, changes in the social environment, urbanisation, and a disruption of settled and traditional patterns. Labour migrations, for instance, have had an important impact on patterns of courtship and on illegitimacy rates. Changes in the organisation of the economy have affected the relative social situation of men and women, shifted their relations of dominance and subordination and altered the significance, materially and ideologically, of the family. We shall not argue that any particular mode of production 'demands' in a simple way a particular form of sexuality, but the rhythm of economic, and consequent social, transformation do provide the basic preconditions and the ultimate limits within which social forms are organised and reorganised.

3. Changing forms of 'social regulation'

Within a wider social framework, we need to study both the formal and informal modes of the regulation of sexuality. At the formal level this must involve the operations of Church and state, the regulation of marriage, divorce, illegitimacy, incest, sexual unorthodoxy and so on. But we must not forget also the changing role of the state. The growth of social intervention and the emergence of a welfare state have all profoundly affected the patterns of sexual behaviour.

Informal methods of control can be as important. Peer-group regulation of adolescent courtship can substantially affect the patterns of sexuality, keeping the illegitimacy rates low, for instance, regulating the timing of marriage and the importance given to celibacy and restraint. Traditional rituals of public shaming (such as the 'charivari') can regulate unorthodox or socially undesired behaviour. We must be sensitive to all forms of what can loosely be termed 'social control'.[35]

4. The political moment

There is no necessary connection between political decision making and moral change: politics is not a simple reflection of changes in society. But the political context in which decisions are made – to legislate or not, to prosecute or ignore – can be important in promoting shifts in the sexual regime and these must be analysed both in terms of long-term shifts and in conjunctural terms.

An important mechanism here is that of the 'moral panic'. Stan Cohen defined it as follows in his book *Folk Devils and Moral Panics*:

Societies appear to be subject every now and then to periods of moral panic. A condition, episode, person or group of persons emerges to become defined as a threat to societal values and interests; its nature is presented in a stylized and stereotypical fashion by the mass media; the moral barricades are manned by editors, bishops and politicians and other right-thinking people; socially accredited experts pronounce their diagnoses and solutions; ways of coping are evolved, or (more often) resorted to; the condition then disappears, submerges or deteriorates . . . . Sometimes the panic is passed over and forgotten, but at other times it has more serious and long term repercussions and it might produce changes in legal and social policy or even in the way in which societies conceive themselves.[36]

This definition was used by Cohen to explain the response to youth in the 1950s and 1960s but it can be similarly applied to moral crises in the more distant past – one may refer by way of example, to the nexus of fears generated by the French Revolution, which significantly shaped the contours of 'Victorian' sexuality, or the anxieties which produced the legislative restructuring of the 1880s and 1900s, or the fears generated by the cold war in the 1950s. The moral panic crystallises widespread fears and anxieties, and often deals with them not by seeking the real causes of the problems and conditions which they demonstrate but by displacing them on to 'Folk Devils' in an identified social group (often the 'immoral' or 'degenerate'). Sexuality has had a peculiar centrality in such panics, and sexual 'deviants' have been omnipresent scapegoats.

But combating on the political terrain are a variety of more established political forces whose influence cannot be ignored. Over the long term we can detect three broad tendencies: the conservative, authoritarian often expressed in the actions of social morality campaigns; the liberal often in the vanguard of reforming activity; and the radical, libertarian; the first asserting the importance of absolute moral standards; the second by and large seeking relaxation within a traditional framework of family values; and the third advocating a transformation of values. They are present in varying degrees throughout the period of this book; the degree of their influence, their role in the construction of social consensus or in unifying disparate social forces is another factor that must be taken into account. The political moment – that period when moral attitudes are transformed into formally political action – can be of key importance in nuancing the regulation of sexuality, and at crucial times a moral schema has been of prime significance in political propaganda.

5. Cultures of resistance

It is all too easy to assume that formal regulation has an immediate unilinear impact, but in actuality the history of sexuality is as much a history of an avoidance of, or resistance to, the moral code, as of a simple acceptance and internalisation. Cultures of resistance may stretch from the folk knowledges and information networks which sustained an awareness of abortion and birth control when they were tabooed or unlawful, to the specific subcultures of stigmatised sexual minorities. In more recent years the resistances have often adopted more explicitly political forms as sex-reform organisations or as sexual liberation movements. They are as much a part of a history of sexuality as the grander organisation of sexual codes.

This somewhat schematic listing will serve to illustrate that sexual behaviour and its regulation cannot be reduced to a simple explanatory factor; nor can there be a simple, straightforward history. But, as Foucault has indicated, we *can* trace a series of long-term strategies at work which are related to the cultural significance given to sexuality. The remainder of this book will explore the major phases in this development, while attempting to bring into play the schema suggested above. The next four chapters (Ch. 2–5) chart the complexities of 'Victorian' sexuality: its ideological weight, its class specifities, its legislative effects. Chapter 6 explores the construction of the category of the homosexual, important both as an illustration of the wider tendencies of sexual categorisation at work, and as an illustration of a specific sexual experience, and the efforts at social organisation and regulation it evokes. The following four chapters (Ch. 7–10) look at aspects of the delineation of the field of sexuality: in relation to debates over population, in its construction as an area of specialised knowledge, and in relation to organisations and movements that challenged the sexual *status quo* in the nineteenth century and first third of the present century. The final four chapters (Ch. 11–14) examine the phases in the political and social reorganisation of sexuality in the twentieth century: in relationship to the weakening of the authoritarian consensus; as part of the social restructuring attendant on the growth of the welfare state; in terms of the transforming effects on long-term changes in the social structure, which gave rise to the short era of 'permissiveness'; and finally the last chapter offers a brief description of the political and moral conjuncture in which the book was written.

I do not claim that this book is in any way a final or even comprehensive analysis of its subject matter. Historians still have before them the difficult task of charting the area before they can properly explore its hidden riches. So this book is by way of a clearing of the ground for later work, rather than a definitive study, and hence its concentration on particular *aspects* of the regulation of sexuality. But that, I would argue, is an important task in itself, for it points towards the importance of studying in its particular application what is the major theme of this book: the central symbolic and moral significance assigned to sexuality in our culture.

References

1. **Vern L. Bullough**, 'Sex in History: A Virgin Field', *The Journal of Sex Research*, Vol. 8, No. 2, May 1972, p. 101.
2. The discussion that follows is based on a rather long one in my paper 'Discourses, Desire and Sexual Deviance: Problems in a History of Homosexuality', in **Kenneth Plummer** (ed.), *The Making of the Modern Homosexual*, Hutchinson, London, 1981.
3. In **Kenneth Plummer**, *Sexual Stigma: An Interactionist Account*, Routledge and Kegan Paul, 1975.
4. **Gordon Rattray Taylor**, *Sex in History*, Thames and Hudson, London, 1953, p. 13.
5. **Lawrence Stone**, *The Family, Sex and Marriage in England 1500–1800*, Weidenfeld and Nicolson, London, 1977, p. 666. Stone rejects, in fact, the idea that the id 'is the most powerful of all drives and has not changed over the ages' (p. 15). He argues that changes in protein diet and physical exhaustion and psychic stress all have their effect. But he goes on to speak in essentialist terms of the superego at times repressing and at times releasing the drive which does not fundamentally break with the views which I challenge. See also **Edward Shorter**, *The Making of the Modern Family*, Fontana, London 1977, Introduction.
6. **Steven Marcus**, *The Other Victorians: A Study of Sexuality and Pornography in Mid Nineteenth Century England*, Basic Books, New York, 1966; Weidenfeld and Nicolson, London, 1967.
7. **Richard von Krafft-Ebing**, *Psychopathia Sexualis*, F. A. Davis, Philadelphia and London, 1892, p. 1; **William McDougall**, *An Outline of Abnormal Psychology*, S. Scribner's, New York and Boston, 1926, p. 322.
8. **J. H. Gagnon** and **William Simon**, *Sexual Conduct: The Social Sources of Human Sexuality*, Hutchinson, London, 1973, p. 26.
9. For a recent discussion of the interactionist and labelling approaches see **Kenneth Plummer**, *Symbolic Interactionism and Sexual Differentiation: An Empirical Investigation*, Unpublished report to the Social Science Research Council, February 1979. On trends in psychoanalysis see **Jacques Lacan**, *The Four Fundamental Concepts of Psychoanalysis*, The Hogarth Press, London, 1977; **Juliet Mitchell**, *Psychoanalysis and Feminism*, Allen Lane, London, 1974; and for an irreverent discussion of the intellectual context see **Sherry Turkle**, *Psychoanalytic Politics: Freud's French Revolution*, Burnett Books, London, 1979. For **Michel Foucault** the central text is *The History of Sexuality*, Vol. 1, *An Introduction*, Allen Lane, London, 1979.
10. Michel Foucault, *op. cit.*, p. 152.

11. *Ibid*, p. 153.
12. Gagnon and Simon, *Sexual Conduct*, p. 17.
13. There is a sympathetic study of Foucault which explores the implications of the genealogical approach by **Colin Gordon**, 'Other Inquisitions', *I and C*, No. 6, Autumn 1979.
14. See for example, the work of **Judith Walkowitz** on Victorian prostitution, especially *Prostitution and Victorian Society: Women, Class and the State*, Cambridge University Press, 1980. My own earlier work has also been very much influenced by this approach. See **Jeffrey Weeks**, *Coming Out: Homosexual Politics in Britain from the Nineteenth Century to the Present*, Quartet, London, 1977.
15. **Meaghan Morris** and **Paul Patton** (eds) *Michel Foucault. Power, Truth, Strategy*, Working Papers Collection 2, Feral Publications 1979, Sydney, p. 8.
16. Foucault, *op. cit.*, p. 107.
17. **Michel Foucault**, *Discipline and Punish: the Birth of the Prison*, Allen Lane, London, 1977; and Part Five, 'Right of Death and Power over Life', in *The History of Sexuality*, Vol. 1.
18. Foucault, *The History*, p. 146.
19. **Rosalind Coward**, '"Sexual Liberation" and the Family', in *M/F*, No. 1 1978, p. 20. There is an ever-expanding literature on Foucault. For a clear and sympathetic summary of his views see Colin Gordon, *op. cit.*; and **Alan Sheridan**, *Michel Foucault. The Will to Truth*, Tavistock, London, 1980. For a sharp critique from the left see **Peter Dews**, 'The *Nouvelle Philosophie* and Foucault', *Economy and Society*, Vol. 8, No. 2, May 1979.
20. Foucault, *The History*, p. 95.
21. *Ibid*; and in Morris and Patton, *op. cit.*, p. 55.
22. Foucault, *The History*, p. 149.
23. Cf. the comments of Dews, *op. cit.*
24. **Nicos Poulantzas**, *State, Power, Socialism*, New Left Books, London, 1978, p. 44.
25. Foucault, *The History*, p. 157.
26. This is discussed in Chapter 2, pp. 25–7.
27. See Foucault, *op. cit.*, pp. 82 ff. For a comment on these lines see Rosalind Coward, *op. cit.*
28. **Robert A. Padgug**, 'Sexual Matters: On Conceptualising Sexuality in History', in *Radical History Review*, No. 20 Spring/Summer 1979, p. 9. This article, in particular, discusses the problems raised in this chapter in a broadly similar fashion, while the issue of the *Review* as a whole examines the theoretical and research problems that follow.
29. A good introduction to these issues is **Ann Oakley**, *Sex, Gender and Society*, Temple Smith, London, 1972.
30. The development of the private/public division is sketched in a suggestive way in **Eli Zaretsky**, *Capitalism, the Family and Personal Life*, Pluto, London, 1978.
31. Padgug, *op. cit.*, p. 11.
32. A very stimulating discussion of the factors examined here is provided by **Ellen Ross** and **Rayna Rapp**, 'Sex and Society: A Research Note from Social History and Anthropology', to be published in *Comparative Studies in Society and History*. I am grateful to the authors for allowing me to read a typescript of this paper.

33. Mitchell's work has produced a host of comments and discussions, focusing especially on her discussion of the significance of kinship patterns in ordering the cultural acquisition of psychological masculinity and femininity under 'Patriarchy', and in shaping the compulsion towards heterosexuality. Some of these themes are taken up in Chapter 7 below. But see also the discussions in *Working Papers in Sex, Science and the Culture*, Vol. 1, No. 1, January 1976, and Vol. 1, No. 2, November 1976; and **Veronica Beechey**, 'On Patriarchy', *Feminist Review*, No. 3, 1979.
34. See **Mia Campioni** and **Liz Gross** 'Little Hans; the Production of Oedipus', in **Paul Foss** and **Meaghan Morris** (eds), *Language, Sexuality and Subversion*, Feral Publications, Darlington NSW, 1978. See also the discussion in **Gilles Deleuze** and **Felix Guattari**, *Anti-Oedipus: Capitalism and Schizophrenia*, Viking Press, New York, 1977; and **Roisin McDonough** and **Rachel Harrison**, 'Patriarchy and Relations of Production', in **Annette Kuhn** and **Ann Marie Wolpe**, *Feminism and Materialism. Women and Modes of Production*, Routledge & Kegan Paul, London, Henley and Boston, 1978.
35. I do not subscribe unproblematically to the concept of 'social control'; I mention it here to indicate a problem rather than to suggest any particular approach. See the discussion on the difficulties in the concept in **Gareth Stedman Jones**, 'Class Expression *versus* Social Control?', *History Workshop Journal* No. 4, Autumn 1977; and the debates in **A. P. Donajgrodzki** (ed.), *Social Control in Nineteenth Century Britain*, Croom Helm, London, 1977, particularly the editor's introduction and Richard Johnson's article on education.
36. **Stan Cohen**, *Folk Devils and Moral Panics*, MacGibbon and Kee, London, 1972, p. 9.

Chapter Two

'That damned morality':
Sex in Victorian ideology

Victorian sexuality: myths and meanings

The 'Victorian Age' has long been a synonym for a harsh and repressive
sexual puritanism. A long critical tradition, stemming from writers such
as Grant Allen, Edward Carpenter and Havelock Ellis at the end of the
nineteenth century, continuing through the liberal *avant garde* of the
inter-war years, and culminating in the sexual reformers of the 1950s
and 1960s, alive to the demands of permissiveness, has analysed the
contradictions and absurdities of the moral code of the nineteenth century. It has been portrayed as the era when rigid puritanism allied with
moral hypocrisy, verbal and visual delicacy marched arm in arm with a
flourishing pornography. The authoritarian paterfamilias presided over
the institutionalisation of the double standard, while the pedestalised
mother and wife depended for her purity on the degradation of the fallen woman. It was the age when sex was publicly, indeed ostentatiously
denied, only to return, repressed, to flourish in the fertile undergrowth.

Yet simultaneously and apparently paradoxically it was during the
nineteenth century that the debate about sexuality exploded. Far from
the age experiencing a regime of silence and total suppression, sexuality
became a major social issue in Victorian social and political practice.
There was indeed a reign of euphemism and of ostensible delicacy
which prevented for instance the novel from being too explicit, bowdlerised Shakespeare's plays, alluded to prostitution as the 'social evil'
and gonorrhoea and syphilis as the 'social diseases'. Sodomy and birth
control for the first two-thirds of the century were '*nom nominandum
inter christianus*', or 'crimes against nature', too horrible to be named.

But even the refusal to talk about it, as Michel Foucault has noted,
marks it as *the* secret and puts it at the heart of discourse. From the end
of the eighteenth century with the debate on over-population and the
hyperbreeding of the poor, sexuality pervades the social consciousness:
from the widespread discussions of the birthrate, deathrate, life expec-
tancy and fertility in the statistical forays of the century to the urgent
controversies over public health, housing, birth control and prostitution. The reports of the great Parliamentary Commissions, which in the

1830s and 1840s investigated working conditions in factories and mines, were saturated with an obsessive concern with the sexuality of the working class, the social other, displacing in the end the acute social crisis from the area of exploitation and class conflict, where it could not be coped with, into the framework of a more amenable and discussable area of 'morality'. From the 1850s sexuality, particularly in the wide area of venereal disease and prostitution (allied to fears that Britain would follow Rome into imperial decline) enters the heart of Parliamentary debate. The controversy over the Contagious Diseases Acts, passed in the 1860s to impose compulsory medical examination and registration on working-class women suspected of being prostitutes in designated garrison and naval towns, generated an avalanche of controversy and publications. The Acts were the subject of repeated Parliamentary enquiries, while the repeal organisations alone published at least 520 books and pamphlets on venereal disease and prostitution. Between 1870 and 1885, 17,367 petitions against the Acts, with 2,606,429 signatures were presented to the House of Commons, and over 900 public meetings were held by supporters of repeal.[1]

Other legislative changes produced their own effects. The divorce act of 1857 evinced a flurry of interest in the next decade in stories of bigamy and adultery: a special paper, *The Divorce News and Police Reporter*, was founded to cater for specialised tastes, but other Victorian papers, like their more familiar twentieth-century offspring, were full of divorce cases and other sexual scandals. This prurient exposé of other people's sex lives was complemented by a slow trickle of neo-Malthusian birth-control propaganda from the 1820s, and a torrent of advertisements in the popular press for potions for, or to safeguard against, potency, abortion, masturbation, etc. Some of the popular writings it seems had a huge circulation: Samuel Solomon's *Guide to Health, or Advice to Both Sexes* ran to 66 editions between 1782 and 1817, and editions were still appearing in the later nineteenth century. It has been estimated that each edition after 1800 probably ran to over 30,000 copies.[2] And beneath these streams was the subterranean river of pornography. Steven Marcus has suggested that: 'Pornography, in the sense that we understand it today, is a historical phenomenon; it begins to exist *significantly* some time during the middle of the eighteenth century, and flourishes steadily – though with periodic fluctuations in intensity – throughout the nineteenth and twentieth centuries.'[3] The mid-nineteenth century saw a major increase in the market and supply of pornography: its concerns (flagellatory, the cross-class seduction of servants and young girls, and so on) were often different in substance from our own (there was little homosexuality for instance), but they illustrate a growing demand for fantasy fulfilment in the very heart of 'respectability'.

Alongside all this, gaining momentum in the second half of the century, was a new taxonomic and labelling zeal which attempted to classify 'scientifically' the characteristics and increasingly the aetiologies of the forms of sexual variety, and in so doing helped construct them as objects of study and as sexual categories. It may or may not be of significance that the Oxford English Dictionary can find no instance of the word 'pornography' being used before 1864 (in a decade, it may be noted, which also saw a generalised use of the term 'capitalism'). But it is most certainly of major conceptualising importance that the word homosexuality was first invented, by the Hungarian Benkert, in 1869; its adoption into English usage in the 1880s and 1890s was a vital stage in the articulation of a modern concept of the homosexual (see Ch. 6). Other words which designated sexual traits, such as nymphomania, narcissism, autoeroticism, kleptomania, urolagnia and many others, began to seep into scientific discourse by the end of the century and the beginning of the twentieth century, indicating a new concern with detailing sexual variations, and with using sex as a distinguishing mark between individuals.

Evidence such as this serves to undermine the apparently monolithic edifice of Victorianism. There was no final triumph of censorship or purity during the nineteenth century, whatever the efforts of the social morality crusaders; and the continuing concern of moral conservatives over the flood of unexpurgated literature, street ballads, music-hall songs, dubious pamphlets and advertisements attests to their continuing presence as much as to the concern of the moralists.[4] Moreoever, far from being simply denied in the nineteenth century, sex acquires a peculiar significance in structuring ideology and social and political practices, and in shaping individual responses. Havelock Ellis cites the case of:

A married lady who is a leader in social purity movements and an enthusiast for sexual chastity, (who) discovered through reading some pamphlets against solitary vice, that she had herself been practising masturbation for years without knowing it. The profound anguish and hopeless despair of this woman in the face of what she believed to be the moral ruin of her whole life cannot well be described.[5]

This is an excellent example of the way in which social definitions can subtly mould and transform the personal meaning given to sexual activity; or indeed can make 'sexual' what had hitherto seemed acceptable. A harmless pleasure can become the gateway to nameless hells when for whatever reasons it begins to carry a significant symbolic meaning. What is particularly revealing in this anecdote is the existence in the ideology of a strong concept of what is desirable and undesirable, what is moral and immoral.

The obvious question arises, of how different was this from what went before. We are not suggesting a sharp break at the turn of the nineteenth century or at the accession of Queen Victoria or whatever. On the contrary, the changing symbolic role of sexuality was a product of long and complex changes, and unevenly enforced over the population as a whole. Moreover, there were strong elements of continuity, especially with regard to the central organising significance of Christianity which from the early days of Christendom to the present has structured basic beliefs and formed the framework within which law and custom (if not always behaviour) have operated. But to stress the role of Christian tradition as the *primum mobile*, and as the dominant force, as many early sexologists, such as Havelock Ellis did, is to miss the actual complexity of developments. Even in the mid-seventeenth century, when Puritan dominance over the moral code was strongest, there is some evidence that the courts were willing to acquiesce in a more pragmatic code, provided public order was sustained.[6] We may, schematically, suggest the long-term co-residence of three separate layers of attitudes and beliefs. Providing the general boundary was the Christian, Pauline, tradition, sustained through the institutionalisation of the Church, and fertilised from the sixteenth century by the Puritan and dissenting traditions. The moral code here was clear, even as its application was uneven. At its strongest, sexuality within holy matrimony was only justified as a necessary part of reproduction. The holiest state was celibacy; but it was better to marry than to burn. In the Puritan tradition this was modified. Married love was a duty, and a grace that permitted, and alone permitted, the fulfilment of conjugal rights. But sex in turn existed to bring man and woman closer together. Within marriage sex was a positive, even a spiritual binding force.[7]

But the actual implementation of this Christian philosophy often fell far short of these standards, and throughout the modern era we can trace a second layer, summed up in the phrase 'the double standard', which enjoined chastity on the female while allowing a large degree of sexual freedom for the male. This at times, before the nineteenth century, was almost the 'respectable' standard, though it never went unchallenged.[8]

But a third layer was even more removed from the formal standards, the popular morality of the vast majority, which was no less strict for being only loosely Christian in a formal sense. As G. R. Quaife has put it, 'God does not loom large as a damper on lower-class sexual activity.'[9] This should not be taken to imply that there was in any sense an unrestrained licence for peasant sexuality; there was no 'amorality' in a fundamental sense. There was, on the contrary, an often strict morality, enforced through various informal and traditional methods such as those of public shaming, the charivari and skimmington rides. But it was a *social* morality, in which the potential economic burden to the community of bastards mattered more than the 'immorality' of premarital sex. There is no lack of evidence for the litigious nature of the pre-industrial population over sexual matters. In the early seventeenth century, for instance, all sorts of cases were fought to the courts, from the seduction of wives to the incidence of prostitution. Moreover, the actual life and manners of the peasantry are by no means clear, and the historians are divided over whether the late age of marriage, dictated by the impossibility of marriage before an economic slot opened for the

man, meant compulsory restraint or a social toleration of masturbation, oral and anal sex, and homosexuality. But what does seem
clear is on the one hand the absence of any straightforward link between
sexual activity *per se* and social morality; and on the other, the inability
and sometimes unwillingness of the ecclesiastical authorities to enforce
stricter single standards. In distinction to this, morality, for the Victorians and increasingly for the generations that have come after, has
been to a significant degree organised around concepts of sexuality, so
that even when moral attitudes were authoritarian and restrictive, as the
dominant notions were for much of the nineteenth century, sexuality
had a vigorous presence.

For the historian, then, the problem becomes one of discovering the
contours of Victorian sexual *mores* without surrendering to facile generalisations, for despite a plethora of studies we are still woefully ignorant of general trends in the development of sexual attitudes, of their
effects on individual lives, and of the particular meanings given to their
activities by the sexual subjects in all their variety – by class, by gender,
by generation and by region. Many historians prefer of course the overarching pattern. Lawrence Stone, for instance, in his massive book, *The
Family, Sex and Marriage*, speaks in terms of a long development
towards modern sexual 'permissiveness' from the eighteenth century.
Interrupted by what he terms a second wave of moral regeneration
and repression in the nineteenth century, it resumes its onward march
from the 1860s, to the present.[10] This is helpful in pointing to long-term
shifts in sexual norms in the last century (though its dating is misleading), but it combines both an evolutionist teleology (with the present
appearing as little more than a culmination of ineluctable historical
trends) and a use of the metaphor of repression which in the end is
emotive rather than analytical and obscures more than it reveals. The
linkage of a pressure-cooker view of sexuality (which sees sex as a
natural force constrained by societal norms) with a cloud-of-dust theory
of ideology (which assumes that ideas are inevitably sifted downwards
through society at large) suggests that the 'sexual revolution' is in the
end just about more sexual activity. But surely a much more central
question concerns the different ways being developed of organising sexual behaviour. What seems to be happening in the nineteenth century,
in response to major social changes (rapid industrialisation and urbanisation, the disruption of old class patterns and the rise of capitalist
social relations, the development of new and sharp class conflicts with
their related social and intellectual manifestations) is a continuous battle over the definition of acceptable sexual behaviour within the context
of changing class and power relations. And there are different rhythms
in this process. There was no blanket imposition of 'repression'. Not
until the 1880s did 'social purity' have any major legislative purchase;
and it is significant that it is from this period that the earliest critiques of
'Victorianism' stem.[11]

The domestic ideology

Various forces were at work in the process of definition and redefinition – from ideological articulation to medical and legal practices and moral endeavour. These forces intersected at that crucial site for modern ideology, the family, which they both helped to build and sustain. The increasing specification of sexual behaviour outside the family which was a product of nineteenth-century sexology and criminal practice, served only to enhance the importance of those definitions which traversed the domestic hearth. The family, as Josephine Butler put it, was in accordance with the law of God, and the claim that every person should live in accord with their instincts was a departure from 'the sternness of the moral law'.[12] It was a key element in the dominant ideology of the nineteenth century in all the major capitalist countries. Indeed the so-called 'Revolution Bill', the *Umsturzvorlage* proposed by the German government in 1894 to ward off the threat of revolution, made criticism of the family as an institution punishable by drastic penalties.[13] To the chagrin of rationalists such as John Stuart Mill, the family, not the individual, was regarded as the basic unit of society and increasingly a substitute for lost faith, so that even positivists like Frederic Harrison, who rejected supernatural religions, supported an almost Catholic orthodoxy of marriage as the gateway to family responsibility.[14]

By the nineteenth century there was a wide acceptance, at least amongst the upper classes, of the single marriage code though its origins in fact were comparatively recent. Not until after 1753 with Lord Hardwick's Marriage Act did the church wedding as opposed to verbal spousehoods become the single legally binding form, with compulsory registration in the parish register, parental consent enshrined up to the age of 21 and enforcement transferred to the secular authorities.

The new marriage laws (especially those after 1836, which granted the right to marry to nonconformist chapels as well as civil registrars) had the effect of making the betrothal less binding and of sharply differentiating the married from the unmarried, hence making the difference between licit and illicit sex more important.[15] Earlier traditions survived in rural areas and amongst the unorganised and disrupted working class, but marriage became increasingly the gateway to respectability and stability. It was buttressed by an increasing idealisation of domesticity, a growing specification and rationalisation in the censure of extra-marital sex (partly articulated by what one sex reformer called 'the continued extension of the criminal law') and by the difficulty of divorce. The 1857 Matrimonial Causes Act, which set up secular courts and procedures, established no new principle not involved in the old form of divorces by petitions in Acts of Parliament. The only principle abandoned in 1857 was the propriety of making legal remedies for marriage difficulties available for the aristocracy while withholding them from the growing upper middle class.[16] Change was slow: divorce rose from an annual average of 148 in the decade after 1851 to 582 in the decade before 1900; and divorce remained a strong social stigma. Even innocent parties were excluded from court until 1887. In the working class, though the stigma might be less, the difficulties were even greater and divorce was quite out of the question for most.

It is likely then that marriages, at least amongst the propertied, in fact lasted longer during the Victorian period than ever before or since. The decline in mortality rates, which had traditionally cut off marriage after about twenty years, was not yet offset by rising divorce rates. So it was only in the nineteenth century when all the loopholes had been stopped up that marriage became in fact what it had always been in theory, indissoluble. The Victorian family was the first family form in history which was both long-lasting and intimate.[17] It was this which gave the family its peculiar importance in the surveillance, and control, of sexual behaviour.

The relationship of the nuclear family to wider social forms has troubled the historian for a long time. Most historical accounts have been influenced by a long sociological tradition going back to Frederic le Play's *L'Organisation de la Famille selon le vrai modele signalé par l'histoire de toutes les races et de tous les temps* (1871), which saw a broad change in the family from the extended form in the middle ages to nuclear form in modernity. The cohesive solidarity of the medieval kin was ruptured by the impact of industrialisation and the result was a family form reduced to its essential core, of parents and offspring. This model has influenced most subsequent studies, whether in the functionalist accounts of Talcott Parsons and his followers (who see economic 'modernisation' as the agent of change) or in the orthodox Marxist version (which sees change as an effect of capitalism).[18] In the work of the French Marxist Louis Althusser, the family, as an 'ideological state apparatus', becomes the scene of the operation of ideological processes whereby the reproduction of existing social relations of production is secured, but even this more sophisticated version assumes a functionalist fit between intention and effect. In all these versions the family is seen as having a direct relationship with the wider society, being that social form within which people are assigned a place in society and where they internalise the values of that place and which shapes sexual attitudes to conform to wider social needs. The family is therefore the site of both primary socialisation of children and the continuing socialisation of adults, so that 'socialisation' becomes a deterministic notion of the way in which people are manipulated by existing structures of society. In both the Parsonian model and in the orthodox Marxist version, the function of the family is to secure the maintenance of the existing social order economically, ideologically and sexually.

Aspects of these various models have been challenged more recently by historians, especially those interested in family reconstitution. Peter Laslett, for instance, has attempted to show that the average household size from the late sixteenth century to the twentieth century was 4.75

persons (that is, always 'nuclear'), and he has used this data to challenge the notion that the nuclear model is a product of 'modernisation'. This has generated a considerable debate on the size of the household, its class basis and the changing meanings given to it. Laslett in turn has been challenged for ignoring the effects of the life-cycle in altering family size through generations, for by-passing evidence which suggests that other kin lived with the conjugal unit, and for rejecting changing ideologies of the family.[19]

What most versions have in common, however, is basically an essentialist view of the family as a discrete historical object, usually a biological reality which society acts upon. Mark Poster has recently suggested that 'historians and social scientists in general have gone astray by viewing the family as a unitary phenomenon which has undergone some type of linear transformation'. He argues instead that the history of the family is discontinuous, evolving several distinct family structures each with its own emotional pattern. Moreover, these structures are the creation of a variety of social practices: economic, ideological, educational, medical and legislative.[20] If this is the case, what this points to is the construction of various family forms, both in ideological definition and in social practice. We can see in fact some evidence of this process at work in eighteenth-century history. By the late eighteenth century, according to Stone, the four key features of the modern family were strongly entrenched in the upper sections of society. These were intensified affective bonding at the expense of neighbours and kin, a strong sense of individual autonomy, weakening of the association of sexual pleasure with sin and guilt, and a growing desire for physical privacy. Another historian, Randolph Trumbach, has further argued that even by the late seventeenth century there was a growing stress amongst aristocratic families on romantic love in the establishment of marriage alliances, though this tended to favour sons rather than daughters, still valuable as makers of alliances between families. What is being suggested here is a distinct historical switch in notions of the family, away from traditions which stressed the links with kin and the importance of lineage (being part of a family with a long history which marriage sought to sustain) towards a new stress on sexual choice as the basis for alliance. It seems that by the end of the eighteenth century sexual love was enshrined as a central element in the making of families and this was integrated into the bourgeois familial ideology of the nineteenth century, though whether this new ideology originated in the aristocracy or amongst the aspiring bourgeoisie is still a point of major historical debate.[21] It seems more likely, however, to have been the result of major historical transformations, including the separation of work from home, and the growing centrality of the individual in the economy and the general ideology, than to have derived from developments intrinsic to a landed class.

But this stress was only one of several strands in the ideological construction of the bourgeois family, for sexual choice was hemmed in by simultaneous emphases on property, the survival (and even accentuation) of a differentiated standard of morality, and the growth of the ideology of 'respectability', with all its class connotations. Through the conduit of 'respectability' the new stress on sexual choice linked with the puritan heritage, particularly as mediated through the evangelical tradition. Puritanism, after all, had always stressed the significance of sexuality in cementing happy family life. The result of these complex influences was a family model that carried heavily ideological concepts of what the distribution of power should be in the family and how sexuality should be expressed, interpreting, in particular, female sexuality as secondary, and deriving from the maternal instinct, and severely regulating childhood sexuality.

So, although it would be wrong to derive the family form directly from developments in capitalism, the new domestic ideal was not a completely autonomous development. It was inextricably intertwined with wider social and political forces and changes. The conscious articulation of the ideology was a product both of political crisis – the fear of social disintegration for which the breakdown of familial and sexual order became a striking metaphor – and of the self-development of an increasingly dominant class. One important element can be traced to the evangelical revival of the late eighteenth century which laid the foundations of Victorian domesticity and challenged ruling-class immorality. The attack on aristocratic moral excesses simultaneously became a demand for a new stable order as a buttress against social collapse. The evangelical Hannah More, in her *Thoughts on the Importance of the Manners of the Great to General Society* in 1788, noted that: 'Reformation must begin with the GREAT or it will never be effectual. Their example is the fountain from where the vulgar draw their habits, action and characters.'[22]

These warnings were given a sharp resonance by the horrors to the aristocratic and respectable bourgeois mind, of the French Revolution. A correspondent writing to the *Public Ledger* in 1816 expressed the view very clearly: 'That the French Revolution, with all its constant horrors, was preceded by a total revolution of decency and morality, the virtuous qualities of a mind being sapped and undermined by the baneful exhibition of pictures, representing vice in the most alluring and varied forms, to a depraved mind, is a truth that unfortunately will not admit of doubt.'[23] Sexual collapse seemed the necessary path of social revolution; sexual and family decorum a vital part of social stability. Evangelical propaganda was thus able to achieve a sharp impact: while evangelicals like James Plumptree and Thomas Bowdler produced expurgated songs and literature, evangelical intellectuals like William Wilberforce, Hannah More and others such as Thornton and Stephen associated in the Clapham sect set up as moulders of a new ideology of domesticity, which not only proposed the family as a Christian haven in a disrupted world, but put forward a code of rules and regulations for the governing of individual lives.

The regency delayed the full application of the new moral code on the aristocracy until the coming of peace, but by 1820 with the furore generated by Queen Caroline's trial for adultery, there was clearly a new pressure for purity to which the aristocracy had to bend their knee. By 1825 Hannah More could remark: 'It is a singular satisfaction to me that I have lived to see such an increase in genuine religion among the higher classes of society. Mr. Wilberforce and I agree that where we knew one instance of it thirty years ago, there are now a dozen or more.'[24]

In the aristocracy this was often external obeisance, but even this was significant, for it underlined the new power of the bourgeoisie, industrially powerful, and from the 1830s politically influential but often morally anxious, particularly under the impact of political instability and economic uncertainty. The ideal of domesticity thus appeared as an important social cement. By the 1840s, as many acute observers like John Stuart Mill were noting, bourgeois opinion was coming to dominate even the actions of the upper classes.[25]

But the prime task of the new ideology of home and the family was less to influence others than to articulate the class feelings and experiences of the bourgeoisie itself. During the first half of the nineteenth century the domestic ideal and its attendant images became a vital organising factor in the development of middle-classness, and in the creation of a differentiated class identity. It became, indeed, an expression of class confidence, both against the immoral aristocracy, and against the masses, apparently denied the joys of family life and prone to sexual immodesty, and vice, 'fit only for sleep or sensual indulgence', as W. R. Greg put it firmly. The norms of domestic life it set forth drew a clear ideological boundary between rational members of society and the feckless. Not surprisingly, the bourgeois ideology of domesticity had a major impact on the subordinate elements in the bourgeois coalition itself, those class fractions and groups who aspired to its social standards and standing, the middle and lower bourgeoisie. By the end of the nineteenth century the lower middle classes were actually seen as the bulwark of respectability. The ideology of family life embedded in the wider notion of 'respectability' was to become therefore an important element in the establishment of bourgeois leadership in society at large.[26]

The ideology was composed of a series of rules relating to marriage, the family and Home that for the evangelicals were rooted in Christianity but were also clearly related to wider social and economic aspirations. A central part of this was expressed in two catchwords of the bourgeoisie: prudence and postponement, ritualistic guidelines to the bourgeoisie at this stage of its history but also presented secondarily as models for the poor. The importance of living up to what was required by one's status and what one had been used to came out over and over again in the discussions of the time, and 'prudence' became a moral imperative in the process of becoming axiomatic in the 1830s and 1840s.

As J. Wade put it in 1842, 'The immorality of marrying without the means of supporting a family is a doctrine of recent promulgation.'[27] The average age of marriage for men between 1840 and 1870 was just over 29 years, a fact that had important consequences, especially with regard to the market for prostitution. Indeed, social morality leaders came to believe that earlier marriages would discourage resort to prostitution. The rise of the average age of marriage in the nineteenth century underlines an important switch. Traditionally it had been the poor who had deferred marriage until they could become independent in an economy of the margins, but the early impact of industrialisation appears to have broken the pattern. The young working-class man in industrial employment could expect his income to reach its peak in early manhood and stay constant thereafter, barring disasters such as unemployment. The middle-class man, on the other hand, could predict a rising income for much of his life. Postponement of marriage was thus a judicious policy and a vital element in his standard of living.

Once marriage had been entered into, the home became an even more vital element in the desired way of life. Many have observed the emotional pressure behind the Victorian view of home which is not present in the eighteenth-century view. In the writings of such men as John Ruskin as for the evangelicals earlier, the home is invested with a religious imagery and dogmatic assurance which brooks no opposition. Home, he wrote in 1865, is: 'The place of Peace; the shelter, not only from all injury, but from all terror, doubt and division . . . . a vestal temple, a temple of the hearth watched over by Household Gods.'[28] Such an elevated tone was obviously not universal. But in all social discourse a stable home was seen both as a microcosm of stable society and a sanctuary from an unstable and rapidly changing one. It testified to the moral and financial respectability; it secured the legitimacy of the children; it offered cheaper and safer pleasures than the outside world and, as an additional boon, it was a source of virtues and emotions that could be found nowhere else, least of all in business or society. 'Here and here alone', as E. J. Hobsbawm has put it, 'the bourgeois and even more the petit-bourgeois family could maintain the illusion of a harmonious, hierarchic happiness.' Linked to this, a central factor in the familial ideology, was the increased ideological separation of home from work, based as it was on the withdrawal of the lady from social labour. This was an indispensable prelude to the development of the concept of personal life, a sphere of individuality and self-development, based on material prosperity, but focused on the cultivation of individuality, which in its turn was to have important consequences on the specification of sexuality.[29]

But these ideological concerns carried clear economic connotations. As Dr Johnson noted, upon the chastity of women 'all property in the world depends'. The middle-class capitalist required the legitimacy of all his children not only to protect his possessions from being enjoyed by the offspring of other men but to ensure the loyalty of his sons who might be business partners, and of his daughters who might be essential in marriage alliances.

That 'damned morality' which disturbed Lord Melbourne did not result from religious enthusiasm only. Differing provisions for the inheritance of family property were an important factor too. The sexual waywardness of the territorial aristocracy did not endanger the integrity of succession of estates which were regulated by primogeniture and entail. Countless children of the mist played happily in Whig and Tory nurseries where they presented no threat to the property or interest of heirs. The middle class families handed on their accumulating industrial wealth within a system of partible inheritance which demanded a more severe morality, imposing higher standards upon women than upon men. An adulterous wife might be the means of implanting a fraudulent claimant upon its property in the heart of the family; to avoid this ultimate catastrophe, middle class women were regulated to observe an inviolable rule of chastity.[30]

Female sexuality was necessarily therefore defined within these social and economic considerations, and it was in this context that the 'double standard' became an important adjunct of respectability.

The life style of the bourgeois lady was purchased at the expense of a large class of servants, often prone to sexual depredations, and an equally vulnerable group of prostitutes. The ideological division of women into two classes, the virtuous and the fallen, was already well developed by the mid-eighteenth century: its reality was to have a vivid impact on the Victorian imagination. Nor did it go unchallenged. The evangelical and puritan strands vigorously opposed the double standard, and by the last decades of the century were able to pose a significant challenge to its easy acceptance. Nonetheless, it is inescapably true that the familial ideology was accompanied by, and often relied on, a vast underbelly of prostitution, which fed on the double standard and an authoritarian moral code.

Other tensions were clearly focused in the bourgeois family, belying its apparently 'natural' and harmonious imagery. Juliet Mitchell has argued that 'it is against a background of the remoteness of the kinship system that the ideology of the biological family comes into its own'.[31] In fact, one of the major tensions was precisely that between the residual kinship patterns and the new form of relationships that were being constructed in the course of the nineteenth century. Randolph Trumbach has illustrated this point by reference to the otherwise baffling controversy over the ban on marriage to a deceased wife's sister. He argues that there was in force in England from the Restoration to the early twentieth century a system of marriage that approved cousin marriage (that is, to someone of one's blood) and discouraged marriage to affins (that is a relation by marriage, including *inter alia*, the deceased wife's sister). The established system conceived of marriage as an act of incorporation which maintained social status; it kept the family name from being lost and the family property from being distributed. The other system stressed that alliances could be maintained by remarriage and could be used to improve social standing. Inevitable conflicts developed. The law upheld the first system as long as the aristocracy was supreme. The ban against marriage to a deceased wife's sister was rescinded in 1907, another sign that the middle classes had come into their own.[32] Whatever the merits of this argument, what it points to is the way in which the complexities of these tensions found their focus in the questions of sexuality.

Another sign of the tension was the growing concern over incest in nineteenth-century culture. Indeed, by the end of the nineteenth century the incest taboo was seen as the very key to culture in anthropological works and occupied a pivotal position in Freud's theorisation of the dynamic unconscious. These intellectual breakthroughs actually coincided with a new social anxiety over incest throughout Europe. France, for instance, saw a systematic administrative and judicial hunting down of incest between 1889 and 1898, and the enactment of laws depriving defaulting parents of their paternal rights.[33] In England there was a particular concern over the effects of housing conditions in creating the possibility for incest in the working class, a concern voiced by the 1884 Housing Commission. Beatrice Webb was shocked when working for Booth in 1888 to hear working-class people tease each other about having babies by their fathers and brothers, and discussing the violation of little children. 'To put it bluntly', she wrote, 'sexual promiscuity, and even sexual perversion, are almost unavoidable among men and women of average character and intelligence crowded into the one-room tenement of slum areas.'[34]

Unlike Scotland, where incest was punishable by death up to 1887, or several American states, England had no civil law on incest in the nineteenth century, although the Matrimonial Causes Act of 1857 did include incestuous adultery as grounds for divorce. A growing feeling, encouraged by bodies such as the National Society for Prevention of Cruelty to Children, as to the social obnoxiousness of incest was finally expressed in the Criminal Law in 1908 which marked the tardy acceptance of a recommendation made over three centuries earlier. The 1908 Punishment of Incest Act made incest (by men) punishable by imprisonment for up to seven years and not less than three.

There were obvious problems resulting from the overcrowding of working-class homes but we may speculate that the social-purity agitation over incest reflected middle-class anxieties and tensions concerning the sanctity of the family rather than the objective reality of working-class conditions. For an essential paradox of the bourgeois family was that it was both the privileged location of emotionality and love, the only source in respectable ideology where it could be tolerated, and simultaneously an effective policeman of sexual behaviour. Childhood sexuality, especially, within this harbour of emotional and sexual restraint (ideologically at least), posed a particular challenge, and was met by simultaneous (and of course, contradictory) denial and control. The family, in other words, succeeded both in exalting sexuality, via the indispensable marriage bond, and in severely regulating it. The paradox was that the more ideology stressed the role of sex within conjugality, the more it was necessary to describe and regulate those forms of sexuality which were outside it.[35]

Sex and class

Sexuality thus had an extremely complex and vital symbolic role in what became the dominant ideology in the nineteenth century. First and foremost, sexual respectability expressed the aspirations and lives of the middle class. Only secondarily was it for export to other classes. It is here that theorisations which see the nuclear family as a means for controlling the working class in the 'interests of capitalism' can be seen to be inadequate.

Nevertheless, during the nineteenth century the working class was the recipient of various phases of evangelism and attempted colonisation. The aim clearly was to bring the masses into accord with the perceived notions of naturalness and stability that the bourgeoisie adhered to, and to which the lower middle classes aspired. Underlining this was not only a sense of what was proper but also a sense of what was politically and socially wise. The major phases of ruling-class concern with the moral behaviour of the masses, such as the 1790s, the 1830s and 1840s, the 1880s and 1890s, coincided with periods of political and social disruption. The words of evangelicals such as Hannah More could have a greater resonance in the context of the French Revolution when all the proprieties seemed lost, and political fear too could feed Malthusian fears of the growth of the working class outstripping resources. In a period of rapid change the family was an obvious model of traditional, ordered society with its pattern of authority and dependence.

What is peculiar about the evangelical advocates of this ideology is their social location. They were more often intellectuals than big industrialists, being what Robert Gray has called 'urban gentry', removed from the direct world of production and distinguished from other bourgeois groups by the rigours by which they set forth their views.[36] Often they demonstrated a rigid belief in iron laws of political economy, and hence their defence of the 1834 Poor Law and their evangelical attitudes to the working class. From their social position, the conditions of the working class could be conceived in absolute terms and compared with an abstract model of ordered familial life. The moral decay of the working class was seen above all in terms of its deficient pattern of family life, the apparently absent values of domesticity, family responsibility, thrift and accumulation. Hence the growth of the paradoxical phenomena of leisured middle-class ladies encouraging the education of working-class women in the virtues of housewifery, with the development of sewing schools, cooking classes, and so on, from the 1840s. The trend towards a form of social colonisation was accentuated throughout the nineteenth century by the perceived otherness of the working class, condemned, it was believed, to sexual rampancy and immorality, and often even physically different from the more leisured classes. The fascination of a middle-class man such as A. J. Munby with the hands and the boots of the working-class women, or 'Walter's' fascination with working-class girls in the anonymous sexual chronicle *My Secret Life* are signs of the complex sexual meanings that frequently resulted.[37]

Nevertheless, despite the earnest evangelical endeavours it is probably true to say that many bourgeois groups had little direct interest in working-class morality, as long as work relationships were secured. In the debate over the great Commissions of Inquiry of the 1830s and 1840s, divisions amongst the bourgeoisie were quite clear. Neither the interpretations nor the prognostications of men such as Lord Ashley were universally acceptable and the 'colonising' efforts were largely unsuccessful. By the 1890s the seats of sexual respectability were seen by reformers such as Grant Allen to rest in the lower middle class[38] and the upper working class, but in the latter there was no simple acceptance of middle-class norms. What was taking place was much more complex, and the working-class patterns of family and sexual life that were brought to the twentieth century were as much the product of working-class adaptation to rapid change in the context of a ruling set of ideas as a successful colonisation. Nevertheless, the existence of this vast and strange symbolic other served to confirm the rightness, indeed righteousness, of the moral code. It is in this context that we can appreciate the truth of Foucault's dictum that 'sexuality' was originally and fundamentally bourgeois in origins. It was in the great middle classes that sexuality, albeit in a morally restricted and sharply defined form, first became of major ideological significance.

References

1. See **E. M. Sigsworth** and **T. J. Wyke**, 'A Study of Victorian Prostitution and Venereal Disease', in **Martha Vicinus** (ed.), *Suffer and be Still*, Indiana University Press, Bloomington and London, 1972, p. 77.
2. **F. Barry Smith**, 'Sexuality in Britain, 1800–1900: Some Suggested Revisions', in **M. Vicinus** (ed.), *A Widening Sphere: Changing Roles of Victorian Women*, Indiana University Press, Bloomington and London, 1977, p. 193.
3. **Steven Marcus**, *The Other Victorians: A Study of Sexuality and Pornography in Mid-Nineteenth Century England*, Weidenfeld and Nicolson, London, 1967, p. 212. I do not concur with Marcus's general theoretical position, that 'the impulses and fantasies with which pornography deals are transhistorical' (p. 282), but I do think he points to the fact of change in the nature of erotica. Its social function changes when sexuality is defined as a private and sacred activity. For a critique of Marcus's views on pornography see **Ned Polsky**, *Hustlers, Beats and Others*, Penguin, Harmondsworth, 1971, pp. 199–200. I am indebted to Colin Buckle for this reference.

4. For general discussion of the forms and contradictions of 'Victorian' sexual ideology and behaviour, see **Eric Trudgill**, *Madonnas and Magdalens: The Origins and Development of Victorian Sexual Attitudes*, Heinemann, London, 1976; Marcus, *op. cit.*; F. B. Smith, *op. cit.*; **Brian Harrison**, 'Underneath the Victorians' (review of Marcus), *Victorian Studies*, Vol. X, No. 3, March 1967; **Peter T. Cominos**, 'Late Victorian Sexual Respectability and the Social System', *International Review of Social History*, No. 8, 1963; and 'The Late Victorian Revolt', Unpublished Oxford D.Phil. thesis, 1958; and essays in the two volumes edited by Martha Vicinus, cited above.

5. **Havelock Ellis**, *Studies in the Psychology of Sex*, Vol. 1, Random House, New York, 1936 (4-volume edition), p. 464.

6. See **G. R. Quaife**, *Wanton Wenches and Wayward Wives. Peasants and Illicit Sex in Early Seventeenth Century England*, Croom Helm, London, 1979; and more generally, **Jean Louis Flandrin**, *Families in Former Times. Kinship, household and sexuality*, Cambridge University Press, Cambridge, 1979, pp. 174 ff.; and Stone, *The Family, Sex and Marriage*.

7. Flandrin, *op. cit.*, pp. 166 ff. Cf. **Kathleen M. Davis**, 'The Sacred Condition of Equality – How Original were Puritan Doctrines of Marriage?', *Social History*, No. 5, May 1977, which suggests a continuity of puritan attitudes to marriage with those of the pre-reformation pious bourgeoisie. The Puritans believed that in rejecting abstinence in marriage they were breaking with Romish practices.

8. Quaife, *op. cit.*, argues the point.

9. *Ibid.*, p. 245. For other discussions of 'pre-industrial' *mores* amongst the peasantry, see **Peter Laslett**, *The World We Have Lost*, Methuen, London, 1st edn 1965, 2nd edn 1971; and *Family Life and Illicit Love in Earlier Generations. Essays in Historical Sociology*, Cambridge University Press, Cambridge, 1977; **P. Laslett** and **Richard Wall**, *Household and Family in Past Time*, Cambridge University Press, Cambridge, 1972; **David Levine**, *Family Formation in an Age of Nascent Capitalism*, Academic Press, New York and London, 1977. See also Chapter 4 below.

10. Stone, *op. cit.*

11. See Chapter 5 below.

12. *The Sentinel*, April 1885, p. 441.

13. Cf. **Richard J. Evans**, 'Prostitution, State and Society in Imperial Germany', *Past and Present*, No. 70, Feb. 1976.

14. Cominos, 'The Late Victorian Revolt', p. 371.

15. On the Hardwicke Marriage Act see Stone, *op. cit.*, p. 35. Two Acts in 1836, An Act for Marriage in England, and An Act for Registering Births, Deaths and Marriages, established a Central Registry Office, with registrars throughout the country who had the power to celebrate civil marriages, while nonconformist chapels were licensed to conduct marriages. On the effects see **Olive Anderson**, 'The Incidence of Civil Marriage in Victorian England and Wales', *Past and Present*, No. 69, Nov. 1975, pp. 50–87; and the Debate: **Roderick Floud** and **Pat Thane**; Rejoinder from **Olive Anderson**, *Past and Present*, No. 84, Aug. 1979. Anderson argued that as a result of the 1836 Act a significant proportion of the population chose civil marriage in preference to the rites of religious denominations, suggesting either the survival of old traditions or the adoption of new ways of behaviour.

16. **O. R. McGregor**, *Divorce in England: A Centenary Study*, Heinemann, London, 1957, p. 19.

17. Cf. Stone, *op. cit.*, p. 679; and **Elizabeth Wilson**, *Women and the Welfare State*, Tavistock, London, 1977.

18. Flandrin, *op. cit.*, pp. 50 ff. discusses le Play and other contributors to this debate thereafter. For a critique of functionalist Marxism from within a Marxist perspective see **Annette Kuhn**, 'Structures of Patriarchy and Capital in the Family', in **Annette Kuhn** and **Ann Marie Wolpe** (eds) *Feminism and Materialism: Women and Modes of Production*, Routledge and Kegan Paul, London, 1978. Stone, *op. cit.*, clearly has a functionalist position in which the family serves to channel sexual drives.

19. See Peter Laslett's work, cited above; Flandrin, *op. cit.*, pp. 50 ff., summarises Laslett's views and basically supports them. These views in turn are criticised in **L. Berkner**, 'The Stem Family and the Development Cycle of the Peasant Household', *American History Review*, Vol. 77, No. 2, 1972, pp. 398–418; and **Arlen Skolnick**, 'The Family Revisited: Themes in Recent Social Science Research', *Journal of Interdisciplinary History*, Vol. V, No. 4., Spring 1975. See also **Michael Verdon** 'The Stem Family: Towards a General Theory', *Journal of Interdisciplinary History*, Vol. X, No. 1, Summer 1979. **Christopher Lasch** discusses theories of the family in his review article 'The Family and History', *New York Review of Books*, 13 November 1975; see also his book, *Haven in a Heartless World*, Basic Books, New York, 1977. The whole relevance of the theme is discussed in **Rayna Rapp**, **Ellen Ross** and **Renate Bridenthal**, 'Examining Family History', *Feminist Studies*, Vol. 5, No. 1, Spring 1979, which gives extensive and valuable references.

20. **Mark Poster**, *Critical Theory of the Family*, Pluto Press, London, 1978, p. xvii. There is a critique of this book by **Ellen Ross**, 'Rethinking "The Family"', *Radical History Review*, No. 20, Spring/Summer 1979. For a theory which discusses the construction of the family through various social practices see **Jacques Donzelot**, *La Police des Familles*, Les Editions de Minuit, Paris, 1977; trans. as *The Policing of Families*, Hutchinson, London, 1980.

21. Stone, *op. cit.*, p. 89; **Randolph Trumbach**, *The Rise of the Egalitarian Family. Aristocratic Kinship and Domestic Relations in Eighteenth Century England*, Academic Press, New York, San Francisco, London, 1978; and 'Europe and its Families: A Review Essay of Lawrence Stone', *Journal of Social History*, Vol. 13, No. 1, Fall 1979. Flandrin, *op. cit.*, p. 8, has found the first indisputable use of the term 'family' as applying to parents and children only (the nuclear case) as being no earlier than 1829 in England (it was earlier in France) and argues (p. 9): 'The concept of the family, therefore, as it is most commonly defined today, has only existed in our western culture since a comparatively recent date.'

22. Trudgill, *Madonnas and Magdalens*, p. 164. The best recent discussion of the role of the evangelicals in the shaping of the ideology of domesticity is **Catherine Hall**, 'The Early Formation of Victorian Domestic Ideology', in **Sandra Burman** (ed.) *Fit Work for Women*, Croom Helm, London, 1979.

23. *Public Ledger*, 17 January 1816. Trudgill, *op. cit.*, is good on the various crises and moral panics, e.g. 1797 (p. 166) and during the 1830s and 1840s (p. 43).

24. Quoted in Trudgill, *op. cit.*, p. 173.

25. See Trudgill, *op. cit.*, Ch. 3.

26. This theme is discussed in Trudgill, *op. cit.*, pp. 194 ff.; **Geoffrey Crossick**

Chapter Three

The sacramental family: middle-class men, women and children

Masculinity and femininity

The bourgeoisie and its values shaped official sexual imagery. The hysterical woman was the middle-class woman of leisure deprived of productive labour and imprisoned in dependence on her family. The masturbating child was the middle-class boy trapped within familial concerns and devotion. The perverse adult was the public schoolboy grown up, the infraction of the norm whose existence re-established it. Even when the moralising concern was directed to other individuals or classes, the issues were mainly those germane to the respectable middle class. The concern with the 'immorality' of the working class said more about bourgeois morality than about the working class. The great crusades of the 1880s over child prostitution sometimes answered as much to middle-class anxieties as to gross sexual exploitation.[1]

But the concern and anxiety over sexual behaviour were often genuine. Even when the double standard of morality existed the rules of the game were accepted and when the morality of sexual restraint broke the sense of torment was real. 'The bourgeois world was haunted by sex', Hobsbawm has written, 'but not necessarily sexual promiscuity; the characteristic nemesis of the bourgeois folk myth . . . followed a *single* fall from grace'.[2] Many men battled valiantly with what they conceived of as temptation and strove to live up to a higher ideal of married life, and few women, including leading feminists, would have thought of demanding more. It is in this context that we must read the definitions and practices that constituted Victorian sexuality. Gagnon and Simon in their book *Sexual Conduct* have suggested that 'Social roles are not vehicles for the expression of sexual impulse. . . . Sexuality becomes a vehicle for expressing the needs of social roles.'[3] It is in the construction of the assumptions governing the rules of manhood, femininity and childhood that the definitions of sexuality emerged.

Havelock Ellis suggested that male sexuality was unproblematical, being direct and forceful, based as it was in the original primitive seizure of the female by the male. It was female sexuality that constituted the social problem, because through it the race was perpetuated.[4] But in fact we can see in process in the nineteenth century a quite clear creation of a series of beliefs about male sexuality, beliefs which were inextricably linked to concepts of male self-expression and power. Texts put forth a gospel of real manhood and real womanhood.[5] From the 1830s there was, for instance, a stream of handbooks on how to achieve male self-sufficiency. Self making was seen as a product of will and energy but it was achieved only through struggle. There was a long-standing fear of female sexuality which is expressed by ideologists such as William Acton, the surgeon and moralist in the mid century. For him sex appeared to be a torture, where the only possibility of escape was marriage to unresponsive women. Acton was certainly a minority spokesman and was challenged even by contemporaries in his attitude to female sexuality, but he did express pervasive anxieties. The problem was often of living up to the construction of masculinity. Manhood for Acton was as precious as chastity. Virility he wrote is: 'Much more developed in man than is that of maternity in women. Its existence, indeed, seems necessary to give a man that consciousness of his dignity, of his character as head and ruler, and of his importance, which is absolutely essential to the well being of the family, and through it, of society itself.'[6] A man should be so proud of virility that he should not squander or debase it. Or as Krafft-Ebing put it, 'The sexual functions of men exercise a very marked influence upon the development and preservation of character', so that manliness and self reliance were not the qualities which one would expect from the 'impotent onanist'.[7]

A real anxiety is traceable even amongst the most priapic of men, especially when sex entangled with class. James Boswell in the eighteenth century was generally impotent the first time he slept with women of his own class, though in sex with lower-class girls he could easily prove his manhood.[8] An echo of this could be seen in the fascination expressed by many middle-class men with the physical features of working-class women and in the concurrent attempts at sexual colonisation embodied in prostitution of working-class girls.[9] Sex within one's own class was too hemmed in by respect and propriety. And with this exaltation of male sexual power, Krafft Ebing's all-conquering sexual instinct, went a curious discretion about the act of sex. Many men and women were no doubt happily married, and sexual anxieties were subordinated to other familial and social concerns. Indeed, the happiness of many marriages may in part have been based on mutual sexual satisfaction. But many marriages, like that of the writer J. A. Symonds, got off to an unsteady start as mutual ignorances and shyness inhibited consummation. As W. R. Greg put it, 'The first sacrifice is made and exacted . . . in a delirium of mingled love and shame.'[10] It was, as one historian has noted, like two separate races confronting each other over the marriage bed. And even the apparent libertine, if Walter's *My Secret Life* is in any way an accurate chronicle, had his own anxieties born of sexual discretion: 'Does every man kiss, coax, hint smuttily, then talk bawdily, snatch a feel, smell his fingers, assault and win, exactly as I have done?'[11] And often, accompanying this discretion was a real fear of

of as the almost ungovernable lust of men. Chastity, as Blackwell put it, the government of the passions, is the highest law; and one natural to women.

The portrait sometimes drawn of middle-class women of the nineteenth century as proto-modernisers, the forerunners of the sexually liberated American housewife of the late twentieth century, is therefore misleading. Women were defined not only by convention and religion but by ineffective birth control, fear of venereal disease, and by sexual ignorance, which not surprisingly, the physician and lecturer, Sir James Paget, found to be 'very common among well educated women'.[21] What is strikingly absent in nineteenth-century thought is any concept of female sexuality which is independent of men's. A sense of female identity *was* of course present, often engendered around what were defined as exclusively female concerns. Women were bound together by frequent pregnancies, childbirth, nursing and family care, menopausal anxieties and so on, which worked to establish a physical and emotional intimacy, but there was no sense of an independent sexuality.[22] Male sexuality was defined, both in popular treatises and in sexological works as instrumental, forceful and direct; female generally as expressive and responsive, shaped within the traditional emphasis on female emotionality. Moreover, the new scientific discoveries of the century – such as the discovery of the place of ovulation in the menstrual cycle or advances in gynaecology – far from undermining this view, were used to validate conventional ideas about femininity and women's sexuality.

These concepts, expressed in books and pamphlets, and directly to women, assumed a greater importance because of the professionalisation of medicine and the growing dominance of disease models as explanations for social phenomena. Increasingly, as Charles Rosenberg has suggested, disease sanctions were used as the 'basic framework for exposition and admonition'.[23] A key factor here was the campaign for the improvement of the social position of doctors from the mid-nineteenth century. Efforts to establish professional standards and provide a sound educational basis for doctors were accompanied by anxieties about their status, which led to doctors often adopting, it seemed to their critics, a priest-like role.[24] The increasing demand for medical care on the part of the middle classes combined with a growing perception of medical attention as a status symbol by those below, also added to doctors' social power. Furthermore, in their search for a monopoly of medical knowledge they launched bitter attacks on the quality of popular ('quack') and self-help medicine, in many areas of which women had been dominant.

These doctors expressed a mixture of views about sexuality, often recognising the reality of female sexuality, including the role of the clitoris, but this sometimes coincided with the notion that women were naturally timid creatures and were natural invalids. There was a deep belief, even amongst many women, that biology had incapacitated them, and this was sustained by expert opinion. F. H. A. Marshall's

Physiology of Reproduction (1910), in examining current views, found that menstruation was often seen as a disease symptom so that 'the phenomenon of menstruation must be looked upon as belonging to the borderland of pathology'. Even sex reformers like Havelock Ellis shared in the assumption that menstruation was debilitating, and by some this was seen as an educational disqualification. The *British Medical Journal* in 1907 quoted with approval the view of an American doctor that in higher education 'It is not merely her mind that is unsexed, but her body loses much of that special charm that attracts men. In America the college woman when she does marry is often barren....'[25]

There was of course, still a widespread ignorance, even amongst scientists and doctors, about the processes of human reproduction. In the first half of the nineteenth century it was generally believed the menstrual flow came from an excess of nutrients in the female. Eggs were thought to descend from the ovaries only as a consequence of intercourse. By 1845 it had been discovered that eggs were ejected spontaneously but this largely failed to affect existing views of sexuality. In fact, the belief that menstruation incapacitated women seems to have increased amongst some 'experts', though they were constantly challenged. Knowledge about cyclical patterns of women's sexual feelings were in part dependent on further research in endocrinology, and it was not until 1928 that two scientists working separately, Ogino and Knaus, discovered the hormonal pattern for the menstrual cycle.[26]

The assumption that women were dominated by their reproductive systems (women belonged to nature, while men belonged to culture) was implicit in all medical attitudes. The most extreme example of this was in the surgical treatment sometimes meted out to women. There was, for instance, some attempt to use clitoridectomy as a cure for dysuria or amenorrhoea, for epilepsy, hysteria, sterility and insanity, in the 1860s. It was believed that all of these were produced by sexual arousal so the surgical removal of the clitoris was a sure cure for the disease. The columns of *The Lancet* suggest that the operation was performed, though it aroused fierce opposition, and was soon abandoned.[27] Possibly a more frequent practice was the surgical removal of the ovaries, ovariotomy. It seems that thousands of these operations were performed in America from the 1850s onwards, while in England in 1869 Dr Wells reported in *The Lancet* one hundred cases. Another report spoke of 156 cases of ovariatomy, 61 of which proved fatal, and in 60 of the cases there was no ovarian disease. Other medical advances were often the subject of rather more hesitation. Many doctors expressed doubts as to the propriety of using the speculum. As Dr Bennett, an expert on ovarian and uterine diseases, put it, because of the influence it would have on the character of English women 'it must not be used for virgins'. And another doctor, Tyler Smith, made it clear that 'the natural modesty of women' must be protected in the use of such devices. (It should be said that such views often gained the support

ahead of the textile workers, the first working-class group to show strong limitation.[33]

Various contraceptive methods have always been known, from abortion to coitus interruptus, and by the eighteenth century condoms were available, though they seem to have been usually used as safeguards against venereal disease rather than for birth control. James Boswell, for example, often used them for the former, even occasionally, apparently, for the latter; but never it seems with his wife. During the nineteenth century there was a steady stream of birth-control controversy and propaganda. The publication of Godwin's *Political Justice* in 1793 prompted Thomas Malthus's attempted refutation of his argument, that the cause of human misery was social institutions, in the famous *Essay on Population*. Later utilitarians like Jeremy Bentham and James Mill proposed various forms of birth control. The references in their works were guarded but controversy was stimulated from 1823 by the distribution by Francis Place of handbills explaining in detail methods of contraception – sponge, sheath, withdrawal. William Thompson provided moral and economic justification while Richard Carlile's *Everywomans Book* was in 1826 the first devoted to contraception, advocating those methods propounded by Place, and similar advocacy came with works of Robert Dale Owen and Charles Knowlton.[34]

By the 1840s there was some knowledge of the rhythm method of birth control from discussions by French physicians Pouchet and Raciborski on women's ovulation cycle, though for a while it was believed that the safe period was immediately after menstruation. There is some evidence that practical family planning first began amongst what F. B. Smith calls the 'self instructed classes', not the upper middle classes but those most responsive to radical propaganda.[35] There is no doubt, however, that it was in the 1860s and 1870s that there was a real extension of propaganda for birth control directed at the middle class. Charles Bradlaugh's *National Reformer* carried articles by him and George Drysdale on the subject from the beginning. The audience was limited but many of the articles were reissued in pamphlet form. Books by Robert Dale Owen, Knowlton and Drysdale were reissued several times. George R. Drysdale's *The Elements of Social Science, or Physical, Sexual and Natural Religion* was particularly important and quickly translated into many European languages. It offered a review of the Malthusian doctrine, a discussion of the physiology of sex and a survey of all known venereal diseases; it also briefly analysed preventive intercourse.

The trial of Bradlaugh and Annie Besant in 1876 for republishing one of Knowlton's pamphlets gave the birth-control movement wide publicity and created the demand for more information, and led to the setting up of the first organisation to campaign on birth control, the Malthusian League. Between 1876 and 1881 over 200,000 copies of the Knowlton tract were sold in England. Annie Besant's own *The Law of Population*, published in 1877, sold 175,000 copies by 1891. Never before, as the Banks put it, had the arguments in favour of limiting the size of the family been presented to so large a public. And although one or two other trials, in the 1890s for example, centred around birth control, at no time after 1877 was birth-control propaganda hindered by law. Banks estimates that some 3 million pamphlets and leaflets were circulated between 1879 and 1921 urging family limitation, while over 1 million between 1876 and 1891 gave details of contraception.[36]

Though propaganda was important in disseminating information, it was not decisive. It also needed a second factor, a change in the general attitude to family size, and this seems to have begun well before the 1870s. A crucial factor in this does seem to have been changes in the role of women within the family. When Drysdale established a short-lived *Political Economist and Journal of Social Science* in 1856, letters appeared in his columns from women supporting the birth-control crusade. One reported that many had read Drysdale's work:

Numbers of young women have told me that they look upon life in quite a different light now that they learn that nature has not been so cruel to them, as to give them but the choice of a married life, in which probably all the highest aims of life must be sacrificed, and the wife reduced to the level of a breeding animal, or a life of celibacy.[37]

Another correspondent asked for cheap tracts which she could distribute to the poor as the middle class were already knowledgeable. Many feminists were also interested in birth control as an issue although discretion dictated a public silence (see Chapter 8). But there are no easy ways of determining the actual role of women in decision making in the use of birth control. It seem improbable that it was an entirely autonomous female decision, particularly given the absence of sex instruction for girls. The Banks have speculated on the possibility of the husband and wife debating the use of contraception, and certainly, as they suggest, the very use of contraceptive techniques required some minimum level of discussion about sexual matters. Others have suggested that the deliberate limitation of family size was one of the principal contributions of middle-class women to the modernisation process of women generally. But the portrait that has been drawn of respectable women rising from the marriage bed to insert the sponge or to draw the condom over the 'burning machine', seems unlikely to have been the norm.[38]

Rather than 'domestic feminism' being central in encouraging the use of birth control methods, it is much more probable that decisions to limit family size came from changing notions of the family. Banks has argued that the main factor in the decision to limit family size was the attempt to maintain the standard of living in more difficult economic circumstances in the late nineteenth century, and in particular the rising cost of servants which altered the middle class way of life.[39] But as the fall in the proportion of domestic servants began after professional families started to limit their families, it seems probable that the limitation of children caused the reduction in domestic service. Family restric-

significant shifts in public attitudes, particularly acting to increase sex segregation and reinforce stereotypes. Linked with this, as a result of the decline in family size and the decline of the family as a working unit, was the increased discontinuity of age-groups within the family. Hall implied that adolescence covered the years from sexual maturity to the end of physical growth in a person's twenties, which was not dissimilar to the early nineteenth-century concept of youth, but all those who followed Hall equated it with the teen years. After Hall, but not before, the major emphasis was on puberty as marking the onset of adolescence, whereas earlier popular definitions had taken their cue from social status, not physiology.

As the image of home became more sentimentalised in the nineteenth century, one's entry into the world of affairs appeared more threatening and the promptings of prudence suggested deferred gratification. It was in this context that we can try to understand the switch in focus in the taboo against masturbation, which was increasingly directed at infants and young adolescents. It has to be seen, it may be suggested, as an aspect of the effort to control these age-groups. The nineteenth century anxiety about the centrality of sex in people's lives was redirected towards the burgeoning physical potentialities of young people.

The various works on the subject are very revealing about the images of young people that prevailed. Henry Maudsley in the 1860s, for example, developed the notion that masturbatory insanity was characterised by intense self-regard and conceit, extreme perversion of feeling and corresponding deranging of thought, and later by failure of intelligence, nocturnal hallucinations, and suicidal and homicidal propensities, all characteristics which doomed the boy to social disaster. Another doctor, Edward Spitzka, believed that an unwillingness to work at an appointed task was itself a symptom of masturbatory insanity.[46] These emphases, particularly as brought out in the typical case histories in a host of texts, revealed, we may suggest, the fear of masturbation as actually fixed in the minds of middle-class parents, disturbed by their sons' unwillingness to live by the respectable sexual ideology, and attend to their duties and to future marriage. Writers like Maudsley and Spitzka represent a form of scientific morality which simultaneously reinforces and promises to alleviate parental sexual anxieties, while underlining parental authority within the middle-class family against the demands of adolescent youth for sexual and personal autonomy. The connotations of this in the creation of manhood were made clear by Baden Powell, founder of the Scout movement, who observed that masturbation checks the semen from getting its full chance of making the strong, manly man: 'You are throwing away the seed that has been handed down to you as a trust instead of keeping it and ripening it for bringing a son to you later on.'[47]

The popularity of physical sanctions to prevent masturbation, including the development of elaborate machines which sensitively responded to erections or physically prevented masturbation, has been

well documented.[48] More important probably was the guilt induced by
the constant strictures, which made the struggle against one's wicked
urges a constant and exhausting effort of will. For young women the
disease sanctions were even stronger and tended to be linked with
childbearing threats, with the possibility opened up of cancer, insanity
and TB, or at the least frigidity or nymphomania. There was undoubtedly seen to be a growing problem regarding adolescent girls because they were maturing a little earlier[49] and marrying later, around
25, and it was in this context that such horrors as clitoridectomies could
be developed. Perhaps another manifestation of the growing concern
over adolescence, for boys this time, was the new mania for circumcision among the upper and professional classes of Britain and America
in the 1890s. Dr Remondino attacked the 'debateable appendage' in his
History of Circumcision (1891), and compared circumcision to 'a well
secured life annuity', 'a better saving investment', making for a greater
capacity for labour, a longer life, less nervousness, fewer doctors' bills.
By the 1930s at least two-thirds of public schoolboys were circumcised,
(compared to only one-tenth of working-class boys), and by then perhaps one-third of the male population was circumcised, with very little
medical justification.[50]

Changes in attitudes to masturbation were manifest by the end of the
nineteenth century. Maudsley modified his 1867 comments and in 1895
argued that masturbation was a product of a particular form of insanity, due to the processes of adolescence. There was a greater emphasis
on masturbation as a symptom rather than as a cause. Masturbation did
not become respectable, but there was a new stress on its ability to rob
adolescence of real fulfilment, and this was even echoed in the work of
sex reformers such as Havelock Ellis and expressed in G. Stanley Hall's
two volumes on adolescence. But despite this slight shift in the taboos,
as late as the 1920s Havelock Ellis and Albert Moll were still able to
recommend little metal suits of armour fitted over the genitals and
attached to a locked belt as prophylaxis for masturbation, and sex education books continued to inveigh against the solitary vice well into the
second half of the century. Pre-adult sexuality remained something to
be organised and controlled.

The middle-class family was a peculiar combination for it both
stressed the innocence of childhood, its asexuality, *and* its potentiality
for sexual corruption, with all the horrors that opened up. This was
clearly expressed as late as 1913 by the Reverend Edward Lyttleton,
headmaster of Eton:

Those who are working and hoping, however feebly, to encompass the lives of
boys and girls with wholesome atmosphere must know that in regard to sexuality
two factors stand out. First, that in proportion as the adolescent mind gets absorbed in sex questions, wreckage of life ensures. Secondly that sanity and up-
right manliness are destroyed, not only by the reading of obscene stuff, but *by a
premature interest* in sex matters, however it be excited.[51]

It was, it seems, to prevent this 'premature interest' that the family, and its moralists, were so anxious to concern themselves with sexual manifestations. But by a typical return, the anxiety and concern created rather than alleviated the 'problem', for the incitement that Lyttleton so worried about was a product of middle-class obsessions themselves.

References

1. This point is dealt with more fully in Chapter 5, below. It is worth noting (I am grateful to Colin Buckle for pointing this out to me) that one of the best known advocates of this position, F. B. Smith ('Sexuality in Britain'), has recently modified his position: **F. B. Smith**, *The People's Health*, Croom Helm, London, 1979, p. 303.
2. E. J. Hobsbawm, *The Age of Capitalism*, p. 234.
3. Gagnon and Simon, *Sexual Conduct*, p. 45.
4. **Havelock Ellis**, *Studies in the Psychology of Sex*, Vol. 1, Part 2, *The Sexual Impulse in Women*, Random House, New York, 1936, p. 189.
5. See **G. J. Barker Benfield**, *The Horror of the Half Known Life. Male Attitudes towards Women and Sexuality in Nineteenth Century America*, Harper and Row, New York, 1976; and 'The Spermatic Economy', in *Feminist Studies*, Vol. 1, No. 1. Cf. Trudgill, *Madonnas and Magdalens*, pp. 54 ff.; and **Malcolm Tozer**, 'Manliness. The Evolution of a Victorian Ideal', unpublished Ph.D., University of Leicester 1978. The fears of sex were pervasive. There was a fear both of indulging and of not indulging. For the latter, see the diseases listed by Drysdale for abstinent men, including spermatorrhoea and impotence, in **George R. Drysdale**, *The Elements of Social Science*; 1st edn (under the title *Physical, Sexual and Natural Religion* by a Student of Medicine) 1885; 4th edition, by a Graduate of Medicine, E. Truelove, London, 1861. There were 12 editions between then and 1874, and another 23 by 1904.
6. **William Acton**, *The Functions and Disorders of the Reproductive Organs in Youth, in Adult Age, and in Advanced Life*, John Churchill, London, 1857, p. 74.
7. Krafft-Ebing, *Psychopathia Sexualis*, p. 13.
8. See Stone, *Family, Sex and Marriage*, p. 593.
9. See Chapter 2, note 37, pp. 36–7.
10. For Symonds, see **Phyllis Grosskurth**, *John Addington Symonds: A Biography*, Longmans, London, 1964. For Greg, see *Westminster Review*, Vol. LIII, July 1850, p. 473. **Carol Christ**, 'Victorian Masculinity and the Angel in the House', in Vicinus (ed.) *A Widening Sphere*, shows how the poets Patmore and Tennyson, like other writers, sought to resolve their ambivalence about manhood through idealising the 'Angel of the House' – locating (as in John Ruskin) moral qualities to compensate for man's aggressiveness. Behind this she detects a fear of sexual energy and a desire to escape the burdens of action and sexuality.
11. *My Secret Life*, quoted in Marcus, *The Other Victorians*, p. 163.
12. **John R. Gillis**, *Youth and History: Tradition and Change in European Age Relations, 1770 – Present*, Academic Press, London and New York, 1974 – on which part of this discussion is based.

13. Discussed in **Brian Harrison**, *Separate Spheres: the Opposition to Women's Suffrage in Britain*, Croom Helm, London, 1978.
14. The Boy Scouts had a course of warnings on sex from the age of 8. By 11 they had learnt that semen had to be hoarded. By 17, in *Rovering to Success*, they were recommended to bathe the 'racial organ' in cold water daily. The *Handbook for Girl Guides* warned that 'secret bad habits' led to hysteria and lunacy.
15. Quoted in Marcus, *The Other Victorians*, p. 31. Marcus's book makes the most strenuous efforts to define Acton's central role, but he was not the first. There are clear signs of the attempt to construct the importance of Acton, to build a bogeyman who can then be mocked as a typical 'Victorian', in Havelock Ellis, *The Psychology of Sex*, Heinemann, London, 1933 (10th impression 1946), p. 287: 'less than a hundred years ago the English surgeon Acton wrote a book which until the end of the last century was the standard authority on sexual questions . . .'.
16. *London Medical Review*, Vol. 111, No. 3, September 1862; Jacob Bright, quoted in Smith, 'Sexuality in Britain', p. 186.
17. Quoted in **Angus McLaren**, *Birth Control in Nineteenth-Century England*, Croom Helm, London, 1978, pp. 96–7.
18. **Carl N. Degler**, 'What Ought to Be and What Was: Women's Sexuality in the Nineteenth Century', *American Historical Review*, Vol. 79, No. 5, December 1974, p. 1486.
19. With regard to divorce, a man could after 1857 obtain a divorce for simple adultery on the part of the wife; the wife had to prove desertion, cruelty or sodomy. See McGregor, *Divorce in England*, p. 20. On property rights (the more equitable Married Women's Property Act was passed in 1882), see **Lee Holcombe**, 'Victorian Wives and Property. Reform of the Married Women's Property Law, 1857–1882', in Vicinus (ed.), *A Widening Sphere*. On the middle-class lady's domestic duties see **Patricia Branca**, *Silent Sisterhood*, Croom Helm, London, 1975; and *Women in Europe since 1750*, Croom Helm, London, 1978. See also Trudgill, *Madonnas and Magdalens*, p. 69, for a discussion of female dependency.
20. **Elizabeth Blackwell**, *The Human Element in Sex*, 4th edn, J. and A. Churchill, London, 1885, p. 44.
21. Quoted in Cominos, 'The Late Victorian Revolt', p. 405. Branca, *Silent Sisterhood*, most clearly advances the modernisation thesis; as I make clear, I believe her views to be somewhat exaggerated.
22. The now almost classic discussion of this theme (using American evidence) is **Carroll Smith-Rosenberg**, 'The Female World of Love and Ritual: Relations Between Women in Nineteenth-Century America', *Signs*, No. 1, Autumn 1975. Cf. **W. R. Greg**, *Westminster Review*, July 1850, to the effect that in women 'desire is dormant, if not non-existent, till excited; always till excited by undue familiarity; almost always till excited by actual intercourse'.
23. **Charles E. Rosenberg**, 'Sexuality, Class and Role in 19th-Century America', *American Quarterly*, May 1973.
24. See **F. P. Cobbe**, 'The Little Health of Ladies', *Contemporary Review*, January 1878, when she argues that the medical profession occupies 'with a strangely close analogy, the position of the priesthood of former times, assumes the same airs of authority . . . and enters every family with a latch key of private information'. On professionalisation and its effects, see **Jean**

L'Esperance, 'Doctors and Women in Nineteenth Century Society: Sexuality and Role', in **John Woodward** and **David Richards**, *Health Care and Popular Medicine in Nineteenth Century England. Essays in the Social History of Medicine*, Croom Helm, London, 1977; and **Angus McLaren**, 'The Early Birth Control Movement: An Example of Medical Self Help', in *ibid.* For a more optimistic view see Branca, *Silent Sisterhood*, pp. 63 ff.

25. **F. H. A. Marshall**, *The Physiology of Reproduction*, Longman & Co., London, 1910, Vol. 1, p. 192; **P. Geddes** and **J. A. Thomson**, *The Evolution of Sex*, Contemporary Science Series, London, 1889; Havelock Ellis, *Studies in the Psychology of Sex* (Random House, 1936 edn) Vol. 1, Part 1, Appendix A; *British Medical Journal*, 2 March 1907. There is a very useful discussion of the theme in **Elaine** and **English Showalter**, 'Victorian Women and Menstruation', in M. Vicinus (ed.), *Suffer and be Still*.

26. See Showalter, *op. cit.*, p. 38; Branca, *op. cit.*, p. 71; and see the further discussion in Chapter 8 below.

27. **Lorna Duffin**, 'The Conspicuous Consumptive: Woman as an Invalid', in **Sara Delamont** and **Lorna Duffin** (eds), *The Nineteenth Century Woman. Her Cultural and Physical World*, Croom Helm, London, 1978, on which this section is based. Dr Isaac Baker Brown, a London surgeon, popularised the clitoridectomy after 1858. Colin Buckle estimates that some 600 such operations were conducted 1860–66, but Baker Brown was excoriated for his efforts.

28. **Carroll Smith Rosenberg**, 'The Hysterical Woman: Sex Roles and Role Conflict in 19th-Century America', *Social Research*, Vol. 39, No. 4, Winter 1972.

29. *British Medical Journal*, 13 January 1900; 21 March 1914. See also *British Medical Journal*, 27 March 1909.

30. L'Esperance, *op. cit.*, p. 117.

31. Drysdale, in *The Elements*, was the first doctor to openly advocate birth control. Even he attacked coitus interruptus, as likely to lead to sexual enfeeblement, while he claimed the sheath produced impotence.

32. **Angus McLaren**, *Birth Control in Nineteenth-Century England*, Croom Helm, London, 1978, p. 132, describes the incident, and gives an excellent discussion of the mixture of medical attitudes and motives in Ch. 7, pp. 116 ff. One reason, of course, was the fear that birth control would allow 'indiscriminate debauchery' and undermine the single standard. For this reason many, like Elizabeth Blackwell, opposed contraception, preferring abstinence and male restraint.

33. J. A. Banks, *Prosperity and Parenthood*, is the classic discussion of this issue.

34. McLaren, *op. cit.*; **William M. Langer**, 'The Origins of the Birth Control Movement in England in the Early Nineteenth Century', *Journal of Interdisciplinary History*, Vol. V, No. 4, Spring 1975, pp. 669–86.

35. F. B. Smith, 'Sexuality in Britain'.

36. See **J. A. Banks** and **Olive Banks**, 'The Bradlaugh–Besant Trial and the English Newspapers', *Population Studies*, Vol. VIII, 1954–5, pp. 22, 24; Langer, *op. cit.*

37. *Political Economist*, 11 January 1857, p. 85.

38. **J. A.** and **Olive Banks**, *Feminism and Family Planning in Victorian England*, Liverpool University Press, p. 127; **Daniel Scott Smith**, 'Family Limitation, Sexual Control, and Domestic Feminism in Victorian America', *Feminist Studies*, Vol. 1, Nos. 3–4, Winter/Spring 1973; Patricia

Branca, *Silent Sisterhood*, pp. 132, 137. Branca challenges the conventional view (endorsed, for example, by McLaren, *op. cit.*) that family limitation was achieved by pre-industrial methods such as coitus interruptus, abstention and abortion. She argues both that the late nineteenth century saw a mass-production and advertising of contraceptive devices (p. 130) and that there was a conscious involvement of women (p. 114 ff.). But the evidence she cites in support of the latter is scanty. For the woman actually using the sponge, she only cites Richard Carlile's *Every Woman's Book* (p. 132), which is clearly more prescriptive than descriptive. There is no convincing evidence either for the mass use of artificial, manufactured, contraceptives.

39. Banks, *Prosperity and Parenthood*, p. 12 and *passim*; Branca, *op. cit.*, p. 4., challenges him; cf. also **Paul Thompson**, *The Edwardians: The Making of British Society*, Granada, St Albans, 1977, pp. 289–90.
40. **J. H. Plumb**, 'The New World of Childhood in Eighteenth-Century England', *Past and Present*, No. 67, May 1975, p. 93. Childhood in the eighteenth century is also discussed in Stone, *Family, Sex and Marriage*; and Trumbach, *The Rise of the Egalitarian Family*, p. 187. On the relationship between changing attitudes to childhood and birth control, see Stone, *Family, Sex and Marriage*, p. 418; and J. A. Banks, *Prosperity and Parenthood*, p. 173.
41. **Philippe Ariès**, *Centuries of Childhood*, Penguin, Harmondsworth, 1973. For a critique see Elizabeth Wilson, *Women and the Welfare State*, pp. 15 ff. **Emmanuel Le Roy Ladurie**, *Montaillou: Cathars and Catholics in a French Village, 1294–1324*, p. 213, remarks that there was not such a large gap between modern and medieval concepts as Ariès, amongst others, suggests.
42. On this theme see Foucault, *The History of Sexuality*, p. 27. The theme has been developed by **John Hood-Williams** in an unpublished paper, 'Sexualised Children', Institute of Education, 1979.
43. On the sheath see McLaren, *op. cit.*, p. 26; on pre-eighteenth century views see Stone, *op. cit.*, p. 512, Trumbach, *op. cit.*, p. 260. For discussions of masturbation, see **E. H. Hare**, 'Masturbatory Insanity: The History of an Idea', *The Journal of Mental Science*, Vol. 108, No. 452, January 1962; **Robert H. MacDonald**, 'The Frightful Consequences of Onanism: Notes on the History of a Delusion', *Journal of the History of Ideas*, Vol. XXVIII, No. 3, July–September 1967; **R. P. Neuman**, 'Masturbation, Madness and the Modern Concepts of Childhood and Adolescence', *Journal of Social History*, Spring 1975.
44. F. B. Smith, 'Sexuality in Britain', pp. 27–8 argues this point; Neuman, *op. cit.*, p. 4., sees the late eighteenth century as the key period of masturbation being associated with adolescence.
45. **G. Stanley Hall**, *Adolescence: Its Psychology, and its Relation to Physiology, Anthropology, Sociology, Sex Crimes, Religion and Education*, D. Appleton and Co., New York, 2 Vols, 1904; John R. Gillis, *Youth and History*, offers the best discussion of changing nineteenth-century concepts. See also **Joseph F. Kett**, 'Adolescence and Youth in Nineteenth-Century America', in **Theodore K. Rabb** and **Robert I. Rotberg**, *The Family in History. Interdisciplinary Essays*, Harper Torch Books, New York, 1973. Stone, *op. cit.*, p. 377, strongly rejects the view that there was no concept of adolescence before the nineteenth century. I merely argue here that its social meaning changed in the nineteenth century.
46. See Gillis, *op. cit.*, p. 158; Neuman, *op. cit.*, pp. 10–11.

47. Quoted in Hare, *op. cit.*, p. 431, note 35. For a discussion of masturbation and homosexuality see Chapter 6 below, and Jeffrey Weeks, *Coming Out*, pp. 23 ff. For the relationship of masturbation to male role anxieties see Charles Rosenberg, *op. cit.*, p. 145.

48. See, for example, **Alex Comfort**, *The Anxiety Makers*, Panther Books, London, 1968. Ch. 3, 'The Rise and Fall of Self-Abuse'.

49. On age of maturity, see **Laslett**, 'Age of Menarche in Europe since the Eighteenth Century', in Rabb and Rotberg, *op. cit.*, p. 29. It fell from 17.5 in the 1830s, to 16.5 in the 1890s. On strictures against female masturbation in America, see Rosenberg, *op. cit.*, p. 146.

50. **P. C. Remondino**, *History of Circumcision from the Earliest Times to the Present*, F. A. Davis, Philadelphia and London, 1891.

51. E. Lyttleton in letter to the editor, *The Times*, 22 November 1913. The literature of moralistic tracts is vast. For a discussion see **Edward J. Bristow**, *Vice and Vigilance. Purity Movements in Britain since 1700*, Gill and Macmillan, Dublin 1977, Ch. 6.

Chapter Four

Sexuality and the labouring classes

Middle-class myths, working-class realities

If middle-class moralities invoked peculiar anxieties, the development of a huge working class throughout the nineteenth century posed immense moral problems of its own. The fundamental problem as conceived by the middle-class moralists was the effect of industrialisation and urbanisation, and in particular factory work, on the working-class family and the role of the woman within it. The issue had long exercised the evangelicals but became central in the 1830s and 1840s, coinciding in fact with the crisis of the domestic system in textile areas. Most of the evidence used in the debates of that period relate to this area. The alleged lack of virtues and sense of shame of women cotton operatives was deplored alike in parliamentary debate and government blue books, in contemporary novels and in newspapers. Ashley (later Lord Shaftesbury) wrote with regard to women's labour in the cotton mills:

You are poisoning the very sources of order and happiness and virtue; you are tearing up root and branch all relations of families to each other; you are annulling, as it were, the institution of domestic life decreed by Providence Himself, the wisest and kindest of earthly ordinances, the mainstay of social peace and virtue and therein of national security.[1]

Contemporary observers, including radicals like Friedrich Engels, painted a picture of destruction of working-class family life. Peter Gaskell, in his *Artisans and Machinery: The Moral and Physical Conditions of the Manufacturing Population*, wrote of the family disrupted by machinery and factory working where 'recklessness, improvidence, and unnecessary poverty, starvation, drunkenness, parental cruelty and carelessness, filial disobedience, neglect of conjugal rights, absence of maternal love, destruction of brotherly and sisterly affection, are too often its constituents.'[2] Half a century later Dr Barnardo could write in similar tones: 'The East End of London is a hive of factory life and *factory* means that which is inimical to *home* . . . . There is bred in them (factory women) a spirit of precocious independence which weakens family ties and is highly unfavourable to the growth of domestic virtues.'[3] Many complained of a promiscuous mingling of sexes, and a witness before the Factory Commission in 1833 declared: 'It would be no strain on his conscience to say that threequarters of the girls between fourteen and twenty years of age were unchaste.'[4]

Novels such as Mrs Gaskell's represent the factory girls as too low to be taken into a lady's house as servants and claimed that immoralities were rooted in the conditions of the mills. The lack of sex segregation and the late hours moreover, had bad effect not only on unmarried but also on married women. Peter Gaskell wrote: 'The chastity of marriage is but little known or exercised amongst them: husband and wife sin equally, and an habitual indifference to sexual vice is generated which adds one other item to the destruction of domestic habits.'[5]

It is clear that two factors were of particular symbolic importance and concern to these bourgeois intellectuals, both relating to women: their sexuality and their economic autonomy. Because of the developing ideology of woman's role in the family and her very special responsibility for society's well being, it was women working outside the home who received the most attention from the parliamentary commissioners in the 1830s and 1840s. Moreover, most attention was paid not to the conditions of work as such but to the moral and spiritual degradation said to accompany female employment. Ashley wrote, 'In the male the moral effects of the system are very sad, but in the female they are infinitely worse . . . . It is bad enough if you corrupt the man, but if you corrupt the woman, you poison the waters of life at the very fountain.'[6]

It was largely because of these alleged conditions that the working class was the recipient of sustained evangelism throughout the nineteenth century, from Christian organisations, Sunday schools, educational charities, philanthropic societies, organisations like the Salvation Army, settlement houses and the like. The views of people like Ashley were determined very clearly by their own class experiences, and partook of the orthodox middle-class view that the free congregation of the sexes inevitably led to dangers. But class fears in fact considerably exaggerated the situation. Apart from anything else, mill life actually inhibited social intercourse, particularly with the perpetual noise, the physical separation of machines, and the power of overseers, all of which was fully recognised at the time.[7] Much of the evidence used was contradictory. Gaskell made a distinction between intercourse before marriage in agricultural areas, when marriage is tacitly understood as coming later, and the promiscuity of the town, which he condemned, but in fact there was probably little difference, as we shall see. The same misreading of the evidence is apparent in the controversy over the alleged lack of prudence of the working class, particularly as manifested in the younger age of marriage. This was blamed by many on the factory system and the alleged promiscuity it bred in women, but this ignored the fact that the highest percentage of young people who married between the ages of 15 and 20 was in Durham, where women did not work. Margaret Hewitt has calculated that in Lancashire between 1861 and 1871, the districts showing the highest proportion of young married women were not centres of cotton industries. In 1911 the fertility census recorded that textile workers actually married later.[8] In fact, working women were more independent and less likely to marry early; and the real significance of this controversy was what it revealed about the ideological assumptions of ruling-class men.

This should not lead us in turn, however, to ignore the impact of industrialisation or more generally proletarianisation on sexual *mores*. The point is that disruptions and adaptations were complex, not unilinear. It is important to grasp two complementary elements: first of all the persistence into industrial society of old habits of thought about sex amongst the working class, and their gradual, not immediate, transformation throughout the nineteenth century in the context of working-class experience. Secondly, related to this, we must be sensitive to the development of quite distinct working-class strategies, designed above all to preserve family structures in the new conditions of urbanisation and industrialisation. It was the complex interaction of these two factors that shaped the sexual *mores* of the majority of the population.

Tradition, illegitimacy and proletarianisation

E. P. Thompson, in criticising Lawrence Stone's reconstruction of *The Family, Sex and Marriage*, warned that: 'the point of history is not to see their occasions through the mist of our feelings, nor to measure them against the Modern Us. It is first of all to understand the past: to reconstruct those forgotten norms, decode the obsolete rituals, and detect the hidden gestures'.[9] What this indicates is the necessity of understanding class moralities within their own terms. Acute social divisions may indeed have induced violence, a disruption of settled married life and so on, but there is no need to assume that relationships within the working class were intrinsically any more lacking in feeling than relationships amongst other classes, just because they took different forms. Many historians have tended to stress the instrumental nature of sexual relationships and the conflicts inherent in working-class patterns of life,[10] and no doubt much of this was often true; but because we cannot now identify with the exact meanings given to activities, this does not mean that strong feelings of warmth and mutual support did not exist. Such feelings developed very much within the context of the lived experience of the mass of the population. Engels argued that: 'Sex love and the relation of husband and wife is and can become the rule only among the oppressed classes, that is, at the present day, among the proletariat, no matter whether this relationship is officially sanctioned or not.' He based this on the belief that only where property considerations were absent – as by definition they were in the proletariat – could 'true sex-love' develop. Lawrence Stone has suggested that this sort of argument is misconceived precisely because 'sex love' as the basis of relationships was first ideologically articulated in the bourgeoisie.[11] In a sense both writers are, in their very different ways, probably correct. What the dispute pinpoints is that different social situations and considerations breed quite different sets of values, which cannot be glibly conflated. Take for instance pre-marital sex.

Differences in attitude to pre-marital sex in the working class itself were noted throughout the nineteenth century. Charles Booth for instance, towards the end of the century wrote: 'With the lowest classes premarital relations are very common, perhaps even usual . . . . I believe it to constitute one of the clearest lines of demarcation between upper and lower in the working class.' And a little later Havelock Ellis noted (also citing Booth) that: 'The advantage for women of free sexual unions over compulsory marriage is well recognised in the case of the working classes in London, amongst whom sexual relationships before marriage are not unusual and are indulgently regarded.'[12] The problem is: how do we interpret such statements? Far from being 'immoral' or promiscuous, there is plentiful evidence that in fact the working class, partly inheriting structures from their rural predecessors, had a very clear set of ethics of their own which survived for a considerable time. Ancient customs such as 'bundling', intimate but fully clothed and ritualistic forms of petting, cuddling and courtship in bed, which had been policed by local traditions in rural society, continued into industrial society. They remained common amongst the poor in Wales and Scotland well into the nineteenth century though they occasioned bafflement amongst middle-class observers. (The social investigator Henry Mayhew came across bundling practices while touring Germany in the 1860s, which he took to be 'licentious'.)[13] Even traditional methods of public shaming such as the charivari and skimmington rides, which were deeply rooted in the close village societies, and were concerned to prevent transgressions of the moral customs, survived into the new society. In an area like Cambridgeshire, courtship habits remained highly ritualised and infraction of the informal norms brought social disapproval and public shaming even into the present century. There, it seems, pregnant unwed women were still being serenaded by 'rough music' at the time of the First World War.[14]

Accompanying the maintenance of old standards, even though social conditions were changing, often dramatically, was the survival amongst many sections of the working class (especially the rural) of the tradition that sexual relationships could begin at betrothal to a steady boyfriend and the corollary was that a pregnant woman would be married by the father, though as we shall see, social transformations were to weaken this. Despite the new marriage codes, common-law partnerships also remained popular – and may even have increased in the nineteenth century.[15] Some sections of the working class, especially where child labour was a necessity, might still prefer evidence of a woman's fertility, but even when such utilitarian motives were absent, informal ties were often preferred. Mayhew described the costermongers living in the coster districts of London with wives to whom they were not legally married although they remained permanently attached, and these are only the most famous of such alliances. 'Chastity' may not have had the same social meaning for a working-class girl, accustomed to different court-ship and marriage patterns, as for a middle-class young lady. Many women who moved into occasional prostitution through economic nec-essity had probably already had previous sexual experience,[16] and for many the distinction between occasional sex with a young wooer and clandestine prostitution may have remained fluid. Generalisations about working-class attitudes to sexuality should not be easily drawn, precisely because it is very difficult to enter into the subjective and customary meanings. Patterns varied from area to area, differed be-tween industrial and rural areas, and between city and city, and a host of social factors have to be taken into account.

The problem is that much of the evidence is contradictory, as a major example will illustrate. One of the most puzzling features for his-torians has been the apparent rise in illegitimacy, a European-wide phe-nomenon, in the late eighteenth and early nineteenth century, which has given rise to various interpretations of working-class sexual life. Illegiti-mate births formed only a small number of the total registered births before 1750, but by the end of the eighteenth century an illegitimacy ratio of 5 per cent was common and by the middle of the nineteenth century 20 per cent was often the norm. Peter Laslett has written that 'Bastard babies must have been commoner between 1810 and 1850 than at any other time in our past for which details are known before our own permissive generation.'[17] Recently Edward Shorter, in a series of articles and in his book *The Making of the Modern Family*, has at-tempted to explain this phenomenon in general terms. In his work, theoretically relying both on Freudianism and on variations of Parso-nian functionalism, which sees the biological, egalitarian family as the culmination of the modernising process, he argues that the rise in ille-gitimacy can be traced to a change in the attitude towards sex of lower-class women, a change so great as to amount to a sexual revolution. 'This illegitimacy explosion clearly indicates that a greater number of young people – adults in their early twenties, to go by the statistics on the age of women at the birth of their first illegitimate child – were en-gaged in premarital sex more often than before. There were slip-ups, and the birth of illegitimate children resulted.' And he sees this change as demonstrating a 'transformation of eroticism from manipulation to expression'.[18]

Working within the confines of modernisation theory and using chiefly German, French and Scandinavian sources, Shorter relates these changes to the urbanisation and economic transformation that Europe experienced in the late eighteenth and early nineteenth century. He ar-gues that as the economy modernised and more and more women left their rural communities and their kin to seek employment in the cities, so they left behind 'traditional values' that stressed that pre-marital sex was wrong. Here they also found the values of the market place, which stressed personal independence and self-gratification, and began to search for a sexual fulfilment which, Shorter says, they found in illicit sexual encounters. From this stemmed the rise in illegitimacy. He also stresses that the new female values encouraged marriage for love rather than for prudential considerations, and maintains that women's increasing search for sexual fulfilment pushed up the general fertility rate of lower-class marriages in the nineteenth century.

Shorter's arguments have quite rightly been vigorously questioned. Several historians for instance have challenged Shorter's notion of the emancipating effect of women's work and have shown that even during industrialisation, it was performed in the context of the family economy and therefore did not necessarily free women from the control of either their families or traditional values. Nor is there much evidence that women's attitudes towards sex changed significantly during this period.[19] The only evidence Shorter has of changing sexual attitudes is the rise in illegitimacy itself and this can be in large part explained, as we shall see, as the product of a persistent traditional sexual attitude in the changing economic context of proletarianisation.

Cissie Fairchild, through investigating the statements of French women who gave birth to illegitimate babies, has challenged Shorter on his own terms. She argues that the rise in illegitimacy occurs in none of the places where we might have expected it if Shorter's hypothesis of the sexual revolution were correct.[20] It appears primarily amongst women who were born and remained in a rural area, and she detects a striking rise in rural illegitimacy. This has bearing in England because, although like the Continental upsurge, the rise in illegitimacy began around 1750, the illegitimacy rates of English cities were, unlike the European cities, beneath those of the surrounding countryside and were in fact lower than European figures. In London in 1859 the illegitimacy rate was 4 per cent of all births, compared with Vienna where illegitimate births apparently exceeded legitimate.[21]

This, on the surface, puzzling preponderance of rural over urban illegitimacy rates, does in fact give us a key to the understanding of the very complex factors that shaped sexual behaviour. For it was not so much the 'immorality' of the great anonymous industrial town or city that changed behaviour patterns as the impact of the changing social relations of a developing industrial capitalism on the society as a whole. The key factor seems to have been proletarianisation rather than urbanisation, that is the generalisation of the wage–labour relationship.

A major element in the pre-industrial economy was the deferred marriage: in essence, as historians of demographic behaviour have argued, young men of the lower classes tended to defer marriage until there was an economic slot for them, usually through inheriting land or a smallholding, or on the retirement of the parents. This dictated a prudential attitude, for marriage was often impossible without that economic placing and independence. When marriage did take place, older brides were often preferred, as they tended to be both more useful as work partners, and have less childbearing years before them. Consequently, as Levine has put it, the age of marriage was 'the lynchpin of pre-industrial demographic equilibrium'.[22] These prudential factors, in turn, shaped the norms of the rural communities, governing the rules of courtship and pre-marital sexual activity. Pre-marital pregnancy was therefore generally an anticipation of marriage and by and large the local community could, if necessary, enforce marriage through its repertoire of informal rules, on a reluctant young couple. The chief aim was to avoid a needless economic burden on the parish through bastardy (and laws of settlement and the Poor Law provisions only guaranteed relief to those born within the parish); and to achieve a population equilibrium which would not outrun local resources. But in a wage–labour economy the labourer was freed from such constraints; he was now dependent on employment opportunities on the market rather than on inheriting a small holding, and tended to reach a maximum income relatively early. Moreover, in such an economy marriage and children could be a positive asset, as sources of domestic labour and increased income. As a result the disincentive to marriage was removed. But decision making was also now, to a large extent, outside his control, for his livelihood was no longer dependent on the vagaries of nature but on the vagaries of the market. This nexus of factors had two important effects. In the first place, as the age of marriage decreased, the years of potential childbearing for the wife increased, and this in turn eventually led to a shortening of the intervals between generations, so increasing the proportion of the population likely to get pregnant. The result was potentially a geometric increase in the birthrate without any necessary basic increase in the natural fertility.

This is probably one of the major factors behind the explosive rise in the birthrate and population (the 'demographic transition') from the late eighteenth century. The population grew rapidly from the 1770s, doubled in the half century after 1780, and doubled again between 1841 and 1901.

A second result was to weaken customary control over pre-marital sexual relations and in the context of increased mobility the inevitable result was that the impulse to marry in the event of a pregnancy was either weakened or thwarted. As one historian has put it, illegitimacy was the result of 'Marriage Frustrated, not Promiscuity Rampant'.[23] A young couple might well anticipate marriage in the complacent and deeply rooted assumption that a pregnancy would be followed by a regularisation of the tie, but in the new economic and social situation the irregularities of the economy might well snatch away the spouse.

This account is, of course, on a high level of generality. It needs to be filled out by detailed evidence from local studies. The pattern, both of population increase, illegitimacy and of formal marriage varied enormously: from region to region, depending on the type of industry, the sex and age ratios of the population, the play of market forces; and over time, depending on the rhythms of economic development.[24] But the general truth of the picture is borne out by the local studies that have been done. David Levine's study of four villages between about 1600 and 1850 with different social and economic profiles, has shown the complexity of the factors at work. The evidence from the Leicestershire textile village of Shepshed, as he puts it, 'supports the argument that the acceleration of economic activity after 1750 was the prime agent breaking down the traditional social controls that previously maintained a demographic equilibrium in which population size was kept in line with resources.'[25] The population increase in turn affected the finely balanced domestic economy, forcing women and children out to work, and by the end of the period, with the crisis of the framework knitters, there is some evidence, when faced with major economic problems, of a use of restraint to limit births. Procreating patterns, in other words, were highly responsive to material factors.

Slightly different factors were at work in the Essex village of Terling, dependent on the London market. The impact of the ending of job opportunities in an overcrowded London, combined with the effect of the Speenhamland system of subsidising wages under the old Poor Law, produced an underpaid, stable, demoralised and pauperised work force by the early nineteenth century which reached its maximum income relatively early. The disincentive to early marriage was lost, even though the economic level was relatively low. The situation changed with the passing of the Poor Law Amendment Act in 1834, which ended the system of subsidising wages. Labourers began to scramble for the available employment; unemployment increased; while labourers still continued to anticipate marriage. But in the new situation its social underpinnings were less secure, and there was a consequent increase in illegitimacy in this Essex village in the 1840s.[26]

These range of influences meant that settled relationship patterns and habits were disrupted by social changes. For instance, increasing geographical and occupational mobility enabled men more easily to abandon women they had seduced, while traditional premarital sexual experiences were more precarious in the light of unstable employment possibilities. The testimony of abandoned women to Henry Mayhew in the mid-nineteenth century indicated the breakdown of traditional contexts which had ensured marriage in the event of an unplanned pregnancy. He describes how in one case a girl from a poverty-stricken background went to live with a man who promised to marry her. Her sister 'made mischief' however, and they parted, by which time she was pregnant. After this, 'Many young girls at the shop advised me to go wrong.... Could I have honestly earned enough to have subsisted upon, to find me in proper food and clothing, such as is necessary, I should not have gone astray.... To be poor and to be honest, especially with a young girl, is the hardest struggle of all.'[27]

The struggle cannot have been a unique one. Working-class girls were probably less socially protected than they had been in pre-industrial communities, and a variety of influences could come into play, including the temptation of the streets. Female domestic servants, for instance, who were often prevented by householders from having 'followers' (which dictated caution, even secrecy when the alternative was dismissal), were often very vulnerable to being abandoned. The vast increase in the number of servants living in households in England and Wales (which rose from 847,000 in 1851 to 1.3 million in 1881; the number of general female servants rose by 33 per cent) also provided new opportunities for sexual exploitation. In this context *My Secret Life*, with its vivid anecdotes describing sexual liaisons between masters and servant girls, offers an insight into the situation in which the opportunity for temptation, seduction and rape was often pervasive. Ironically, while many rescue workers and feminists saw domestic service as a solution for unattached young girls, this was in fact one of the main sources of prostitution. In towns such as Dundee, which was a major centre of women's employment in the jute industry, prostitution was almost unknown. But it must have been a temptation in poor working-class communities, where virginity in any case was not sacred, where the stigma against extra-marital sex was weak, and where a prostitute could earn in half an hour what a respectable girl might earn in a week.

There was again no uniformity about this pattern. Many girls in difficult positions resisted prostitution, whether formal or informal. Different areas maintained different patterns. Mayhew noted the chaste nature of Roman Catholic Irish coster girls in London, and similarly Irish girls in the South Wales coalfields were conservative in behaviour. All sorts of moral, customary and even 'personal' factors played their part. Even the most 'degraded' of women in terms of bourgeois ideology, those subjected to the Contagious Diseases Act, were capable of vigorously defending themselves.[28] But young women were often vulnerable, and despite vigorous efforts to maintain a sexual independence, were in exposed positions. Changes in the general moral climate therefore had their inevitable effect. It is probable that eighteenth- and early nineteenth-century law, custom and employment encouraged women's confidence in their ability to deal with pre-marital sex, but increasingly the transformations of the nineteenth century altered the picture. The effects of the New Poor Law, after 1834, suffused as it was with an assumption that the stable two-parent family was the norm, were probably less to encourage female sexual autonomy, and a 'sexual revolution' than to diminish female control. Under the New Poor Law practice, unmarried mothers were always more likely to be sent to the workhouse than granted outdoor relief, and once there were left in no doubt of their shameful condition. It also made it more difficult to obtain maintenance – and this emphasised the stigma of bastardy. As a result, illegitimacy and irregular marriage possibly receded in the second half of the century as working-class women sought refuge in chastity and conventional marriage. The decline of pre-marital pregnancy during the late nineteenth century was probably therefore less the product of adoption of middle-class values than the consequence of the felt loss of control over the consequence of heterosexual relations.[29]

Other forms of disruption attendant upon rapid social changes also set the conditions for working-class sexual attitudes. Amongst transient communities of working men, with no obvious home situation, irreligion and blasphemy and a casual attitude to life were usual, and in such circumstances what was termed sexual 'promiscuity' was rife, as for example amongst sailors, railway navvies, residents of common lodging houses and the like. For those who worked in barracks, on ships, in shanty towns around the periphery of cities, or in open countryside, short-term cohabitation or prostitution were common, legal marriage the exception. The demand for cheap labour indeed caused marriages to be forbidden in certain working-class occupations, and it was a common complaint in the 1850s that the British army officers were allowed to marry, but not their men.[30] Similarly, as we have seen, householders often insisted that female domestic servants must remain single.

The living conditions of working-class people also had a profound effect on sexual habits. The lack of privacy in working-class homes, for example, was obviously a major determinant of mores. In Leeds in the early nineteenth century the average cottage was fifteen foot square. In Nottingham an average of five persons occupied tiny three-floor houses, with upper floors for communal sleeping. In no decade during the period were the working classes adequately housed, and in the overcrowded conditions under which many working-class people lived it was very difficult indeed to retain the moral refinement demanded by the upper strata of society. It was in this context that the scare over incest in the late nineteenth century developed. As Sir John Simon put it in the *Report on the Sanitary Conditions of the City of London 1849–50*, 'It is no uncommon thing, in a room of twelve foot square or less, to find three or four families *styed* together . . . in the promiscuous intimacy of cattle.'[31]

Other problems proliferated. The absence of any accepted divorce procedures, for instance, was probably one of the reasons for the rituals of 'wife sales' in the nineteenth century, continuing until at least the 1880s.[32] Even after the reform of the divorce laws in 1857, most working-class people were denied the possibility of easy divorce; in the 1900s petitions for divorce from the working class were still extremely rare, largely because of the cost. The perceived difficulty of ending marriages was doubtless one of the reasons for the increased concern with wife-battering which was of major import in the 1860s and 1870s. Francis Power Cobbe's pamphlet of 1878, *Wife Torture*, which was basically concerned with crimes of violence in working-class districts, especially in cases of men against their wives, was a major influence leading to the drafting of the Matrimonial Causes Act of 1878, which gave magistrates powers to grant separation orders and maintenance to a wife whose husband was convicted of aggravated assault, plus custody of children under ten. A series of Acts followed which strengthened the powers of magistrates. Between 1897 and 1906, magistrate courts granted over 87,000 separation and maintenance orders in England and Wales at the rate of some 8,000 separations per year, and these became the working-class norm.[33]

The patterns of family life

But undoubtedly the most important focus for nineteenth-century working-class sexual attitudes *was* the family, and it is in the context of specific family strategies and patterns that sexual *mores* developed and were transformed. Michael Anderson has recently argued that in many areas factories offered a type and range of employment that could keep the family together, for co-residency of kin was complemented by the practice of hiring relatives in factories. Tilly and Scott have argued in partial amplification of this that the traditional rural family defined women's work situation and contributed to actually changing the work situation in urban areas. The experience of peasant families was repeated by sending daughters into similar social situations in domestic service and piecework. Both positions endorse Neil Smelser's view in *Social Change in the Industrial Revolution* that the family as a work unit was incorporated into the factory in the 1820s. Smelser argues that male trade-union agitation against married women's employment after the 1830s was due to the enforced decline of employment opportunities for children and hence the need for an adult presence in a newly constituted home life.[34]

The implication of this is that the traditional view of the collapse of the working-class family under the impact of industrialisation, as Engels, for instance, suggested in *The Condition of the Working Class in England*, is misleading. Anderson, for instance, suggests that the strong family cohesion amongst some groups in rural areas was maintained by migrants into Lancashire cotton plants like Preston though largely for fairly calculative reasons rather than out of emotional loyalty to kin. But the relations that developed were much more than simply instrumental; when families did survive it was more than a product of what Stone called, for an earlier period, 'psychic numbing'. Married women who entered the labour force to supplement the family income tended for example, to display all the traditional self-sacrificing attitudes. A good example of this well into the twentieth century is the evidence of the Women's Co-operative Guild investigation into *Maternity* during the First World War, which found that pregnant working-class women often saved for the coming confinement by stinting on food, and there is plentiful evidence of similar attitudes earlier. Marriages might of necessity be in the first place a business agreement – an exchange of goods and services – but this did not mean that deep feelings did not enter it.[35]

The family patterns that developed did, however, have different ef-

fects for women and men. Marriage was essential for the young working-class girl, indeed an economic necessity, for she could scarcely have
survived unmarried. Factory girls usually married in their early twenties; it was unlikely to happen over the age of 25, and only in textile
areas, where there was a long tradition of employment, did women
generally prolong their independence, though conditions varied in different industries and areas.[36] This had variable effects on work patterns. The exclusion of women from the paid labour force became in
many areas an important part of the development of both working-class
'respectability' and of notions of working-class *manhood*. 'Manhood'
indeed became synonymous with being able to maintain one's family,
an important element in virility. So from the mid century onwards
many working-class women seem to have retreated into the home, and
by the end of the nineteenth century a conscious ideology was constructing the role of housewife and mother. But of course this varied from
place to place, from time to time, and it is still not clear how far working-class men and women did accept the domesticated role of married
women, even in the diluted version which social circumstances could
allow to become part of their lives. Very large numbers of married
women did, for various reasons, remain in paid labour.[37] But Henry
Broadhurst at the 1877 Trades Union Congress expressed what was to
become a very important element in working-class respectable ideology.
The men, he said,

had the future of their country and their children to consider, and it was their
duty as men and husbands to use their utmost efforts to bring about a condition
of things, where their wives would be in their proper sphere at home, instead of
being dragged into competition for livelihood against the great and strong men
of the world.[38]

Implicit in this is both a fear of female competition for scarce jobs and a
sense of the need of a woman's domestic labour at home. As a result,
the female working-class role was very much seen as one of maintaining
the family and here was her emotional and sexual destiny. A woman's
sexuality indeed was in many ways the key to her economic survival.

The conception of the family as a 'refuge', which apparently echoed
middle-class views, therefore carried a different weight and intensity in
the working class when the world from which the family formed a retreat was the daily experience of class exploitation and potential poverty. The family had a strong social value because it was an absolutely
necessary social institution, an essential mutual-aid society in a world of
rapid change, and in this the woman's contribution was pivotal.[39]

These factors shaped distinctive family patterns in the working class.
There was, for instance, a general distrust of middle-class interest in
sexuality and the whole export of the moral apparatus to the working
class. This can be traced in the working-class response to birth-control
propaganda, which was often extremely hostile. This went back to the
development of working-class antipathy to Thomas Malthus, who was

seen as giving scientific justification to ruling-class opposition to reform, for after all the aim of his famous moral restraint was to convince
the working class to postpone marriage as long as possible. Radical pioneers of birth control in the 1820s like Richard Carlile believed that a di-
minshed workforce, by reducing competition, would benefit wages, but
such arguments often received short shrift.

Cobbett wrote with regard to Carlile, 'He's a tool, a poor half mad
tool, of the *enemies of reform*. He wants no reform, for the end of his
abominable book is to show that the sufferings of the people do not
arise from the want of reform; but from the *"indiscreet breeding of
women"*.' And as the Chartist Bronterre O'Brien wrote, 'In spite of the
Devil and Malthus, the work people are resolved to live and breed.'[40]
The bulk of the working-class press continued to argue that discussion
of contraception only hindered the advancement of social reform. It
seems likely, from the small amount of information available, that the
press was successful in fixing in working men's minds the idea that contraception was a highly individualistic act prompted by self-interest.
Many working-class radicals saw the percolation downward of birth-
control methods as a sign that aristocratic decadence was spreading de-
basement to the people as a whole. Outraged articles on the sexual
habits of the wealthy became a familiar feature of the popular press.
Underlying much working-class opposition was a hostility often born of
an older moralism: it was their willingness to interfere with the workings of God, Providence or Nature that made the suggestions of the
birth controllers sometimes appear even more shocking than those of
Malthus. But at the same time many, like Cobbett in *Rural Rides*, believed they were tackling the wrong problem in the wrong way. It was
not population but poverty that was the real problem.[41]

But despite this controversy, methods of birth control were not in
fact alien to the working class and in the use of contraception we can
again see distinctive patterns. We have evidence from at least the seventeenth century of restraint of births,[42] and there is clear evidence of a
planned decline of working-class family size from the end of the nineteenth century. The textile workers were in the vanguard of the process
from the 1850s, though not alone, and after 1900 the process was much
more rapid. Amongst certain workers the average number of children
born to a family fell by nearly 35 per cent between 1900 and 1911.[43] It is
important to grasp birth control very much within the context of the
particular customs and needs of groups of workers, and it is notable,
for instance, that the poor and the unemployed generally had a high
birthrate. For those on the margins or in casual labour the extra mouths
to feed in infancy was more than compensated for by the potentially increased sources of income and domestic help in childhood and adoles-
ence. For many, large families were economically rational.

Other factors also came into play. Miners, for example, maintained
large families, 3.6 children in 1911, despite the rapid general reduction
in birthrate, and in the early twentieth century they were the only large

category of workers whose families averaged over 3. Here a series of influences – the isolation of mining communities, the absence of any opportunities for female work outside the home in an area like South Wales – were important in establishing a firm familial tradition, while a high infant mortality rate, 50 per cent higher than for most factory workers, meant that women had to bear 4½ children to achieve the average family size in 1911.[44] The higher infant mortality rate among the working class was probably a major element throughout the nineteenth century in encouraging frequent pregnancies.

It has been suggested that there are three factors that determine population control: family ideals, both material and non-material; knowledge of bodily functions, reproduction, health, hygiene, childcare, etc.; and thirdly, access to contraception.[45] Following this last point it is significant that the birthrate tended throughout the nineteenth century to be highest in areas where employment opportunities for women were lowest, for it is likely that knowledge was more easily acquired by factory workers than by those in service or those who stayed at home. The *Maternity* letters illustrate the ignorance even of the facts of life amongst many women. One respondent wrote: 'About a month before the baby was born I remember asking my aunt where the baby would come from. She was astounded, and did not make me much wiser.'[46] There were, of course, sources of information. Folk myths and wisdoms survived for a long time. For example, the (now held to be correct) notion that prolonged lactation was likely to delay impregnation had a long resonance. It is likely also that works like *Aristotle's Masterpiece*, which went through at least 25 editions between 1684 and 1930, were a common form for the distribution of sexual knowledge, until attacked by the medical profession in the 1930s. The *Masterpiece*, a collection of folklore about the body and its functions, was probably the single most popular source of information on sex relations and childbirth, and the continuing publication of this work was possibly the last remnant of a much stronger popular demand and usage that began to grow in the nineteenth century with increasing literate audiences demanding knowledge. Its various editions are full of myths and anachronisms based on a 'humoral pathology'.[47] On the other hand, it was for a very long time the only kind of popular medical and natural science handbook which was available to laypeople, who possessed little knowledge of such matters other than their own experiences and the tales of other. What was probably most important to such an audience was not so much the unlikely explanation of a phenomenon as its very mention, reducing fears of the unknown and of apparently inexplicable events such as changes in female physiology during pregnancy.

There was nothing on contraception in the *Masterpiece* but new information from the radical proponents of birth control was available to the working class from the 1820s onwards, much of it aimed at dissuading women from having abortions. Despite such efforts, it is likely that abortion played a major part in the regulation of family size amongst the working class, especially in factory districts, where knowledge of abortifacient techniques was widespread.[48]

A new sensitivity to the subject is suggested by the series of laws and practices concerning it in the nineteenth century. Abortion was a common-law crime until 1803, when it was made a statutory offence. The law was further tightened in 1828, 1837 and 1861. It seems, moreover, that from the 1830s and 1840s there was a distinct switch in literary representation of the type of women who had recourse to abortion: no longer was it just the seduced domestic, but the married and unmarried working women, particularly factory women in the textile areas of Lancashire.

If, as we have suggested, the working woman's goal was one of maintaining and protecting her family, abortion could be one means of attaining that end. Life was often too difficult for working-class mothers to be overscrupulous about the birth of children. Combined with this was the continuance of traditional beliefs that life only began 40 to 80 days after conception, with 'quickening'. The Birkett committee of 1937 which examined the question of abortion was informed that many working-class women were not aware that abortion was illegal. They assumed that it was legal before the third month, and only illegal when procured. A further importance of abortion was that it gave women some control over their own fertility, especially given the hostility of many men to birth control. Moreover, abortion as a method allowed decision making to be delayed until material circumstances could be assessed. It is likely, then, that the abortion method of control was particularly applicable in specific times and places, such as in the situation in which married women worked outside the home, as in textile factories, and enjoyed a key role in determining the family's economic stability.

Certainly Havelock Ellis in the early part of this century was able to write that it 'scarcely appears to excite profound repulsion in a large proportion of the population of civilised countries',[49] and he mentioned specifically that working-class women often resorted to it. Most of the advertisements for 'female pills', which were thinly veiled abortifacients, were directed at working-class women. One used by the infamous Chrimes brothers, who were involved in a notorious scandal and subsequent trial in the late 1890s gives the flavour.

Ladies Only.
THE LADY MONTROSE / – MIRACULOUS – /
– FEMALE TABULES.
Are positively unequalled for all
FEMALE AILMENTS. The most OBSTINATE
obstruction, Irregularities, etc.
of the female system are removed in a few doses.[50]

The pills themselves it seems were actually quite harmless and probably useless. But by 1898 the Chrimes brothers had on their ledgers over

10,000 names of women who had responded to their advertisements and these they then used for blackmail. In pursuance of this, 8,000 letters were sent out in 1898 and nearly 3,000 replies were received within a short space of days. When they were eventually brought to trial, the most revealing thing that came out was that thousands of women were seeking, by a variety of means, to terminate their pregnancies. The trial of the Chrimes brothers in December 1898 brought the subject to public discussion. *The Lancet*, for instance, had a long series of articles on various medications that paraded as abortifacients. But advertisements continued to appear in a large number of local London papers and provincial papers and even a religious publication, *The Rock*. A paper like *Illustrated Bits* contained advertisements for 'Ottley's Strong Pills' and Towle's Penny Royal and Steel Pills for Females, alongside *Aristotle's Masterpiece* in its report of the Chrimes trial.[51] *Reynolds* newspaper declared it surprising that any respectable paper should advertise such wares. In the same issue, however, there were a dozen advertisements for surgical appliances and five for abortifacients. Similar advertisements also appeared in the *Labour Leader* and the *Freewoman*.

The *Malthusian* of June 1914 estimated that 100,000 women a year took drugs to induce miscarriage, and there were suggestions at the time that there were few mothers of large families who had not attempted abortion. Methods used to procure abortions included traditional herbal remedies, savin, ergot of rye, penny royal, slippery elm, squills and hierpicra; compounds of aloes and iron; and compounds of iron and purgative extracts. Sometimes self-discovered methods were used: for example, after an epidemic of lead poisoning in Sheffield in the early 1890s it was noted that those who were poisoned had aborted. The idea stuck that doses of lead could induce miscarriage: hence the use of diachylon, a lead compound widely available as an antiseptic, became widespread in Sheffield, Leicester, Nottingham, Birmingham and later Barnsley and Doncaster.[52] There was strong evidence of a slow but methodical spread of this knowledge. By 1906 it had reached South Yorkshire and the North Midlands; by 1914 Lancashire.

The importance of this discussion of birth control, particularly abortion, is what it reveals about the patterns of working-class family life. In the first place we can see a reliance on self-help and often pre-industrial techniques, given new meaning in transformed social circumstances. But secondly we can see the continued autonomy of working-class patterns. They were shaped within a world dominated by respectable values, but even when the patterns approximated (as they did in the eventually declining birthrate) they did so for reasons which had a different rationale in each class.

Respectability and social control

Changes can be discerned in family patterns by the end of the century.

By the 1890s the social habit of marrying later, which had originally been confined to the upper middle classes, was being adopted by higher-paid artisans. And in view of the later age of marriage and often long engagements of the Edwardian years, it seems likely that by the end of the nineteenth century there was a new degree of sexual restraint amongst many young adults of the working class.[53] The general illegitimacy rates as a proportion of all live births fell from 6 per cent in the mid-nineteenth century to 4 per cent in 1900, despite the later marriages. Figures for the first pregnancies conceived before marriage show the same trend, falling from around the 40 per cent in the early nineteenth century to under 20 per cent in the early twentieth century. In addition, as we have just seen, there was a growing control of family size. The effect of these changes on the establishment of stable family patterns and the emotional lives of the members of the family are difficult to work out. As in the middle-class family it is likely that the declining infant mortality and the smaller sizes of family encouraged parents to make an increased emotional investment in each child. But tensions between young and middle-aged adults were acute in many families. By their mid teens young people were able to earn, and were sexually mature, but had not taken on independent economic responsibilities. Parents were reluctant for them to leave home too early – particularly because of the loss of income to the family budget that would ensue – and there was a fear also of the independent youth culture with its sexual rituals, such as the 'monkey parade', public courting areas where youth proudly proclaimed both its independence and sexuality. Tensions there had been throughout the century but there is some evidence of a conscious 'respectable' assault on this precarious independence by the end of the nineteenth century.[54] The street culture of working-class youth was often attacked directly by the police; and changes in the education system after the introduction of state elementary education after 1870 also had its effects. Many parents bitterly objected to their loss of control over their children (and particularly to the violence of ritualised corporal punishment). But it also had the effect of increasing dependence. Until the end of the century the lowest legal age for leaving school was 10, though some cities like London had bye laws fixing a higher age. By 1900 the official leaving age was 14. Moreover, so successful were the numerous methods for delaying marriage (the mean age of which, by the early twentieth century was higher than at any other time in British history, 27 for men and 25 for women), that for the typical Edwardian the gap between leaving school and the full independence of marriage was twice as long as it is today. This inevitably produced family and sexual tensions.

There is some evidence that outside the upper working class, in the poorest families, attitudes were not particularly authoritarian or rigid in roles, and children were often left to pick up sexual attitudes for themselves. Certainly formal sex education remained poor. Nevertheless, in the last decades of the nineteenth century we can observe a greater decorum amongst the working class as a whole, and the articulation of clear respectable standards amongst important strata of it. Indeed, a working-class culture, the passing of which was to be lamented by social commentators in the 1950s, was being largely created in these closing decades of the nineteenth century, and the new or transformed working-class standards were to become deeply embedded.[55] The hard-working, God-fearing, nonconformist working man and 'labour aristocrat' of the northern industrial cities, with his Sunday best, neat front parlour, non-working wife and high morality, was to become the epitome of the respectable proletarian. There were, inevitably, contradictory elements in this mode of life. On the one hand, the respectable standard asserted the social superiority of the labour aristocrats, over the 'residuum', as the moralists chose to call it, and approximated to the middle-class standard. But on the other hand, this respectable ideology was deeply rooted in the general experience of working-class life. As R. Q. Gray has put it:

the style of life created by the upper artisan strata may be seen, from one point of view, as a transmission of middle class values – certainly as an assertion of social superiority, a self conscious cultural exclusion of less-favoured working class groups. On the other hand, the very pursuit of 'respectability', especially in so far as it involved claims to status recognition and participation in local institutions, was a source of social tension, a focal point in the growth of class identity.[56]

For what it often meant was a claim to full citizenship on behalf of skilled workers as a whole; and it was located in a strong sense of class pride. So the patterns of moral respectability, far from being a simple assimilation of the middle-class norm, were effects of specific class experiences and a growing sense of class identity. There are even signs, by the end of the nineteenth century, of increased intermarriage between the skilled worker and other strata of the working population, a sure indication of a diminishing sense of social distance.[57]

Even in a city like London, with no large industrial base and a preponderance of casual labourers, we can see in the last half of the nineteenth century, as Gareth Stedman Jones has put it, the 'emergence of a working class culture which showed itself impervious to middle class attempts to guide it', even as it remained politically conservative, and it developed deeply rooted family patterns of its own. The most striking example of this was the giving way of a work-centred culture to a home-centred one, as a result of a diminishing working day, the institution of the free weekend, the introduction of Bank Holidays, and the growing geographical separation of home from work as, in many towns, the working class followed the middle class out of the inner, industrial areas. The removal of many married women from wage labour, the innovations such as the Education Act of 1870, and ideological forces, also tended to rigidify the gender divisions. Homes remained often uncomfortable of course, and the pub was still a major centre of social life, but the late nineteenth century also saw the growth of a greater emphasis on home, and of new leisure opportunities for both adults which in London particularly is best epitomised in the music hall. Such forms of entertainment, moreover, sharply reflected many of the contradictions of working-class marriage and sexual life. As Stedman Jones has shown, marriage was often portrayed as a 'comic disaster'; marriage was necessary, especially for the woman, but was best to be resisted for as long as possible by the man. At the same time there was a recognition that despite the horrors of mothers-in-law and squalling children the family was an essential bulwark for survival, against the vagaries of the economy and the all too likely threat of the (sexually segregated) workhouse in poverty or old age.[58]

The middle-class evangelism which attempted to transform working-class moral habits, which had continued throughout the century, accentuated in the last decades under the stress of perceived social tensions. This 'civilising mission' both endorsed legislation which could help create a physical and institutional environment in which undesirable working-class habits and attitudes would be deterred (as long as it was not too expensive), and encouraged private philanthropy, which could undertake active propagation of a new moral code. Habits of regularity could be increased by regular payments of rent, slums and immoral haunts could be demolished, bawdy songs and games could be suppressed. From the 1860s organisations such as the Charity Organisation Society, the Salvation Army, Church and many other philanthropic missions, through their direct intervention in working-class life attempted to mould it to conform to a middle-class norm. These efforts were bolstered by the firm belief in the civilising effect of personal relations between the classes which reached their peak in the 'settlement houses' in slum areas of London in the 1880s.

But the question remains of how far the middle-class onslaught changed and influenced working-class attitudes and behaviour. Several historians recently have suggested that it was certainly not in the way that had been intended.[59] By the Edwardian period it had become inescapably clear that middle-class evangelism had failed to create a working class in its own image; the great majority of London workers, particularly, were not Christian, provident, chaste or temperate by middle-class standards, while the artisan and skilled worker had developed social and political patterns of their own. All this suggests that the institutions of more stable family patterns should not be seen as evidence of the success of an effort at 'social control'. The most effective ideological influences came not from evangelical social reform but from more complex processes by which elements similar to those of the ruling ideology were produced from deeply felt experiences of the class itself. Thus the weight given to values such as thrift and respectability may have been articulated in terms of the dominant ideology, but they still have to be understood as outcrops of a distinctive social experience. What happened was what has been called a 'negotiated redefinition' on

the part of the respectable working class: there was no passive acceptance. As a result we can observe the emergence in the last decades of the
nineteenth century of a working-class culture whose prevailing tone was
not one of political combativity, and yet which had firm moral standards of its own. Middle-class moralists might be ardent, even strident,
but working-class patterns continued to be remarkably resistant and
independent.

References

1. *Hansard*, 3rd series Vol. LXXIII, 1844, Col. 1100.
2. **Peter Gaskell**, *Artisans and Machinery: The Moral and Physical Condition of the Manufacturing Population*, John W. Parker, London, 1836, p. 89.
3. T. J. Barnardo in 1889, quoted in Davidoff, L'Esperance and Newby, 'Landscape with Figures', p. 167.
4. Quoted in **Harold Perkin**, *The Origins of Modern English Society*, Routledge and Kegan Paul, London, 1969, p. 150.
5. **P. Gaskell**, *The Manufacturing Population of England*, Baldwin and Cradock, London, 1833, p. 147. See **Margaret Hewitt**, *Wives and Mothers in Victorian Industry*, Rockcliff, London, 1958. The Children's Employ-ment Commission, *First Report of the Commissioners (Mines)*, 1842, is a good example of the prurience of investigators as it detailed the use of female labour, often working naked with naked men. See **U. Henriques**, *Before the Welfare State*, Longman, Harlow, 1979, pp. 108–9. For a later worry, about sewing machines inducing female masturbation, see **Langdon Down**, *British Medical Journal*, 12 Jan. 1867.
6. Quoted in **Sally Alexander**, 'Women's Work in Nineteenth Century Lon-don; A Study of the Years 1820–50', in Juliet Mitchell and Ann Oakley, *The Rights and Wrongs of Women*, p. 62.
7. See for example, Perkin, *op. cit.*, pp. 150–2; and Hewitt, *op. cit.*
8. Hewitt, *op. cit.*, p. 54, p. 42, p. 30.
9. **E. P. Thompson**, 'Happy Families', *New Society*, 8 September 1977, p. 501, reprinted in *Radical History Review*, No. 20, Spring/Summer 1979.
10. **Michael Anderson**, *Family Structure in Nineteenth Century Lancashire*, Cambridge University Press, 1971.
11. **F. Engels**, *The Origins of the Family, Private Property and the State*, Lawrence and Wishart, London, 1972, p. 135; L. Stone, *Family, Sex and Marriage*.
12. **Charles Booth**, *Life and Labour of the People in London*, William and Norgate, 1892, Vol. 1, pp. 55–6; **Havelock Ellis**, *Studies in the Psychology of Sex*, Vol. VI, *Sex in Relation to Society*, F. A. Davis, Philadelphia, 1920, p. 388 (Ellis discusses the theme at length, pp. 386 ff.)
13. Stone, *op. cit.*, pp. 605–7; Gillis, *Youth and History*, p. 35. On bundling in Scotland, see **T. C. Smout**, 'Aspects of Sexual Behaviour In Nine-teenth Century Scotland', in **A. A. McLaren** (ed.), *Social Class in Scotland: Past and Present*, Edinburgh, John Donald, pp. 76–8.
14. Gillis, *op. cit.*, p. 35. On the phenomenon see **E. P. Thompson**,, 'Rough Music: Le Charivari Anglais', *Annales*, 27 Annee, No. 2, March–April 1972; **Natalie Zemon Davis**, 'The Reasons of Misrule; Youth Groups and Charivari in Sixteenth Century France', *Past and Present*, No. 50, Feb. 1971; and the discussion on charivari and the lower middle class by **Richard**

N. **Price** in **G. Crossick** (ed.), *The Lower Middle Class in Britain 1870–1914*, Croom Helm, London, 1977, p. 91: 'The essence of charivari . . . is the collective assertion of values or a morality that has been violated or transgressed. It involved the humiliation or mockery of its victims, and was the collective voice of those who generally went unheard.'

15. On the tradition of pre-marital pregnancy, see **P. E. H. Hair**, 'Bridal Pregnancy in Earlier Rural England', *Population Studies*, Vol. 24, 1970, pp. 59–70, which on the basis of a study of parish registers 1540–1820 suggests that one-fifth of all brides, 1540–1700, and two-fifths in later centuries were pregnant on marriage. Havelock Ellis, *Sex in Relation to Society*, p. 380, discusses the custom of free marriage unions made legal before the birth of a child, which he says is common practice in rural parts of England. **Louise A. Tilly** and **Joan W. Scott**, *Women, Work and Family*, Holt Rhinehart and Winston, New York, 1978, p. 97 discusses the frequency of common-law unions.

16. This point is made in **Judith R. Walkowitz** and **Daniel J. Walkowitz**, ' "We are not Beasts of the Field"; Prostitution and the Poor in Plymouth and Southampton under the Contagious Diseases Acts', in *Feminist Studies*, Vol. 1, Nos. 3–4, 1973, p. 84.

17. **Peter Laslett**, *The World We Have Lost*, Methuen, London, 1st edn 1965, 2nd edn 1971, p. 143. Illegitimate births as a percentage of registered births were as follows: 1811–50, 5.3–7.0; 1851–80, 4.7–7.6; 1881–1900, 4.2–4.7; 1900–40, 3.9–5.4; 1941–5, 5.4–9.3; 1947–60, 4.7–5.4; by 1962 reaching 6.6 (p. 142). Stone, *op. cit.*, p. 613, suggests the rural illegitimacy ratio rose from 2½ per cent in the 1720s to 4½ per cent in the 1760s, and 6 per cent after 1780.

18. **Edward Shorter** 'Illegitimacy, Sexual Revolution, and Social Change in Modern Europe', in **T. K. Rabb** and **R. I. Rotberg**, *The Family in History: Interdisciplinary Essays*, Harper Torchbooks, New York, 1973, p. 49; *The Making of the Modern Family*, Collins, London, 1976, Fontana paperback, 1977.

19. **Joan W. Scott** and **Louise A. Tilly**, 'Women's Work and the Family in Nineteenth Century Europe', *Comparative Studies in Society and History*, Vol. 17, 1975; **Louise A. Tilly**, **Joan W. Scott** and **Miriam Cohen**, 'Women's Work and European Fertility Patterns', *Journal of Interdisciplinary History*, No. 6, Winter 1976; Tilly and Scott, *Women, Work and Family*, Ch. 5.

20. **Cissie Fairchilds**, 'Female Sexual Attitudes and Rise of Illegitimacy: A Case Study', *Journal of Interdisciplinary History*, Vol. VIII, No. 4, Spring 1978.

21. **Albert Leffingwell**, *Illegitimacy and the Influence of the Seasons upon Conduct*, London, 1892, pp. 85–7, quoted in **Peter Laslett**, *Family Life and Illicit Love in Earlier Generations: Essays in Historical Sociology*, Cambridge University Press, 1977, p. 105, Note 2. See also Tilly and Scott, *Women, Work and Family*, pp. 97. Smout, *op. cit.*, pp. 62 ff., discusses bastardy figures in Scotland and shows that on the basis of 1889 figures, out of 17 countries in Europe, Austria had the highest illegitimacy ratio (that is, the proportion of illegitimate to total births); Scotland was 10th, England 14th.

22. **David Levine**, *Family Formation in an Age of Nascent Capitalism*, Academic Press, New York, San Francisco, London, 1977, p. 11, on which the following discussion is based. For a discussion of the Hardwicke Marriage Act's impact in redefining marriage, and hence legitimacy,

see **B. Meteyard**, 'Illegitimacy and Marriage in Eighteenth Century England', *Journal of Interdisciplinary History*, Vol. X, No. 3, Winter 1980.

23. Levine, *op. cit.*, title of Ch. 9.

24. **Michael Anderson**, 'Marriage Patterns in Victorian Britain: An Analysis based on Registration District Data for England and Wales 1861', *Journal of Family History*, Vol. 1, No. 1, Autumn 1976, suggests that changes in agricultural relations of production and in the proportion of women in domestic service were the most likely factors to have affected marriage chances and marital fertility. Population sex ratios were also important. Industrialisation and urbanisation by contrast had comparatively little effect. See also his *Family Structure*, pp. 132—4.

25. Levine, *op. cit.*, p. 5; on the use of birth control, see p. 66.

26. *Ibid.*, p. 134. See **John R. Gillis**, 'Servants, Sexual Relations and the Risks of Illegitimacy in London, 1801–1900', *Feminist Studies*, Vol. 5, No. 1, Spring 1979, Note 2, p. 169, for references on regional variations in illegitimacy rates; and T. C. Smout, *op. cit.*, for an enlightening discussion of causes of illegitimacy in Scotland.

27. **E. P. Thompson** and **Eileen Yeo**, *The Unknown Mayhew*, Merlin Press, London, 1971, p. 148.

28. See F. B. Smith, 'Sexuality in Britain', on servants; Smout, *op. cit.*, p. 73, on Roman Catholic customs; Walkowitz and Walkowitz, 'We are not Beasts of the Field', on the 'resistance' of prostitutes.

29. Gillis, 'Servants, Sexual Relations and the Risks of Illegitimacy', argues this point very forcibly. On the impact of the 1834 Poor Law Amendment Act, see **U. R. Q. Henriques**, 'Bastardy and the New Poor Law', *Past and Present*, No. 37, July 1967. She describes (pp. 118—19) how the Poor Law was seen by some men as giving them a new licence to avoid marrying pregnant brides. But there was no complacent acceptance. The opposition to the bastardy clauses was dramatised in the Welsh Rebecca Riots. One of the complaints against the New Poor Law was that the enforced segregation of the sexes was intended to reduce population; another was that food was being adulterated with bromide to reduce fertility: see Henriques, *Before the Welfare State*, p. 52. For this stigmatising effect of the Poor Law, and its effect on women, see **Pat Thane**, 'Women and the Poor Law in Victorian and Edwardian England', *History Workshop*, No. 6, Autumn 1978.

30. **Hugh McLeod**, *Class and Religion in the late Victorian City*, Croom Helm, London, 1974, pp. 55—6; Brian Harrison, 'Underneath the Victorians', p. 237; **Terry Coleman**, *The Railway Navvies*, Hutchinson, London, 1965.

31. Simon, quoted in Sally Alexander, *op. cit.*, p. 406, Note 4; see also Margaret Hewitt, *op. cit.*, p. 56; and Stone, *op. cit.*, p. 605. The Royal Commission on Housing in 1884 spent a great deal of its time discussing the connections between overcrowding, intemperance and sexual offences. See **Gareth Stedman Jones**, *Outcast London*, Clarendon Press, Oxford, 1971, p. 223.

32. Not, it should be said, real sales, but more a ritualised exchange of partners by mutual consent, and apparently designed to minimise the shame to the abandoned spouse. Moreover, far from being a 'survival' the ritual was probably developed in the eighteenth century. There is an excellent discussion of these 'sales' in **E. P. Thompson**, 'Folklore, Anthropology, and Social History', *Indian Historical Review*, Vol. III, No. 2, January 1978,

pp. 247–66. See also Stone, *op. cit.*, p. 40; Ellis, *Sex in Relation to Society*, p. 403.

33. **Frances Power Cobbe**, *Wife Torture*, London, 1878; O. R. Mc-Gregor, *Divorce in England*, pp. 23 ff.
34. Michael Anderson, *Family Structure*; Tilly and Scott, *Women, Work and Family*; **Neil J. Smelser**, *Social Change and the Industrial Revolution: An Application of Theory to the British Cotton Industry*, University of Chicago Press, 1959.
35. See **Margaret Llewelyn Davies**, *Maternity: Letters from Working Women*, first published G. Bell, London, 1915, republished Virago 1978. Anderson, *op. cit.*, p. 62, speaks of the lack of spontaneous warmth amongst his working-class families, as do Shorter, *op. cit.*, and Stone, *op. cit.* On female self-sacrificing attitudes, see the discussion in **Peter N. Stearns**, 'Working-Class Women in Britain, 1890–1914', in M. Vicinus (ed.), *Suffer and Be Still*; **Laura Oren**, 'The Welfare of Women in Labouring Families: England, 1860–1950', *Feminist Studies*, No. 1, 1973.
36. Tilly and Scott, *op. cit.*, p. 95, show how the age of marriage varied a great deal as a result of the availability of certain types of jobs; see also Anderson, 'Marriage Patterns', and Note 24 above. Cf. **N. F. R. Crafts**, 'Average Age at First Marriage for women in Mid Nineteenth Century England and Wales', *Population Studies*, No. 32, pp. 21–5.
37. See particularly **Sally Alexander**, **Anna Davin** and **Eve Hostettler**, 'Labouring Women: A Reply to Eric Hobsbawm', *History Workshop*, No. 8, Autumn 1979. Also Sally Alexander, *op. cit.*, and **Dorothy Thompson**, 'Women and Nineteenth Century Radical Politics: A Lost Dimension', also in Mitchell and Oakley, *The Rights and Wrongs of Women*, p. 115. On ideological pressures at the beginning of the twentieth century see Chapter 7 below.
38. Quoted in **M. Ramelson**, *The Petticoat Rebellion: A Century of Struggle for Women's Rights*, Lawrence and Wishart, London, 1967, p. 103.
39. There has been a long discussion on the role of female unpaid domestic labour in servicing the male proletariat and in contributing to the creation of surplus value under industrial capitalism. For a summary of the debate see **Maxine Molyneux**, 'Beyond the Domestic Labour Debate', *New Left Review*, No. 116, July–August, 1979.
40. Quoted in **Angus McLaren**, 'Contraception and the Working Classes: The Ideology of the English Birth Control Movement in its Early Years', *Comparative Studies in Society and History*, No. 18, 1976, pp. 245–6. McLaren, *Birth Control in England*, gives the best comprehensive account of the whole controversy. For contemporary French views see McLaren, 'Sex and Socialism: the Opposition of the French Left to Birth Control in the Nineteenth Century', *Journal of the History of Ideas*, Vol. XXXVIII, No. 3, July–September, 1976.
41. **W. Cobbett**, *Rural Rides*, Penguin, Harmondsworth, 1967, p. 317.
42. The classic evidence is given in **E. A. Wrigley's** essay on the Devonshire village of Colyton, 'Family Limitation in Pre-Industrial England', *Economic History Review*, 2nd series, Vol. XIX, 1966; reprinted in **M. Drake** (ed.), *Population in Industrialisation*, Methuen, London, 1969. Levine, *op. cit.*, revisits Colyton and finds the population decline in the second half of the seventeenth century a result not so much of 'instinctive providence' as of a rational response to de-industrialisation.
43. See **N. L. Tranter**, *Population since the Industrial Revolution*, Croom

Helm, London, 1973; and McLaren, *Birth Control in England.*
J. A. Banks takes McLaren to task in reviewing his book for ignoring the
fact that textile workers did not have the lowest birthrates; wives of
coachmen, grooms, domestic gardeners and domestic indoor servants had
lower birthrates 1851–91, *Victorian Studies*, Vol. 22, No. 4, Summer 1979.
44. See below, p. 204. For a discussion of birth-control strategies see **J. Matras**,
'Social Strategies of Family Formation: Data for British Female Cohorts
Born 1831–1906', *Population Studies*, Vol. 19, 1965–6, pp. 167–82. See
also **Pierre Bourdieu**, 'Marriage Strategies as Strategies of Social Reproduction', in **Robert Forster** and **Orest Ranum**, *Family and Society.*
F. B. Smith, in a review article, suggests that the spread of compulsory
elementary education and legislative restrictions on child employment,
together with the improved infant survival rate, may well have been crucial
incentives to family limitation in the working class from the late 1870s:
Social History, Vol. 5, No. 1, Jan. 1980. p. 51.
45. See **Diana G. Gittins**, 'The Decline of Family Size and Differential Fertility
in the 1930s', unpublished M. A. Thesis, University of Essex, Sociology
Department, 1974.
46. Llewelyn Davies, *op. cit.*, p. 30.
47. **Janet Blackman**, 'Popular Theories of Generation: The Evolution of
Aristotle's Works. The Study of an Anachronism', in Woodward and
Richard, *Health Care and Popular Medicine.*
48. In this discussion I follow McLaren, *op. cit.* For discussions amongst doctors in the 1860s suggesting that abortion and infanticide were on the increase, see Banks and Banks, *op. cit.*, p. 86.
49. Ellis, *Sex in Relation to Society*, p. 601. Abortion was not just a working-
class method, of course. J. A. Banks, *Prosperity and Parenthood*, discusses middle-class resort to abortion. See also **Patricia Knight**, 'Women
and Abortion in Victorian and Edwardian England', *History Workshop*,
No. 4, Autumn 1977.
50. McLaren, *op. cit.*, pp. 232 ff.
51. *Illustrated Bits*, 22 November 1898.
52. Ellis, *op. cit.*, p. 603; McLaren, *op. cit.*, p. 390.
53. Cominos, 'The Late Victorian Revolt', p. 354; **Paul Thompson**, *The Edwardians: The Remaking of British Society*, Paladin, St Albans, 1977,
p. 77.
54. See **Thea Vigne**, 'Parents and Children 1890–1918; Distance and Dependence'; and **Paul Thompson**, 'The War with Adults', both in *Oral History*,
Vol. 3, No. 2, Autumn 1975; and **John R. Gillis**, 'The Evolution of
Juvenile Delinquency in England, 1890–1914', *Past and Present*, No. 67,
May 1975. Cf. **Leonard Barlanstein**, 'Vagrants, Beggars and Thieves:
Delinquent Boys in Mid Nineteenth Century Paris', *Journal of Social
History*, Vol. 12, No. 4, Summer 1979.
55. Here I follow **Gareth Stedman Jones**, 'Working-Class Culture and
Working-Class Politics in London, 1870–1900; Notes on the Remaking of
a Working Class', *Journal of Social History*, Vol. 7, No. 4, Summer 1974.
56. **R. Q. Gray**, *The Labour Aristocracy in Victorian Edinburgh*, Clarendon,
Oxford, 1976, p. 142.
57. *Ibid.*, pp. 118, 169; **Geoffrey Crossick**, *An Artisan Elite in Victorian Society: Kentish London 1840–1880*, Croom Helm, London, 1978, p. 142.
58. Stedman Jones, *op. cit.*, p. 491.
59. *Ibid.*; Gray, *op. cit.*

Chapter Five

The public and the private: moral regulation in the Victorian period

Forms of moral regulation

The last decades of the nineteenth century saw the coming together of all the major themes of its sexual discourses: class pride and evangelism, moral certainty and social anxiety, the double standard and 'respect-ability', prurience and moral purity. Moral reform, from the 1870s, came close to the centre of political debate – much more so than struc-tural social reform ever did in the nineteenth century. Individual con-duct and moral reformation were seen as the key to public health. The Austrian Krafft-Ebing evoked a European-wide theme: 'The material and moral ruin of the community is steadily brought about by debauch-ery, adultery and luxury.'[1] The problem was, how to establish a frame-work within which moral reform could take place.

Victorian morality was premised on a series of ideological separa-tions: between family and society, between the restraint of the domestic circle and the temptations of promiscuity; between the privacy, leisure and comforts of the home and the tensions and competitiveness of work. And these divisions in social organisation and ideology were re-flected in sexual attitudes. The decency and morality of the home con-fronted the danger and the pollution of the public sphere; the joys and the 'naturalness' of the home countered the 'corruption', the artificial-ity of the streets, badly lit, unhygienic, dangerous and immoral. This was the basis of the dichotomy of 'the private' and 'the public' upon which much sexual regulation rested.

The double standard of morality relied upon this separation between the public and the private. The private was the nest of domestic virtues: the public was the arena of prostitution, of vice on the streets. So as the struggle against the double standard developed, particularly amongst social-purity crusaders from the 1860s onwards, one of the prime tar-gets in trying to establish a single standard of morality (the morality essentially of the chaste woman) was the drive against public manifesta-tions of vice. The division between the private and the public sphere, which was located both in economic development (the separation of work and home) and in social ideology, was by the end of the nine-teenth century at the heart of moral discourse; as a corollary, not surprisingly, the development of social purity was to have profound effects between the 1880s and the First World War on the regulation of sexual behaviour.

To fully understand the significance of these developments we must attempt, firstly, to grasp the role of the state, for its work in regulating sexual behaviour is central but complex. It does so directly, obviously, through legislation on marriage and divorce, through the regulation of extra-marital sex, and through the moral assumptions of its agencies, such as the Poor Law; and indirectly through its various forms of support for particular familial and household types, the education system, its role in encouraging or discouraging prosecutions, its omissions as well as its commissions. What it does not seem to have shown in the nineteenth century is any ready acceptance of a formal role in moralising the nation.

The general moral framework was unquestionably that of the Christian tradition. This provided the language within which morality (even the morality of non-believers) was articulated, and many of the formal practices which actually regulated sexual behaviour. Not until 1908, for instance, did state legal regulation replace ecclesiastical in the control of incest. Changes in sexual regulation we may hypothesise were more a product of changing patterns of class power and alliances, various, and changing forms of pressure, and shifting perceptions of the moral needs of classes and masses rather than the result of any firm, moralizing policy. There was no single strategy at work, no automatic response to the needs of the economy or social change.

Important shifts did nevertheless take place in ways which profoundly reshaped the organisation of sexuality. There were, in the first place, important changes in the property laws, in large part a result of the move towards industrial capitalism and this, as was suggested in Chapter 2, had its effects in family patterns. Until the eighteenth century aristocratic landed property was generally governed, under common law, by primogeniture and entail, which worked to secure large estates. Some provision was generally made for the scions of the family – the 'portion' for the younger sons, the dowry for the daughters – but primogeniture was essential. By the eighteenth century there was some move towards acceptance by the smaller landlords of partible inheritance, and the shift into industrial capitalism led to legal changes which increased freedom of testation, allowing a business man greater choice in securing his business fortune.[2] In theory, daughters could now more easily inherit, though marriage law, prior to the 1882 Married Women's Property Act, still dictated that a daughter's property must pass to her husband on marriage. This suggests again the close connection between property regulations and marriage patterns. The 1882 Act in one respect served to grant to middle-class women the rights in property enjoyed by the middle-class male. But of course these rights were contained within an ideological framework which stressed domesticity and in many ways, as we know, worked to restress the importance of female chastity.[3]

Secondly, there was throughout the nineteenth century a gradual assumption by the state of many of the responsibilities formerly held by the Church, particularly in regard to marriage – Lord Hardwicke's Marriage Act in 1753, the 1836 Act which introduced civil marriage, the reorganisation of divorce and separation procedures in 1856 and 1878, with further Acts in 1884, 1886, 1895. Marriage was obviously not simply a religious union but had profound social consequences and these were recognised in the formal legal changes of the nineteenth century.

Thirdly, there was a highly uneven, but nevertheless very important formal assumption of responsibility by the state for many areas of sexual unorthodoxies, not simply, as often hitherto, in terms of enforcement, but also in terms of actual organisation, as for example with obscenity (1857), prostitution and homosexuality (1885, 1898), and indecent advertising (1889).

These shifts were not without their contradictions and sustained challenges: they were products of complex pressures, and subject to various influences. The economically equitable assumptions behind changes in the property law often, for instance, came into conflict with inherited beliefs about the proper division of labour in the family and ideologies of femininity – and the latter usually won. It was no accident that this was a major area of feminist endeavour. There was moreover a great reluctance to intervene in the family itself. As Whately Cook Taylor put it in 1874, 'Hitherto, whatever the laws have touched, they have not dared invade the sacred precinct',[4] and such reluctance dictated the hesitations over passing the incest law until 1908. The family remained ostensibly a privileged domain, even while it was being legally and ideologically constructed and unified.

Simultaneously, state agencies were often uncertain about the effects of the legal regulation of extra-marital sex, and enforcement was sporadic and uneven.[5] As the legislative attitude to prostitution indicates, there was an underlying implicit acceptance of the double standard for much of the century, and a tacit assumption that the function of the machinery of the state, local and national, was to regulate the public sphere and not the private. Even the moral reformer was primarily concerned – at least in terms of practical politics – with encouraging greater efforts in the regulation of the public arena, though imperceptibly many began to attempt to evangelise in the private too, in a tradition that had a considerable history, and a long future. The importance of the morality organisations lay not so much in their mass membership as in the specific influence they could demonstrate in moments of crises, the forces they could mobilise, the pressures they could bring to bear, the ears they could bend, the opportunities they could seize, and here conjunctural political factors played an important part. The major political groupings themselves had different attitudes towards moral regulation in the later part of the century. Liberals generally sought to defend the family by promoting education and temperance and by opposing the Contagious Diseases Acts; Conservatives pursued similar aims by encouraging a host of voluntary and philanthropic organisations, which worked to instil habits of sobriety and respectability in the working class.[6]

As Brian Harrison has pointed out, the peculiar nature of the problem as conceived by the moral reformers – as an individual moral failing from which social consequences flowed – meant that it was difficult to evolve administrative machinery to carry out their aims. They constantly used interventionist language, but this often involved little more than a legislative declaration in favour of good, and they relied to an extraordinary degree on individual and voluntary effort.[7] Voluntary organisations in many cases became the effective agents of enforcement, as well as pressure groups constantly campaigning for further intervention, and here they became quasi-state apparatuses, a pattern which had a long history. Nevertheless, there was, *in toto*, an increase in legal regulation and public surveillance.

Private morality, public vice

As far back as the 1690s, with the establishment of the Society for the Reformation of Manners in London and the provinces, moral transgressors, including violators of the Sabbath, profane swearers, prostitutes, keepers of bawdy houses, actors in indecent plays and buggers, had been subject to sustained efforts at moral control, while public officials in the royal court encouraged the societies as an important contribution to the woefully inadequate police.[8] But the regulation of sexual behaviour also became a way of policing the population at large, and this combination of factors is clearly manifest again in the social morality crusades of the nineteenth century. From the early part of the nineteenth century, until absorbed in the new social purity movements of the 1880s, the Society for the Suppression of Vice (founded in 1802 and known universally as the Vice Society) remained the Victorian's basic legal force against the obscene, and its work demonstrates the often close relationship between private vigilance and public authorities. It was the persuasion of the Vice Society that led Lord Chancellor Campbell to push through the Obscene Publications Act of 1857, an Act which was to remain in force for a hundred years, and this was followed by the establishment of the first (and short-lived) Obscene Publications police squad in London.[9] A similar pattern of pressure and response can be seen in the moral restructuring of the last decades of the century.

It was prostitution which was the main focus of the debate and moral reforming efforts from the 1850s, and this best illustrates the various elements at work. The widespread tolerance of prostitution was reflected in the absence of any serious legislative attack on the problem until the 1860s, with the passing of the Contagious Diseases Acts. These, moreover, were designed not to prevent prostitution but to provide a degree of state regulation, with the aim of curtailing venereal disease. Medical men, as well as the military and defenders of the double standard, were strong proponents of the Acts. The act of prostitution itself has never been illegal. As the Home Secretary Ritchie put it in 1901, 'To get rid of prostitution by legal enactment or by official interposition is out of the question – so long as human nature is what it is, you will never entirely get rid of it . . .',[10] and measures such as the Vagrancy Act, 1824, and the Metropolitan Police Act of 1839 were designed to regulate public nuisance rather than prostitution itself.

There can be no doubt of the symbolic importance of prostitution to the Victorians. The use of terms such as 'social evil' and the 'social diseases' suggests a widespread fear of the social implications of prostitution, and by the middle years of the century this fear was becoming part of a general social anxiety. Between 1838 and 1859 over a dozen important books were published on the subject as well as a host of articles. By way of contrast we may note that between 1939 and 1959, years which saw a major debate and official investigation of the subject, there were only two major books.[11] It is difficult to assess the number of prostitutes actually involved. Even in the late eighteenth century Colquhoun estimated that there were 50,000 London prostitutes; in the 1830s and 1840s others fixed the total at some 80,000, while the *Westminster Review* fixed the national totals at anything between 50,000 and 368,000. Police estimates were rather more conservative, suggesting about 7,000 prostitutes in London in the 1850s, with a national total of something under 30,000.[12] The degree and meaning of prostitution was an important issue in itself (one estimate would have made prostitution the fourth largest female occupation) but more important, given the double standard, was the reservoir of venereal disease especially syphilis, that it was perceived as constituting, a threat particularly to the efficiency of the armed services, and it was concern over this that led to the passing of the Contagious Diseases Acts (in 1864, 1866, 1869).[13]

The incidence of syphilis itself, though a real problem, was actually declining from the 1860s while the Acts were manifestly unfair, for they took for granted the double standard and consequently sought to control working-class women while ignoring the major source for the spreading of the disease, the men. But the response at first was muted, for the Acts seem to have been *ad hoc* responses to a perceived crisis rather than an expression of a coherent programme. The working of the Acts themselves was instrumental in crystallising and shaping the situation. Only as they were put into operation, piecemeal, were their assumptions clarified, and their aims consciously formulated and defended by regulationists. And only as the operation of the Acts was perceived did a groundswell of opposition develop.[14] Neverthless, the apparent acceptance of prostitution in the Acts evoked a strong response from feminists, led by Josephine Butler, and from social moralists, which was directed particularly against the state regulation of vice. Throughout the 1870s and 1880s the 'abolitionists', as they were called, were a major social force, and the stimulus for the emergence of vigorous social-purity organisations, such as the National Vigilance Association, which survived in many cases into the 1950s and 1960s.[15] They also touched a nerve of public anxiety.

The last decades of the nineteenth and the first decade of the twentieth centuries saw a major attempt at moral restructuring which had its effects both in legislation and in the tone of public life. The evangelical and moral reforming endeavour was not, as we know, new, and throughout the century it had a significant impact on the manner of public life. But from the 1870s, following what was seen as a decline in standards in the 1850s and 1860s, a new confidence in the moralistic ethic can be detected, as if the hesitations that had governed earlier attempts were cast off. In the early decades of the century, evangelicals had been constrained by the fear of revolution. No such fears limited them in the 1880 and 1890s. Moreover a series of causes and scandals sustained them – from the iniquities of the Contagious Diseases Acts to the scandalous leniency meted out to high-class 'madams',[16] from the exploitation and abduction of young girls in the White Slave Trade to the marriage and other scandals of those in high places: the divorce case of Charles Dilke in 1886; of the Irish leader Parnell in 1890; the scandal of the Cleveland Street homosexual brothel, 1889–90, said to involve the eldest son of the heir to the throne; and the Tranby Croft gambling scandal of 1891, which involved the Prince of Wales himself.

There was, too, a constituency ready to be stirred by such scandals, in the lower middle class and the respectable working class. At the very time when the former was achieving a settled status, their values were being attacked by radicals, libertarians and libertines. The novelist Walter Gallichan spoke of *The Blight of Respectability* in the 1890s, and it was indeed their most central values that were most flagrantly challenged. The ideology of respectability had been in the process of articulation throughout the century. Its stress on values such as self-help and self-reliance, the value of work, the need for social discipline, the cohering centrality of the family, were all challenged by public immorality. Here was a strong social basis for social purity, which could be effectively mobilised by moral entrepreneurs.[17]

The working of the Contagious Diseases Acts themselves also served to mobilise many a radical working man against the exploitation of working-class women, and an important alliance developed between this radicalism and feminists, which had the additional effect of providing for the latter a social support which enhanced their authority within the repeal movement.[18]

Behind this, giving a tremendous dynamism to the campaigns was an evangelical revival, bringing large sections of the feminist movement into alliance with nonconformity, an alliance sealed in outrage against the double standard. Many of the leaders of the campaigns of the 1880s were products of this Christian revival. W. T. Stead described himself as 'a child of the revival of 1859–60' which had swept across the Atlantic and won hundreds of thousands of converts (over a hundred thousand in Ulster alone). William Coote, who was to play a major role in social purity up to the 1920s, went through a typical adolescent conversion experience in the 1860s and 1870s. The same pattern is manifest in the new outbreak of social morality fervour in the decade before the outbreak of the First World War. Again its leadership was provided by many of the converts of the last great series of revival missions sponsored by the Free Church Council in 1901 and 1902.[19]

But social purity was also able to mine very deep fears of a more secular kind. 1885, an *annus mirabilis* of sexual politics, was also the year of the expansion of the electorate, fears of national decline following the defeat of General Gordon, anxieties about the future of Ireland, and all this in the context of a socialist revival and feminist agitation. The Reverend J. M. Wilson called for social purity, 'for the good of your nation and your country', and warned that 'Rome fell; other nations are falling'. So moral purity became a metaphor for a stable society: 'In all countries the purity of the family must be the surest strength of a nation; and virtue from above is mighty in its power over the homes below.'[20]

By 1885 social purity was able to tap an anxiety which found a symbolic focus in the 'twin evils' of enforced prostitution and the exploitation of minors, young girls. W. T. Stead's sensational exposé of the latter in his articles on 'The Maiden Tribute of Modern Babylon' generated a sense of outrage with which a wide spectrum of public opinion found itself in sympathy. By the summer of 1885, Anglican bishops, freethinkers and socialists found themselves able to work together in a short-lived coalition against sexual abuse of children. Stead's dramatisation of the issue of sexual exploitation not only stilled for the moment many fundamental conflicts of interest between participants in the agitation, but it also obscured the contradictions inherent in the ideology that informed this agitation against child prostitution.[21] But under the impact of this pressure Parliament belatedly passed the long-delayed Criminal Law Amendment Act which attempted to suppress brothels, raised the age of consent for girls to sixteen, and introduced in Section 11 new penalties against male homosexual behaviour – significantly both in private as well as in public. Further changes, in the 1898 Vagrancy Act and the 1912 Criminal Law Amendment Act, underlined the new legislative involvement with prostitution and homosexuality.

The problem we have to grapple with in trying to understand the significance of the events is the contradiction between the ostensibly humanitarian instincts of those who campaigned for legal change, and the controlling impact they had on people's lives, particularly working-class girls and homosexuals. Often seen as a major stage in the humanisation of sexual relations and in the development of a single standard of mo-

rality, which was certainly the intention of feminists such as Josephine
Butler, the changes nevertheless involved an extention of social regulation of sexual behaviour.[22]

Reformers in 1885 had no doubt that their cause was righteous: a
crusade against 'a dark and cruel wrong'. Young girl prostitutes were
portrayed as sexually innocent, as passive victims of individual evil
men. As Deborah Gorham has pointed out, what this sort of approach
ignored was the very origins of prostitution in the economic system and
the opportunities that prostitution offered to young girls as a way out of
acute poverty and dismal career possibilities.[23] Reformers were directing their energies, as we can see now, at many of the wrong targets,
illustrating the typical nineteenth-century preference for moral campaigns rather than for structural social reforms. In directing it at the
targets they did, however, they produced effects that feminists such as
Josephine Butler might have eventually found abhorrent. The most important element was the difficulty that reformers had in distinguishing
between their desire to protect the young girls who were the objects of
their concern and their desire to control them. And behind this there
were those unresolved problems on childhood, adolescence, maturity,
and the different conditions of working-class children which we discussed earlier. Implicit in the rhetoric of those who campaigned for stif-
fer age-of-consent legislation (and the campaign went on into the 1930s
to raise it above 16, even to 21)[24] was the assumption that young working-class girls were ignorant and defenceless and could not decide for
themselves. But in fact those they sought to protect often did not act as
if they were passive. The majority of young girls who went into prostitution had not been dragged or coerced into 'shame'; often it was the
only course that seemed open.

What cemented the temporary alliance between feminists, like
Josephine Butler, and moral repressionists, such as Alfred Dyer, was a
rejection of the double standard that lay behind the speeches and pressure of most of their parliamentary opponents. Most of the men who
wished to keep the age of consent at 12 and 13 accepted as a matter of
course an outlook in which young girls from the working class were perceived to be easy sexual targets. For many upper-class men, prostitution
appeared both necessary and inevitable; and their objections to raising
the age of consent often arose from the fear that either they or their
sons might be threatened by new legislation. One member of the House
of Lords put it succinctly in 1884: 'Very few of their Lordships . . . had
not, when young men, been guilty of immorality. He hoped they would
pause before passing a clause within the range of which their sons might
come.'[25]

Confronted with this sort of attitude it is easy to see why even such a
reformer as Butler, who was usually extremely sensitive to the issue of
the personal rights of individuals, responded with outrage to attempts
to block age-of-consent legislation. To her, such opposition was a fla-
grant example of the pernicious belief that 'a large section of female

society' should be set aside 'to administer to the irregularities of the excusable men'. In this sort of atmosphere the arguments of those like Charles Hopwood, MP for Stockport, who accepted social-purity arguments about prostitution but opposed the Criminal Law Amendment Act, were drowned. He opposed the Criminal Law Amendment Bill on the grounds that 'repressive legislation of this kind is not calculated to improve public morals'. He opposed raising the age of consent above 13 largely because it violated the right of free choice, and he opposed the provisions of the Bill relating to street soliciting. He was also the most vigorous opponent in the House of the attempts of some purity advocates to amend the Bill by including punishment by flogging for certain types of offenders, a provision that was renewed in a similar atmosphere of hysteria in 1912.[26]

There were in fact two separate but overlapping strands in the social-purity alliance. These were, first of all, those who believed that the purpose of legislation was to force people to be moral. Prostitution, said the Rescue Society in 1880, 'should be completely suppressed and houses of ill fame utterly rooted out'. On the other hand, there were those feminists represented by Josephine Butler who believed that prostitution was evil because it destroyed human dignity but who also believed the prostitute had a right not to be harrassed, and if she was an adult she even had a right to choose to become a prostitute. But the legislative changes of the 1880s and afterwards were to have effects probably quite different from those that reformers such as Butler intended, and much more in the direction of increased control rather than of assertion of individual choice.

Reform or control?

The history of prostitution particularly illustrates this combination of reform and control; reform, indeed, as a means of control. The Contagious Diseases Act which had been so bitterly opposed by feminists like Butler, had extended well beyond sanitary supervision of common prostitutes. As single women, residing often outside their families, women registered under the Acts were perhaps the most vulnerable members of their community. As a result, official intervention into their lives offered police an easy opportunity for general surveillance of the poor neighbourhoods in which they resided. As Judith Walkowitz has pointed out, in the districts where the Acts were enforced, petty theft, the seasonal migration of the poor into the countryside to pick hops and strawberries, and prostitution, were all means by which the chronically under-employed endured through hard times. The Contagious Diseases Acts, alongside their formal aim, can also be seen as part of the legal effort to contain this occupational and geographical mobility.[27]

The fragile social equilibrium between the toleration and segregation of marginal social behaviour which was necessary to the survival of the very poor in the working-class community was almost certainly upset by the enforcement of the Contagious Diseases Acts. On the one hand, the Acts generated an extensive public resistance amongst the women in their community. On the other, by forcing prostitutes and their neighbours publicly to acknowledge what had previously been informally tolerated they introduced a stricter redefinition of acceptable behaviour, thereby facilitating the social isolation of prostitutes. One of the effects of the Contagious Diseases Acts was to define more sharply the categories of acceptable social and sexual behaviour. And in fact public shaming was one of the principal functions of police registration and surveillance. What probably bothered respectable neighbours was not so much the 'immorality' of a young woman as the notoriety which her social exposure and labelling brought. The dictates of self-preservation often ensured that the respectable young working woman dissociated herself from the known prostitute, since association with prostitutes rendered a woman's character suspect to the police and could lead to her name being placed on the registration list.

Repressive public sanctions would make the move into prostitution a different kind of choice than when it could constitute a temporary and relatively anonymous stage in a woman's life. But ironically the repeal of the Contagious Diseases Acts in the 1880s accentuated rather than diminished this tendency, for police and judicial measures, combined with the efforts of moral reformers, were making ever clearer that distinction between respectable and unrespectable behaviour. Control of the lives of accused prostitutes did not end with the repeal of the Acts; it was merely transferred to new agencies, often with similar personnel to those who had enforced the Contagious Diseases Acts. Social-purity legislation, such as the Industrial Schools Amendment Act of 1881, which allowed children of prostitutes to be committed to an industrial school, and the 1885 Act, gave further powers to the police in their surveillance over women and children.

So far from wiping out vice, whether in public or private, social-purity legislation almost certainly merely contributed to changing its form. Just as the closing of the pleasure houses of the 1870s had thrown prostitutes onto the streets, so the suppression of brothels after 1885 probably increased street prostitution, at the same time pushing prostitutes into massage parlours and flats, and into the arms of 'bullies', who became mythical figures of popular fears in the new moral panic over the white slave trade before 1912.[28] In addition, by drawing more firmly the line between respectable and disreputable behaviour, social-purity legislation certainly encouraged the emergence of a much clearer subculture of prostitution, and a similar development can be observed with regard to male homosexuality (see Chapter 6 below).

In the years following 1885 there was a considerable increase in prosecutions for sexual offences. The Editor of the *Criminal Statistics* for 1896 noted this and added, 'The growth of public sentiment with regard to sexual crime, of which the (Criminal Law Amendment) Act was one manifestation, is no doubt responsible also for the more vigorous prose-cution of offences.'[29] Stricter enforcement, allied to the creation of new categories of crime (defilement of girls under 13, gross indecency be-tween men), marked a new inflection in the sexual regime. There were cross-currents; for instance, books banned in the 1880s reappeared in the 1890s,[30] but social purity remained vigorous through the 1890s and 1900s, particularly through voluntary organisations, such as local vigilance committees, public morality organisations and bodies like the Salvation Army, bringing closure orders against brothels, hunting out displays of vice, prosecuting obscene books, and promoting wholesome literature.

There was a willingness on the part of public authorities, not surpris-ingly, to allow voluntary bodies such as the National Vigilance Associa-tion to carry out the (often unpopular) duties of moral surveillance, though the practices of police and magistrates varied. In a place like Liverpool the police were willing to prosecute prostitutes for soliciting without independent corroboration of nuisance, and the magistrates backed this up. In 1901 the Home Office adopted a similar tougher policy for the Metropolitan area, and the next five years saw an intense clean-up. But clean-ups and purges were less a sustained policy than a reaction to popular events and anxieties.

After the suspension in 1883 and later repeal (in 1886) of the Conta-gious Diseases Acts, the state effectively abandoned any attempt to reg-ulate (and hence lend official backing to) prostitution and adopted the traditional policy of tacit acceptance of it as an inevitable evil. By the early part of the century the policy of the state was quite clearly to regu-late, as best it could, public vice, but to ignore, as outside its purview, private adult heterosexual liaisons: whether conjugal or involving pros-titution. Legal intervention in the private sphere concentrated on acts involving children, acts of incest (after 1908) and male homosexuality, where the private/public distinction was not applied. The state re-mained reluctant to initiate legislation to enforce morality, though by the 1880s it was clearly responsive to its perception of public pressure. At the huge demonstration in Hyde Park on 22 August 1885, prior to the passing of the Criminal Law Amendment Act, a speaker expressed the hope that 'our public men shall be pure'. By 1895, with the sensa-tional trial of Oscar Wilde (one of those 'writers of elegant and glitter-ing literature, glossing over vice', denounced by the Reverend Richard Armstrong of the Social Purity Alliance), the government felt obliged to prosecute *because* a relative of one of its members was mentioned in the case.[31] Effectively, social purity had been politically appropriated.

But the mention of Wilde also serves to remind us that social purity never succeeded in totally silencing its opponents. Indeed, there is a strong case to be made that the moralistic campaigns around sexuality encouraged, as a response, a more radical position on sexuality. A Drysdale could argue that it was the repression of sex that led to insan-ity. A James Hinton, the mystical inspirer of Havelock Ellis and others,

saw sex as suffusing and enhancing the whole of life. Radicals like
Grant Allen, Ellis, Edward Carpenter, the 'new women' in fiction, the
mannered libertarianism of Wilde and his circle, discovered sexuality as
a positive value or as a subversive force which challenged the tyranny of
respectability. All this was to feed into the stream of sexual radicalism
in the early twentieth century.[32] And at the other extreme, the success of
social purity never silenced the defenders of the double standard. Mrs
Ormiston Chant's valiant efforts to close the infamous promenade of
the 'Empire' Music Hall in London in 1894 were, we must remember,
countered by an impassioned group of upper-class rowdies, led by the
young Winston Churchill.[33] There was, as we have said before, no final
triumph for puritanism.

But undoubtedly, a new mood is detectable from the 1880s and
1890s, and 1895 is a particularly symbolic year because the reaction to
Wilde's downfall was indicative of the new mode in public discourse.
Throughout 1895 the attack on the 'sex mania' of the new fiction developed, marking the 'return of the Philistines'. And the danger of the
'flaunting' of immorality was underlined by the publication of Max
Nordau's book, *Degeneration*, evoking individual and national collapse
under the impact of immorality.[34] It was not a final closure and by the
new century a younger generation was challenging the social-purity consensus. But they in turn provoked a new fear of the obscene. St Loe
Strachey, editor of *The Spectator* attacked H. G. Wells' *Ann Veronica*
as undermining

the sense of continence and self control in the individual which is essential to a
sound and healthy State. . . . Unless the citizens of a State put before themselves
the principles of duty, self sacrifice, self control and continence . . . the life of
the State must be short and precarious. Unless the institution of the family is
firmly founded and advanced, the State will not continue.[35]

These themes constantly recur up to the First World War. In 1912
Havelock Ellis complained that: 'During the past ten years one of those
waves of enthusiasm for the moralisation of the public by the law has
been sweeping across Europe and America.'[36] Anxieties about moral
standards reflected a deep belief that the roots of social stability lay in
individual and public morality. So an agitation, like that over the international white slave trade in the 1900s, mined rich seams of anxiety: on
the position of women, dramatised by feminism; about the consequences of domestic and international migration; and on the effects of
rapid urban and industrial growth. They had their apotheosis in a moral
resolution. Again in 1912 feminists allied with social purity to press on a
reluctant government a new criminal law amendment act, 'The White
Slave Act'.[37] More significant than its provisions (which tightened up
the law regarding 'bullies', procurers and brothel keepers, and reaffirmed flogging, which chiefly affected homosexuals) was what it reflected: a deflection we would argue, of real, and urgent, anxieties, the
product of major social disruptions, on to the sphere of sexuality.

Once the moral gesture had been made, the immediate panic dissipated, though the problems it addressed did not. Sexual behaviour had in the course of the previous century become a symbol of much wider social features. This is perhaps the main contribution of the sexual economy of the nineteenth century to that of the twentieth.

References

1. **Krafft-Ebing**, *Psychopathia Sexualis*, p. 6.
2. See **Rachel Harrison** and **Frank Mort**, 'Patriarchal Aspects of 19th Century State Formation: Property Relations, Marriage and Divorce, and Sexuality', in **P. Corrigan** (ed.), *Capitalism, State Formation and Marxist Theory*, Quartet, London, 1980. I am grateful to the authors for allowing me to read their paper before publication. For a detailed discussion, see **F. M. L. Thompson**, *Landed Society in the Nineteenth Century*, Routledge and Kegan Paul, London, 1963, p. 119; see also **Albie Sachs**, 'The Myth of Male Protectiveness and the Legal Subordination of Women – An Historical Analysis', in **Carol Smart** and **Barry Smart** (eds), *Women, Sexuality and Social Control*, Routledge and Kegan Paul, London, 1978; and **Albie Sachs** and **Joan Hobb Wilson**, *Sexism and the Law*, Martin Robertson, Oxford, 1978.
3. See the discussion in Chapter 2, above, pp. 29 ff. On property concerns of the women's movement see **I. Minor**'s article in **D. E. Martin** and **D. Rubinstein**, *Ideology and the Labour Movement*, Croom Helm, London, 1979, p. 105.
4. Quoted in Margaret Hewitt, *Wives and Mothers,* p. 154.
5. On hesitations about the prosecution of private homosexuality, see pp. 103–4 below. On the hesitations with which the Home Office came to see the need for legislation on incest, see Victor Bailey and Sheila Blackburn, 'The Punishment of Incest Act'. On prostitution, see below.
6. **Brian Harrison**, 'For Church, Queen and Family: The Girl's Friendly Society 1874–1920', *Past and Present*, No. 61, November 1973. This essay is an excellent account of one major Tory voluntary organisation.
7. **Brian Harrison**, 'State Intervention and Moral Reform in Nineteenth-century England', **Patricia Hollis** (ed.), *Pressure from Without in early Victorian England*, Edward Arnold, London, 1974.
8. Cf. **Edward J. Bristow**, *Vice and Vigilance: Purity Movements in Britain since 1700*, Gill and Macmillan, Dublin, 1977, pp. 32–50.
9. *Ibid.*, pp. 46–7.
10. Public Record Office: HO 45: B13517/35/41. For a recent study of the subject which seems to accept its inevitability, see **Abraham A. Sion**, *Prostitution and the Law*, Faber and Faber, London, 1977. For an acute dissection of the ideological assumptions underlying such an approach see **Mary McIntosh**, 'Who Needs Prostitutes? The Ideology of Male Sexual Needs', in Smart and Smart (eds), *op. cit.*
11. A point made by **H. R. E. Ware**, 'The Recruitment, Regulation and Role of Prostitution in Britain from the Middle of the Nineteenth Century to the Present Day', unpublished London University Ph.D. thesis 1969, p. 10.
12. See **E. M. Sigsworth and T. J. Wyke**, 'A Study of Victorian Prostitution and Venereal Disease', in M. Vicinus (ed.), *Suffer and Be Still*, pp. 78—9.
13. On this and on the fear of venereal disease, see *ibid.*; Judith Walkowitz,

Prostitution and Victorian Society; and **F. B. Smith**, 'Ethics and Disease in the later Nineteenth Century: The Contagious Diseases Acts', *Historical Studies* (University of Melbourne), No. 15, 1971. H. R. E. Ware, *op. cit.*, has an Appendix on venereal disease in the nineteenth century. See also **Paul McHugh**, *Prostitution and Victorian Social Reform*, Croom Helm, London, 1980, for a detailed account of the passing and operation of the Contagious Diseases Acts.

14. Walkowitz, *op. cit.*

15. The National Vigilance Society was founded in 1885, in the midst of the agitation for the passing of the Criminal Law Amendment Act, to ensure its passage and, thereafter, effective operation. It amalgamated with *inter alia* the Minors' Protection Society and the Vice Society in its early days, and with the National Committee for the Suppression of Traffic in Women in 1953 to form the British Vigilance Association. This was disbanded in 1972. Josephine Butler's organisation, founded in 1869, was originally known as the Ladies' National Association for the Abolition of State Regulation of Vice. The words 'and for the Promotion of Social Purity' were added after repeal. In 1915 after amalgamations it became the Association for Moral and Social Hygiene, under which title it was known until 1953, when it became the Josephine Butler Society. Other organisations, such as the Social Purity Alliance, White Cross, and denominational organisations are discussed in Bristow, *Vice and Vigilance*.

16. The case of Mrs Jeffries in 1885 became notorious because of the suspicion that she received lenient treatment because of the people in high places she could name. See *The Sentinel*, No. 74, June 1885.

17. See references in Chapter 2. The challenge to lower-middle-class respectability is discussed in **Richard N. Price's** article in G. Crossick (ed.), *The Lower Middle Class in Britain*; and also in Trudgill, *Madonnas and Magdalens*, pp. 194 ff. For a discussion of the relationship between class, status fears and public morality crusades, see **J. R. Gusfield**, *Symbolic Crusade: Status Politics and the American Temperance Movement*, University of Illinois Press, Urbana, 1972, and references for Ch. 14, p. 289, Notes 20–2, below.

18. See Walkowitz, *Prostitution and Victorian Society*; **P. Dwyer**, 'The Repeal Movement Against the Contagious Diseases Act 1866 with Special Reference to Working Class Agitation', unpublished thesis for History Diploma, Ruskin College 1971; and P. McHugh, *Prostitution and Victorian Social Reform*.

19. See **Deborah Gorham**, 'The "Maiden Tribute of Modern Babylon" Re-Examined: Child Prostitution and the Idea of Childhood in Late-Victorian England', *Victorian Studies*, Vol. 21, No. 3, Spring 1978; Bristow, *op. cit.*

20. **Rev. J. M. Wilson**, *Sins of the Flesh*, Social Purity Alliance, London, 1885, p. 7; **Rev. W. Arthur**, 'The Political Value of Social Purity', *The Sentinel*, September 1885, p. 480.

21. Stead's articles appeared in early July 1885. This discussion is based on Gorham *op. cit.* For a qualification see Note 1, p. 52.

22. This point is made forcefully by **George Ives**, *The Continued Extension of the Criminal Law*, London, 1922.

23. Gorham, *op. cit.* For a recent discussion of poverty as a major root of prostitution, see **Frances Finnegan**, *Poverty and Prostitution: A Study of Victorian Prostitutes in York*, Cambridge University Press, 1979.

24. The age of consent for girls rose from 12 in 1861, to 13 in 1875, to 16 in

1885. There were attempts to amend the age in agitation for new Criminal Law Amendment Acts in 1912, 1917–19, 1921–22, and in the 1930s. There is evidence in the National Vigilance Association papers of some people wanting to raise the age to 21. In 1925 a Departmental Committee on Sexual Offences Against Young Persons advocated the raising of the age of consent to 17, and the National Vigilance Association (unsuccessfully) supported this. But by 1936 there was a feeling that to raise the age from 16 would not increase but actually decrease convictions. (National Vigilance Association papers, Fawcett Library, City of London Polytechnic.)

25. Quoted in Gorham, *op. cit.*, p. 366.

26. *Ibid.*

27. **Judith Walkowitz**, 'The Making of an Outcast Group: Prostitutes and Working Women in Nineteenth-Century Plymouth and Southampton', in M. Vicinus (ed.), *A Widening Sphere*; see also Walkowitz, *Prostitution and Victorian Society*; and Walkowitz and Walkowitz, ' "We are not beasts of the field" '.

28. See Trudgill, *Madonnas and Magdalens*, pp. 191 ff., on the closure of former London pleasure haunts from the 1870s, partly through economic factors (the decline of the 'gent', the rising property prices from suburban development), and partly from moral pressure. Bristow, *op. cit.*, Ch. 7, discusses the changing forms of prostitution. Cf. the changes in the 1960s, p. 244 below.

29. Quoted in **Hermann Mannheim**, *Social Aspects of Crime in England between the Wars*, George Allen & Unwin, London, 1939, p. 50. See also **R. S. Sindall**, *Aspects of Middle Class Crime in the 19th Century*, unpublished M.Phil. thesis, Leicester University, 1974, p. 215: 'the Criminal Law Amendment Act of 1885 caused a sharp increase in the number of recorded indictable offences against the person'.

30. See Trudgill, *op. cit.*, pp. 338 ff. The publisher Viztelly was prosecuted in 1888 by the National Vigilance Association for publishing allegedly pornographic works, especially Emile Zola's *La Terre*; the following year he was prosecuted again, and this time imprisoned for publishing Flaubert. But by 1891 Zola, if not Viztelly, was being warmly feted in London. Other writers to be hysterically abused included Ibsen and Thomas Hardy. Oscar Wilde's works were of course effectively blacked for a while after 1895, and works featuring homosexuality were in a particularly vulnerable position. See p. 104 and p. 116 below.

31. *The Sentinel*, September 1885, p. 473; **Rev. Richard Armstrong**, *Our Duty in Matters of Social Purity*, Social Purity Alliance, London, 1885.

32. See Chapters 8 and 9.

33. **Mrs Ormiston Chant**, *Why we Attacked the Empire*, Marshall and Son, London, 1895; **Winston L. S. Churchill**, *My Early Life. A Roving Commission*, Thornton Butterworth, London, 1930, p. 71; G. Stedman Jones, 'Working Class Culture', p. 495; Bristow, *Vice and Vigilance*, pp. 213–14.

34. See *Westminster Gazette*, March 1895; *Contemporary Review*, Vol. LXVII; *Reynolds News*, 21 April 1895; Trudgill, *op. cit.*, p. 145. **Max Simon Nordau**, *Degeneration*, W. Heinemann, London, 1895 (trans. from 2nd German edn of *Entartung*, Berlin, 1892).

35. Quoted in Bristow, *Vice and Vigilance*, p. 217.

36. Havelock Ellis, *Sex in Relation to Society*.

37. Bristow, *op. cit.*, pp. 189–93, gives a full account of the moral panic of 1912.

Chapter Six

The construction of homosexuality

Homosexuality: concepts and consequences

Most works on the history of sex tend to concentrate on the major forms of sexual experience to the exclusion of the minority forms. This is not surprising given the centrality in our society of the great rituals of birth, maturation, pair-bonding and reproduction. But to ignore extra-marital, non-reproductive, non-monogamous, or even non-heterosexual forms is to stifle an important aspect of our social history. Nor indeed are they independent aspects. The regulation of extra-marital sex has been a major concern for the forces of moral order throughout the history of the West, whether through the canonical controls of the church over adultery and sodomy in the medieval period, or the state's ordering of prostitution and homosexuality in the modern.

Of all the 'variations' of sexual behaviour, homosexuality has had the most vivid social pressure, and has evoked the most lively (if usually grossly misleading) historical accounts. It is, as many sexologists from Havelock Ellis to Alfred Kinsey have noted, the form closest to the heterosexual norm in our culture, and partly because of that it has often been the target of sustained social oppression. It has also, as an inevitable effect of the hostility it has evoked, produced the most substantial forms of resistance to hostile categorisation and has, consequently, a long cultural and subcultural history. A study of homosexuality is therefore essential, both because of its own intrinsic interest and because of the light it throws on the wider regulation of sexuality, the development of sexual categorisation, and the range of possible sexual identities.

In recent years it has become increasingly clear, first to sociologists, and belatedly to historians, that it is essential to distinguish between on the one hand, homosexual behaviour, and on the other homosexual roles, categorisations and identities.[1] It has been apparent to anthropologists and sexologists since at least the nineteenth century that homosexual behaviour has existed in a variety of different cultures, and that it is an ineradicable part of human sexual possibilities. But what has been equally apparent are the range of different responses towards homosexuality. Attitudes towards homosexual behaviour are, that is to say, culturally specific and have varied enormously across different cultures and through various historical periods. What is less obvious, but is now central to any historical work, is the realisation not only that *attitudes* towards same sex activity have varied but that the social and subjective meanings given to homosexuality have similarly been culturally specific. Bearing this in mind it is no longer possible to talk of the possibility of a universalistic history of homosexuality; it is only possible to understand the social significance of homosexual behaviour, both in terms of social response and in terms of individual identity, in its exact historical context. To put it another way, the various possibilities of same sex behaviour are variously constructed in different cultures as an aspect of wider gender and sexual regulation. The physical acts might be similar, but their social implications are often profoundly different. In our culture homosexuality has become an excoriated experience, severely socially condemned at various periods, and even today seen as a largely unfortunate, minority form by a large percentage of the population. It is this that demands explanation.

The general tendency is still to assume that 'deviance', and especially sexual unorthodoxy, is somehow a quality inherent in the individuals, to which the social then has to respond. Over the past twenty years, however, it has been increasingly recognised that the social not only defines, but actually in part constructs the deviance. The classic statement of the impact of social labelling was made by Edwin Lemert, who drew a distinction between what he termed 'primary' and 'secondary' deviance, the first being intrinsic, for whatever reason, to the individual, the second the result of social definition.[2] This suggests that there are two levels of analysis, one of which is more susceptible to historical understanding than the other. First of all there is the question of the actual creation of gendered and sexed individuals, whether as heterosexual or homosexual. Recent advances in social psychology and in neo-Freudian thought have suggested that the development of heterosexual or homosexual propensities at the level of the young human are not a product of inherent biological imperatives but are the effect of historically conditioned familial and other social influences channelling the sexual possibilities which exist in the young child.[3] It is quite possible, that is to say, that changing family forms, changing notions of childhood, of the role of parents and so on actually have profound effects in the construction of individual heterosexuals, homosexuals or other sexual categorisations. Emotions are differentially structured according to different social forms and pressures. But even if primary differences were biologically formed, this would not fundamentally alter the argument. For secondly, what makes this *historically* important are the social reactions to the sexed individuals that emerge in any particular form of society, and the ways in which these shape individual meanings. For to feel or experience something is not the same thing as to adopt a specific social identity, with all its often problematical effects. The historical problem therefore is to explain the various sources of the social stigmatisation of homosexuality, and the individual and collective response to this broadly hostile regulation. But the way to do this is not to seek out a single causative factor. The crucial question must be: what are the conditions for the emergence of this particular form of regulation of sexual behaviour in this particular society? In our own history this must involve an exploration of what Mary McIntosh pinpointed as the significant problem: the emergence of the notion that homosexuality is a psychological or emotional condition peculiar to some people and not others, and the social implications of this conceptualisation.

Mary McIntosh herself has theorised this, in a highly suggestive essay, in terms of the emergence of what she describes as a 'homosexual role'.[4] That is to say, under specific historical circumstances, which McIntosh traces to the late seventeenth century, there emerges a specific male (and it has usually been a male) role, a specialised, despised and punished role which 'keeps the bulk of society pure in rather the same way that the similar treatment of some kinds of criminal helps keep the rest of society law abiding'.[5] Such a role has two effects: it helps to provide a clear-cut threshold between permissible and impermissible behaviour; and secondly, it helps to segregate those labelled as deviant from others, and thus contains and limits their behaviour patterns. In the same way, a homosexual subculture, which is the correlative of the development of a specialised role, provides both access to the socially outlawed need (sex) and contains the deviant.

This insight has been enormously influential but, as in all exploratory essays, it has left many questions unanswered. More recent work has attempted to challenge it both in terms of its relationship to role theory and functionalism generally, and because of its apparent denial of any pre-given sexual orientation.[6] This however is to misconstrue its real importance. The essay itself suffers from the usual defects of a structuralist functionalist approach, particularly in the purposive effort at social control that it implies. But what it points to is an approach that can bear much historical fruit, indicating the necessity of studying homosexuality (as with other forms of sexual behaviour) both in terms of the social categorisation that shapes the experience, and in terms of the response itself, which in relationship to homosexuality has, over a long historical development, given rise to complex cultural and subcultural forms, and a distinctive series of sexual identities. These identities must, however, be understood in all their specificities, historical, class and gender. This last point is particularly important because though social scientists and historians have, by and large, sought to explain male and female homosexualities in terms of the same aetiologies and characteristics, their social histories, though obviously related, are distinctive. For both male and female homosexualities are social and historical divisions of the range of sexual possibilities and as such have to be understood in terms of their social implications.[7]

Moral, legal and medical regulation

There is a long tradition in the Christian West of hostility towards homosexuality, although this usually took the form of the formal regulation of male homosexual activity rather than of lesbian. The West during the Christian era was in fact unique in its taboo against all forms of homosexuality. Cross-cultural evidence demonstrates very clearly that other cultures have successfully integrated some forms at least of homosexual behaviour into its sexual *mores*, whether in the form of the socially accepted pedagogic relations common to ancient Greece, or in the development of the transvestite (berdache) roles in certain tribal societies.[8] But though persistent, the Christian taboos against homosexuality have varied in strength throughout time and have had differential effects on male and female homosexual behaviour. In England before 1885 the only legislation which *directly* affected homosexual behaviour was in fact that referring to sodomy. This 'sin against nature', the crime not to be named amongst Christians, evoked acute horrors. The classic position was summed up by the jurist, Sir William Blackstone, in the late eighteenth century, who felt that its very mention was 'a disgrace to human nature'. But this defiance of nature's will was not a solely homosexual offence. The 1533 Act of Henry VIII which first brought buggery within the scope of statute law, superseding ecclesiastical law, adopted the same criterion as the church: all acts of buggery were equally condemned as being 'against nature', whether between man and woman, man and beast, or man and man. The penalty for 'the abominable vice of buggery' was death, and the death penalty continued on the statute books, formally at least, until 1861. This enactment was the basis for all homosexual convictions up to 1885 in England and Wales. Other forms of homosexual activity were subsumed under the major form either as assault or as attempts at the major crime. The central point we must grasp was that the law was directed against a series of sexual acts, not a particular type of *person*, although in practice most people prosecuted under the buggery laws were probably prosecuted for homosexual behaviour (sodomy). It seems likely that homosexuality was regarded not as a particular attribute of a certain type of person but as a potential in all sensual creatures. The prime task seems to have been protection of reproductive sex in marriage. The law against sodomy was a central aspect of the regulation of all non-procreative sex and it was directed at men. Though lesbian behaviour was variously condemned its threat was less explicitly recognised in legal regulation, in Anglo-Saxon cultures at least.[9]

The 'sin against nature' seems to have evoked a peculiar hostility. One of the sailors court-martialled for buggery on HMS *Africaine* in 1815 spoke of 'a crime which would to God t'were never more seen on earth from those shades of hellish darkness whence to the misery of Man its propensity has been vomited forth'.[10] The epithet 'sodomite' was certainly one to be feared throughout the nineteenth century. In the early part of the century there is some evidence of great public antipathy towards convicted sodomites, while in 1895 Oscar Wilde was stirred into his disastrous libel case against the Marquis of Queensberry after being accused of posing, in his inimitable misspelling, as a 'somdomite'. As Lord Sumner put it in 1918, setting the stamp of an admired judge on social stigmatisation, sodomites were stamped with 'the hallmark of a specialised and extraordinary class as much as if they had carried on their bodies some physical peculiarities'.[11]

Despite this evidence it is difficult to trace in any detail the actual enforcement of the sodomy law or to understand the sorts of sexual identities that those prosecuted under it developed. Its enforcement varied throughout time and between different social classes. There seems to have been a spate of convictions at the end of the seventeenth century and in the 1720s, coinciding significantly enough with morality crusades and the emergence of a distinctive male homosexual subculture in some of the larger cities. And there appears to have been an increase in prosecutions in the first third of the nineteenth century when more than 50 men were hanged for sodomy in England. In one year, 1806, there were more executions for sodomy than for murder, while in 1810 four out of five convicted sodomists were hanged.[12] The law appears to have been particularly severe on members of the armed forces, where it was often employed with particularly dramatic and exemplary results. In 1811 Ensign John Hepburn and Drummer Thomas White were 'launched into eternity' before a 'vast concourse of spectators' including many notables and members of the Royal Family. And in February 1816, four members of the crew of the *Africaine* were hanged for buggery after a major naval scandal. Buggery has been mentioned in the articles of war since the seventeenth century and was treated as seriously as desertion, mutiny or murder.[13]

There does seem to be a pattern, certainly in the early nineteenth century, of an increase in the prosecution of buggery related to whether or not Britain was at war or in a state of social turmoil; as in later periods, homosexual behaviour was often a funnel for wider social anxieties. Efforts to remove the death penalty for sodomy were generally unsuccessful. Sir Robert Peel reaffirmed it in his reforms, in 1826; and when Lord John Russell attempted to remove 'unnatural offences' from the list of capital crimes in 1841 he was forced to withdraw through lack of parliamentary support. In practice, however, the death penalty was not applied after the 1830s, and was finally removed in 1861 (to be replaced by sentences of between ten years and life imprisonment).

Severe as the law was in theory, it was a catch-all rather than a refined legal weapon, reflecting a generalised legal control rather than detailed individual surveillance. As late as 1817 a man was sentenced to death under the sodomy laws for oral sex with a boy (he was later pardoned), and the term 'unnatural crimes' often covered a multitude of meanings, from bestiality to birth control. The uncertain status of sodomy was underlined in the notorious prosecution of the two transvestites, Ernest Boulton and Frederick William Park, who with others were tried for conspiracy to commit sodomite acts in the early 1870s. Police, legal and medical attitudes were manifestly confused. When Boulton and Park were arrested in 1870 for indecent behaviour (constituted by their public cross-dressing), they were immediately examined, without authorisation, for evidence of sodomy. It becomes clear from the transcripts of the trial (itself a major public event, held before the Lord Chief Justice in Westminster Hall and producing saturation press coverage) that neither the police nor the court were familiar with the patterns of male homosexuality. The opening remarks of the Attorney General hinted that it was their transvestism, their soliciting men as *women* which was the core of their crime. A Dr Paul, who examined them for sodomy on their arrest, had never encountered a similar case in his whole career. His only knowledge came from a half-remembered case history in Alfred Swaine Taylor's *Medical Jurisprudence*. But even Dr Taylor himself, who gave evidence in the case, had had no previous experience apart from this case, and the other doctors called in could not agree on what the signs of sodomitical activity were. The Attorney General observed that: 'It must be a matter of rare occurrence in this country at least for any person to be discovered who has any propensity for the practices which are imputed to them.[14] Their only recourse to the 'scientific' literature that was by then appearing was to the French, and then reluctantly. Dr Paul had never heard of the work of Tardieu, who had investigated over two hundred cases of sodomy for purposes of legal proof, until an anonymous letter informed him of its existence. The Attorney General suggested that it was fortunate that there was 'very little learning or knowledge upon this subject in this country'. One of the defence counsel was more bitter, attacking Dr Paul for relying on 'the newfound treasures of French literature upon the subject – which thank God is still foreign to the libraries of British surgeons'.[15]

What is striking in all this is that as late as 1871, concepts of homosexuality were extremely undeveloped both in the Metropolitan Police and in high medical and legal circles, suggesting the absence of any clear notion of a homosexual category or of any social awareness of what a homosexual identity might consist of. Certainly from the early seventeenth century, if not earlier, there was a widespread appreciation of the existence of a sort of transvestite and male prostitution subculture, and by the early nineteenth century it was often assumed in court cases that a married man was less likely to be guilty of buggery offences with another man.[16] But even this issue was a matter of debate in the Boulton and Park case in 1871. Such popular notions as did exist invariably associated male homosexual behaviour with effeminacy and probably transvestism as well. The counter-evidence that was present always produced surprise. The author of *The Phoenix of Sodom*, published in 1813, was amazed to discover that males who prostituted themselves were often not effeminate men, but coalmerchants, police runners, drummers, waiters, servants, and a grocer.[17] There was no awareness of homosexuality constituting the centre of a life 'career'. Even Jeremy Bentham, the utilitarian philosopher, who had produced extraordinarily advanced views at the turn of the eighteenth and nineteenth centuries, almost always conceived of sodomites as 'bisexual', capable of marriage, and attracted to adolescent boys, rather than as adult men who love other adult men.[18]

The latter part of the nineteenth century, however, saw the clear emergence of new conceptualisations of homosexuality although the elements of the new definitions and practices can be traced to earlier periods. The sodomite, as Foucault has put it, was a temporary aberration. The 'homosexual', on the other hand, belonged to a species, and it is this new concern with the homosexual person, both in legal practice and in psychological and medical categorisation, that marks the crucial change, both because it provided a new subject of social observation and speculation, and because it opened up the possibility of new modes of self-articulation. It is precisely at this period that we see the development of new terms to describe those interested in the same sex. The adoption in the last decades of the nineteenth century of words like 'homosexual' or 'invert', both by sexologists and by the homosexuals themselves, marked as crucial a change in consciousness as did the widespread adoption of the term 'gay' in the 1970s. Changing legal and medical attitudes were important elements in this development. The 1861 Offences Against the Person Act represented a formal move towards civilisation and removed the death penalty for buggery (replacing it by sentences of between ten years and life). In the next twenty years there is clear evidence in the Home Office files of attempts to distinguish the various forms of buggery, which in practice meant a separation of bestiality from homosexual activity, which was being more closely defined as an individual trait.[19] This in turn was being more directly controlled. By the famous Labouchère Amendment to the Criminal Law Amendment Act of 1885, acts of gross indecency between men were as 'misdemeanours' made punishable by up to two years' hard labour, and this in effect brought within the scope of the law all forms of male homosexual activity. In 1898 the Vagrancy Act tightened up the law relating to importuning for 'immoral purposes' and this was effectively applied exclusively against homosexual men. By a further Criminal Law Amendment Act in 1912, the sentence for this offence was set at six months' imprisonment with flogging for a second offence, on summary jurisdiction.[20]

Henry Labouchère stated that his stimulus to introduce this amendment was a report on male prostitution sent to him by W. T. Stead, and he argued that its introduction was essentially to facilitate proof.[21] The new laws were of course formally less repressive than the sodomy law, which still carried for a while a maximum of life imprisonment. Moreover the application of the laws varied throughout time and between different places at different times, with juries still reluctant to convict.

There was even some opposition at governmental level to the fact that the Labouchère Amendment applied to private as well as public behaviour. The Director of Public Prosecutions noted in 1889 'the expediency of not giving unnecessary publicity' to cases of gross indecency; and at the same time he felt that much could be said for allowing 'private persons – being full grown men – to indulge their unnatural tastes in private'. Often it seems juries were reluctant to convict, while the police directed a blind eye to private activity before the First World War, as long as 'public decency' was not too offended.[22] When the law was applied however, as it was for instance in the case of Oscar Wilde in 1895, it was applied with rigour, with the maximum penalty of two years' hard labour under the 1885 Act often being enforced. Similarly, the clauses against importuning were vigorously applied. Compared to the forty shillings fine imposed on female prostitutes under the Vagrancy Act, the maximum sentence of six months' imprisonment for men under the same provision ground particularly hard on male homosexuals, particularly as a prosecution was usually associated with social obloquy and moral revulsion. As a libertarian writer observed in the 1930s, speaking of private enforcements by the Public Morality Council, 'It is gratifying to note that in respect of female soliciting action is only taken where actual annoyance or disorderly conduct are apparent. All cases of importuning by male persons are however reported.'[23] The law did not *create* hostility, but as part of a wider restructuring of the social regulation of sex, it helped shape a new mood, particularly in its operation. Perhaps even more important than the individual prosecutions were the outbursts of moral panic that often accompanied some of the more sensational cases. This was particularly exemplified in the furore surrounding the 'Three Trials' of Oscar Wilde in 1895. The downfall of Oscar Wilde was a most significant event for it created a public image for the 'homosexual', a term by now coming into use, and a terrifying moral tale of the dangers that trailed closely behind deviant behaviour. The Wilde trials were in effect labelling processes of a most explicit kind drawing a clear border between acceptable and abhorrent behaviour. But they also of course had paradoxical effects. As Havelock Ellis said of the Oscar Wilde trials, they appeared 'to have generally contributed to give definiteness and self-consciousness to the manifestations of homosexuality, and to have aroused inverts to take up a definite stand'.[24] It seems likely that the new forms of legal regulation, whatever their vagaries in application, had the effect of forcing home to many the fact of their difference and thus creating a new community of knowledge, if not of life and feeling, amongst many men with homosexual leanings. There was clear evidence in the later decades of the nineteenth century of the development of a new sense of identity amongst many homosexual individuals, and a crucial element in this would undoubtedly have been the new public salience of homosexuality, dramatised by the legal situation.

The changing legal situation was intricately associated with the emergence of a 'medical model' of homosexuality which helped provide theoretical explanation for the individualising of the crime. The most commonly quoted European writers on homosexuality in the mid-1870s were Casper and Tardieu, the leading medical and legal experts of Germany and France respectively, and both seemed to have been primarily concerned with the need to define the new type of 'degenerates' who were coming before the courts, and to test whether they could be held legally responsible for their acts.[25] The same problem was apparent in Britain. Most of the works on homosexuality that appeared up to the First World War were directed, in part at least, at the legal profession. Even J. A. Symonds's privately printed pamphlet *A Problem in Modern Ethics* declared itself to be addressed 'especially to medical psychologists and jurists', while Havelock Ellis's *Sexual Inversion* (1897) was attacked for its opposite policy, for not being published by the medical press and being too popular in tone. The medicalisation of homosexuality – a transition from notions of sin to concepts of sickness or mental illness – was a vitally significant move, even though, like the new legal model, its application was uneven. Around it the poles of scientific discourse raged for decades: was homosexuality congenital or acquired, ineradicable or susceptible to cure, to be quietly if unenthusiastically accepted as unavoidable (even the liberal Havelock Ellis in his pioneering study of homosexuality found it necessary to warn his invert readers not to 'set himself in violent opposition' to his society), or to be resisted with all the force of one's Christian will?[26] Older notions of the immorality or sinfulness of homosexual behaviour did not of course die in the nineteenth century. But from the nineteenth century they were inextricably entangled with would-be scientific theory which formed the boundaries against and within which homosexuals had to define themselves.

What in effect many of the pioneering sexologists of the late nineteenth and early twentieth centuries were doing was to develop the notion that homosexuality was the characteristic of a particular type of person. Karl Westphal, for instance, in the 1860s described a 'contrary sexual feeling' and argued that homosexuality was a product of moral insanity resulting from 'congenital reversal of sexual feeling'. Karl Ulrichs, a German lawyer and writer and himself homosexually inclined, who pioneered congenital theories in Germany from the 1860s, argued that the 'urning' was the product of the anomalous development of the originally undifferentiated human embryo, resulting in a female mind in a male body or vice versa. The theories of an intermediate sex popularised by Edward Carpenter in the early twentieth century were logical extensions of Ulrichs's ideas. On a more scientific level, the great German sexologist Magnus Hirschfeld was able to develop notions of a third sex and to integrate into this notion discoveries of the significance of hormones in the development of sexual differentiation. Hormonal explanations also supplement Ellis's congenital theories. Many of these ideas in turn were taken up by homosexual apologists to form the basis for an explanation of homosexuality which was free of the pejorative implications of the sin or moral-weakness theories.

Alongside these congenital theories, environmentalist notions of corruption or 'degeneration' continued to flourish. And discussion continued as to whether, as liberals like Havelock Ellis agreed, homosexuality was a congenital and relatively harmless 'anomaly', or whether it was evidence of moral insanity or mental sickness. The sickness theory of homosexuality was to have profound social reasonance from the 1930s onwards, but even earlier many homosexuals themselves had a deeply rooted belief that they were sick. Oscar Wilde complained in prison that he had been led astray by 'erotomania' and extravagant sexual appetite which indicated temporary mental collapse.[27] Sir Roger Casement, the Irish patriot, thought his homosexuality was a terrible disease which ought to be cured, while Goldsworthy Lowes Dickinson, a liberal humanist famed for his rationalism, believed his homosexuality to be a misfortune: 'I am like a man born crippled'.[28] With such a deeply rooted self-conception often went a willingness to accept a hegemony of (often dubious) medical knowledge and that in turn encouraged would-be cures, from hypnotism through to chemical experimentation and in the 1960s to aversion therapy.[29] But in the early decades of the twentieth century the medical model still to a large extent stayed at the level of theory and most doctors seemed to have been indifferent to or ignorant of the phenomena, reflecting as usual all the prejudices of the wider society. The old morality rather than the new psychology retained its influence until at least the inter-war years. Nevertheless, the existence of a medical model was profoundly to shape the individualisation of homosexuality, and contribute to the construction of the notion of a distinct homosexual person.

Although the theorising of homosexuality applied indifferently to males and females, it is striking that it was male homosexuality that was chiefly subject to new regulation. Lesbianism continued to be ignored by the criminal codes. An attempt in 1921 to introduce provisions against lesbianism similar to those of the Labouchère Amendment ultimately failed to get through Parliament, and the reasons were instructive. Lord Desart, who had been Director of Public Prosecutions when Wilde was indicted, opposed the provision with the comment: 'You are going to tell the whole world that there is such an offence, to bring it to the notice of women who have never heard of it, never thought of it, never dreamt of it. I think that is a very great mischief.' Lord Birkenhead, the Lord Chancellor made the same point: 'I would be bold enough to say that of every thousand women, taken as a whole, 999 have never even heard a whisper of these practices. Among all these, in the homes of this country . . . the taint of this noxious and horrible suspicion is to be imparted.'[30] It is clear in such comments that there was both an awareness of the contradictory effect of severe laws against homosexual behaviour, and a belief that the control of male homosexuality was of greater social salience than of female. It was not that lesbian behaviour was approved – but it did not enter the same domain of debate as male homosexuality.

It is this preoccupation with male sexuality that allows us to indicate at least some of the concerns which acted as preconditions for the refinement of social regulations in the latter part of the nineteenth century. These cannot be understood by trying to locate a simple programme of social control. On the contrary, it seems likely that the changes in attitudes towards homosexuality were often unintended consequences of other major changes. What was happening was that the ensemble of traditional assumptions was meeting new categorisation and together being transformed by a series of intersecting influences.

An important factor here was the renewed emphasis in the social-purity campaigns of the latter part of the nineteenth century on the dangers of male lust, and on the necessity for public decency. It is striking that the social-purity campaigners of the 1880s saw both prostitution and male homosexuality as products of undifferentiated male desire and it is significant in this respect that the major enactments affecting male homosexuality from the 1880s (the Labouchère Amendment, the 1898 Vagrancy Act, the 1912 Criminal Law Amendment Act) were aspects of the general moral restructuring, and were primarily concerned with female prostitution. Indeed, as late as the 1950s it was still seen as logical to set up a single government committee – the Wolfenden Committee – to study both prostitution and male homosexuality. In the debates before the 1885 Criminal Law Amendment Act was rushed through Parliament, male homosexual behaviour was quite clearly linked with the activities of those who corrupted young girls. What was at stake was on the one hand the uncontrolled lusts of certain types of men, and on the other the necessary sanctity of the sexual bond within marriage.[31]

At this point several apparently extraneous themes intervene, which in particular demonstrate the influence of the new attitudes towards childhood and adolescence. The progress of civilisation, the headmaster of Clifton College, Bristol, the Reverend J. M. Wilson, intoned in the 1880s, was in the direction of purity. This was threatened by sins of the flesh which undermined both the self and the nation. He advised his students to 'strengthen your will by practice: subdue your flesh by hard work and hard living; by temperance; by avoiding all luxury and effeminacy, and all temptation'.[32] Such beliefs and adjurations constantly invade the discussion of and responses to homosexuality.

In the scandals around the Cleveland Street brothel in 1889/90 and in the Oscar Wilde scandal, the corruption of youth was again a central issue. The Director of Public Prosecutions, reflecting on the Cleveland Street scandal, observed that there was a duty 'to enforce the law and protect the children of respectable parents taken into the service of the public . . . from being made the victims of the unnatural lusts of full grown men'.[33] The efforts through the raising of the age of consent for girls to 16 to prevent the seduction of minors was therefore paralleled by the regulation of male homosexual behaviour. In the mythology of the twentieth century the homosexual, as the archetypal sexed being, a person whose sexuality pervaded him in his very existence, threatened to corrupt all around him and particularly the young. The most pervasive stereotype of the male homosexual was as a 'corrupter of youth.'

Another vital complex of attitudes, those associated with imperialist sentiment, also entered the development of attitudes towards homosexuality. Here there was a complex pattern related not only to the notion of corruption and degeneration but also to the vital importance of the family to imperial security. Attitudes to homosexuality have of course long been linked to fears of imperial decline, from Gibbon's description of the decline and fall of the roman empire, through to those who opposed homosexual law reform in the 1960s. These had no more relevance in the 1880s than at other times. But to the social-purity advocate it was lust which threatened both the family and national decay. 'Rome fell; other nations have fallen; and if England falls it will be this sin, and her unbelief in God, that will have been her ruin.'[34] The puritan emphasis on the family, and on sexual life as being necessarily confined to the marital bed, offered an antidote to social crisis and a counter to the fear of decline.

But there is an even wider factor that needs to be emphasised. Homosexuality only becomes a matter for social concern when sexuality as a general category becomes of major public importance. The debates on 'natural' sexuality in the nineteenth century, and particularly the focusing on the sanctity of the marital bond in social-purity discourse, by a necessary rebound demands the more refined control of extra-marital sexuality, however trivial. Sodomy was a catch-all which marked the distinction between non-reproductive and reproductive sexuality, but whose character, as description and as legal category, remained vague. Homosexuality and the other categories that were so intricately described by Krafft-Ebing and others in the late nineteenth century spoke of the pleasures and dangers of sex in general, in all its forms, pleasures and dangers that not only addressed reproductive sexuality but also the privileged role of sex in cementing the marriage alliance. As sex was ideologically privatised, in the privileged domain of the sacramental marriage, as its discretion and 'control' became *the* mark of respectability, so its variant forms needed ever more refined definitions and control – and ever more discussion and debate and analysis. But inevitably, simultaneously, they also provided the space for new sexual localisations: for, indeed, sharper sexual identities. The inevitable contradictory effect was that a growing awareness of homosexuality, an ever-expanding explosion of works about it, accompanied its more detailed organisation and control; and this in turn created the elements of resistance and self-definition that led to the growth of distinctive homosexual identities.

Identities

Social regulation provides the conditions within which those defined can begin to develop their own consciousness and identity. In the nineteenth century, law and science, social *mores* and popular prejudice established the limits but homosexual people responded. In so doing they created, in a variety of ways, self-concepts, meeting places, a language and style, and complex and varied modes of life. Michel Foucault has described this process in the following way:

There is no question that the appearance in nineteenth century psychiatry, jurisprudence, and literature of a whole series of discourses on the species and subspecies of homosexuality, inversion, pederasty, and 'psychic hermaphrodism' made possible a strong advance of social controls into this area of 'perversity'; but it also made possible the formation of a 'reverse' discourse: homosexuality began to speak on its own behalf, to demand that its legitimacy or 'naturality' be acknowledged, often in the same vocabulary, using the same categories by which it was radically disqualified.[35]

But this 'reverse discourse' was by no means a simple or chronologically even process. It is difficult to fit homosexual behaviour into any preconceived mould; on the contrary, it pervades various aspects of social experience, and as the recent work from the Kinsey Institute of Sex Research has indicated, despite the plethora of definitions and social regulations there is not a single homosexuality but on the contrary, 'homosexualities': 'There is no such thing as *the* homosexual (or *the* heterosexual, for that matter) and (that) statements of any kind which are made about human beings on the basis of their sexual orientation must always be highly qualified.'[36]

It is the social categorisation which attempts to create the notion of uniformity, with always varying effects. The very unevenness of the social categorisation, the variations in legal and other social responses, meant that homosexual experiences could be absorbed into a variety of different lifestyles, with no necessary identity as a 'homosexual' developing. The casual encounter, for instance, perhaps in the context of wider sexual experiences, rarely touches the self-concept. It can easily be dismissed as a drunken aberration or a passing phase or even the deliberate attempt to explore a new experience. A classic example of this is provided by the author of *My Secret Life*, who experimented with homosexuality after years of compulsive sex with all manner of women. There is no suggestion that his own basic self-concept was in any way disturbed. 'Have all men had the same letches which late in life have enraptured me?' he asked.[37] The implication was that homosexuality was not something that was solely the prerogative of any particular type of being.

A second type of homosexual involvement which avoids all the problems of commitment and identity was the highly individualised, deeply emotional and possibly even sexualised relations between two individuals who were otherwise not regarded, or did not regard themselves as 'homosexual'. It was widely accepted in Victorian society that strong and indeed often emotional relationships between men were normal. W. T. Stead was appalled at the consequences of the Wilde trial, precisely because he argued a greater publicity concerning homosexuality would make such relationships more difficult. He wrote to Edward Carpenter: 'A few more cases like Oscar Wilde's and we should find the freedom of comradeship now possible to men seriously impaired to the permanent detriment of the race.'[38] But while male friendship became more suspect with a greater public discussion upon homosexuality, no one questioned the legitimacy of strong emotional relationships between women, and indeed highly personalised relationships, with a negligible development of lesbian self-concepts, probably remained the most common form of female homosexual relationships until very recently.

A third type of homosexual behaviour can best be described as 'situational': activities which were often regarded as legitimate, or at least acceptable, in certain circumstances, without affecting self-concepts. Classic examples of this were provided by the prevalent schoolboy homosexuality in public schools which became a matter of major concern for a number of social-purity advocates from the 1880s onwards. By the mid-nineteenth century, indeed, homosexuality seems to have been institutionalised in some of the major schools. J. A. Symonds described his horror at the situation in Harrow, where every boy of good looks had a female name and was either a 'prostitute' or a 'boy's bitch'. A little later Goldsworthy Lowes Dickinson described Charterhouse as a 'hothouse of vice'. Other examples of such situational homosexuality occurred then, as now, in the army, the navy and prison, each giving rise to specific rituals and taboos. The Brigade of Guards was notorious for its involvement in male prostitution from the eighteenth century, and as one practitioner put it, 'as soon as (or before) I had learnt the goose step, I had learnt to be goosed'.[39] Such situational homosexuality possibly revealed more clearly than anything else a constant homosexual potential which could be expressed when circumstances and the collapse of social restraints indicated; but for that reason demanded elaborate strategies of evasion to avoid entering into a stigmatised identity.

The absorption of the various types of homosexual experiences into 'a total way of life' was more problematical. The notion that 'a homosexual', whether male or female, could live a life fully organised around his sexual orientation is consequently of a very recent origin. Even the most famous homosexual of the nineteenth century, Oscar Wilde, who appears to have participated in a wide range of homosexual subcultural activities, was respectably married with an upper-middle-class family life, and indeed in many ways the only difference between him and many others of his social status was that his casual sexual encounters were with working-class youths rather than young women. The experiences of Sir Roger Casement, the Irish patriot, who was executed for treason in 1916, are perhaps even more typical. His diaries record various homosexual encounters in Africa, South America, as well as in London and Dublin. He records the sexual liaisons, all of which appear to have been casual, with great pleasure, noting the size of the organs of his pick-ups as well as their cost in his financial accountancy. But there is no sense, in his diary, of his seeing the possibility of a full homosexual lifestyle. On the contrary, his lifestyle was that common to his class and public career, on the surface at least. His homosexuality was a matter of secrecy and furtiveness even though in the colonial offshoots as well as in the streets of London, Casement had no difficulty in meeting sexual partners.[40]

Homosexuality has existed in various types of societies, but it is only in some cultures that it becomes organised into distinctive subcultures, and only in contemporary cultures that these became public. Homosexual behaviour in the Middle Ages and after was no doubt recurrent, but only in certain closed communities was it ever probably institutionalised: in some monasteries and nunneries, as many of the medieval penitentaries suggest; in some of the chivalric orders; in the courts of certain monarchs, such as James I and William III; and in and around the theatrical profession, and such like fringe cultural activities. Other homosexual contacts are likely to have been casual, fleeting and undefined. The development of wider, more open subcultures was probably of a comparatively recent origin. Though in Italy and France there is evidence for some sort of male homosexual subculture in the towns in the fourteenth and fifteenth centuries, in Britain there was no obvious public subculture, bringing together various social strata, until the late seventeenth century. Certainly by the early 1700s there were signs of a distinctive network of overlapping homosexual subcultures in London associated with open spaces, pederastic brothels, and latrines. From the eighteenth century these were known as 'markets', reflecting in part the current heterosexual usage, as in the term 'marriage market'.[41] But it does underline what seems to have been characteristic of these subcultural formations well into the twentieth century: their organisation around forms of prostitution, the exchange of money and services between unequals, rather than peer partnerships. It seems quite likely that the only frequent or regular participants in these subcultures were the relatively few 'professionals'. The evidence of the trials from the eighteenth century suggest that a wide variety of men from all sorts of social classes participated in the subculture, but very few organised their lives around them. The most distinctive aspect of these small subcultures were the stereotyped 'effeminacy' and transvestism often associated with them, a mode which still characterises the relatively undeveloped subcultures of areas outside the major cities of Western Europe and North America. In the nineteenth century J. A. Symonds described the homosexual stereotype: 'lusts written on his face . . . pale, languid, scented, effeminate, oblique in expression'. This imagery was reinforced by the words used for homosexuals: 'molly', 'marjorie', 'maryanne', characteristic terms of abuse for generations.[42]

The Boulton and Park scandal in 1871 revealed to a startled and agog public a group of people whose transvestism became a way of life for them, socially justified in terms of the participants' involvement in 'theatricals'. In the case of Ernest Boulton, his parents had known and accepted his transvestism from a very early age. The notion that a homosexual lifestyle necessarily involved elements of cross-gender behaviour, of effeminacy, persisted well into the twentieth century and the humour known as 'camp' partook of its ambiguity precisely because of this. Camp was not just a vehicle of communication between peers, but a way of presenting oneself to the 'straight' world. It was deeply ambivalent because it celebrated effeminacy while retaining a sharp awareness of conventional values. It could become a form of 'minstrelisation', an ambiguous playing to the galleries, the homosexual variant of the negro stereotype in the films and plays of the 1930s to 1950s; but in other ways it provided a subcultural language within which the elements of identity could cohere.

The concern with how to behave in public was a characteristic of another form of the homosexual subculture, a specific homosexual slang known as 'palare'. Derived from theatrical and circus slang, it was language for evaluating appearances and mannerisms and in which to gossip. It was not so much concerned with sex, what people did in bed, as with how to behave in public. By the end of the nineteenth century there was a widespread and often international homosexual argot suggesting a widely dispersed and organised subculture.[43]

But the most common form of homosexual social intercourse was not so much subcultural as 'coterie' orientated. There is abundant evidence for the existence of networks of homosexual friendships, which sometimes acted as mutually supportive picking-up networks. The circle of which Oscar Wilde was part around Charles Taylor was a good example of this – and not surprisingly it soon encountered legal attention.[44]

By the latter decades of the nineteenth century we can see the emergence of groups of people with a much more clearly defined sense of a homosexual identity. From the 1860s the poet and critic John Addington Symonds was attempting to grapple with the new theories on inversion which were appearing in Europe. His essay *A Problem in Greek Ethics*, privately printed in 1883, examined homosexuality as a valid lifestyle in Ancient Greece and this emphasis on the Greek ideal, despite its transparent anachronisms, was a very important one for self-identified homosexuals into the twentieth century. His essay *A Problem in Modern Ethics*, privately published in 1891, was a synthesis of recent views and a plea for law reform. With Havelock Ellis he began the preparation for the first comprehensive British study of the subject, *Sexual Inversion*, which appeared after his death, and after his family had withdrawn their consent, under Ellis's name alone. Although married, with children, there is no doubt that J. A. Symonds was striving to articulate a way of life quite distinct from those which had gone before. Edward Carpenter and his circle of socialists and libertarians provide another example of the development of a distinctive homosexual identity, in his case associated with politico-social commitment. From the 1890s he lived a relatively open homosexual life with his partner, George Merrill.[45] Oscar Wilde and his circle also constitute an example of a social network where a sense of a homosexual way of life was developing. Individuals from these interlocking circles, such as George Cecil Ives, later became important in the small-scale homosexual reform movements which began to develop in the early years of the twentieth century, and saw themselves very much as fighting for 'the Cause' against legal and moral repression.[46]

Most homosexual encounters were, however, casual, non-defining, less articulate and typically furtive. For many indeed the excitement and danger of this mode was an added incentive: Oscar Wilde's fascination for 'feasting with panthers' was only the most outrageously expressed. But for many others, participation in the homosexual world was accompanied by a deep shame and sense of guilt and anxiety as the moral and medical ideologies penetrated. The rather frenetic life of the better-off homosexual world might establish the norms, but they were by no means universal. The common element, pulling men of different classes together, was simply a desire for sexual contact and often there was little else. The use of the term 'trade' for any sort of sexual transaction, whether or not money was involved, indicates this graphically and it certainly seems to have been used in this sense by the mid-nineteenth century, as a vivid metaphor for the sexual barter. In such a world, particularly given the great disparities of wealth and position of participants, the cash nexus with all its class resonances pervaded all sorts of relationships. It is likely that there was a much more clearly defined homosexual sense of self-identity amongst men of the upper and middle classes and a greater possibility, through mobility and money, of frequent homosexual encounters, as could be seen in the career of Roger Casement, but also of many others. J. R. Ackerley and Tom Driberg in their memoirs during the mid-twentieth century record the type of possibilities that existed.[47] And despite the wide social range of the subculture, from pauper to peer, it was the sexual ideology of the male upper classes which seems to have dominated. One indication of this was a clearly observable and widely recognised, upper-middle-class fascination with crossing the class divide, a fascination which indeed shows a direct continuity between male heterosexual *mores* and homosexual. The patterns for instance of the heterosexual narrator of *My Secret Life* are stikingly paralleled by the evidence for the behaviour of homosexual men of the same class.

J. A. Symonds might disapprove of some of his friends' compulsive chasing of working-class contacts, but it was undoubtedly a major component of the subculture, as the major scandals revealed to a delightedly shocked Victorian public. It was a world of promiscuity, particularly if you had the right contacts, and many sections of the working class were drawn in, often very casually, as the Post Office messenger boys in the Cleveland Street scandal of 1889–90 and the stable-lads, newspaper sellers, bookmaker's clerks in the Wilde trials vividly illustrate. One participant in the Cleveland Street brothel described how casually money and sex might overturn youthful scruples. The young Charles Ernest Thickbroom, aged 17, recounted how he was asked 'If I would go to bed with a man. I said "no". He said "you'll get four shillings for a time" and persuaded me.'[48] The moving across the class barrier, on the one hand the search for 'rough trade', and on the other the belief in the reconciling effect of sex across class lines, was an important and recurrent theme in the homosexual world. Lasting partnerships did of course develop, but in a world of relatively easy casual sex, in a society where open homosexuality was tabooed, promiscuity was a constant temptation, and this in turn reflected complex emotional patterns. One homosexual, who had many homosexual friends from the First World War onwards, found it difficult to have sex with his friends. He had a fascination with Guardsmen, suffering, as he put it, from 'scarlet fever': 'I have never cared for trading with homosexuals . . . . I have always wanted to trade with men . . . . I don't say I never went with homosexuals because I did. But I would say that as a rule I wanted men.'[49] As this suggests, two factors closely interacted: the desire for a relationship across class lines, a product largely of a feeling that sex could not be spontaneous or natural within the framework of one's own moralistic and respectable class; and a desire for a relationship with a 'real' man, a heterosexual. E. M. Forster wanted 'to love a strong young man of the lower classes and be loved by him'. J. R. Ackerley felt that 'the ideal friend . . . should have been an animal man. The perfect human male body always at one's service through the devotion of a faithful and uncritical beast.'[50]

There are very complex patterns recurring here which historians have largely ignored. What they underline again are the class differentiation of identities and attitudes. In the writings on homosexuality of the late nineteenth century there was a widespread belief that the working class was relatively indifferent to homosexual behaviour, partly because they were 'closer to nature', and the two great swathes of male prostitution, with working-class youths in their teens, and with Guardsmen, notorious from the eighteenth century throughout Europe for their easy prostitution, seemed to justify this belief. Havelock Ellis noted the almost 'primitive indifference' to homosexuality of the Guardsmen. Or, as one regular customer observed, 'they were normal, they were working class, they were drilled to obedience'.[51] These class and gender interactions (working class = male = closeness to nature) were to play important roles in the homosexual world affecting in particular the rituals of prostitution.

Prostitution was an indispensable part of the male homosexual, though, unlike female prostitution, no distinctive subculture of male prostitution seems to have developed in the nineteenth and early twentieth centuries. Jack Saul, a notorious 'professional Maryanne' in the 1880s and 1890s, observed that he 'did not know of many professional male sodomites',[52] and such evidence as exists confirms the picture of a basically casual prostitution, with participants beginning usually in their mid-teens and generally leaving the trade by their mid-twenties. And the routes out were numerous, from becoming a kept boy, either in a long-term relationship or in successive relationships, to a return to ordinary heterosexual and family life. At least two of the boys involved in the Cleveland Street affair, despite their early traumas, seem to have led successfully heterosexual lives and to have entirely lost contact with the world of homosexuality.[53] In most cases the decisive factors were likely to be the willingness of the participants to accept perilous self-concepts as homosexual and as prostitute.

The keynote of the homosexual world was ambivalence and ambiguity. It *was* possible to lead a successful homosexual life within the interstices of the wider society. Nor was the life entirely shaped by legal repression. Jack Saul in his deposition in 1889 was asked:

'Were you hunted out by the police?'

'No, they have never interfered. They have always been kind to me.'

'Do you mean they have deliberately shut their eyes to your infamous practices?'

'They have to shut their eyes to more than me.'[54]

Probably more important than the legal situation was the social stigma that attached to homosexual behaviour and that seems to have increased in the late nineteenth and early twentieth centuries. It is this which gives social significance to the development of the small-scale and secretive homosexual reform movement. One circle associated with the criminologist George Cecil Ives, the Order of Chaeronea, appears, on the evidence of his three-million-word diary, to have been active from the early 1890s in succouring homosexuals in trouble with the law. It developed an almost Masonic style and ritual, insisting on secrecy and loyalty, and developed international 'chapters'.[55] Many of the participants in this Order, men like Ives and Laurence Housman, were active in the British Society for the Study of Sex Psychology, founded on the eve of the First World War to campaign for general changes in attitudes towards sexuality. One of the major planks of the society was reform of the law relating to homosexuality, and in the 1920s this too became part of an international movement for sex reform.[56] It is characteristic of these movements that although they were generally founded and operated by homosexuals they were not ostensibly homosexual organisations. On the contrary, their ability to remain publicly respectable was an important part of what success they gained.

Despite the ambiguities, it is clear that by the end of the nineteenth century a recognisably 'modern' male homosexual identity was beginning to emerge, but it would be another generation before female homosexuality reached a corresponding level of articulacy. The lesbian identity was much less clearly defined, and the lesbian subculture was minimal in comparison with the male, and even more overwhelmingly upper class or literary. Berlin and Paris might have had their meeting places by the turn of the nineteenth century and there is clear evidence of coteries of literary lesbians such as those associated with the Paris salon of Natalie Clifford Barney.[57] A chronicler of homosexual life in the early part of this century mentions various lesbian meeting places, including the London Vapour Bath on ladies' day, and by the 1920s the better-off lesbians could meet in some of the new nightclubs. But it is striking that the best-recorded examples of a lesbian presence referred to the defiantly 'masculine appearance and manner' of the participant. The novelist, Radclyffe Hall, for instance, became notorious for her masculine appearance. Only by asserting one's identity so vehemently, as Radclyffe Hall recognised, could you begin to be noticed and taken seriously.[58] But the numbers who could dress this way and could afford to defy conventional opinion were tiny and the lives of the vast majority of women with lesbian feelings were unknown, perhaps unknowable. Even the enthusiastic categorisers of early twentieth-century sexology stopped short of female homosexuality. In 1901 Krafft-Ebing noted that there were only fifty known case histories of lesbianism, and even in the early 1970s, two modern writers on homosexuality could note that 'the scientific literature on the lesbian is exceedingly sparse'.[59] Writers like Magnus Hirschfeld and Havelock Ellis whose scientific and polemical interest in the subject was genuine seem to have found it difficult to discover much information, or many lesbians whose case histories they could record.

No doubt the absence of any legal regulation of lesbian behaviour and a consequent absence of public pillorying and scandal was an influence in shaping the low social profile of female homosexuality, but the basic reason for the indifference towards lesbianism is probably more fundamental. It relates precisely to different social assumptions about the sexuality of men and women and in particular to dominant notions of female sexuality. Havelock Ellis, whose wife was lesbian, felt the need to stress that female homosexuals were often particularly masculine, and in Radclyffe Hall's *The Well of Loneliness*, a major novel of lesbian love published in 1928, it is the 'masculine' woman in the story who is the true invert. Stephen, masculine in name and behaviour, is forced to endure the agonies of her nature, the biologically given essence, while the feminine Mary in the story is in the end able to opt for a heterosexual married life.

This concern with the masculinity of lesbians can only be explained in terms of the overwhelming weight of assumptions concerning female sexuality. As J. H. Gagnon and William Simon have put it, 'the patterns of overt sexual behaviour on the part of homosexual females tends to resemble those of heterosexual females and to differ radically from the sexual patterns of both heterosexual and homosexual males'.[60] Several intertwined elements determined attitudes to lesbianism, and the consequent possibilities for lesbian identity: the roles that society assigned women; the ideology which articulated, organised and regulated this; the dominant notions of female sexuality in the ideology; and the actual possibilities for the development by women of an autonomous sexuality. The prevailing definitions of female sexuality in terms of the 'maternal instinct', or as necessarily responsive to the stimulation of the male, were overwhelming barriers in attempts to conceptualise the subject. Ideology limited the possibility for even an attempt at scientific definition of lesbianism. But even more important, the social position of most women militated against the easy emergence of a distinctive lesbian identity. It remained very difficult for respectable young ladies to be 'independent'. So it is likely that most women with lesbian inclinations fitted inconspicuously into the general world of women. There is as we have seen abundant evidence in eighteenth- and nineteenth-century diaries and letters that women as a matter of routine formed long-lived emotional ties with other women. Such relationships ranged from a close supportive love of sisters, through adolescent enthusiasms, to mature avowals of eternal affection. Many of the early writers on lesbianism spoke of the greater emphasis on cuddling, on physical warmth and comforting, of kissing and holding hands between female homosexuals, at the expense of exclusively sexual activity. This was precisely the line of continuity between all women whatever their sexual orientation. Deep and passionate declarations of love recur without any obvious signs of sexual expression.[61] The conditions for a polarity between 'normal' female sexuality and 'abnormal' were almost non-existent and it is this which makes it presumptuous to attempt to explore female homosexuality in terms of categories derived from male experiences.

It is striking that it is amongst the new professional women of the 1920s that the articulation of any sort of recognisable lesbian identity became possible for the first time, and it was indeed in the 1920s that lesbianism became in any way an issue of public concern, following a series of sensational scandals. Towards the end of the First World War the criminal libel prosecution brought by the dancer Maude Allan against the right-wing Member of Parliament, Noel Pemberton Billing, who had accused her of being on a German list of sexual perverts, was a *cause célèbre* which brought lesbianism to the headlines. In 1921 there were attempts, as we have seen, to bring lesbianism into the scope of the Criminal Law. During the 1910s and 1920s a series of novels, and even a film, portrayed lesbian experiences; and in 1928 came the most famous event of all, the banning and prosecution of Radclyffe Hall's lesbian novel, *The Well of Loneliness.* As Lord Birkett, who appeared for the publishers, later pointed out, the Chief Metropolitan Magistrate, Sir Chartres Biron, found against the novel largely because Radclyffe Hall 'had not stigmatised this relationship as being in any way blameworthy'.[62] Nevertheless, paradoxically, and in line with the impact of the Oscar Wilde trial, the prosecution gave unprecedented publicity to homosexuality. This perhaps is the outstanding feature of the case: the publicity it aroused did more than anything to negate the hopes of reticence expressed by Lords Desart and Birkenhead in 1921. Thousands of lesbian-inclined women wrote to Radclyffe Hall. She more than anyone else during this period gave lesbianism a name and an image. As a lesbian of a later generation put it, 'When . . . I read *The Well of Loneliness* it fell upon me like a revelation. I identified with every line. I wept floods of tears over it, and it confirmed my belief in my homosexuality.'[63]

In any study of homosexuality the important point to observe is that there is no automatic relationship between social categorisation and individual sense of self or identity. The meanings given to homosexual activities can vary enormously. They depend on a variety of factors: social class, geographical location, gender differentiation. But it is vital to keep in mind when exploring homosexuality, which has always been defined in our culture as a deviant form, that what matters is not the inherent nature of the act but the social construction of meanings around that activity, and the individual response to that. The striking feature of the 'history of homosexuality' over the past hundred years or so is that the oppressive definition and the defensive identities and structures have marched together. Control of sexual variations has inevitably reinforced and reshaped rather than repressed homosexual behaviour. In terms of individual anxiety, induced guilt and suffering, the cost of moral regulation has often been high. But the result has been a complex and socially significant history of resistance and self-definition which historians have hitherto all too easily ignored.

References

1. Or as the French theorist **Guy Hocquenghem** puts it, between 'desire', and homosexuality as a psychological category: See his *Homosexual Desire*, Allison and Busby, London, 1978. A Preface by Jeffrey Weeks discusses the general placing of his theories. For a major discussion of the distinctions drawn here see the essays in **Kenneth Plummer** (ed.), *The Making of the Modern Homosexual*, Hutchinson, London, 1981. A longer theoretical exploration of the issues referred to in this chapter can be found in **Jeffrey Weeks**, 'Discourses, Desire and Sexual Deviance: Problems in a History of Homosexuality', in that volume. See also **Kenneth Plummer**, *Sexual Stigma: An Interactionist Account*, Routledge & Kegan Paul, London, 1975, which is the most important British work of sociology on these themes.

118   *Sex, Politics and Society*

2. **Edwin M. Lemert**, *Human Deviance, Social Problems and Social Control*, Prentice Hall, Englewood Cliffs, New Jersey, 1967, p. 40.
3. These are themes discussed in Hocquenghem, *op. cit.*, and in Deleuze and Guattari, *Anti-Oedipus: Capitalism and Schizophrenia*, Viking Press, New York, 1977.
4. **Mary McIntosh**, 'The Homosexual Role', *Social Problems*, Vol. 16, No. 2, Fall 1968; republished in Plummer (ed.), *The Making*, with additional comments by McIntosh. (The page references given are to the original journal version.)
5. McIntosh, *op. cit.*, p. 184.
6. Compare **Frederick L. Whitam**, 'The Homosexual Role: A Reconsideration', *The Journal of Sex Research*, Vol. 13, No. 1, February 1977; and **Randolph Trumbach**, 'London's Sodomites: Homosexual Behaviour and Western Culture in the 18th Century', *Journal of Social History*, Fall 1977.
7. This point is forcefully argued by **Annabel Faraday**, 'Liberating Lesbian Research' in Plummer (ed.), *The Making*.
8. The anthropological and cross-cultural data is summarised in McIntosh, 'The Homosexual Role', and in Trumbach, 'London's Sodomites'. The most comprehensive discussion of ancient Greek attitudes is in **K. G. Dover**, *Greek Homosexuality*, Duckworth, London, 1978. On the berdache see **Donald G. Forgey**, 'The Institution of Berdache Among the North American Plains Indians', *The Journal of Sex Research*, Vol. 11, No. 1, February 1975. On a different form of cross-dressing see **Martin Baumi Duberman**, **Fred Eggan** and **Richard Clemmer** (eds), 'Documents in Hopi Indian Sexuality: Imperialism, Culture, and Resistance', *Radical History Review*, No. 20, Spring/Summer 1979.
9. For a general discussion of the legal situation, see **Jeffrey Weeks**, *Coming Out: Homosexual Politics in Britain from the Nineteenth Century to the Present*, Quartet, London, 1977, Chs 1–3. (This present chapter is a development of themes discussed in that book.) For a further discussion of the legal situation, see **D. J. West**, *Homosexuality Revisited*, Duckworth, London, 1977, Ch. 10. On the general taboo on sodomy, see **Michael Goodich**, *The Unmentionable Vice*, Clio, Oxford, 1978; and **John Boswell**, *Christianity, Social Tolerance and Homosexuality*, University of Chicago Press, Chicago and London, 1980; and on the confusion in the use of the term in another, though related culture, see **Robert F. Oaks**, ' "Things Fearful to Name": Sodomy and Buggery in Seventeenth Century New England', *Journal of Social History*, Vol. 12, 1978. On reasons for the absence of legislation relating to lesbian behaviour, see the statement of the British government, quoted in *Gay News*, No. 144, June 1–14, 1978, p. 3: 'the question of homosexual acts by females has never – so far as the government of the United Kingdom are aware – been generally considered to raise social problems of the kind raised by masculine homosexuality'.
10. Quoted in **A. N. Gilbert**, 'The Africaine Court Martial', *Journal of Homosexuality*, Vol. 1, No. 1, Fall 1974.
11. Quoted in **Sir L. Radzinowicz**, *A History of the English Criminal Law*, Vol. 4, *Grappling for Control*, Stevens and Son, London, 1968, p. 432.
12. On the eighteenth century, see Trumbach, 'London's Sodomites'; on the early nineteenth century, see **A. D. Harvey**, 'Prosecutions for Sodomy in England at the beginning of the Nineteenth Century', *The Historical Journal*, Vol. 2, No. 4, 1978; see also Radzinowicz, *Grappling for Control*; and the review article by **Louis Crompton**, *Victorian Studies*, Winter 1979,

pp. 211–13. Crompton makes the point that in no other Western country was the law so severe. No executions elsewhere have been documented after 1784. And the policy of *sentencing* to death continued to the eve of repeal. In the years 1856–59, 54 men were sentenced to death for sodomy, though the capital punishment was not carried through.

13. See Gilbert, *op. cit.*; 'Buggery and the British Navy 1700–1861', *Journal of Social History*, Vol. 10, No. 1, Fall 1976; 'Social Deviance and disaster during the Napoleonic Wars', *Albion*, No. IX, 1977.

14. Public Record Office: DPP4/6. Transcript of the trial, Day 1, p. 21. This account is based on the manuscript transcript.

15. *Ibid.*: Day 2, p. 276; Day 1, p. 82; Day 3, p. 299.

16. McIntosh, 'The Homosexual Role'; Trumbach, 'London's Sodomites', p. 18.

17. *The Phoenix of Sodom or the Vere Street Coterie*, Robert Holloway, London, *c.* 1813, p. 13.

18. **Louis Crompton**, 'Jeremy Bentham: Essay on "Paederasty": An Introduction', *Journal of Homosexuality*, Vol. 3, No. 4, Summer 1978, p. 386.

19. See for example 'Opinions of certain judges on Unnatural Offences Cases', Public Record Office: HO 144/216/A 49134/2. Mr Justice Hawkins suggested with regard to bestiality that 'for the most part that crime is committed by young persons, agricultural labourers etc. out of pure ignorance. The crime of sodomy with mankind stands upon a different footing . . .'. See also HO 144/216/A 49134/4, a memorandum from the Under Secretary. I am grateful to the Departmental Record Officer at the Home Office who gave me access to the hitherto closed files in the HO 144 series.

20. See Weeks, *Coming Out*, Ch. 1; D. J. West, *op. cit.*; and **G. C. Ives**, *The Continued Extension of the Criminal Law*, London, 1922.

21. On Labouchère's motive see his Parliamentary statement, *The Times*, 1 March 1890, and his comments in *Truth*, 30 May 1895; and the discussion in **F. B. Smith**, 'Labouchère's Amendment to the Criminal Law Amendment Act', *Historical Studies*, Vol. 17, No. 67, 1976.

22. For the DPP's comments, see Public Record Office: DPP 1/95/1: 20 July 1889, and 14 September 1889. On the reluctance of juries to convict (sometimes because they could not believe respectable people could commit such deeds), see **H. Montgomery Hyde**, *The Other Love: An Historical and Contemporary Survey of Homosexuality in Britain*, Mayflower Books, London, 1972, p. 19. On police attitudes in the early twentieth century, see **Havelock Ellis**, *The Task of Social Hygiene*, Constable, London, 1912, p. 272.

23. **Alec Craig**, *The Banned Books of England*, George Allen & Unwin, London, 1937, p. 86. *The Report of the Royal Commission upon the Duties of the Metropolitan Police*, Cd 4156, London, HMSO 1908, Vol. 1, p. 119, makes clear that there is nothing in the 1898 Act which would have inhibited prosecuting of men soliciting women; in practice it was never used for this purpose. It was effectively directed against homosexual offences. For the flogging provision of the 1912 Act, see Bristow, *Vice and Vigilance*, p. 193; **Ian Gibson**, *The English Vice: Beating, Sex and Shame in Victorian England and After*, Duckworth, London, 1978, p. 161; **Hermann Mannheim**, *Social Aspects of Crime in England between the Wars*, George Allen & Unwin, London, 1939, Table V, p. 51.

24. **Havelock Ellis**, *Studies in the Psychology of Sex* (4 Vols), Vol. 2, *Sexual Inversion*, Random House, New York, 1936, p. 352.

25. **Arno Karlen**, *Sexuality and Homosexuality*, Macdonald, London, 1971, p. 185.
26. For a fuller discussion see Weeks, *Coming Out*, Ch. 2.
27. See Wilde's petition for reducing his sentence, 2 July 1896, HO 144/A 56887/19. The eloquence of his petition, as the prison staff did not fail to point out, contradicted his supposed mental weakness.
28. **Dennis Proctor** (ed.), *The Autobiography of G. Lowes Dickinson*, Duckworth, London, 1973, pp. 10–11; **Brian Inglis**, *Roger Casement*, Coronet, London, 1973, pp. 67–8; Public Record Office: Casement Diaries, entry for 17 April 1903.
29. See below, Chapters 11 and 12, for a discussion of the acceptance of medical theories. For an excellent summary of theories of intersexuality, the incorporation of hormonal theories, and the debate over 'cures', see **Max Hodann**, *History of Modern Morals*, William Heinemann, London, 1937.
30. See Hyde , *The Other Love*, pp. 200 ff.
31. For a fuller discussion of these ideas see Weeks, *Coming Out*, Ch. 1.
32. **Rev J. M. Wilson**, *Social Purity*, Social Purity Alliance, London, 1884; *Sins of the Flesh*, Social Purity Alliance, London, 1885, p. 7.
33. Quoted in **L. Chester**, **D. Leitch** and **C. Simpson**, *The Cleveland Street Affair*, Weidenfeld & Nicolson, London, 1976, p. 73.
34. Wilson, *Sins of the Flesh*, p. 7. 'This sin' in fact referred to masturbation, but masturbation (not surprisingly, given the public-school tradition) was intimately linked to homosexuality. Cf. **V. L. Bullough** and **M. Voght**, 'Homosexuality and its Confusion with the "Secret Sin" in pre-Freudian America', *Journal of the History of Medicine*, Vol. XXVII, No. 2, April 1973.
35. Michel Foucault, *The History of Sexuality*, Vol. 1, p. 101. There is now a growing corpus of works on the history of homosexual resistance and self-definition. For a general discussion see **Vern L. Bullough**, 'Challenges to Societal Attitudes toward Homosexuality in the late Nineteenth and early Twentieth Centuries', *Social Science Quarterly*, Vol. 58, No. 1, June 1977. On Britain, Weeks, *Coming Out*, is the only full-length book. On America, see **Jonathan Katz**, *Gay American History: Lesbians and Gay Men in the USA*, Thomas Crowell Co., New York, 1976. On Germany, see **John Lauritsen** and **David Thorstad**, *The Early Homosexual Rights Movement*, Times Change Press, New York, 1974; and **James D. Steakley**, *The Homosexual Emancipation Movement in Germany*, Arno Press, New York, 1975.
36. **Alan P. Bell** and **Martin S. Weinberg**, *Homosexualities: A Study of Diversity among Men and Women*, Mitchell Beazley, London, 1978, p. 23.
37. 'Walter', *My Secret Life*, Amsterdam, privately printed 1877, Vol. 1, p. 14.
38. Stead to Edward Carpenter, Ms 386–54(1–2), June 1895, Edward Carpenter collection, Sheffield City Library.
39. **J. A. Symonds**, *Memoirs*: unpublished manuscript in the London Library; **Proctor** (ed.), *The Autobiography of G. Lowes Dickinson*, p. 8; *The Sins of the Cities of the Plain: or the Recollections of a Mary-Ann*, London, privately published 1881, Vol. 1, p. 84. (The ostensible memoirs of the male prostitute, Jack Saul.)
40. See the Casement Diaries, Public Record Office.
41. Trumbach, 'London's Sodomites'.
42. Quoted in **Brian Reade**, *Sexual Heretics: Male Homosexuality in English Literature from 1850–1900*, Routledge and Kegan Paul, London, 1970, p. 251.

43. **Mary McIntosh**, 'Gayspeak', *Lunch*, No. 16, January 1973; **Joseph J. Hayes**, 'Gayspeak', *Quarterly Journal of Speech*, Vol. 62, October 1976.
44. **R. Croft-Cooke**, *The Unrecorded Life of Oscar Wilde*, W. H. Allen, London, New York, 1972.
45. See **Phyllis Grosskurth**, *John Addington Symonds*, Longman, London, 1964; Weeks, *Coming Out*, Ch. 6, 'Edward Carpenter and Friends' (see also Chapter 9 below).
46. On Ives, see Weeks, *Coming Out*, pp. 118 ff.
47. **J. R. Ackerley**, *My Father and Myself*, The Bodley Head, London, 1968; **Tom Driberg**, *Ruling Passions*, Jonathan Cape, London, 1977; see also **Christopher Isherwood**, *Christopher and His Kind*, Eyre Methuen, London, 1977; **Michael Davidson**, *The World, the Flesh and Myself*, Mayflower-Dell, London, 1966.
48. Public Record Office: HO 144/X24427/1, copies of depositions.
49. In an interview with the author.
50. **E. M. Forster**, *The Life to Come and Other Stories*, Penguin, Harmondsworth, 1975, p. 16; J. R. Ackerley, *My Father and Myself*, p. 218.
51. Ellis, *Sexual Inversion*, p. 9; Ackerley, *op. cit.*, p. 135.
52. *Sins of the Cities of the Plain*, Vol. 2, p. 109. For a general discussion of this topic see **Jeffrey Weeks**, 'Inverts, Perverts and Mary-Annes: Male Prostitution and the Regulation of homosexuality in England in the Nineteenth and early Twentieth Centuries', *Journal of Homosexuality*, Vol. 6, Nos 1 and 2, 1981.
53. Chester *et al.*, *The Cleveland Street Affair*, p. 225.
54. Public Record Office: DPP 1/95/4, File 2: Saul's deposition.
55. See Weeks, *Coming Out*, pp. 122 ff.
56. See below, p. 184 ff.
57. See **George Wickes**, *The Amazon of Letters: The Life and Loves of Natalie Barney*, W. H. Allen, London, 1977; **Gayle Rubin**, Introduction to **Renee Vivian**, *A Woman Appeared to Me*, New York, 1976; **Blanche Wiesen Cook**, 'Women Alone Stir My Imagination: Lesbianism and the Cultural Tradition', *Signs: Journal of Women in Culture and Society*, Vol. 4, No. 4, 1979; and 'The Historical Denial of Lesbianism', *Radical History Review*, No. 20, Spring/Summer 1979. See also Weeks, *Coming Out*, Chs 7–9.
58. **Lovat Dickson**, *Radclyffe Hall at the Well of Loneliness*, Collins, London, 1977.
59. Gagnon and Simon, *Sexual Conduct*, p. 176, Note 1.
60. *Ibid.*, p. 180.
61. **Carroll Smith-Rosenberg**, 'The Female World of Love and Ritual: Relations between Women in Nineteenth Century America', *Signs: Journal of Women in Culture and Society*, Vol. 1, No. 1, Autumn 1975. See also **Blanche Wiesen Cook**, 'Female Support Networks and Political Activism: Lillian Wald, Crystal Eastman and Emma Goldman', *Chrysalis*, No. 3, Autumn 1977; reprinted as a pamphlet by Out and Out books 1979. For similar British references see Weeks, *Coming Out*, Ch. 7.
62. See Weeks, *Coming Out*, Ch. 9; and pp. 217–18 below.
63. Quoted in **Charlotte Wolff**, *Love Between Women*, Duckworth, London, 1971.

Chapter Seven

The population question in the early twentieth century

Population politics

By the beginning of the twentieth century, the sexual question was being inextricably linked with the politics of population. The problem of 'population' recurs in all the major discussions of the time, from the 'social question' to the threat of national decline, from issues of unemployment to the threat of war.

At the heart of the debates was the increasing belief that the health, hygiene and composition of the population were the keys to progress and power. And sex was the key to the question of population. It was the point of access both to the health and status of the individual and to the future of the population as a whole. The political and theoretical debates over personal morality and national fertility, physical deterioration and a differential birthrate, major topics in the early decades of this century, all raised the twin questions of the population and the role and significance of sexuality. Sex, wrote Patrick Geddes and J. Arthur Thomson in their little book of that title, is 'a cardinal fact of life and one of the prime movers of progress'. Consequently, irregularities of sexual behaviour had to be judged not just by their influence on the individual, 'but by their influence on the race'.[1]

So, before examining the organisation of sexuality during the first half of the twentieth century, we must disentangle the complex strands within which this took place. It is the premise of this chapter that the various (largely unsuccessful) strategies designed to develop a national population policy which appear in this period offer a particularly valuable context in which to trace the construction of a new sexual economy. Two sometimes conflicting strategies are particularly representative: the new inflection in the emphasis on the functions of motherhood; and the burst of enthusiam for direct intervention in the planning of reproduction associated with the eugenics movement. The discussion will therefore focus on these themes.

The issue of population was not, of course, new in the twentieth century. The concern with the population, in the sense of an organised, regulated and policed domain, and as a major concern of political theory, can be traced back at least to Plato.[2] It recurs in most of the major English theoretical texts from Sir Thomas More's *Utopia* to the great works of the political economists in the nineteenth century. But from the late eighteenth century the population takes on a new significance, because it begins to be quantified: it becomes an object in its own right, an entity that can be measured and described.[3]

From the first census in 1801, and with growing strength from the 1830s, with compulsory registration of births, marriages, etc., statistics in ever growing numbers could indicate changes, chart trends and pinpoint problems. Birth and death rates, life expectancies and fertility rates, all could be laid out to show the population trends.

Coinciding with this was a politicisation of the question of population associated with the work of Thomas Malthus and his supporters. Malthus's argument, in reply to Godwin's, that as food supplies move in arithmetic progression while the population moves in geometric progression, the population would soon overshoot the food supply, to be swamped by vice and misery, had clear political, social and sexual connotations. It suggested that because no social remedy was possible, the poor were responsible for their own poverty, the major cause of which was therefore moral: reckless overbreeding. Charity or reform were valueless: the only conceivable remedy was to educate the worker in the secrets of political economy and in particular to get them to see the importance of sexual self-restraint and of deferring marriage. The direct political implications of this were demonstrated in the debates over the old Poor Law, in which Malthus's supporters were prominent. These debates focused attention on the population issue, and as a result the new Poor Law of 1834, with its strict adherence to the laws of political economy had, as we have seen, important effects on the regulation of sexual morality.

The fundamental purpose of Malthusian doctrine, it has been well said, was to establish 'a new moral economy'. Its peculiar strength came from its basic belief that the laws of population (like the laws of political economy) were inscrutable, and from its claim to be based on objective and scientifically proven facts. Social life could only be satisfactorily established on the basis of subservience to the facts of social existence, and these could not be changed by lay interference. The result was an inherent pessimism in Malthusianism proper. Its function was to instil awareness of these 'facts', not fruitlessly to try to change them. Its passivity before the laws of population influenced many others who were not strict Malthusians. Utilitarians, for example, who argued, unlike Malthus, for the use of contraceptive methods, accepted his demographic data, and this passivity, determinism even, led to the dominant nineteenth-century belief, amongst Malthusians and Spencerians alike, that population arrived naturally at its own correct level.[4]

The population issue remained a significant undercurrent from the 1830s but it was not until the 1870s, with the revival of the debate over contraception, that it again became a central political question. One major sign of this was the re-emergence of neo-Malthusianism in an organised form (the Malthusian League was formed in 1877) attempting to induce in the educated classes a conviction of the truth of Malthusianism with the hope that this awareness would penetrate to the feckless. Another sign was the development of theoretical arguments, which were to crystallise in eugenics at the beginning of the new century, about the possibilities of direct intervention in the planning of population. We can observe, in other words, a more generalised move away from *laissez-faire*, with its pessimism over population, to a new interventionism, often wildly utopian and scientistic. Its aim was control over the population.

A number of closely related themes recur throughout the population debates of the late nineteenth and early twentieth centuries: the problem of 'degeneracy'; the multiplication of the 'unfit'; the question of a differential birthrate. And these themes were given a peculiar reverberation because of external referrents to which they were thought to be linked: poverty and urban problems; and the fear of national decay.

The theme of degeneracy was evoked in the 1880s to try to explain the results of urban change. Behind it was a fear, particularly amongst the urban middle class, that Britain might have taken a major wrong turning in becoming an urban, industrial society. Commentators looked with alarm at the casual labourers and the slum inhabitants of the big cities – almost another race – who were increasing at a disturbing rate and were refusing to respond to legislation and charity to improve them. Degeneration was, as Gareth Stedman Jones has put it, 'a mental landscape within which the middle class could recognise and articulate their own anxieties about urban existence',[5] but it became an explanatory tool to justify the existence of a residuum of people who did not seem to respond to the blandishments of self-improvement.

The social investigation of Charles Booth and Seebohm Rowntree from the 1880s pinpointed the problem: many believed that what was happening was a reverse natural selection, producing a distinct subspecies of people, unable to accept the social norm, a residuum of the 'unfit'.[6] Of course, the perception of class inequality and of poverty could as easily lead to political theories arguing for radical social change, but it was within a hereditarian discourse that many of the debates were actually played out.

Degeneration represented a falling away from type. It was a general condition of a section of the population which nevertheless manifested itself in many different forms of individual behaviour. In this context sexual variations could readily be seen as part of the same core problem as poverty. Dr Rentoul of Liverpool, one of the more extreme eugenicists, could easily lump together lunatics, neurotics, kleptomaniacs, alcoholics and sexual perverts as all being examples of degenerate stock.[7] *Reynolds' Newspaper* made the relevant connection in commenting on Tarnowsky's book, *The Sexual Instinct*: 'A perusal of these pages will reveal the fact that many so-called sexual "crimes" are simply irresistible impulses of degeneracy, an illustration of the doctrine of heredity, a theory which none more than British scientists have done so much to popularise.' It went on to suggest that 'the earnest seeker after the truth' should present these facts to the public, 'in the interests of his species'.[8]

The major perceived problem was the rapid multiplication of 'unfit' people producing more and more inadequates. Thus Arthur Newsholme, not a rigid eugenicist, could worry that: 'the birth rate at present is disproportionately high among the wage earning and probably also among the poorer classes. Also, that this implies the survival of a disproportionate number who are relatively ill-fed, ill-nourished, and brought up under conditions rendering them less fitted to become serviceable citizens.'[9] There was a strong belief, which pervaded various types of political discussion, that since the 1870s the race was being threatened with decline as a result of the differential birthrate, which threatened to reproduce these degenerates more readily than healthy stock. As the National Birth Rate Commission, an unofficial body set up to study this question, pointed out, amongst the upper and middle class there were around 119 births per 1,000 married males under 35, while for the skilled workmen the figures were 153, and the unskilled 213.[10] The result, Karl Pearson argued, was that 25 per cent of the population threatened to produce 50 per cent of the next generation. Consequently, the racial mixture of the population was undergoing a fundamental change: the worst stock were reproducing busily, while the best were dying out.

Even when the arguments were not taken to this extreme, the larger size of the working-class family (with an average of over 4 children) was seen as being a major source for the perpetuation of poverty. One leading neo-Malthusian could not understand how Parliament could enact a legal minimum wage, without at the same time enacting 'a Legal Maximum Family', while Havelock Ellis believed there to be a correlation between large families and abnormalities: large families tended to be degenerate.[11] What was inevitably taking place was a slide in the argument, from questions of quality of the population as a whole to a rough equation of genetic worth with social standing. It was the working-class which was breeding over-rapidly, and within that the unrespectable who were reproducing most quickly. And as Lord Rosebery suggested, 'in the rookeries and slums which still survive, an imperial race cannot be reared'.[12] These debates crystallised around the turn of the century precisely because they seemed to touch on the question of national survival: 'an empire such as ours requires as its first condition an imperial race'.[13]

The impact of the Boer War gave this issue a special centrality, for the war brought to light what was perceived as the drastic unfitness of the imperial race. The reports of the Inspector General of Recruiting, which suggested that 3 out of 5 men presenting themselves for enlistment in Manchester in 1899 had to be rejected as physically unfit, aroused widespread concern, and he commented in his 1902 report on the 'further gradual deterioration of the physique of the working classes'.[14] Major-General Sir Frederick Maurice made this apparent deterioration a major issue by publishing an anonymous article in the *Contemporary Review* for January 1903 in which he indicated that ill health was a result of early marriages and the ignorance of mothers.

The Interdepartmental Committee set up to investigate physical deterioration in 1904 in fact decided that actual deterioration remained unproven, though working-class health and the appalling infant mortality figures left much to be desired. It made 53 recommendations, most of which dealt with the environment (overcrowding, the lack of open spaces, pollution, bad housing) or with working-class conditions (unemployment, adulteration of food, insurance). Overwhelmingly, however, these environmental issues were ignored in the ensuing debates.[15] The recommendations generally endorsed and underlined both the hereditarian as opposed to the environmentalist flavour of the discussions, and the new stress on the role of motherhood, especially those covering the instruction of girls and women in cooking, hygiene and child care.

Maternalism

What was taking place, indeed, was a partial shift in the dominant ideology, away from the nineteenth-century stress on woman as wife towards an accentuated (though not of course new) emphasis on woman as mother. Women's traditional domestic responsibilities were being ideologically reshaped to accord with new perceived problems. A good index of this is an observable change in the recommended reasons for marriage at the turn of the century. A representative manual of the 1860s, for instance, stressed the need for a young woman to find someone to support her, to protect her, to help her, and who was qualified to guide and direct her. There was no mention of children. A 1917 book, concerned with young women and marriage, on the other hand, offered three main reasons for marriage: mutual comfort and support; the maintenance of social purity; and the reproduction of the race.[16] Motherhood, it seemed was a major key to a healthy population. As the Swedish feminist Ellen Key put it, 'as a general rule the woman who refuses motherhood in order to serve humanity is like a soldier who prepares himself on the eve of battle for the forthcoming struggle by opening his veins'.[17] The new ideological inflection was undoubtedly a cross-class phenomenon. As Havelock Ellis put it: 'Women's function in life can never be the same as man's, if only because women are the mothers of the race . . . the most vital problem before our civilisation today is the problem of motherhood, the question of creating human beings best suited for modern life'.[18] But it had a particular nuance when directed at the 'unfit' working class, with its high infant mortality and arguable physical deterioration. It was not poverty that was seen as the cause, but poor maternal training. What were needed were better mothers. Bad hygiene, dirty bottles and dirty homes, and the general question of working-class ignorance were tackled with a fervour by the host of unofficial voluntary bodies that sprang up in the years before the First World War often directed at working-class mothers. These included the Institute of Hygiene (1903), the Infants' Health Society (1904), the National League for Physical Education and Improvement (1905) (later known as the National League for Health, Maternity and Child Welfare), the Eugenics Education Society (1907), and the Women's League of Service for Motherhood (1910).[19]

Patrick Geddes and J. A. Thomson welcomed as a further notable sign of progress the rise of Colleges of Domestic Economy, with 'their vast crowds of girl students', 'Parallel to the admirable revolutionary outbreak of boy-scouting, there is growing up for girls a corresponding novitiate of domesticity.'[20] At the same time, the relationship between the family and the state was subtly changing along with the ideologies. Child rearing was no longer seen as just an individual moral duty: it was a national duty, and this was reflected in the new spirit of interventionism on the part of the state. Compulsory education had already undermined the pure doctrine of parental rights, and the Poor Law Act of 1899 had given the Guardians power to remove children from unsuitable parents. Measures in the early twentieth century, many associated with the Liberal reforms after 1906, accentuated the trend. The provision of school meals for the needy in 1906; medical inspection in schools; the 1907 requirement for the notification of births within six weeks, so that health visitors could be sent round; the Children Act of 1908, making detailed provisions regarding child welfare, and the introduction of maternity insurance in the 1911 Health Insurance Act; all these betokened a new state intervention in the regulation of maternal duties, with particular regard to questions of health and hygiene.[21]

This new interventionism was not a full-scale state assumption of responsibility. It offered rather, a generalised supervision, and the provision of a safety net. The real everyday responsibility still belonged to the mother. Nor was it the product of a conscious adoption of a national policy for motherhood. Most of the policies adopted were *ad hoc* responses rather than part of a national strategy. Continuance of older policies, such as the Poor Law with its less eligibility clauses, meant that at no time before the Second World War did the state assume direct responsibility for the health of the population as a whole. Nevertheless, the new policies, whatever their source, did contribute to an improvement in health, particularly underlined by a reduction in infant mortality and the growth of child-welfare centres after the war.[22]

But what also has to be measured is the balance between the improvement in health, and the subtle tightening of the ideology of motherhood that accompanied it. The improvement of medical care in childbirth went side by side with the loss of control by women over its management. The elevation of the professional expert involved the denial of the neighbourly amateur. Science extinguished the benefits of tradition. Above all, the triumph of medicine represented in practice the assumption by men of many of the traditional responsibilities exercised by women, which in turn could easily mean the imposition of professional middle-class values over working-class traditions.[23]

These new ideological and political interventions are clearly reflected in the specification of female sexuality. At its most extreme, the implication was that sexual intercourse was a racial duty. Havelock Ellis believed that every healthy woman should at least once in her lifetime exercise the vocation of motherhood. Those, like Beatrice Webb, who rejected, for various reasons, individual motherhood, could easily accept the notion of 'racial motherhood', particularly given the expanding opportunities for women in health and social administration. For Mrs Webb, as for many others, the alternative to physical motherhood was celibacy and social activity, 'so that the special force of womanhood – motherly feeling – may be forced into public work'.[24] The period indeed saw a significant reassessment of female sexuality, and the accentuated ideologies of motherhood were to be of prime significance in this redefinition. It is no accident that the influential work of Marie Stopes in the 1920s should be simultaneously a celebration of female sexuality, a paean to parenthood, and a rehearsal of eugenics' arguments. Her intellectual formation was precisely during this period.

Eugenics

If maternalism was one stream feeding population policy in the early decades of the century, eugenics was another which more coherently attempted to transform national policy and intellectual debate, though its degree of success is open to doubt. Many eugenicists were in fact maternalists as well. Havelock Ellis and C. W. Saleeby are two important examples. Other leading eugenicists, such as Karl Pearson, were more worried about the possible dysgenic effects of preserving too many infant lives, particularly the lives of the offspring of the unfit. Such views remained influential for decades, and as late as the end of the 1920s the *Eugenics Review* could comment that 'from every point of view, we can best afford to lose the lives of infants', for by their very death they 'offered a strong possible presumption of inherent worthlessness'.[25]

It was never an undifferentiated approach. But there was a unifying belief behind eugenics, a conviction that it was possible to intervene directly in the processes of producing the population. It was, as its earliest leading proponent, Sir Francis Galton, put it, 'the study of agencies under social control that may improve or impair racial qualities of future generations either physically or mentally'. And as Havelock Ellis added, it was 'the effort to give practical effect to those agencies by conscious and deliberate action in favour of better breeding'.[26] The perceived problem was how to induce in the population a new sense of 'sexual responsibility' so as to direct sexual selection into appropriate channels to ensure racial progress.

Behind this was no mere dispassionate belief that 'science' could take over where individuals or 'stocks' had failed (though this was present). Science in the eyes of the leading advocates of eugenics was married with a messianic optimism and fervour. Galton called for a 'Jehad', a holy war, to be declared on the survival of ancient dysgenic customs, and urged that eugenics – 'a virile creed' – should become a 'religious tenet' of the future. Ellen Key, no less an enthusiast, believed that men and women would eventually devote the same religious fervour to propagating the race as Christians devoted to the salvation of souls.[27] The National Council of Public Morals ('for Great and Greater Britain') adopted a similar note of millenarian hope in introducing its 'New Tracts for the Time': 'The supreme and dominant conception running through these Tracts is the Regeneration of the Race. They strike, not the leaden note of despair, but the ringing tones of a new and certain hope. The regenerated race is coming to birth; the larger and nobler civilisation is upon us.' The titles in the series underlined the complex concerns within eugenics, marrying public morality with the higher 'science'. C. W. Saleeby's *The Methods of Race Regeneration* and Havelock Ellis's *The Problem of Race-Regeneration* marched arm in arm with J. A. Thomson and P. Geddes's *Problems of Sex*, the Rev F. B. Meyer's *Religion and Race-Regeneration*, Mary Scharlieb's *Womanhood and Race Regeneration* and Sir Thomas Clouston's *Morals and Brains*. Social purity, sex reform, racial hygiene and scientific advance could all find a home with eugenics.

Eugenics was a particular social strategy which while drawing on pre-existing beliefs effectively transformed them into a new approach.[28] Hereditarian beliefs were not absent from social reform before eugenics, particularly with the adoption (for example by the philosopher, Herbert Spencer) of Lamarckian beliefs in the inheritance of acquired characteristics. But such beliefs were used to argue for environmental reform; bad conditions, drunkenness and drug abuse, for instance, were held to have bad effects on the next generation. Social reform, Spencerians believed, could improve the next generation.

But behind eugenics, giving it practical impetus, was the conviction either that social reform had failed, or that it was totally insufficient to improve the race. What was needed were policies designed to produce a new sense of citizenship based on the planning of sexual behaviour. Ellis, always a sound weathervane, observed that the progressive movement was beginning to see that comparatively little could be affected by improving the conditions of life of adults. The need was to switch from concentration on the point of production to the source of the problem: 'the point of procreation', 'the regulation of sexual selection between stocks and individuals as the prime condition of life'.[29]

This activism also distinguished eugenics from neo-Malthusianism,[30] which still adhered to the strict economic arguments of its founder, and therefore believed that all that was necessary was to demonstrate the validity of Malthus's arguments, making recourse to social controls unnecessary (though in practice and quite logically Malthusians were to be more activist than early eugenicists in promoting contraceptive knowledge – see below). Eugenicists like Karl Pearson felt that whatever its pretensions, Malthusians directed their effective propaganda at the middle classes (who after all had already limited their birthrates) and bypassed the poor.

Leading neo-Malthusians, on the other hand, claimed that the Malthusian League had always in fact been eugenically minded, in as much as its main goal was to limit the birth of the poor.[31] But whatever the considerable overlap, both in policies and personnel (several leading neo-Malthusians joined the Eugenics Education Society), the theoretical origins of eugenics were quite different.

Eugenics in any recognisable form, can be said to have originated with Charles Darwin. His central concept, that Man is a product of natural selection, led in an 'age of science' quite logically to the hope that Man could participate consciously in the evolutionary process. Darwin's response to the developing eugenics ideas of his cousin, Sir Francis Galton, was in fact cautious. He stopped short of endorsing them in his *Descent of Man* (1871), where he discussed some of the ideas. In other ways, however, eugenic ideas could be said to be in the air. Many eugenicists later claimed to have come to their ideas before Galton publicised them. The American utopian communitarian, John Humphrey Noyes, had, for instance, practised what he called 'stirpiculture' in the Oneida Community, where monogamy was frowned upon and where the number of births each year was strictly controlled. He had first published his views in the 1830s with his *Battleax Letter*. But he later borrowed from Galton to scientificise his views in his book *Scientific Propagation* in 1873.[32]

Galton, however, and most of his followers were much more respectable than this. Galton had been working on eugenicist lines since the 1860s (his *Hereditary Genius* was published in 1869) but it was not until the end of the century that eugenics as a programme of scientific breeding achieved a degree of plausibility: until, in fact, biologists had gained a sufficient grasp of heredity to be able to explain how parents could transmit their genetic qualities to their offspring. First of all there was the break with Lamarckian theory of the inheritance of acquired characteristics, a break associated with the theories of the German biologist August Weismann on the continuity of the germ plasm. Adumbrated in the 1880s, it rapidly became the starting point for further studies.[33] The basis of Weismann's arguments was the distinction he drew between the germ cells which controlled reproduction, and the body or somatic cells. Germ cells were independent of somatic cells and could not be affected by any modification caused by disease or injury.

From this, eugenics drew the conclusion not only that acquired characteristics could not be inherited but that environmental reforms could only have a limited effect: only selective breeding could improve quality.

The second major theme was Galton's development of the concept that the laws of heredity were solely concerned with deviations expressed in statistical units. From this emerged the biometric approach, which sought to measure mathematically the genetic variations, and which was destined to be vastly influential in the growth of statistics and of intelligence testing. He was able to demonstrate, to his own satisfaction at least, a rigorous statistical relationship between heredity and degeneration. For Galton eugenics always meant applied biometrics, and under his closest supporter, Karl Pearson, this became a central element of eugenics.[34]

The third major breakthrough was the rediscovery in the late 1890s of Mendelian genetics; though Galton never felt much enthusiasm for this aspect. A group of biologists led by William Bateson observed that certain physical traits in human beings observed the simple laws of gametic segregation which the Abbé Mendel had analysed in sweet peas in the 1860s. This was seen as a key to the unlocking of the genetic structure of human life, which in turn offered the possibility of applying genetic engineering to individual lives: the aim was not so much to change individuals as to change the balance of the stock. Eugenics was therefore conceived of as applied genetics.[35]

Theoretically then, eugenics welded together a hereditarian theory of population, population statistics and population genetics to develop a distinctive theory of population regulation.[36] This was to find various forms of institutional expression in the first decade of the century. A Eugenics Records Office was set up in 1907 which became the Eugenics Laboratory under Pearson's direction, and this was accompanied by a chair in eugenics, endowed by Galton's will, at University College London in 1911. Pearson was its first incumbent, and he was widely influential. The Eugenics Education Society was founded in 1907 to propagate eugenic views, and this published its own review. By 1914, it had a membership of 634, including a number of highly influential intellectuals,[37] though Galton held aloof for a while, and Pearson remained hostile.

The eugenics movement thus institutionalised was to have a wide, but diffuse, influence. It was probably more important in setting the context for policy making than in influencing detailed policies themselves, but a wide spectrum of people, from far right to socialist left, worked until the 1930s and even beyond (see Chapter 12) within a eugenics framework, or at least with a eugenics terminology. As befitted the prevailing social mood of its period, and as a response to the anxieties that gave it its resonance, clear imperialist and patriotic themes can be discerned. Galton himself spoke of the need to arrest a 'very serious and growing danger to our national efficiency' in the growth of the feeble-minded, while F. S. Schiller argued that 'the nation which first subjects itself to a rational eugenical discipline is bound to inherit the earth'.[38] Pearson went further, accepting the full logic of social imperialist views (as early as the 1880s): 'If child-bearing women must be intellectually handicapped, then the price to be paid for race-predominance is the subjection of women.'[39] But it would be wrong to see eugenics simply or straighforwardly as an apologia for imperialism. Many supporters of eugenics, like Havelock Ellis, were not imperialists, arguing that what they were after was not population quantity but quality. Nor were all eugenicists in agreement with Pearson's view that a nation could be 'kept up to a high pitch of external efficiency by contest, chiefly by way of war with inferior races, and with equal races by the struggle for trade routes and for the sources of raw material of food supply'. Many felt that war was a waste of 'germ plasm', and was fundamentally dysgenic.[40]

Nor was the heart of eugenics its constant evocation of the language of race. There was undoubtedly an unthinking assumption that the white races were superior to the coloured, and many explicit racists, like Arnold White could inveigh against 'Rule by foreign Jews' or the influx of 'diseased aliens'. But others, like Ellis, stressed that they were talking not about specific races, but about the human race.[41]

More central than any of these factors were the class connotations of eugenics.[42] There is a problem here. It is tempting to see eugenics straightforwardly as the ideology of a particular social stratum, which on the basis of the social background of most of its supporters would be the professional middle class, and particularly what could be termed its 'modern' sector. We then have to face the question of whether it is the *expression* of the social needs of that class: whether, in fact, eugenics was little more than a class-specific ideology, limited in its effectiveness by that very fact. There is undoubtedly an emphasis in eugenics on the social importance of the middle-class expert, that is the very type who gave eugenics allegiance, and from Galton's *Hereditary Genius* onwards there is a suspicion both of inherited wealth and of the titled nobility, as well of course of the working class. But we cannot explain eugenics simply in these class reductionist terms, because though eugenics ideas may have had a class-specific origin, they were presented as a strategy for the whole ruling class to adopt, and support was gained from outside the professional classes, just as opposition to eugenics came from within it.

Nevertheless, the class origins or locations of most active eugenicists are clear and important, and they help to explain some of their assumptions. The bulk of the active members of the Eugenics Education Society were from the new professional middle class, that is from the intellectual, creative and welfare professions: they were university teachers and scientists, writers and doctors. 'Sociologists' were prominent[43] (the inaugural meeting of the Sociological Society had been addressed by Galton in 1904), and the majority of biologists were also members of the Society. On the other hand, business men and the aristocracy were not prominent, no more than were the working class. The older professions, such as law and the churches, were also sparsely represented. Women, however, were highly represented, constituting more than half the total membership of the Society in 1913.

Given this balance, not surprisingly, the heroes of the eugenicists were generally professional people, and at various times the Eugenics Education Society clearly took up the interests of the professional middle class. They protested, for instance, at the burden of income tax on professional people, arguing that it discouraged parenthood, and they advocated rebates for each child. On the outbreak of war the Society helped in the setting up of a Professional Classes War Relief Council. Eugenicists were, however, rather uninterested in business: business acumen did not figure in their criteria of mental ability, and they often attacked the plutocracy as well as the hereditary aristocracy. They were also, by and large, and not unexpectedly, hostile to *laissez-faire* capitalism. Galton was generally highly conservative politically, but Karl Pearson had described himself as a socialist from the 1880s (though social imperialist might be a more appropriate description). The general assumption was that eugenics as such was a neutral, scientific doctrine, and the adoption by the state of eugenic policies was to the general good of the body politic. Nevertheless, it was clear that a eugenic society would, necessarily, be administered by eugenic experts, that is by people similar to middle-class professionals who were putting forward eugenic views.

From their point of view, the task of state policy was to encourage methods to induce a sense of sexual responsibility in the population at large. Theoretically, there were two ways to do this: by encouraging the best to breed, or by discouraging the worst. But in practice, social policy had to be directed at the latter – who, as we have seen, were inevitably seen in class terms.

Eugenics not surprisingly made a strong appeal to many Fabian socialists, many of whom came from a similar social background and who shared the same distrust of the masses and faith in professional administrators as many leading eugenicists. H. G. Wells had a burst of enthusiasm on hearing Galton and advocated the 'sterilisation of failures'. Sidney Webb, more soberly, as was his *métier*, warned that unless the decline of the birthrate was averted the nation would fall to the Irish and the Jews.[44] What Fabians and eugenicists shared then, and what is characteristic of their appeal, is their belief in planning and control of population.

It was inevitable that the Fabians would extend their belief in social regulation to fertility: reproduction was obviously too important to be left to individuals, and Sidney Webb believed it could not safely be left to the residuum to regulate their lives with Malthusian prudence. In 1907 a Fabian Tract on *The Decline of the Birth Rate* (the product of a sub-committee set up in 1905) had warned of the dangers of the differential birthrate, where the thrifty limited their families, and the residuum did not. Webb had argued that the state should adopt social policies, which would induce the right sort of people to assume parenthood. Eugenics might be useful in eliminating the biologically feeble, but only social policies could enable the socially disadvantaged to improve their lot. So there was an important difference between the Fabian approach and the eugenic, whatever the class, and rhetorical similarities. Webb advocated policies – such as the endowment of motherhood – which eugenicists thought were dysgenic, while the main thrust of the Fabian approach was to differentiate between the thrifty and the residuum in order to encourage the *social* advance of the former. George Bernard Shaw's call, in his inimitable way, for the 'elimination of the mere voluptuary from the evolutionary process', and his advocacy of a State Department of Evolution to pay women for their child-rearing services, and if necessary to regulate a 'joint stock human stud farm',[45] had social efficiency as their purport. Pure eugenicists on the other hand were uninterested, as we have seen, in such flipperies or in reform. Their aim was to purify the stream of life at its source, to eliminate not so much the social causes of evil, but the core biological defects. Hence the twin poles of their arguments, 'positive' and 'negative' eugenics, the centre of their efforts to control the processes of procreation.

Positive eugenics stressed the need to breed a better race, a race of Shakespeares and Darwins. Beatrice Webb, though feeling she and Sidney could contribute little to the process themselves, believed 'the breeding of the right sort of man' to be the most important of all questions.[46] Few eugenicists actually went so far as to recommend breeding experiments, however.

Galton feared that in man's present state of ignorance, attempts to arrange eugenic marriages would do more harm than good. There was a realisation that human life was somewhat different from the stock yards, despite the verbal flourishes. Moreover, some eugenicists realised that if it became possible to breed supermen, it might also become possible to breed mutants.

There was the further problem of selecting the criteria which were to be developed. Galton believed there was a correlation between physical health and academic worth; Pearson's researches found only a low correlation.[47] And what was to be the response to the less than eugenic qualities of many recognised 'geniuses': Keat's consumption, Beethoven's deafness? Then there was the problem of whether to favour 'genius' or all-round civic worthiness; if everyone was a genius, who was to do the manual labour?

But the core question was who was to decide which groups to control, and how? Havelock Ellis felt that the state had no more right to ravish a woman than a man,[48] but Galton's faith that each group would regulate their own fertility policies was scarcely practical. So as C. W. Saleeby argued, 'the *positive* methods of regeneration, at any rate under anything like present social conditions, will be mainly educative'.[49] He rejected therefore compulsory mating, 'and anything else that involves the destruction of marriage'. But this acceptance of conventional morality meant that in the end he was left with little besides education for parenthood, and the encouragement of eugenic marriages.

Galton developed various fancy schemes to do the latter, including financial incentives to encourage eugenic marriages, low-cost housing for 'exceptionally promising young couples'; pressure of public opinion and the award of honours; 'and above all else the introduction of motives of religious or quasi-religious character'.[50] Marriage certificates and financial bonuses from the state to parents of fit offspring found a more general favour. Ellis believed that marriage certificates would one day become like university degrees, and allow individuals to select the properly qualified partner. Pearson thought that the state should follow the policy of the Indian civil service and take parenthood into account in determining salaries of public servants.[51]

But the problem that eugenicists faced was that many efforts to encourage better breeding, such as subsidies for motherhood, might actually encourage the unfit to breed even more. Similarly, proposals for the penalisation of bachelors might actually encourage undesirable single people to enter dysgenic relationships. Consequently, the most favoured approach was to alter the tax system in favour of married couples with dependent children. The beauty of this was that as only the middle class generally paid substantial income tax, it would not needlessly encourage the unfit. The Liberal Government's introduction in 1909 of an allowance of £10 to income-tax payers for every child below 16 was heralded as a major triumph for eugenic principles.

Positives eugenics, however, offered a double problem: it was both technically difficult to achieve, and it did not tackle the core problem: the multiplication of undesirables. Hence the greater emphasis, particularly from the early 1920s, on negative eugenics, the elimination of the unfit. Galton had foreshadowed this possibility as early as his 1906 Huxley lectures. In Britain few actually advocated their actual physical destruction. When the Mayor of Brighton in 1909 advocated putting to death the unfit, if three doctors recommended it, there was a furore in which eugenic luminaries joined. They were similarly shocked in 1910 when George Bernard Shaw, in his usual mischievous manner, seemed to be advocating, while addressing them, 'an extensive use of the lethal chamber'. Most respectable eugenicists, like Saleeby, thought it necessary to underline their rejection of all synonyms for mutilative surgery and murder.[52]

The other drastic remedy was compulsory sterilisation of the unfit, advocated in particular by Dr Robert Reid Rentoul of Liverpool. Few were prepared to support him, though many were prepared to back voluntary sterilisation, especially of those suffering from hereditary defects. It would, it was pointed out, be cheaper than custodial care.

The prohibition of marriage or its limitation to those with medical certificates, was another possibility floated. But this, it was pointed out, would not prevent degenerates from coupling. Segregation, therefore, 'the permanent care under humane medical supervision' of defectives, seemed a possibility.[53]

But as with positive eugenics, so with negative: education in eugenic principles seemed the only practical way forward. Out of this was to come the beginnings of genetic counselling. But another logical step was the advocacy of deliberate birth control. Many of the leading supporters of birth control in the 1920s and 1930s, like Stopes, had strong eugenic backgrounds.[54] But many felt contraception was dysgenic, as it was the middle class who generally controlled their fertility, and *that* was the major problem. Others felt that by so directly entering the sexual debate, rather than maintaining a scientific stance, the whole moral tone of eugenics was threatened. Still others, however, like Ellis and the socialist feminist F. W. Stella Browne, were quite prepared to use eugenic arguments to garner support for birth control, and their influence passes through into later debates.

The influence of eugenics

Having described the approaches of eugenicists we must, finally, attempt to assess their practical influence, particularly on the actual regulation of the processes of procreation and sexual behaviour. In terms of practical policies adopted they cannot be said to have been spectacularly successful. Several government policies were heralded as triumphs of eugenic principles. Ellis saw the Liberal reforms and the 1908 Notification of Births Act as the 'national inauguration of a scheme for the betterment of the race', and as a triumph for 'national efficiency', while the provision of the National Insurance Bill of 1911 which established 'Maternity Benefits' was welcomed by Saleeby as a 'red letter day in real politics'.[55] The origins of the latter, however, owed nothing to direct eugenic propaganda. Similarly, the Mental Deficiency Act of 1913 which was trumpeted as the major triumph of eugenics before the war, had relatively little eugenics content. Eugenics arguments played an important part in the development of the concept of the feeble-minded,[56] and the report of the Royal Commission on the Care and Control of the Feeble Minded in 1908 had backed eugenic fears that their fertility was way above average. Segregation was recommended to control them. But the actual Act that followed had few obviously eugenic elements, despite intensive lobbying. Eugenic thought was never without its severe critics, even from within the professional middle class. Many liberals, such as L. T. Hobhouse, could accept similar arguments on, say, the feeble-minded, but believed that progress was ethical not racial. Roman Catholics were particularly hostile, especially because of eugenic claims to control life, but also because of its pretensions to be a new religion.

On the other hand, eugenic statements can be traced in all sorts of unexpected sources, and came from all parts of the political spectrum. Not surprisingly, Conservative politicians like A. J. Balfour lent them prestige and such intellectual distinction as they possessed. But even militant socialists, not scarred like the Fabians by social imperialism, were enthusiasts. Maurice Eden Paul, a prominent left-wing socialist before the First World War, and later a member of the Communist Party, believed that 'unless the socialist is also a eugenicist, the socialist state will speedily perish from racial degradation' and suggested that the ability to earn the minimum wage should be the precondition for becoming a parent.[57] Even J. B. S. Haldane, the leading left-wing and Communist Party scientist of the 1930s, looked forward to the creation of 'a classless society' where 'far-reaching eugenic measures could be enforced by the state with little injustice', though adding that 'Today this would not be possible.'[58] More directly influential were men like Sir William Beveridge, architect of the Welfare State, who held strong eugenic views, while liberal and radical theorists from Goldsworthy Lowes Dickinson to H. J. Laski at various times expressed eugenic sentiments. Traces can also be located in a host of approaches and policies put forward during the inter-war years, from family planning and family allowances to National Insurance and taxation, and it reappeared in Fabian population policies in the 1940s. Its rhetoric was even to reappear like a myth that never dies, in the quite different circumstances of the 1970s in the 'new conservatism' of Sir Keith Joseph and others (see below).

Nevertheless, as an *organised* strand of thought, eugenics lost its impetus after the First World War. Before the war eugenics offered an appealing strategy to remove what was conceived of as a residuum. But in the light of mass unemployment after the war, more drastic *social* policies seemed necessary. The *ad hoc*, but consistent policies of selective intransigence and co-option adopted by governments from the 1920s to deal with working-class discontent owed nothing to eugenics.[59] The Eugenics Society itself gradually became a learned society rather than a propaganda body (and as such still survives) and by the 1930s felt it necessary to distinguish itself from the more extreme eugenicism practised in Nazi Germany.[60]

What eugenics fundamentally wanted was the adoption of a national policy for the population which would regulate sexual behaviour in the interests of the race. But Britain never during this period adopted anything that could be termed a formal population policy. This does not mean of course that informal population policies did not exist. A host of government actions, from its taxation and housing policies to its attitudes to birth control, had vital effects on decision making. But these were *ad hoc* policies rather than the result of strategic planning. In these, eugenic notions often played a significant, but by no means decisive, part. It is as a current of thought, colouring a variety of debates, that the real influence of eugenics has to be sought. This will become apparent in the succeeding chapters.

References

1. **Patrick Geddes** and **J. A. Thomson**, *Sex*, Home Universal Library, London, 1914, p. 196.
2. Cf. **Nikolas Rose**, 'The Psychological Complex: Mental Measurement and Social Administration', *Ideology and Consciousness*, No. 5, Spring 1979, p. 28. This is an important discussion of many of the themes in this chapter, within a theoretical framework derived from Michel Foucault.
3. Michel Foucault, *The History of Sexuality*, Vol. 1, Ch. 5.
4. Angus McLaren, *Birth Control in Nineteenth Century England*, pp. 43 ff.
5. **Gareth Stedman Jones**, *Outcast London*, Clarendon Press, Oxford, 1971, p. 151.
6. **Geoffrey R. Searle**, *Eugenics and Politics in Britain 1900–1914*, Noordhof International, Leyden, 1976, pp. 20 ff. Most of the non-attributed factual information in this chapter derives from this work.
7. Quoted in *ibid.*, p. 19.
8. Quoted in **Jacobus X** (pseud. for Louis Jacolliot), *The Ethnology of the Sixth Sense*, Charles Carrington, Paris, 1899, p. 425. For a comment on degeneracy and homosexuality see Anomaly, *The Invert, and his Social Adjustment*, Baillière, Tindale and Cox, London, 1927, p. 24: 'It has been argued that inversion is the result of racial degeneration. If this is the case it is difficult to account for its presence in every race, climate and caste.' For a semi-official index of the passing away of the term in the 1930s ('we need no longer concern ourselves with the possible interpretations of these vague terms') see **W. Norwood East**, *Medical Aspects of Crime*, J. and A. Churchill, London, 1936, pp. 420–1.
9. **Arthur Newsholme**, *The Declining Birth Rate*, Cassell and Co., London, 1911, pp. 52–3.
10. Searle, *op. cit.*, p. 26.
11. **C. V. Drysdale**, *The Malthusian*, June 1906; **Havelock Ellis**, *Studies in the Psychology of Sex*, Vol. 4: *Sex in Relation to Society*, Random House, New York, 1936, p. 591 (first published 1912).
12. **Lord Rosebery**, *Miscellanies. Literary and Historical*, Vol. 11 (ed. John Buchan), Hodder and Stoughton, London, 1921, p. 250.
13. *Ibid.* See **G. R. Searle**, *The Quest for National Efficiency 1899–1914*, Blackwell, Oxford, 1971.
14. Searle, *Eugenics*, p. 23.
15. Interdepartmental Committee on Physical Deterioration, PP. 1904, XXXII. See **Anna Davin**, 'Imperialism and Motherhood', *History Workshop*, No. 5, Spring 1978, pp. 26–7.
16. *Ibid.*, p. 13.
17. Quoted, with approval, in Havelock Ellis, *Sex in Relation to Society*, p. 587.
18. **Havelock Ellis**, *The Task of Social Hygiene*, Constable, London, 1912, p. 186.
19. Anna Davin, *op. cit.*, p. 12.
20. Geddes and Thomson, *Sex*, p. 177, p. 178.
21. Anna Davin, *op. cit.*, p. 13.

22. See **Jane Lewis**, *The Politics of Motherhood: Maternal and Child Welfare in England 1900–39*, Croom Helm, London, 1980; **Carol Dyhouse**, 'Working Class Mothers and Infant Mortality in England, 1895–1914', *Journal of Social History*, Vol. 12, 1978. The maternal mortality rate remained around the 1910 level of 3.56 deaths per 1,000 births until the late 1920s. It rose during 1926–36.

23. Anna Davin, *op. cit.*, p. 13. Ann Oakley gives examples of female opposition to the male-defined concerns in 'Wise Woman and Medicine Man: Changes in the Management of Childbirth', in **Juliet Mitchell** and **Ann Oakley**, *The Rights and Wrongs of Women*, Penguin, Harmondsworth, 1976, pp. 43–4. In the 1920s Eleanor Rathbone noted the increased state supervision of mothers in the home, pointing out that at any time health visitors, school inspectors or rent collectors could drop in unannounced, putting pressure on mothers to improve the quality of the labour power she produced, and holding legal sanctions against her if she failed to meet the prevailing norms: **E. Rathbone**, *The Disinherited Family: a Plea for the Endowment of the Family*, Edward Arnold, London, 1924.

24. Anna Davin, *op. cit.*, p. 51; Angus McLaren, *op. cit.*, p. 190.

25. 'Notes of the Quarter'; *Eugenics Review*, Vol. 21, 1929–30, p. 163.

26. Galton is quoted in Searle, *op. cit.*, p. 1; the Ellis quote is from *The Task of Social Hygiene*, p. 28.

27. Galton is quoted in **B. Semmel**, 'Karl Pearson: Socialist and Darwinist', *British Journal of Sociology*, Vol. IX, No. 2, June 1958, p. 119; references to Ellen Key are in Ellis, *Sex in Relation to Society*, pp. 580–81.

28. Detailed discussion of eugenics can be found in Searle, *op. cit.*, N. Rose, *op. cit.*; **Donald MacKenzie**, 'Eugenics in Britain', *Social Studies of Science*, No. 6, 1976; and Past and Present Society, 'The Roots of Sociobiology', Proceedings of a conference held in Oxford, 1978. For Galton's views see *Hereditary Genius*, Macmillan, London, 1869; *Natural Inheritance*, Macmillan, 1889; *Eugenics*, Sociological Society, 1905.

29. Ellis, *Sex in Relation to Society*, p. 582.

30. For discussion of the difference, see McLaren, *op. cit.*, p. 148; and **Jill Hodges** and **Athar Hussain**, 'La Police des Familles', review article, *Ideology and Consciousness*, No. 5, Spring 1979, p. 115.

31. McLaren, *op. cit.*, p. 148.

32. **J. H. Noyes**, *Essay on Scientific Propagation*, Oneida, New York, 1875; see also his *Male Continence*, 1872. The starting point of 'Scientific' eugenics was **Darwin**, *The Descent of Man. Selection in Relation to Sex*, 2 Vols, John Murray, London, 1871.

33. G. R. Searle, *op. cit.*, pp. 6 ff, for a discussion of these theoretical roots.

34. For an important discussion of this, see Rose, *op. cit.*

35. A point made by **Leonard Darwin**, 'The Aims and Methods of Eugenical Societies', in *Eugenics, Genetics and the Family*, Vol. 1 (Scientific Papers of the Second International Congress of Eugenics, September 22–28, 1921), Wilkins and Wilkins, Baltimore, 1923, p. 16.

36. Cf. Rose, *op. cit.*, p. 27.

37. See Searle, *op. cit.*, Ch. 2, for this institutionalisation.

38. Quoted in *ibid.*, p. 34.

39. Quoted in Semmel, *op. cit.*, p. 119.

40. Searle, *op. cit.*, pp. 36 ff., p. 152.

41. For Ellis see my essay in **S. Rowbotham** and **J. Weeks**, *Socialism and the New Life*, Pluto Press, London, 1977; and below, Chapter 8.

42. MacKenzie, *op. cit.*, is particularly valuable on this theme. See also Searle, *op. cit.*, pp. 45 ff.
43. 'In London, on May 14, 1904, our newly formed Sociological Society was publicly inaugurated by an address on "National Eugenics" from the veteran Francis Galton. Before he had finished I had abandoned all idea of medical practice to follow him.' C. W. Saleeby, *The Eugenics Prospect: National and Racial*, Fisher Unwin, London, 1921, p. 11.
44. Semmel, *op. cit.*, p. 122.
45. McLaren, *op. cit.*, p. 190; on the Fabian approach, see also Rose, *op. cit.*, p. 35.
46. Searle, *op. cit.*, p. 75.
47. *Ibid.*, p. 77.
48. Ellis, *Sex in Relation to Society*, p. 586.
49. C. W. Saleeby, *The Methods of Race-Regeneration*, Cassell and Co., London, 1911, p. 2.
50. Searle, *op. cit.*, p. 83.
51. *Ibid.*, p. 88.
52. *Ibid.*, p. 92, Saleeby, *The Methods of Race-Regeneration*, p. 46.
53. Searle, *op. cit.*, p.96, Saleeby, *The Methods of Race-Regeneration*, p. 48. The Report of the Departmental Committee on Sterilisation, Cmd. 4485, London, HMSO 1934, reported that 'The supposed abnormal fertility of defectives is in our view largely mythical' (p. 18). The mortality rate amongst defectives and their offspring was abnormally high. It argued against compulsory sterilisation, or for the special selecting out of defectives; which led to their recommendation that voluntary sterilisation be authorised, with defectives being encouraged to adopt it. In 1936 the Labour Women's Conference demanded sterilisation laws along the lines of the 1934 report.
54. Searle, *op. cit.*, p. 101; McLaren, *op. cit.*, Ch. 8.
55. Ellis, *Sex in Relation to Society*, p. 29; Saleeby, *The Methods of Race-Regeneration*, p. 31.
56. Searle, *op. cit.*, pp. 106 ff.
57. Eden Paul, *Socialism and Eugenics*, National Labour Press, Manchester, (?1912), pp. 14, 16. See also M. Eden and Cedar Paul (eds), *Population and Birth Control: A Symposium*, The Critic and Guide Co., New York, 1917.
58. J. B. S. Haldane, *The Inequality of Man and Other Essays* (1932), quoted in Gary Werskey, *The Visible College*, Allen Lane, London, 1978, p. 97. Bertrand Russell wrote in 1929: 'It seems on the whole fair to regard Negroes as on the average inferior to white men, although for work in the tropics they are indispensable.' For this and his arguments on eugenics, see *Marriage and Morals*, Allen and Unwin, London, 1929, p. 202. Eugenic ideas bit deep. See also Michael Freeden, 'Eugenics and Progressive Thought: A Study in Ideological Affinity', *The Historical Journal*, Vol. 22, No. 3, Sept. 1979. For a very helpful discussion of the influence of eugenics on the European left, see Loren R. Graham, 'Science and Values: The Eugenics Movement in Germany and Russia in the 1920s', *American Historical Review*, Vol. 82, No. 5, Dec. 1977.
59. This point is made by MacKenzie, *op. cit.* See also comments in Werskey, *op. cit.*., pp. 32, 33.
60. See L. S. Waterman, *The Eugenic Movement in Britain in the 1930s*, unpublished M.Sc. Thesis, University of Sussex, 1975.

Chapter Eight

The theorisation of sex

A new continent of knowledge

The debate over population was an aspect of a general opening up of the question of sexuality, ranging from the issue of genetics to the broader problem of the nature of sex itself, and its complex impact on social life. Though much more muted in Britain than in countries such as Germany, the result was, nevertheless, a significant expansion of writings on sexuality in the late nineteenth and early twentieth centuries. The consequent emergence of sex as an object of study was one of the major features of the social sciences of the period, and stands as a central moment in the constitution of modern concepts of sexuality. As Max Hodann, a German writer on sex, and a former colleague of the great pioneer, Magnus Hirschfeld, observed in the 1930s, 'The focus of conflict and emotional tension for the nineteenth century was the Darwinian theory. In the twentieth, the stress has shifted to the scientific investigation and discussion of sexual matters.'[1]

Most liberal writers over the past generation have been clear on the status of the founders of modern sexology. Professor Flugel argued that the work of men like Havelock Ellis, Magnus Hirschfeld and Freud, by claiming the right to investigate the human sexual life impartially, 'broke up the "conspiracy of silence" that had so largely stifled discussion of this subject in the nineteenth century, and . . . at last awarded it its rightful place in psychology and sociology'. O. R. McGregor, writing in the 1950s, believed that writings such as Havelock Ellis's 'mark the watershed between the Victorians and ourselves'.[2] In considering such comments, however, we must be careful to comprehend the precise context in which they are relevant and meaningful.

A concern with sex-related behaviour was not, of course, new in the late nineteenth century, nor was the reaction to the major figures necessarily hostile. A work such as Krafft-Ebing's encyclopaedia of sexual variations, *Psychopathia Sexualis*, faced few overt dangers when translated into English in the 1890s because it declared its object to be 'merely to record the various psychopathological manifestations of sexual life in man and to reduce them to their lawful conditions'.[3] As a 'medico-forensic study' of the 'abnormal', (its subtitle notes its 'especial reference to the Antipathic Sexual Instinct') directed at the specialist, it set out insights without suggesting licence. Its various editions were translated into English during the 1890s and later, but discretion was maintained. Krafft-Ebing case histories (which in themselves were innovatory, marking an individualising of a condition) tactfully broke into Latin when sex acts were discussed. An example chosen at random will give the flavour: 'An officer of Vienna informed me that men, by means of large sums of money, induce prostitutes to suffer *ut illi viri in ova earum spuerent et faeces et urinas in ova explerent.*'[4]

Other works, of course, were less fortunate in their reception. Iwan Bloch's *Sexual Life of Our Times*, a learned exploration of sexual behaviour, was prosecuted in the 1900s, and many other findings of continental research entered British discourse through the Paris-based publisher of dubious erotica, Charles Carrington, or through summaries in other works.[5] The first volume (*Sexual Inversion*) of Ellis's great seven-volume work, *Studies in the Psychology of Sex*, was labelled 'lewd and obscene' in a court of law in 1897 and Ellis refused to publish further volumes of the *Studies* in English until the 1930s.[6] Freud's work, though welcomed, and even publicised, by writers such as Ellis, produced early wrath from leaders of the medical profession. The *British Medical Journal* thundered in 1908 that 'this method of psychoanalysis is in most cases incorrect, in many hazardous, and in all dispensable'.[7]

There can be no doubts of the difficulties, and many of the most important works on sexuality scarcely attained any respectability before the 1920s, when Ellis and Freud became openly influential – and sex research, still, of course, has its hazards today. But what constitutes the originality and significance of the new sexology is not so much the subject matter as the aim and direction of the work. Ellis, for instance, was criticised for the popular tone of his work, its air of speaking to an intelligent general audience rather than a specialist medico-forensic one. Writers like Magnus Hirschfeld and Havelock Ellis also aroused antagonism as self-conscious reformers who sought to challenge authoritarian sexual norms. Ellis in particular believed that the sex problem, in which he included relations between the sexes, was indeed the most important one facing the social reformers in the nineteenth century. But perhaps the most significant point about the new sexology was its assumption that sexuality deserved serious study not just as an aspect of the treatment of moral laxity or disease but because of its significance for the whole existence of the individual and society. By the 1840s (represented, according to Foucault, by Heinrich Kaan's work) there was a search for the nature of 'sex'. The concern with disparate forms of sexual behaviour, embodied hitherto in a host of social practices, was producing a new unified domain for investigation. Sexology was simultaneously constituting and exploring a new continent of knowledge, assigning thereby a new significance to the 'sexual'.[8]

The major effort of these late nineteenth- and early twentieth-century writers was to isolate and define the nature and characteristics of the specifically sexual instinct or force, and to delineate its social effects. To understand the significance of this we need to unravel very briefly the history of the concept of instinct itself.[9] In a general way, the idea was not, of course, new and is present in Plato and Aristotle, and it reappeared with the revival of Greek philosophy in the Middle Ages, through Thomas Aquinas's theory of natural law. As such it was present in eighteenth-century notions of conscience, benevolence, sympathy and other 'moral sentiments'. It was extended to natural mental endowment, but until late in the nineteenth century it remained a general concept without detailed specification. It was the growth of the biological sciences following Darwin which stimulated the detailed analysis and resultant classifications of the instincts. German biologists, particularly, developed lists of specific instincts, and following the work of Weismann and Mendel these were analysed in purely biological terms, shaving away the possibility of the inheritance of acquired characteristics.

The resulting definition that dominated in the early decades of the twentieth century was that presented by L. L. Bernard as: 'a specific and definite inherited and unlearned response which follows or accompanies a specific and definite sensory stimulus or organic condition that serves as a release to the inherited mechanism'.[10] Instinct, that is, was a biological impulse unmediated by experience.

The question that the early sexologists faced was where did sexuality fit into this schema. The traditional view, endorsed historically by luminaries as diverse as Luther and Montaigne (and accepted by the sexologists Charles Féré as late as 1898) was that the sex instinct was little more than the impulse of evacuation. The obvious corollary of this was the view of sexuality as essentially male and the conceptualisation of women as the hallowed receptacle ('the temple built over a sewer'). An alternative, and perhaps more respectable view, was that sexuality represented the 'instinct of reproduction', a desire for offspring. It was as such (and as nothing else) that sex appeared in all editions of Professor William McDougall's influential textbook, *Introduction to Social Science* until its 8th edition in 1914.[11] Thereafter, it was supplemented by a chapter on the 'sex instinct', in which it was incorporated into his general theory of instincts as being 'innate specific tendencies'. There were obvious difficulties with such a definition – not the least being that in our culture at least, heterosexual sex is only rarely engaged in simply for the sake of procreation; and it failed to offer any way of explaining sexual variations except in terms of degeneration from a given, 'natural', norm. Charles Darwin had, in this as in other fields, opened up the potential new paths to understanding in his development of the theory of sexual selection (in the *Descent of Man*, 1871) and later work was to pursue his leads on the aesthetic, erotic and psychological processes of sexual attraction. Ellis, working from this tradition, saw the prime task of his *Studies in the Psychology of Sex* as precisely the analysis of 'what is commonly called the sexual instinct'.[12] The implication was that there was a complex natural process which underlay a diversity of social experiences.

This project necessarily involved a major effort at labelling and classification. In the great classificatory zeal that produced the complex definitions and aetiologies and the new sexual types of the late nineteenth century (and in which Ellis was the main British participant) we can discern the supplanting of the old, undifferentiated, moral categories of sin, debauchery and excess, by the new, medical and psychological categories of degeneracy, mental illness and disease. The vast majority of the late nineteenth-century pioneers of sex research were concerned, like Krafft-Ebing, with the variations from the norm, and the result was a detailing of even more exotic variations. One of the signal successes attributed to Havelock Ellis was that while not neglecting this, the major (though not always the most controversial) part of his work was a study of the apparently 'normal', which as he partially indicated, was no more than what societies defined as the norm.

There were then two stages to this development. The first was concerned with describing the deviations from a norm which was shrouded in assumptions about its naturalness. Characteristic works include Westphal's essay on 'the contrary sex instinct', Charles Féré's *Sexual Degeneration in Mankind and in Animals*, Albert Moll's *Perversions of the Sex Instinct* and Thoinot's *Attentats aux Moeurs et Perversions du Sens Genital*. Hirschfeld's work developed from his studies of homosexuality, and the first volume of Ellis's *Studies* to appear was on sexual inversion. What was at stake, then, was the construction of new sexual and even psychological categories, definitions, and eventually social practices around these definitions, which increasingly explained sexual 'deviants' in terms of their individual sexual and psychological variations.

The second (though often contemporaneous) stage was more concerned with the manifestations of 'normality', which rapidly demonstrated the problems with the concept of 'the natural'. Both stages have as their central concern the nature of the sexual 'instinct', but the move is towards the recognition of its multifarious and ambivalent nature, even amongst the 'normal'. Patrick Geddes and J. Arthur Thomson capture this very well in their work of popularisation on *Sex*. They noted 'a volcanic element in sex, quite underlying the rest of our nature and for that very reason shaking it from its foundations with tremors, if not catastrophe'. But 'instinct' is not enough to guide us through this jungle of danger and potential disaster, for the 'sex impulses' are relatively undifferentiated: 'The fact is that we have, in regard to sex-functions, very little instinctive knowledge of what various phenomena mean, or of what is normal, or of what is to be carefully avoided.' There are clear contradictions in this and similar positions. On the one hand, Geddes and Thomson clearly believe in the biological 'naturalness' and inevitability of the sexual relationships of man and woman, the basis for all sexual activity. But on the other, this is beset by dangers which only social presumptions, self-control, 'healthy mindedness', 'clean living', and sex education can help us control. All normal human beings, as William McDougall noted in *An Outline of Abnormal Psychology*, are in some degrees liable to perversion under certain circumstances.[13] But this was no longer conceived of as a consequence of 'original sin' as of the nature of sexuality itself. In this approach sex is conceptualised as a biological essence which, if moral suasion fails, can become diverted into perverted channels. Cultural change can weaken the controls on this natural force, but cannot alter its fundamental nature.[14] Sex thus emerges as an independent variable.

A question posed by this new zeal in defining and categorising sexuality is why the effort took place at this particular time. It is obviously an aspect of a much wider trend in social sciences, to order, through scientific description, what previously appeared unclassifiable, but there are also specific factors which influenced the terms of the work on sexuality.[15] First of all, there was the growing concern, associated with agitation over the incidence of prostitution and venereal disease, with personal sexual hygiene. Throughout much of the nineteenth century, indeed, questions of prostitution and venereal disease were seen as the only justification for research into sexuality. At the very least, the public debate over public morality, the double standard and private vice which assumed a new centrality from the 1860s, opened up the question of sex to wider public scrutiny. Secondly, associated with the concern with *personal* hygiene was the wider question of *racial* hygiene, the very issue articulated in the rise of eugenics, which in turn was rooted in post-Darwin biology. Health and racial advance were the issues behind both the population debate and much early sexological work. And these represented a further impulse: towards a new interventionism in sexual matters (whose roots we have traced earlier). The paradox was that the early sexologists, who by and large were also conscious sex reformers, were simultaneously powerful agents in the organisation, and potential control, of the sexual behaviours they sought to describe, for by the inter-war years the new psychology was a potent force in the reconceptualisation of crime and sexual delinquency.

Sex, science and society

Sex research and theorisation, in other words, never worked in a vacuum. Its concerns were dictated by wider social anxieties or aims. Correspondingly, its conceptualisations were shaped by prevailing power relations. It is transparent, for instance, that important advances in theorisation were often integrated into pre-existing assumptions. Conceptions about the inherent 'natural' basis of the separate social roles of men and women, and of the relationship between these roles and sexual behaviour, were deeply rooted, and far from being undermined were actually reinforced by post-Darwinian speculation. Many early sociologists, from Comte to Herbert Spencer, took it as given that social life, and the differences between the sexes, could be explained by reference to biological capacities. Spencer, for instance, concluded that sex differences were a result of the earlier arrest in the woman of individual evolution, necessitated by the reservation of vital powers to meet the cost of reproduction. Female energy was not available for intellectual growth.[16] The break with Lamarckian theories of the inheritance of acquired characteristics bolstered rather than undermined this, as is suggested by the greatly influential work of Patrick Geddes and J. Arthur Thomson, *The Evolution of Sex*, first published in 1889.[17] The germ-plasm, it seemed, had many of the qualities associated with existing middle-class values. Geddes and Thomson were convinced that sex differences should be viewed as arising from a basic difference in cell metabolism. The physical laws concerning the conservation and dissipation of energy applied to all living things. At the level of the cell, maleness was characterised by the tendency to dissipate energy (katabolic), and femaleness by the capacity to store or build up energy (anabolic). By making sperm and ovum exhibit the qualities of katabolism and anabolism, Geddes and Thomson were able to deduce a dichotomy between the sexes which, like Spencer's, could easily be assimilated to the conventional ideal of male rationality and female intuition. The conclusion of this was apparent: male and female roles had been decided in the lowest forms of life, and neither political nor technological change could alter the temperament which had developed from these differing functions. So, what was decided amongst the prehistoric Protozoa could not be annulled by an act of Parliament.

W. Blair Bell in 1916 drew an obvious conclusion from such theorisations: 'it must surely be recognised by all that the male mind and masculine forms are suited to the business of life which so nearly concerns his share in reproduction; while the female mind is specifically adapted to her more protracted part in the perpetuation of the species.'[18]

The view of Geddes and Thomson and their co-thinkers did not go unchallenged in the world of social science, but their approach was a formative pre-Freudian one. Their book was published in Havelock Ellis's influential 'Contemporary Science' series, and many of its assumptions are traceable to his own work. Like theirs, his work can be seen as part of a tradition which expected change to come chiefly from an extension of the area allowed for female sex-determined characteristics. Anything else would challenge what Ellis described in his book, *Man and Woman* (first published in 1893 and frequently published thereafter), as a 'cosmic conservatism', a natural harmony between men and women which had become 'as nearly perfect as possible and every inaptitude is compensated by some compensatory aptitude'.

For a just society, therefore, each sex must follow 'the laws of its own nature'. For Ellis, the fundamental truth of natural life was that the two sexes were separately defined in evolution as a method of favouring reproduction, and this could only partially be overridden. Nature therefore sanctified the social roles that men and women inhabited: 'Woman breeds and tends; man provides; it remains so even when the spheres tend to overlap.'[19]

This did not mean a denial of female sexual needs. Even the relatively conservative Geddes and Thomson recognised a 'physiological base' for female sexuality, though it was more controlled by morality and more fearful of the consequences than the male's, and 'is so constituted that from wooing to consummation it takes longer for the brain to become eroticised'. In the context of permanent monogamy, 'the biological and psychic ideal', love between the partners – and by inference sexual love – is the basis of social morality.[20]

The consciously more reformist Ellis was explicit on the legitimacy of women having their sexual needs satisfied, and attacked male clumsiness and brutality in the sex act. But even Ellis could not resist concluding that female orgasm had a utilitarian and biological function in that it facilitated procreation. His views on lesbianism are relevant here, because while he recognised the legitimacy of female homosexuality (his wife Edith Lees was lesbian), he obviously found it difficult to conceptualise in terms of his sexual theories. His chapters in *Sexual Inversion* on lesbianism are curiously under-nourished compared to his chapters on male homosexuality, and he suggested that while homosexuals were not by and large 'effeminate', lesbians did tend to be 'masculine'. It was as if he could only conceptualise lesbianism as a masculinisation of the woman, whereas today many tend to see female homosexuality as the ultimate in female autonomy from men.[21] Ellis believed that nature dictated that the male must generally take the initiative in sexual matters: 'The female responds to the stimulation of the male at the right moment just as the tree responds to the stimulation of the warmest days in spring.' Thus he held that the sex life of the woman was largely conditioned by the sex life of the man, so that while a youth spontaneously becomes a man, the maiden 'must be kissed into a woman'.[22]

After the turn of the century, advances in the field of endocrinology began to illuminate the question of sexual behaviour, and the nervous model of the causation of human physiology – with its assumptions of closed energy systems – was gradually replaced by a hormonal model. Even so, these advances in knowledge were generally employed to confirm rather than challenge the connections between social characteristics and sexual behaviour.[23] The importance of ovarian hormones was generally accepted by 1908, and by 1916 W. Blair Bell had suggested that the 'essential fact' to be borne in mind is that 'femininity itself is dependent on all the internal secretions'. But more important still was the conclusion that the mental characteristics of women came under the influence of her 'special functions', thus echoing traditional precepts. Hormonal discoveries served to confirm Ellis in his belief in the biological basis of sex differences, and were easily integrated into the views he had already developed on female sexuality and homosexuality.

The same was true of Hirschfeld, whose work was pioneering in this regard.[24] So, while these biological breakthroughs confirmed the existence of an autonomous female physiology, with its own periodic cycles, this understanding did not lead on immediately to any re-theorisation of female sexuality and its different needs and rhythms. In this at least the work of Marie Stopes which is discussed below (Ch. 10) can be seen as pioneering.

The scientific advances penetrated slowly. Not until 1928 did the Japanese and Hungarian scientists Ogino and Knaus locate the interaction of the menstrual hormones (and hence the 'safe period') and as late as 1937 investigations of the effects of menstruation noted that 'no sustained attempt seems to have been made hitherto to obtain systematic records of . . . psychological and . . . subjective physiological changes which accompany the oestrous cycle in women'.[25] Moreover, it is clear that the medical profession, the main transmitters of scientific knowledge, generally did very little to challenge conservative conceptions of female sexuality, and had very little acquaintance with women's feelings or sexual organs and often tended to reinforce sexual ignorance (which of course they often shared). A striking factor was the general downgrading of the significance of the clitoris to women's sexuality despite an earlier literature on the subject. Even Ellis, who noted its importance, played it down, and Freud's ambivalent recognition of its significance in early female development was used by his less radical followers to develop a normative description of it as a 'vestigial penis'. Not until the work of Masters and Johnson and Mary Jane Sherfey in the 1960s did the concept of the 'clitoral orgasm' become a proper focus of serious sexological writings.[26]

Havelock Ellis and sex research

So the theorisations of the early sexologists were contradictory in their impact and this is clearly demonstrated in the work of Havelock Ellis, the greatest of British writers on sexuality, and during the inter-war years probably the most influential. Born in 1859, the year of Darwin's *Origin of Species*, he was the child of nineteenth-century scientific optimism and simultaneously a rebel against its worship of mechanistic laws. He looked forward to a new Renaissance and was himself a late-Victorian polymath, writer on art, literature, travel, criminology, social policy, as well as sexuality. But it was to the understanding of sex that he devoted the greater part of his energy, for it was here, he believed that 'man's organism' was most severely distorted by ancient prejudice and ignorance. Ellis believed in the existence of an essential and basically healthy human nature which was distorted by modern society. His aim was to find ways of chipping away at the residues of the old, to allow this healthy organism to develop, and so to build on the solid groundwork of natural laws. Alongside this went an almost mystical idealisation of sexuality – a stress which was to be singularly influential on the new texts on married love of the inter-war years.

He wrote in his autobiography that 'I have always instinctively desired to spiritualise the things that have been counted low and material,'[27] and the emphasis on the spiritual and social importance of sex pervades his work. In his popular text book, *The Psychology of Sex*, he offered two reasons why sex should not be regarded as commonplace. Firstly, 'it is not merely the channel along which the race is maintained and built up, it is the foundation on which all dreams of the future world must be erected'. Secondly 'amid the sterilizing tendencies of our life the impulse of sex still remains unimpaired, however concealed or despised'. And he quoted Otto Rank to the effect that sex was a last emotional resource. It was the key to a fulfilling life.[28]

Based on these assumptions, his work sets out to do two related things: to describe the roots of sexual behaviour, and to detail the enormous varieties of its manifestations. And to do this he adopts two approaches which were, in the end ultimately contradictory: a form of cultural relativism to describe the variety; and a biological determinism to provide the explanations. This double approach shaped both the radicalism for the period of many of his beliefs (for example on the importance of female sexuality, or the relative harmlessness of homosexuality and other sexual variations) and the ultimate conservatism of his conclusions (for example, on the family and gender divisions).

To Ellis's mind sexuality was not something to be regarded with horror. It was a powerful force which suffused and enhanced the whole of life.[29] 'Auto-eroticism', a term he coined and the subject of the second published volume of his *Studies*, was, Ellis believed, its prime symptom. Auto-eroticism was defined as the sexual energy of a person automatically generated throughout life and manifesting itself without any definite external stimulation. Its typical manifestation was orgasm during sleep and involuntary emissions, though it also included erotic daydreams, narcissism and hysteria. Like Freud, he was to discuss the sexual origins of many apparently disparate phenomena, from hysteria to kleptomania. Sex did not have a simple pre-ordained goal, and might, indeed, have no obvious aim at all.

In the same way Ellis examined, described, and even named, other non-reproductive forms of sex and sex-related behaviour. Coprophilia, undinism, sadism and masochism, frotage, necrophilia, transvestism (eonism), inversion and many others: all were examined with dispassionate interest and with a wealth of historical and cross-cultural detail.

With his passion as a 'naturalist', he refused to either condone or condemn. This did not mean, however, that Ellis adopted a totally relativistic position. With regard to sexual inversion he argued strongly that if inherent it could not be described as anything more than a biological anomaly, one determined, he eventually believed, by hormonal irregularities. At the same time he felt he could not advise people to go too far outside existing norms of behaviour. Similarly, with regard to heterosexual intercourse, he recognised the harmlessness of such activities as cunnilingus, buggery and fellatio. But overarching all was his fundamental belief – which led him towards eugenics – that there was a biological purpose for sexual activity. So, for instance, marital foreplay, however harmless in itself, became 'abnormal' when it substituted itself for the 'real aims of sexuality' – the act by which the race is propagated.

This however, was the central issue. For he sought to relate all the variations of sexual behaviour to a single process, rooted in the biological make-up of men and women, which he called 'courtship'. Courtship was based on the most primitive acts of the animal world, the sexual conquest of the female of the species by the male. It was the process in which sexual excitement was built up in the partners.

He argued that Darwin's two principles of sexual selection – the aesthetic and the erotic – were basically in contradiction, and held that the erotic impulse was most fundamental. Here he took up Albert Moll's theory that there were two components in erotic attraction each of which were uncontrollable – the impulse of detumescence, which was primarily, like a device to empty a full bladder; and the impulse of contrectation, the instinct to approach, touch and kiss another person. Ellis reshaped these components to produce his own theory of 'tumescence' and 'detumescence'; the processes of arousal and release. Into this were written the differences between the sexes. So tumescence was achieved, 'through much activity and display on the part of the male, and long contemplation and consideration on the part of the female'. These were basic and universal processes. Ellis believed that: 'tumescence and detumescence are alike fundamental, primitive and essential; in resting the sexual impulse on these necessarily connected processes we are basing ourselves on the solid bed rock of nature.'[30] All the so-called 'perversions' and variations were, Ellis believed, distortions of this basic activity as a result of the processes of 'erotic symbolism'. Sadism, for example, was just an exaggeration of the pain inherent in the sexual act itself, while transvestism (sexo-aesthetic inversion) was a result of an exaggerated identification with the object of sexual attraction.

On the one hand, Ellis was clearly suggesting a 'continuum' between 'normal' and 'abnormal' sexual phenomena, an idea which has been of profound importance in modern sexual theory (such as in the works of Alfred Kinsey and his successors, who looked upon Ellis as a central, if innumerate, predecessor). But on the other hand was Ellis's deep conviction that the central element in courtship was the *male* wooing the *female* for the sake of procreation. From this flowed his assumptions about the secondary, essentially responsive nature of female sexuality. Ellis quite clearly rejected the notion that sex could be simply identified with an 'instinct of reproduction', preferring the general term 'impulse' to that of 'instinct', 'for an impulse is not analysed by merely stating the end which it may indirectly effect'.[31] Nevertheless, in the end, he retains what was clearly the dominant metaphor of sex: a broad stream from which there are a number of distributaries rather than the potentially more radical image of a sexuality composed of a number of tributaries, what Freud called the 'component instincts', which work to produce a complex pattern in each human subject.

Ellis's influence must be understood within the terms of the crucial differences between his work and Freud's. We can begin to understand this by looking at the effects of Ellis's work on later theorisations and policies. Firstly, we must grasp his centrality as a major influence in the new psychology, and in the categorisation of sexual variations in general and of homosexuality in particular. His book on *Sexual Inversion* was the first, and for a very long time the only major British contribution to the theoretical classification and definition of homosexuality. Its various revisions reflect the changing theorisations, in particular the contributions of hormonal theories and the even more detailed work of Magnus Hirschfeld.[32] His work on homosexuality prefigured his later work on the definition, classification and construction of a range of sexual variations, culminating in a final volume of the *Studies* in the 1920s which explored 'eonism' (transvestism) and other sex-related phenomena.

Ellis's role in publicising the work of co-workers like Hirschfeld, Freud, Moll and many others is his second major contribution. It not only generalised an awareness of the work being carried on, and the rapid developments taking place, but it also centrally contributed to the categorisation of the various sexual phenomena, and provided the starting point for future work. Few of the significant works on the social significance of sex during the inter-war years fail to mention Ellis. His was the major English-language source on the psychology of sex.

His third major contribution is more difficult to evaluate. Put at its bluntest, it was to formulate a social theory of the family and sexuality, which was to have a significant resonance in the period after the Second World War. From his earliest writings, Ellis was clearly a critic of the Victorian family and the marriage system. He likened contemporary marriage to prostitution, in that it subordinated the wife to the authority and whim of the man. He favoured reform of marriage laws, to include liberal divorce laws, and advocated a 'companionate' or ethical union of two people in which the equal rights of both partners would be respected. He believed that men and women were both 'monogamic' and 'polysexual', so he favoured unions which could accommodate both aspects: committed unions of two people which would be flexible enough to allow outside emotional and sexual involvements. A legal marriage would then become necessary, with the state intervening, only when children were involved.

But simultaneously, Ellis, following many contemporary anthropologists[33] believed in the biological roots of monogamy, and by the 1930s the emphasis on marriage in cementing a monogamous union was more pronounced. He stressed that 'marriage is much more than a sexual relationship'. It was, in fact, in his eyes, the key to social policy, for

it was through the family that the future of the human race could be ensured.[34] What he favoured then, was a marriage partnership which
would allow greater complementarity between the sexes but would not
challenge the centrality of the family, and in so doing Ellis's ideas prefigured many of the arguments on the family and sexuality which were
to become part of the ideology of the post-war welfare state, in its
familial and permissive phases. He was, one might say, a major formu-
lator of liberal sexual ideology and therefore, ultimately, a cautious sex
reformer rather than a sexual radical. He was to become almost a
patron saint of the piecemeal but important sex-reforming efforts of the
1950s and 1960s (a Havelock Ellis Memorial Society was established
then to commemorate his work). But as such his significance as a
moulder of a particular way of looking at sex must be heightened rather
than diminished.

The impact of Freud

At the heart of this ideology was a biologism, the major factor shaping
his work, and this was at the core of his differences with Sigmund
Freud. Havelock Ellis was (alongside F. W. H. Myers of the Society
for Psychical Research) one of the first to introduce Freudian concepts
into British discussions in the 1890s, and the interest was mutual. In the
preface to his *Three Essays on the Theory of Sexuality*, Freud acknowledged 'The remarkable volume of Havelock Ellis'. What followed was
a long dialogue, sometimes sharp and polemical, sometimes coopera-
tive, between the two great contemporaries (they were to die within
months of each other in 1939).[35]
    There were fundamental differences of approach and aim. While
Ellis's life work was quite clearly to describe the social significance of
sex, Freud's major object of study and his greatest discovery was just as
clearly the dynamic 'unconscious'. But the resulting recognition by
Freud of the importance of the sexual drives in the aetiology of neuroses
led him directly into the same field as Ellis. Both writers recognised the
importance of infantile sexuality, for instance, and both stressed the
elements of inter-sexuality between the sexes. But differences erupted
over a number of related themes. Ellis felt that Freud, who borrowed
the term 'auto-eroticism' from him, was misusing it to relate to an instinct directed to the self (that is narcissistically). Freud countered that
Ellis himself was distorting his own term by too freely applying it to
phenomena such as hysteria and masturbation, from which it was con-
ceptually different. There were also deep differences over the nature of
bisexuality. Ellis felt that Freud's theory of the Oedipus complex, as
well as being trans-historical and therefore overemphasised, wrongly
suggested that bisexuality ought to be regarded as the basic state, so that
homosexuality arose through the suppression of the heterosexual element. This opened up the possibility of similarly regarding heterosex-

uality as the product of the suppression of homosexual elements, and Ellis felt this fundamentally undermined his concept of the congenital basis of sexual behaviour. 'If a man becomes attracted to his own sex simply because the fact or image of such attraction is brought before him, then we are bound to believe that a man becomes attracted to the opposite sex only because the fact or image of such attraction is brought before him. Such a theory is unworkable.'[36] If he were to accept these views, he believed, then he would also have to accept that the 'most fundamental' human instinct could equally well be adapted to 'sterility' as to the propagation of the race. Such a view, Ellis believed, would not fit into any 'rational biological scheme'.

This was fundamental to the break Freud's work offered with the tradition that Ellis continued to adhere to. For in Freud, despite his debt to other sexologists, the tendency is to see sexuality not as a pre-given essence but as a drive that is constructed in the process of the development of the human animal. As Juliet Mitchell has put it, 'Instead of accepting the notion of sexuality as a complete, so to speak, ready made thing in itself which could then diverge, he found that "normal" sexuality itself assumed its form only as it travelled over a long and tortuous path, may be eventually, and even then only precariously, establishing itself.'[37] The 'drive' itself, as Freud put it, is 'provisionally to be understood as the psychical representation of an endosomatic, continuously flowing source of stimulation. . . . The concept of instinct is thus one of those lying on the frontier between the mental and the physical.'[38] Consequently, what is repressed in the formation of the unconscious is not biological instinct but wishes/desires, mental representations relating to physical possibilities.

The implications of this are profoundly radical because it basically suggests that what comes into play are the *social* concepts of what is sexual at any given time. If we historicise the notion of sexuality and the Oedipal situation, which is the mechanism through which the laws of society are introjected into the individual (to create a sexed, gendered subject), we can begin to pinpoint the social forces that shape the human conscious and unconscious; and the factors that can change them.

Freud was very aware of the fact of historical change, especially with regard to the importance given to sexuality.

The most striking distinction between the erotic life of antiquity and our own no doubt lies in the fact that the ancients laid the stress upon the instinct itself, whereas we emphasize its object. The ancients glorified the instinct and were prepared on its account to honour even an inferior object, while we despise the instinctual activity in itself and find excuses for it only in the merits of the object.[39]

And in this lay the perception of the culturally necessary but never preordained attainment of the heterosexual norm: 'from the point of view of psycho-analysis the exclusive sexual interest felt by men for women is also a problem that needs elucidating and is not a self-evident fact based upon an attraction that is ultimately of a chemical nature'.[40] But these insights were incorporated into a theory which stressed the cultural and trans-historical necessity for the Oedipal moment, and which pessimistically outlined the relationship between civilisation and repression. Consequently, it has been left to the current generation of Freudians to tease out the more radical perceptions.[41]

At the same time, while, as Juliet Mitchell has persuasively argued, Freud was not simply a patriarchal exponent of female inferiority ('anatomy is destiny' is a description not a prescription), there are ambiguities in his theorisation of the relationship between 'masculinity' and 'femininity' on the one hand and biological maleness and femaleness on the other. In the original (1905) edition of the *Three Essays* he made little play with the distinction between the sexes. But by 1915 he was suggesting that the concepts of 'masculine' and 'feminine' are 'among the most confused that occur in science' and that 'observation shows that in human beings pure masculinity or femininity is not to be found either in a psychological or a biological sense'.[42]

At the heart of Freud's analysis is the distinction he draws between the sexual object and sexual aim. He quite unequivocally argues that there is no automatic development towards a heterosexual love object, nor a pre-ordained goal (intercourse). It was only through the hazardous experiences of childhood, and the difficult imposition of cultural standards through the Oedipal process, that heterosexual intercourse became the individual norm in adulthood. Nevertheless, the relationship between biological characteristics and psychic formations is never clearly worked out.

There was sufficient scope in what he did say, or indeed in what he did not say, because his statements on female sexuality are less certain than on male, for his epigones to develop more conservative theories. These in fact showed a distinct return to the biologism of Freud's contemporaries, including Ellis. Two women Freudians, Karen Horney and Helene Deutsch, in the inter-war years, from different points of view[43] attempting to redress the absences in Freud on femininity, but with different conclusions, converged on the notion of an essential femininity. Horney believed that 'masculine narcissism' made women feel their sex organs to be inferior, and set forth the notion of a 'true nature' denied by a masculine civilisation. Helene Deutsch appears to have accepted the conventional definitions of normal contemporary womanhood. But both shared a concept of the biological origins of sex differences. Horney's views were supported by Ernest Jones, and their belief that the biological division of the sexes was directly reflected in mental life constitutes an important break with Freud's emphasis. Freud emphasised that 'we must keep psychoanalysis separate from biology just as we have kept it separate from anatomy and physiology'. Jones on the other hand, argued that the little girl's femininity 'develops progressively from the promptings of an instinctual constitution'. And 'In the beginning . . . male and female created He them.'[44]

For Jones and Horney there is an innate biological disposition to femininity which is expressed in females. For Freud, on the other hand, as Juliet Mitchell has put it, 'society demands of the psychological bisexuality of both sexes that one sex attain a preponderence of femininity, the other of masculinity: man and woman are *made* in culture'. This was, of course, the source of Ellis's disagreements with Freud, and underlines the strength of the approach in which Ellis was representative. It was this form of biologism that was in fact to dominate the psychoanalytic tradition into the 1960s and 1970s. It must be said, however, that the fact that this could be done owes at least as much to the hesitations of Freud's own approach to female sexuality as to the strength of English biologism.[45]

It was indeed in a fairly bowdlerised form that Freudianism made its main penetration into Britain. Despite the pioneering efforts of Ellis, Myers and convinced Freudians like Ernest Jones (whose collected papers were the best general account of psychoanalysis available in Britain until the publication of the English translation of Freud's *Introductory Lectures on Psychoanalysis* in 1922), it took the First World War to provide an entrée for Freudian concepts. The shell-shock and other psychological disorders, and the disturbance of traditional liberal views on human nature that the war produced, opened the way to new forms of treatment. But the popularisation that resulted led to a dilution of the original ideas. A. G. Tansley's *The New Psychology and its Relation to Life* (1920) went through ten impressions in five years, and did much to spread a biologically orientated form of psychoanalysis. Accounts such as this accepted theories of a dynamic unconscious, the principal mental mechanism (repression, sublimation and so on) and conflict, but Freudian metapsychology and libido theory were rejected. What Hearnshaw has noted as 'the final *bouleversement* of Freudian theory' was exemplified in Suttie's *The Origin of Love and Hate* (1935) in which social, not sexual, love becomes the central force, while neurosis and aggressive hate are outcomes of a 'tenderness taboo' and separation from maternal affection.[46]

Orthodox psychoanalysis never achieved a wide following in Great Britain, despite recruiting a number of distinguished people, such as Ernest Jones and J. C. Flugel. The work of Melanie Klein, with its emphasis on an early Oedipus complex, gained a following, and was very influential in child-developmental theories, but was probably too esoteric to arouse a general interest.[47]

A number of recent writers have commented on the way in which Freudian theory both uncovered the role of sexuality in the unconscious and reinforced its centrality in a normalising fashion through the institutions of psychiatry.[48] In the British tradition, what was reinforced through a variety of social practices was essentially the identity between the biological and the social, between anatomical gender and sexual identity. Through this juncture, Freudian and post-Freudian thought in all its increasingly autonomous streams was strongly to influence social thinking, in various fields from mother–child relations and delinquency to questions of femininity. With regard to sexuality, however, though influencing a number of writers from Ellis onwards, and including sexual reformers such as Alec Craig and Reuben Osborn in the 1930s, it was not until the 1970s that the potentially radical implications of Freud's theories were re-asserted. The problem was not that Freud was buried, but that his work became encrusted with the immensely strong, biologically orientated theories of sexuality that Ellis so admirably represented.

References

1. **Max Hodann**, *History of Modern Morals* (trans. Stella Browne), William Heinemann, London, 1937, p. viii.
2. **J. C. Flugel**, *A Hundred Years of Psychology*, Gerald Duckworth, London, 1953 (1st edn 1933), p. 339; **O. R. McGregor**, *Divorce in England: A Centenary Study*, Heinemann, London, 1957, p. 89.
3. **Richard von Krafft-Ebing**, *Psychopathia Sexualis*, Physicians and Surgeons Book Co., New York, 1931 (a translation of the 12th German edn), p. vi.
4. *Ibid.*, p. 115. The *British Medical Journal*, 1893 (p. 1325) regretted that the whole of the book was not veiled in 'the decent obscurity of a dead language'.
5. Carrington catered for the pornographic rather than the learned side of the trade, but he performed a useful service – for the historian at least. The various semi-pornographic volumes he published by 'Jacobus X', gems such as *Untrodden Fields of Anthropology* (1896), *Crossways of Sex* (1904), *Medico-Legal Examination of the Abuses, Aberrations and Dementia of the Genital Sense* (n.d.), are useful if often inaccurately transcribed guides to current literature. On the sexological framework, see **F. J. Sulloway**, *Freud, Biologist of the Mind*, Burnett Books, London, 1979, pp. 277 ff.
6. See below, p. 181.
7. *British Medical Journal*, 11 January 1908, p. 103.
8. See Foucault, *History*, p. 118.
9. The following discussion is based on the note by **L. L. Bernard** in **E. R. A. Seligman** (ed.), *Encyclopedia of the Social Sciences*, Vol. 8, Macmillan, New York, 1935, pp. 81–3. The concept is also discussed in **Jill Conway**, 'Stereotypes of Femininity in a Theory of Sexual Evolution' in **M. Vicinus** (ed.), *Suffer and Be Still*, University of Indiana Press, Bloomington, 1973, pp. 228–9, footnote 17. See also the note in **David L. Sills** (ed.), *International Encyclopedia of the Social Sciences*, Vol. 7, The Macmillan Co. and The Free Press, New York, 1968, pp. 363–71.
10. L. L. Bernard, *op. cit.*, p. 83.
11. Havelock Ellis summarises this debate in his *Studies in the Psychology of Sex*, Vol. III, *Analysis of the Sexual Impulse*, F. A. Davis, Philadelphia, 1920, pp. 1 ff. On McDougall, see Havelock Ellis's comments in *Psychology of Sex*, London, William Heinemann, 1948, (12th impression), p. 13.

12. Ellis, *Studies*, Vol. III, p. 2. See **Charles Darwin**, *The Descent of Man, and Selection in Relation to Sex*, John Murray, London, 2 Vols, 1871.
13. Geddes and Thomson, *Sex*, p. 148, pp. 162, 185. William McDougall, *An Outline of Abnormal Psychology*, p. 323.
14. Cf. Juliet Mitchell, *Psychoanalysis and Feminism*, p. 16.
15. For the general process the work of Michel Foucault is central: *Madness and Civilisation*, Tavistock, London, 1967; *The Birth of the Clinic*, Tavistock, London, 1973; *Discipline and Punishment*, Allen Lane, London, 1978. For analogous works see **Andrew T. Scull**, *Museums of Madness: The Social Organisation of Insanity in 19th Century England*, Allen Lane, London, 1979.
16. Jill Conway, *op. cit.*, p. 14.
17. **P. Geddes** and **J. Thomson**, *The Evolution of Sex*, Contemporary Science series, London, 1st edn, 1889; see also Conway, *op. cit.* Other titles in the Contemporary Science series, edited by Havelock Ellis, include **Ellis**, *The Criminal*; **Lombroso**, *The Man of Genius*; **J. M. Guyau**, *Education and Heredity*; and **August Weismann**, *The Germ Plasm: A Theory of Heredity*.
18. **W. Blair Bell**, *The Sex Complex; A Study of the Relationships of the Internal Secretions to the Female Characteristics and Functions in Health and Disease*, Baillière, Tindall and Cox, London, 1916, p. 108.
19. **Havelock Ellis**, *Man and Woman*, Contemporary Science series, London, 1894, pp. 440, 448.
20. Geddes and Thomson, *Sex*, pp. 19, 192, 142, 181.
21. For a fuller discussion of this, see **Jeffrey Weeks**, 'Havelock Ellis and the Politics of Sex Reform', in Rowbotham and Weeks, *op. cit.* See also p. 285 below. Freud makes a very similar point to this about lesbianism and 'masculine' characteristics in **Sigmund Freud**, *On Sexuality*, Penguin, Harmondsworth, 1977, p. 53.
22. Ellis, *Studies in the Psychology of Sex*, Vol. 1, Part 2, Random House, New York, 1936, p. 24, 69.
23. See Conway, *op. cit.*, p. 151. I am also indebted to Helen Rugen for information on this point. Early studies of the physiology of the nervous system relied on assumptions of a spermatic economy − so that Brown-Sequard, for instance, in the late nineteenth century, believed injection of ejaculate would build up the body. By the turn of the century the internal secretions came to be perceived of as chemical messengers or hormones, and this allowed a more accurate explanation of the physiology of the sex organs. See also **Alfred C. Kinsey** *et al.*, *Sexual Behaviour in the Human Female*, W. B. Saunders Co., Philadelphia and London, 1953, pp. 716 ff., for an account of the discovery of hormones. For a discussion of the influence of hormonal knowledge, see **Merriley Borell**, 'Organotherapy, British Physioiogy and the Discovery of the Internal Secretions', *Journal of the History of Biology*, Vol. 9, No. 2, Fall 1976, pp. 235−68. For a recent defence of deterministic hormonal theories, see **H. J. Eysenck** and **Glenn Wilson**, *The Psychology of Sex*, Dent, London, 1979; see also review by **Morris Fraser**, 'The Dictatorship of the Hormones', in *New Statesman*, 26 October 1979, p. 639. The question of sex and biology is also discussed in **H. A. Katchadourian** (ed.), *Human Sexuality: A Comparative and Developmental Perspective*, Part II, *Biological Perspectives* (Papers by R. Green, J. M. Davidson, A. E. Ehrhardt). University of California Press, Berkeley, 1979.
24. W. Blair Bell, *op. cit.*, pp. 5, 103; **Havelock Ellis**, 'Feminism and

Masculinism', in *Essays in War Time*, Constable and Co., London, 1916, p. 96; **Magnus Hirschfeld**, *Sexual Anomalies and Perversions*, Torch Publishing Co., London, 1946, p. 37.

25. **R. A. McCance** *et al., Journal of Hygiene*, 1973, p. 572, quoted in **Brian Harrison**, *Separate Spheres: The Opposition to Women's Suffrage in Britain*, Croom Helm, London, 1978, p. 61. Hodann, *op. cit.*, pp. 33–4, summarises the developments of knowledge about the female cycle. The key text for the time under review was **F. H. A. Marshall**, *Physiology of Reproduction*, Longman and Co., London, 1910, which set out to collate ideas and research on the oestrous cycle in females; in this menstruation was still not fully related to ovulation. For appropriation of scientific ambiguity for political (i.e. anti-suffrage) purposes, see **Walter Heape**, *Sex Antagonism*, Constable, London, 1913; **Belfort Bax**, *The Fraud of Feminism*, Grant Richard, London, 1913; **Almroth Edward Wright**, *The Unexpurgated Case Against Female Suffrage*, Constable, London, 1913. But similar scientific views could be used to support suffrage (and separate spheres): see **P. Geddes**, in *Nature*, June 1914, p. 346.

26. For the significance of these later views see below, p. 284. Marshall, *op. cit.*, p. 257, emphasised the importance of the clitoris as a sensitive nerve centre.

27. **Ellis**, *My Life*, William Heinemann, London, 1940, p. 363.

28. Ellis, *Psychology of Sex*, p. 124.

29. For a fuller discussion of these themes see Weeks, 'Havelock Ellis'; and **Paul A. Robinson**, *The Modernisation of Sex*, Elek, London, 1976.

30. Ellis, *Psychology of Sex*, p. 15; *Studies*, Vol. 1, p. 24.

31. Ellis, *Psychology of Sex*, p. 14.

32. See discussion in Weeks, *Coming Out*, Ch. 2.

33. **Elizabeth Fee**, 'The Sexual Politics of Victorian Anthropology', in **M. S. Hartmann** and **Louis Banner**, *Clio's Consciousness Raised*, Harper, New York, 1974. The influence of contemporary anthropology on sexual theory was very important. People like Ellis and Freud quite clearly influenced anthropologists such as Westermark and Malinowski. In turn, writers such as these influenced the sexologists – cf. the influence of Sir James Frazer on Freud's *Totem and Taboo*. **Bronislaw Malinowski**'s study of matriarchal cultures in *Sex and Repression in Savage Society*, 1927, was a major text in the critique of the universality of the Oedipus complex. See **R. Coward**, 'On the Universality of the Oedipus Complex. The Jones—Malinowski Debate', *Critique of Anthropology*, Spring, 1980. Simultaneously, **Robert Briffault**, *The Mothers: A Study of the Origins of Sentiments and Institutions*, 1927 initiated an important debate on matriarchal cultures. For the influence of these debates on W. Reich, E. Fromm and other members of the Frankfurt school, see **Martin Jay**, *The Dialectical Imagination: A History of the Frankfurt School and the Institute of Social Research 1923–50*, Heinemann, London, 1973, pp. 94–5.

34. Ellis, *The Task of Social Hygiene*, p. 102, 'The Renovation of the Family', in Ellis's *More Essays of Love and Virtue*, Constable, London, 1931; *Psychology of Sex*, p.231. For comments on this, see Rowbotham and Weeks, *op. cit.*, pp. 179-80

35. For a useful detailing of the relationship between the two men, see **Vincent Brome**, *Havelock Ellis, Philosopher of Sex*, Routledge & Kegan Paul, London and New York, 1978, pp. 208–24. See also P. Grosskurth, *Havelock Ellis*, Allen Lane, London, 1980, the most comprehensive study.

36. Ellis, *Sexual Inversion*, Random House, New York, 1936, p. 304.
37. Juliet Mitchell, *op. cit.*, p. 11. I am aware that I am on controversial ground here. I do not argue that there are not biologistic overtones in Freud's work; but the *tendency* is towards a different view. I part company with Mitchell on the historical specification of this. See Campioni and Gross, 'Little Hans, The Production of Oedipus', *op. cit.* Cf. Sulloway, *op. cit.*, for a more biological interpretation.
38. **Sigmund Freud**, 'Three Essays on the Theory of Sexuality', in *On Sexuality*, Pelican Freud Library, Vol. 7, Harmondsworth, 1977, pp. 82–3.
39. *Ibid.*, p. 61 footnote.
40. *Ibid.*, p. 57.
41. See footnote 33 to Chapter 1 above. **Michèle Barrett** has a very clear discussion of Freud and sexuality in Ch. 2 of her book, *Women's Oppression Today*, New Left Books, London, 1980.
42. Freud, 'Three Essays . . .', p. 142. On the general point, see Mitchell, *op. cit.*, p. 122.
43. The following is based on Mitchell, *op. cit.*, pp. 125 ff.
44. Quoted in Mitchell, *op. cit.*, p. 131.
45. This point is made strongly in **S. Burniston, Frank Mort** and **Christine Weedon**, 'Psychoanalysis and the Cultural Acquisition of Sexuality and Subjectivity', in Women's Studies Group CCCS, *Women Take Issue*, Hutchinson, London, 1978.
46. **L. S. Hearnshaw**, *A Short History of British Psychology*, Methuen & Co., London, 1964, pp. 167, 239. See **A. G. Tansley**, *The New Psychology and its Relation to Life*, Allen and Unwin, London, 1920; and **I. D. Suttie**, *The Origins of Love and Hate*, Kegan Paul, London, 1935.
47. Hearnshaw, *op. cit.*, p. 239.
48. See for example, Deleuze and Guattari, *Anti-Oedipus*.

Chapter Nine

Feminism and socialism

The emergence of the sex question both theoretically and in terms of social policy, had its corollary in the development of campaigns for sex reform, which was now being constituted as an area for conscious intervention. It is tempting to see these campaigns in terms of a reaction against 'Victorianism', as a breath of fresh air in the stifling conformity of late nineteenth century and Edwardian propriety. This, while not wrong, is potentially misleading. The reformers did not come after, or fight against, a *heritage* of sexual repression. They developed their views contemporaneously with the organisation of the social-purity consensus. Consequently, they often shared a host of similar assumptions. Havelock Ellis could simultaneously desire a libertarian revival of primitive man and lend his support to the National Council of Public Morals, with its potent combination of social purity and eugenics. Marie Stopes could combine a generally conservative outlook with being one of the most influential of reformers in the inter-war years. It is not easy, therefore, to single out a clearly demarcated tradition of sex reform. This and the following chapter attempt to trace out some of the major features of sexual radicalism in the late nineteenth and early twentieth century, with the aim of showing both the continuities with conservative thought and the effort at a more radical rupture.

Feminism and sex reform

It is not conventional to discuss early twentieth-century feminisms[1] in the same context as radical sex reform. Whether happily married, like Mrs Josephine Butler, widowed, like Mrs Emmeline Pankhurst or Mrs Millicent Fawcett, or single, like Frances Cobbe or Christabel Pankhurst, most of the leaders of the various campaigns for women's rights were, despite the calumnies of their opponents, models of late-Victorian rectitude with regard to sexual *mores*. Unlike the early English feminists, such as Mary Wollstonecraft,[2] or French independent women, such as George Sands, few of the later leaders of the women's movement could be frontally attacked for their private lives.

This personal respectability was in part a reflection of their class origins and political aims. The suffrage campaigns particularly were led by women from the upper middle class; their families were usually in business or manufacturing, and their religion was often Quaker or Unitarian. They were generally well educated, by a variety of means, some privately, some in schools. And although a powerful impetus behind the women's movement came from the feelings of redundancy experienced by many middle-class single women, denied worthwhile employment outlets (by 1871 there were 3¼ million single women over 15), many of the leaders were married to professional people (lawyers, doctors, clergymen) or businessmen. The major political struggles reflected these social roots: for tertiary education for middle-class women; entry into the professions; the Vote (and most of even the militant suffragettes were prepared to accept the existing property qualifications). The criticisms of the family were directed at questions such as the denial of female property rights, the legal power of the husband over wife and children, custody and taxation questions, rather than at the validity of the institution itself. These aims dictated caution elsewhere. There was a widespread fear that sexual radicalism would undermine the success of these more relevant campaigns. The London feminists split in the 1870s over the wisdom of openly supporting Josephine Butler's campaign against the Contagious Diseases Acts, though none disagreed with its aims. And respectable suffragists like Mrs Fawcett shunned the company of radicals such as Edward Carpenter.[3] (Conversely, when the anarcho-socialist-feminist Emma Goldman arrived in Britain in the 1920s the first two people she decided to see were Edward Carpenter and Havelock Ellis.) Mrs Fawcett believed it to be Mary Wollstonecraft's 'great merit' that 'she did not sanction any depreciation of the immense importance of the domestic duties of women'.[4] Similarly, Elizabeth Blackwell spoke of 'the very grave national danger of teaching men to repudiate fatherhood, and welcoming women to despise motherhood'.[5] Supporting this was the complete acceptance of the view that human sexuality was naturally different in men and women, and played a much less vital role in the lives of the latter. This was behind the appeal to the moral and spiritual superiority of women that was always a strong undercurrent in suffragist literature.

The acceptance of late-Victorian ideals of respectability by leading women reformers must also be seen in the context of their arguments with the anti-feminists. One of the commonest points put forward by their opponents was distaste at the way the feminists attempted to blur any clear distinction between the sexes. And despite the caution of the feminists on such issues, accusations were made in the late-Victorian parliaments, and at the time of suffragette militancy in 1912–13, that suffragist attitudes to the family were subversive.[6] Christabel Pankhurst's morals might be impeccable and her views on sexuality ultra-'Victorian', but her behaviour was unladylike in the extreme.

This sort of criticism was captured by a female anti-feminist in a book published in 1920, but based on lectures given earlier, *Feminism and Sex Extinction*, by Arabella Kenealy (a member of the Eugenics Education Society). She outlined the classic case against the disruptive effects of women claiming equality with men in the latter's field: 'Nature, marvellously prescient in all her processes, has provided that the sexes, by being constituted wholly different in body, brain and bent, do not normally come into rivalry and antagonism in the fulfilment of their respective life-roles.' But feminism, by introducing conflict and competition into the traditional male spheres, 'menace those most excellent provisions and provisions of nature'. The result was the development of what Kenealy called unnaturally 'mixed types', 'more or less degenerate, structurally, functionally and mentally'. The race is then fatally injured: 'Masculine mothers produce emasculate sons by misappropriating the life potential of male offspring.'[7]

The paradox of this type of diatribe is that it was not far removed, except in rhetorical force, from the theoretical views expressed by men like Havelock Ellis, a pro-feminist, who believed the women's movement was making a wrong turn by concentrating on the suffrage rather than on improving women's special sphere, motherhood.[8] But more than this, few leading feminists would have fundamentally disagreed with the basic analysis about the difference between the sexes. The divisions were over the political consequences that followed from this analysis.

Nevertheless, the very existence of agitation for women's rights did raise vital questions about female sexuality, and in confronting these the feminists can be aligned with more obviously radical strands of thought. Questions of women's role in the family could not be divorced from sexual questions. One participant remembered her 'very frequent discussions with older suffragettes of the more sordid problems of sex . . . And a memory comes of a pallid individual who raised her head from her pillow to whisper that her wedding night had been a dreadful revelation to her. . . . .'

In these campaigns the class lines were breached so that middle-class, university-bred suffragists, 'discovered that whether they sold papers in the streets or canvassed households or addressed meetings, they were certain to have stories of erotic troubles poured out to them by suffering women and not seldom by men.'[9] It was inevitable that feminists would be confronted by such questions as sexual ignorance (not least their own), male brutality in the sex act, problems of divorce and prostitution, and by problems about contraception. In their response two factors came into play: firstly, the question of consent, summed up in the term 'voluntary motherhood'; and secondly the question of the nature of female sexuality, and the related issue of sexual pleasure.

On the first question all feminists were in complete agreement: women should not be mothers against their wills. Here we enter a field of some historical controversy. Early observers of the decline of the birthrate from the 1870s had no doubt in accrediting it to the women's movement, and its alleged devaluing of motherhood. More recently, the work of J. A. and Olive Banks sought to disprove this thesis by examining the actual outpourings of leading feminists, and found little interest in the subject of birth control. Feminists were conspicuously silent over the Bradlaugh–Besant trial in 1877, for instance, and unenthusiastic over neo-Malthusianism.[10] But to see the question purely in terms of support for artificial birth control is to misconstrue the actual complexity of the beliefs and feelings that came into play. What unified all feminists was a desire to ease the burdens of motherhood.[11] They agreed on the right of female self-defence against venereal disease, against overbearing male sexual demands, and excessive pregnancies, and this was summed up in the phrase 'voluntary motherhood'. Voluntary motherhood was a basic challenge to the double standard of morality. But where the division amongst the feminists could take place was over the nature of the controls that should be exercised. Some called for complete chastity; others for periods of abstinence and the exercise of male constraint; some for natural methods of birth control; and some (but few in number before the present century) for artificial contraception. The goal in all cases was the same: for women to gain a degree of control of their own bodies, an ambition prefiguring the more overtly radical feminist demands of the 1970s. But the major factor was that in the late nineteenth century, this demand could as easily lead towards social purity as towards sexual libertarianism.

The principle behind feminist social purity was that men should adopt the high (traditional) moral standards of women. If this were to happen, then sexual restraint and honour in themselves were guarantee of a greater female autonomy. The alternative, the adoption of artificial means of birth control, might actually reinforce the double standard. As Linda Gordon has put it, with specific reference to American experiences but with a similar resonance in Britain, 'Legal, efficient birth control would have increased men's freedom to indulge in extra-marital sex without greatly increasing women's freedom to do so.'[12] The reason for this was the continued economic and social dependence of women within the family. In the absence of alternative avenues for middle-class women, their actual survival often *depended* upon a secure legal marriage. To that extent, viewed cynically, the double standard which sanctified the wife while allowing male extra-marital sexuality via prostitution, was less a threat to women's position than the greater sexual freedom that was promised in artificial birth control, which might lead to the break up of marriages. So, the double standard left most feminists convinced that it was in their interests to increase rather than release the taboos against extra-marital sex, and they quite logically then lent support to the social-purity campaigns.[13]

This raises the second question, on the views taken of their sexuality by feminists, for only in this context can we understand the appeal of social purity. Underlying all was the assumption that just as the sex drive in men was directed towards the achievement of sexual intercourse, the same drive in women only appeared where summoned forth by a much stronger instinct, that of motherhood. A quotation from a sympathetic writer, a generation later, succinctly sums up the general view: 'there are two underlying purposes in the sex relationship. The first is reproductive and is the predominating principle amongst women.... The second purpose is the performance of the sex act, which is the predominating principle in the male.'[14]

The fundamental task for feminists was therefore to protect womanhood from male lusts. Although outwardly on the extreme fringe of feminist propaganda, Christabel Pankhurst' pamphlet *The Great Scourge*, published in 1913 (based on a series of articles published earlier in *The Suffragette*) is a useful index of many feminist views on sexuality. The arguments of this tract were clear enough. Male sexual lust was the real reason why men prevented women getting the vote. Ruling-class men wanted to protect prostitution and the sexual abuse of women. Prostitution wasted the energy and health of men, and sacrificed women on the altar of the double standard.[15] The result was the 'scourge' – venereal disease, inflicted on innocent women, and the great cause of physical, mental and moral degeneracy, and ultimately of 'race suicide'. Sexual disease and social disaster were the result of the subjection of women owing to the 'doctrine that women is sex and beyond that nothing'. The only way out of this male nightmare was for women to get the vote, and enforce chastity and the female standard; hence the double slogan which beats through the pamphlet: 'Votes for women and chastity for men.' The main enemy was the male-orientated 'double standard' of morality. Similar themes to this, despite the overheated and emotive tone, can be traced back at least to the anti-Contagious Diseases Acts and social-purity campaigns of the 1870s and 1880s.

There was another possibility, of course, and that was the development of all-female, lesbian relations. For reasons discussed elsewhere, this was not a likely possibility at this period. Close friendships, even love relationships between women, did exist within the feminist struggle. But very few would have become sexualised, and even fewer would have been declared openly. The most famous lesbian of the inter-war years, Radclyffe Hall, seems to have been totally uninterested in the suffrage struggle.[16]

The real alternatives for most feminists were therefore obvious: either a marriage, where the male partner was clearly a supporter of the single standard (as in the case of Mrs Butler, Mrs Fawcett and many others) and where sexuality was subordinated to the moral claims of marriage; or chastity. Kathlyn Oliver intervened in a debate in the feminist journal *The Freewoman* in early 1912 to state firmly: 'How can we possibly be Freewomen if, like the majority of men, we become the slaves of our lower appetites?' She was thirty years old, unmarried and had 'always practised abstinence'.[17] The alternatives to motherhood were clearly not promiscuity but devotion to the public good, to

Beatrice Webb's 'racial motherhood'. Celibacy was an important political position, moreover. In an article written in 1921 entitled 'Confessions of Christabel: Why I never married', Christabel Pankhurst explained that she had never married, not only because she had never met a man who could live up to her high expectations but because her success as a leader of the women's movement depended upon it. Only by remaining unmarried could she have devoted herself single-mindedly to the cause; nor was this necessarily unfulfilling.[18]

It is at least arguable that few alternatives to chastity did exist for most women before the late nineteenth century. Material factors seriously limited female sexual autonomy. At the most basic level, the opportunities for female work, especially for middle-class ladies, were limited until the expansion of clerical opportunities at the turn of the century.[19] And sexual freedom brought serious risks. Most birth-control devices were unpredictable; abortion was dangerous (and illegal). Until the improvements in the 1900s, conditions for maternity were often unhygienic. And there was the ever-present threat of venereal disease. Not until the 1880s were there any advances in knowledge and control of gonorrhoea; not until the 1900s any advance in the control of syphilis. Overarching all was the ideology, embodied in all the social institutions from Church to Poor Law, that equated bastards and female sex outside marriage with unrespectability. Not until the end of the nineteenth century with the expansion of female work opportunities and scientific breakthroughs were the pre-conditions existing for any feminists to feel free in claiming the right to sexual pleasure as opposed to female autonomy from men. It was inevitable that most feminists would work within traditional frameworks. Marie Stopes, because she became so prominent, will serve as an example of the complex factors at work. Born of progressive parents in 1880, her mother a suffragist, she was given no sex education. Her father brought her up to believe that no nice girl would think of marriage before she was 25. Although a scientist, and an independent woman, she remained, out of ignorance, a virgin throughout her first marriage. She was 37 years old, as she bitterly complained, before she experienced intercourse. And she was still a virgin when she wrote her immensely influential book, *Married Love*. Moreover, throughout her life she remained hostile to 'free love' and homosexuality. One of the formative sex reformers of the inter-war years, she was a product, nevertheless, of a conservative sexual-political formation.[20]

Ostensibly more radical voices were occasionally raised. In the early 1890s the 'fiction of sex and the new woman' caused something of a sensation.[21] Grant Allen, with his notorious novel, *The Woman Who Did*, is the most familiar name today, but there were many others – Sarah Grand, 'Iota', George Egerton, Emma Frances Brooke and Mona Caird. The heroines depicted by these popular novelists were 'new women' in the sense that all rejected some features of the conventional female role. They all employed a new degree of frankness about sexual behaviour, and recognised that women had to be freed from the constricting male middle-class view of femininity, though none questioned the existence of fundamental differences. But only Mona Caird, in *The Daughters of Danaus*, went so far as to challenge the 'maternal instinct'. The heroine, Hadria, reflected that throughout history: 'children had been the unfailing means of bringing women into line with tradition. An appeal to the maternal instinct had quenched the hardiest spirit of revolt. No wonder the instinct had been so unimpeded and exalted!'[22]

Some of these themes were taken up in a radical way in the small magazine *The Freewoman* (later *New Freewoman*) in the years 1911–13.[23] This showed a lively interest in female sexuality and opened its pages to controversy on the subject. It carried articles on the relative strength of the male and female sex drives, menstruation and even female homosexuality. One of its contributors was F. W. Stella Browne, an ardent feminist, socialist, pioneer birth controller and later advocate of abortion law-reform, who had replied to Kathlyn Oliver's conservative views in 1912.[24] It was precisely a woman's right to control her own body that involved her, but this included sexual freedom.

In a paper read at a meeting of the British Society for the Study of Sex Psychology in October 1915, she rejected the idea that women have no strong, spontaneous and 'discriminating' sex impulse, and that their sexual life is subordinated to the male. She defended masturbation and questioned whether 'great love is the sole justification of sexual experience'. She also denied that a woman's sex could be equated with maternal instincts. She thus explicitly raised the separation of sex from procreation. With regard to lesbianism, she followed Ellis in arguing that normal sexuality includes the beginnings of most 'abnormal instincts', and felt that society should begin to recognise the 'vital, very often valuable' role of homosexuality in civilisation (thus echoing Edward Carpenter). But, following Ellis again, she makes a sharp distinction between what she sees as 'artificial' inversion, acquired through temporary influences, and 'true' inversion, firmly believed to be congenital. 'Artificial or substitute' homosexuality was, she felt, widely diffused amongst women, 'as a result of the repression of normal gratification and the segregation of the sexes which still largely obtains'. She felt that the suppression of desires and the delay of marriage would encourage homosexuality. Congenital homosexuality was acceptable because unavoidable, but the same was not true for 'artificial' homosexuality: 'I repudiate all wish to slight or depreciate the love-life of the real homosexual; but it cannot be advisable to force the growth of that habit in heterosexual people.'[25] In adopting this abstract division between congenital 'inversion' and artificial 'perversion', Stella Browne was contradicting that exploration of the 'great plasticity of women's sex impulse' which she had earlier suggested. But for the period this was extraordinarily radical. Similar themes occur in the works of other contemporary feminists, of which the best known was the South African novelist, Olive Schreiner. Influenced both by Ellis and Edward Carpenter, with both of whom she was on close personal relations, Schreiner's work was clearly within the feminist radical tradition which, while recognising 'inherent differences' dictated by reproductive divisions and hence the rationale of separate functions, stressed the importance of female eroticism in its own (not male) terms.[26] Such a stress looked forward to the 'new feminism' of the inter-war years rather than back to the older tradition. It was an important but significantly minority response.

The morals of socialism

Most of the explicitly radical writers on sexuality (including feminists like Browne) were, in one way or another, socialists. But this did not mean that most socialists during this period had radical views on sexuality. The criminologist and sex reformer, George Ives, observed in 1904 that:

There is a curious kind of 'Socialism' in this country, which is allied with Christianity and even with Grundyism. That, to my mind, is more hateful than the present order. The socialism to which I belong, and to which solid millions adhere on the Continent, refuses all compromises with the religious parties, all compromises with existing sexual morality, all compromises with the class system in any shape.[27]

The two traditions, a sexual radicalism on the one hand, and either an indifference or an ascetic moralism on the other, coexisted uneasily, and meant that the socialist movement made no attempt to direct the movement for radical sex reform. It was, as Ives suggested, often implicated in delaying it, and this was despite a long alternative tradition.

Engels had noted a 'curious fact'; 'a phenomenon common to all times of great agitation, that the traditional bonds of sexual relations, like all other fetters, are shaken off'.[28] And indeed all great popular movements, from the English revolution of the seventeenth century, through the French Revolution to the Bolshevik revolution of the twentieth century have seen fundamental questioning of attitudes towards marriage, divorce, contraception and sexuality. These major movements of consciousness have had their echoes, on a smaller scale, in the groups, sects, and later, perhaps, mass movements of radicals and socialists who have aspired towards a similar social transformation. The 'New Moral World' aimed at by the English Owenites of the 1830s and 1840s looked forward to the abolition of all relations of power and subordination, including not only those of capitalists over workers, but also those of parent over children and men over women. The feminism of the Owenites was inherited from the eighteenth-century advocates of *egalité*, and rested on the abstract rights of all reasonable creatures to self-determination. And feminism was closely associated with social insurrection, particularly after the publication, and hostile reception, of Mary Wollstonecraft's *A Vindication of the Rights of Women*, which was hailed by the working-class movement as a major radical text. Taking up the themes set forth there, William Thompson and Anna Wheeler's *Appeal of One Half the Human Race* (1825), written in response to the Benthamites' failure to support women's suffrage, advocated the abolition of private property and the patriarchal family.[29] During the 1830s and 1840s hundreds of radical books, tracts, lectures and newspapers discussed everything from collective childcare in new communities to the phrenological evidence for women's innate superiority. Large meetings were held during the same period to discuss Owenite opposition to Christian marriage doctrine. Robert Owen set forth his own rejection of conventional marriage, to be replaced by collective living arrangements, in his *Lectures on the Marriages of the Priesthood of the Old Immoral World* in 1835, and working-class Owenites took up many of these ideas, often performing their own form of marriage service outside the traditional rites.[30] There were limitations to the radicalism of the experiments – men were not, for instance, expected to share the child rearing – but these early socialists looked forward to new ways of living together, and saw socialism as involving a total transformation, and this remained a vital undercurrent.

The other major current of socialists, that of Marx and Engels, generally rejected such utopianism. They were not, of course, primarily concerned in their writings with issues of sexuality, but nevertheless there is clear evidence, at least in their early work, of the influence of the French utopian socialist, Charles Fourier.[31] They did not follow him in his advocacy of various forms of consensual sex – including lesbianism, pederasty and flagellation – but Marx, in his *Economic and Philosophical Manuscripts* of 1844, had echoed Fourier in his belief that the sexual relation of men and women 'reveals the extent to which man's *natural* behaviour has become *human* . . . the extent to which he in his individual existence is at the same time a social being.'[32]

Marx and Engels saw monogamy as a great historical advance, though one which, like all advances, was contradictory. On the one hand, the ideology of monogamy stressed individual choice. But on the other, it reinforced private property in the hands of the male and was monogamy for the woman rather than the man. But from monogamy stemmed, as Engels put it in his *The Origin of the Family, Private Property and the State*, 'the greatest moral advance which we derive from and owe to monogamy . . . namely, modern individual sex love, previously unknown to the whole world'.

What Marx and Engels inherited from the utopian tradition was a classic belief in the all-embracing nature of true love between men and women. Sex love had a degree of intensity and duration which made both lovers feel that non-possession and separation were a great, if not the greatest calamity. This sex love had been distorted by commodity production, particularly because of the double standard, but would flourish on a higher plane under socialism, so that 'monogamy, instead of declining, finally becomes a reality, for the men as well'.[33]

Of course, as a historical materialist, Engels left open the possibility that monogamy as an historical product could just as easily disappear under socialism as survive and flourish, but he generally opted for the belief that individual sex love was such a strong inherent force that it would inevitably become dominant in a future society, freed of artificial restrictions. 'Since sex love is by its very nature exclusive – although this exclusiveness is only fully realised today in the woman – then marriage based on sex love is by its very nature monogamous.'[34]

This did not, however, mean bourgeois monogamy, for sex love could not, by its very nature, be fixed or immutable. What would disappear with private property and its corollary male dominance would be 'the indissolubility of marriage'. Beyond this Engels could not go: it was left to the future society to work out the consequences of the liberation of sex love. What does become clear, however, in the few throwaway remarks he makes on the subject, is that true sex love could not, by definition, embrace non-heterosexual relations. Homosexuality is abhorred by Engels, its expressions seen as 'gross, unnatural vices', a symptom of the failure of sex love, and the degradation of women.[35] It would have been extraordinary in the early 1880s, when the exploration of homosexuality was still in its infancy, had Engels thought otherwise. It represents, nonetheless, a failure to explore the social and historical determinants of sexual and emotional behaviour which underlines another key assumption. Engels, following contemporary views, assumed that the 'personal' was natural and given, and that once the constraints of a society dominated by the pursuit of profit were removed, private life would spontaneously adjust itself to a higher stage of civilisation. There is no concept, that is, of the need for conscious struggle to transform interpersonal relations as part of the transformation necessary for the construction of a socialist society. Within the materialist schema, 'natural man' still flourished.

Marx and Engels' immediate circle, while not ardent sex radicals or feminists as such, supported progressive campaigns. Eleanor Marx, Karl's youngest daughter, was firm that her union with Edward Aveling was a proper marriage and not a free union, unsealed by the law only because of Aveling's previous undissolved marriage. But she was friendly with the young Havelock Ellis, and her commitment to women's emancipation within the context of a socialist transformation was unequivocal.[36]

This was not, unfortunately, true of most of the English 'supporters' of her father's ideas. H. M. Hyndman, the leader of the largest British Marxist organisation, the Social Democratic Federation, between the 1880s and 1914, believed that 'the revolution' was imminent because of the inevitable breakdown of capitalism. All meaningful reforms, consequently, had to await the revolution. He affected to despise those movements which had grown up within capitalism, such as the trade unions

and feminism, as diversions, and would have nothing to do with Engels'
analysis of the family. Behind this was an elevation of women's traditional sphere which can be traced back to the long line of English moralists, through Thomas Carlyle and John Ruskin, and which was to
have its impact on greater Marxists than Hyndman, such as William
Morris.[37] Hyndman, not surprisingly, refused to have any truck with
the suffrage movement, or to interest himself in questions of prostitution or birth control. For Hyndman socialism meant subordination to
the laws of history, and little else: 'I do not want the movement to be a
depository of old cranks, humanitarians, vegetarians, anti-vivisection-
ists, arty-crafties and all the rest of them, we are scientific socialists and
have no room for sentimentalists. They confuse the issue.'[38]

The Marxist philosopher, E. Belfort Bax, shared many of Hyndman's positions and was even more bitterly hostile to the women's
movement and to suffrage than Hyndman. He issued what can only be
described as a series of diatribes against 'The Everlasting Female'. He
blamed the 'new woman's' fear of 'blacklegs' for the outburst of social
purity in the 1880s: 'The Puritan has never learnt to distinguish between
the sacred and the mournful', leading to an overemphasis on the 'quasi-
sacred character of sex'.[39] But as this suggests, his anti-feminism went
with what on the surface, at least, appears to be a curiously liberal attitude to sex. He observed that: 'The root of the whole matter is that we
attach far too much importance to the mere act of copulation *per se*',
and this was because of fear of pleasure and our mortification of the
flesh. But as the aim of socialism was satisfaction of the individual, so,
'satisfaction, not repression, affirmation, not negation, must be our
ethical sheet anchors'.[40]

This leads to a remarkably advanced position on 'sexual offences' in
his book *The Ethics of Socialism*: 'We must be careful in considering
such offences, to eliminate the element of brutality or personal injury
which may sometimes accompany them, from the offence itself. For the
rest I confine myself to remarking that this class also . . . springs from
an instinct legitimate in itself, but which has been suppressed or distorted.' And he goes on to question, with regard to homosexuality,
'whether morality has anything at all to do with a sexual act, committed
by the mutual consent of two adult individuals, which is productive of
no offspring, and which on the whole concerns the welfare of nobody
but the parties themselves.'[41]

This was very close on the surface to the position adopted in the German Social Democratic Party (SPD) which in its theories (based on
August Bebel's investigation of the position of women[42]) and in its
practice (particularly illustrated in Edward Bernstein's materialist
analysis of the Oscar Wilde case[43]) was, as George Ives suggested, far in
advance of the British Marxist movement. Leading Social Democrats
such as Bernstein and Karl Kautsky were very responsive to the new insights of sexologists like Hirschfeld (himself a Social Democrat). Bernstein had warned his fellow socialists that:

Although the subject of sex life might seem of low priority for the economic and political struggle of the Social Democracy, this nevertheless does not mean it is not obligatory to find a standard also for judging this side of social life, a standard based on a scientific approach and knowledge, rather than on more or less arbitrary moral concepts.'[44]

But in the case of Bax, the liberal attitude to sex was vitiated by his fanatical opposition to women's emancipation, on the grounds that the woman was the embodiment of sex, and therefore disqualified from the world of men. Without such emancipation, however, sex reform could as easily lead to reinforcement of the double standard as to its undermining:[45] greater freedom for the male might well involve greater vulnerability for the woman.

In the absence of a strong materialist approach on sexuality, the initiative fell to an older moralistic tradition, bordering at times on asceticism. An exchange the socialist pioneer Edward Carpenter had with Robert Blatchford, editor of the socialist paper the *Clarion*, in the early 1890s points to the difficulties. Blatchford had defended Carpenter, who trailed a whiff of notoriety behind him, and even urged readers to study his works on women. But when Carpenter wrote to Blatchford in late 1893 suggesting that he write on sexual matters, the latter replied: 'I am a radical but . . . the whole subject is nasty to me.' And he underlined his point: 'Now, you speak of writing things about sexual matters, and say that these are subjects which socialists must face. Perhaps you are right, but I cannot quite see with you.'

To justify this, Blatchford put forward arguments which enjoyed a very long currency. First he held that reform of sexual relations would follow industrial and economic change. If this was so, then, secondly, anything which inhibited economic change would also hinder sexual change. And as sex reform was unpopular, it would be best not to raise it at present. 'I think that the accomplishment of the industrial change will need all our energies and will consume all the years we are likely to live.' As a result, sex reform will 'not concern us personally, but can only concern the next generation'.[46] The logic of this was not to do anything, and in this Blatchford's position was a representative one.

Some socialists went further and believed that in a future society the individual would escape the prison of the flesh altogether. We have already noted the views of some leading Fabians (see above p. 134). But even those of a self-consciously militant politics shared much the same outlook. The Glasgow socialist, Guy Aldred, looked forward in 1906 to the day when celibate comradeship would replace the sensuality of existing sexual relations, and in representatively eugenic tones stated as 'a psychological and physiological fact that the tendency of the race, in proportion as it becomes more truly intellectual, is away from sexual passion'.[47] (He was to change his mind later, and become conspicuous as a supporter of artificial birth control in the 1920s.)

The exponents of a more radical, libertarian sexual politics were therefore few in numbers in the late nineteenth century. The outstanding exception was Edward Carpenter, undoubtedly the most significant influence on the next generation of sex reformers. His politics looked back to the conception of the earliest socialists, of socialism as not just a transformation of economic relations but as a whole new way of life. And fundamental to this was his belief that a transformation of ways of living now was a precondition of new socialist relations. Hence his espousal of all those things that Hyndman had dismissed: simple living, dress reform, vegetarianism, mysticism, feminism and homosexual reform. He himself was a homosexual who lived, for the period, a remarkably open life. At the same time, his ideas were informed by the most advanced ideas on sex. He learnt his sexual theories from his friend Havelock Ellis (whom he had met at the socialist Fellowship of the New Life in the 1880s); from German writers such as Otto Weininger, Adolf Brandt and Magnus Hirschfeld; from Lamarckian notions; from Eastern mysticism; and from Western poetry, particularly Walt Whitman whose (only slightly veiled) advocacy of masculine love had inspired Carpenter in his early days. In intellectual terms this eclecticism makes much of his writings appear dated now, but its critique of bourgeois morality, his belief that 'civilisation' stunted natural possibilities and his advocacy of freer sexual relations, was a potent influence in the late nineteenth and early twentieth centuries.[48]

Although an active supporter of feminism and a popular speaker (and organiser) for socialism from the 1880s, it was only in the 1890s as a result of both personal and political changes that he brought together these concerns with a discussion of directly sexual matters.

In 1894 the Manchester Labour Press published an essay by Carpenter on *Homogenic Love and its Place in a Free Society*. By 1895 he had prepared a large-scale work entitled *Love's Coming of Age*, which covered the range of problems in the relationship between the sexes, but had deliberately omitted the chapter on 'Homogenic Love'. Nevertheless, as its author he was immediately caught up in the aftermath of the Wilde affair. Carpenter's publisher, T. Fisher Unwin, withdrew from publication of the book, and Carpenter reported a panic concerning homosexuality in London: 'the "boycott" has set in already. Isn't it a country.'[49] The Labour Press stepped into the breach, so gaining the credit for publishing one of the major radical tracts on sexuality of the late nineteenth century. This was followed by a number of related works, chiefly on homosexual themes, including *The Intermediate Sex*, an expansion of that earlier essay, in 1908.[50]

What distinguishes Carpenter from most of his contemporaries is his willingness to separate sex from procreation, and this had important implications for women as well as homosexuals. He argued in *Love's Coming of Age* that public opinion had been largely influenced 'by the arbitrary notion that the function of love is limited to child bearing; and that any love not concerned in the propagation of the race must necessarily be of dubious character'.[51] Against this, Carpenter stressed the pleasurable nature of sex and its function as a binding fact in social relations; its prime object, as he put it, was *union*. And although he was anxious to stress that emotional love could be transmitted into spiritual, he emphasised that the physical must never be forgotten: without it the 'higher' things can never be realised. His aim was thus to free love from darkness and shame, and to place sex in the vital heart of the new awareness.

For Carpenter, 'Uranians' formed an 'intermediate sex' as bearers of the sexual characteristics of one sex and many of the emotional characteristics of the other: he was thus in the same tradition as many German writers, such as Otto Weininger, as well as, to a lesser extent, Ellis. But whereas Ellis spoke of 'hormones' and used a scientific framework, Carpenter's classification have an almost metaphysical air: 'Nature . . . in mixing the elements which go to compose each individual, does not always keep her two groups of ingredients – which represent the two sexes – properly apart.'[52]

He accepted a theory of sexuality which saw the two sexes as forming in 'a certain sense a continuous group' and he felt that there were many signs of an evolution of a new human type which would be 'median' in character, neither excessively male nor excessively female. Bisexuality might thus become the norm of a new society. He broke away to a large degree from the positivistic and biological model that Ellis favoured, and in his philosophy saw not only a case for toleration of homosexuals, but a positive moral value. He saw 'Uranians' as communicators and reconcilers, bridging the gap between men and women, becoming to a great extent 'the interpreters of men and women to each other', and a 'forward force in human evolution'.[53]

Carpenter's work, like most contemporary views on sexuality, was nevertheless constrained by its devotion to biological assumptions. Carpenter naturally assumed that the division of labour between the sexes was based on inherent biological qualities in men and women, and he agreed with Ellis's analysis in *Man and Woman* that women were more primitive, emotional, intuitive and closer to nature than men. Carpenter believed, however, that society had unnecessarily exaggerated sex differences. For this reason, he argued in *Love's Coming of Age* for the economic and social independence of women, which could only come with the end of the 'commercial system'; for reform of marriage, involving a greater emphasis on spiritual rather than sexual loyalty; and for the central importance of birth control for women. His views on birth control are particularly revealing, especially given the inadequacy of most mechanical methods at the time. He recommended 'Karezza', a method then currently advocated by his American publisher, Mrs A. B. Stockham, which favoured prolonged bodily conjunction between the sexes without orgasmic emission.

Like Ellis's more philosophical efforts, there is a tendency in Carpenter towards emphasising the spiritual. So while he did not, as we have seen, deny the physical, there is a strong moral element in his work which wants to make the purely physical a secondary issue. Carpenter's friend Charles Oates commented that the women he knew were 'either profoundly indignant or highly sarcastic' in response to Carpenter's views, and the very ambivalence of his work caused a mixed response. The radical journal, *The Adult*, criticised him for his devotion to monogamic views, while his friend Kate Joynes, felt there was a 'clergyman's vein' in some of his arguments about sex. More conservative feminists were, however, appalled at the frankness of his arguments, as were many socialists.[54]

Carpenter, who was in many ways a very radical character, was compelled by his beliefs to practise 'propaganda by deed', to live the life that he advocated. So, to a large degree, he was open as a homosexual. By the 1890s many of his friends in the labour movement knew of his homosexuality, though he was always careful to be discreet with a wider public. Inevitably his public position imposed enormous strains. His socialist propagandising of the 1880s was constantly bedevilled by his emotional conflicts. Later, as a major public figure, he was to find his fame a strain in itself. What Edward Carpenter sought above all was a close relationship which would be the focus of a 'body of friends'. It was not until the 1890s that, in his relationships with George Merrill, a young man of working-class origins, he was to find such a focus.

It was a relationship that was to last from their first meeting in the 1890s until Merrill's death in 1928, and was to provide each with necessary emotional support. Not all his friends approved; but others saw Millthorpe, their house near Sheffield, as a focus for that combination of sexual freedom and socialist ideals that they aspired to.[55]

Carpenter's achievements must not be exaggerated. There was a fundamental vagueness in his work, which in part at least accounts for his ambivalent impact on later generations. In Carpenter's total work, the writings on sexuality were part of a radical critique of the values of capitalist 'civilisation'. But the actual emphasis on the personal in his writings on sexuality could easily be detached from the broader context. His work was quietly absorbed, for instance, into the Bloomsbury emphasis on personal relationships, and inserted, through a process of influence and then rejection, into the sexual dialectic of D. H. Lawrence, whose influence was quite oppositional to Carpenter's.[56] But it was in the labour and socialist movements that his influence was most incalculable and ambiguous. His work was clearly and passionately taken up by many feminists and socialists at home and abroad. And when the British Society for the Study of Sex Psychology was established in 1914, Carpenter was the obvious choice as its president.

In the wider labour movement, Carpenter's influence in 'making socialists' must have been vast, especially amongst those who saw socialism as a 'religion' and a new way of relating.[57] But to what degree his sexual radicalism was absorbed is another matter. By the turn of the century, the socialist movement – with its emphasis on the trade unions and parliamentary representation – was already quite different from the millenarian groupings that Carpenter had known in the 1880s, and class politics, as they developed in the complex aftermath of the First World War, had little space for Carpenter's type of sexual radicalism. Nevertheless, his stress that socialism meant a fundamental transformation in all relationships, including sexual ones, has been an important undercurrent in the socialist tradition and one that has reappeared in the revival of Western socialist practice since the late 1960s. Carpenter, however dated his prescriptions, remains one of the outstanding exponents of these necessary connections.

Even before his death, in 1929, however, Carpenter's aspirations seemed part of a different world. The labour movement as a whole was constrained by different demands, and its official leaders were reluctant to take up what were defined as irrelevant – not to say, scandalous – questions. The same was true of the alternative Leninist tradition in Britain. Soviet Russia was after 1918 far in advance of Germany and the Anglo-Saxon countries in terms of sex reform. But the Communist Party of Great Britain was only peripherally interested in issues such as birth control from the 1920s, and apparently not concerned at all with other issues of sex reform.[58] The sexual radicals within the Party in the early 1920s, including Stella Browne and the Pauls, attempted to raise such questions but with little obvious success. Maurice Eden Paul continued into the 1930s to develop theories of marriage, the family and sex reform, but usually within a somewhat esoteric theoretical framework which had little practical influence.[59] Stella Browne seems to have left the Party precisely because of its lack of interest in sex reform, devoting herself in the 1920s to campaigns for birth control and abortion.[60] The Party itself saw sex reform as essentially a secondary matter.

A number of radical intellectuals attempted to combine Marx and Freud in the 1930s, on the model, but without the intellectual strength, of the contemporary Wilhelm Reich and the Frankfurt school (Herbert Marcuse and Erich Fromm particularly). Alec Craig's *Sex and Revolution*, published in 1934, is a useful survey of the need for sex reforms, and a discussion of the advances in the Soviet Union (reforms, alas, soon to be abrogated there). The framework is that biologistic Freudianism very common at the time.[61] Reuben Osborn attempted a similar synthesis in two books in the 1930s, *Freud and Marx* (1937) and *The Psychology of Reaction* (1938).[62] Despite interesting insights, the works are marred by Osborn's loyalty to the Soviet model which produced propaganda rather than analysis. The latter book ends with an attack on Trotsky's maliciousness, 'sustained by strong unconscious drives of a narcissistic character' compared to the remarkable 'stability of character' shown by Stalin.[63] The synthesis of the insights of Marx and Freud, which in the Central European tradition promised new insights into sexual behaviour, was a thin stream in the British school of sexual radicalism.

References

1. I hold to the view that there is not a single feminism which can be simply defined. What unifies feminism is the belief in the necessity for greater autonomy from, and equality with, the male population – economic, legal, political, social and sexual. But within this there is a diversity on class, regional, policy and even generational grounds.
2. For whom see **Margaret Walters**, 'The Rights and Wrongs of Women: Mary Wollstonecraft, Harriet Martineau, Simone de Beauvoir', in Mitchell and Oakley, *The Rights and Wrongs of Women*; **Clare Tomalin**, *The Life and Death of Mary Wollstonecraft*, Penguin, Harmondsworth, 1977. *A Vindication of the Rights of Women* was published in 1792.
3. Bertrand Russell recounted an anecdote of Mrs Fawcett refusing to talk to Carpenter during a suffrage conference in Edinburgh because of his writings on homosexuality: quoted in Rowbotham and Weeks, *Socialism and the New Life*, p. 117. On surplus women, see **J. A. Banks** and **O. Banks**, *Feminism and Family Planning*, Liverpool University Press, 1964, p. 27. More boys than girls were born, but by the age of 15 the balance was redressed (differential mortality, migration, etc.).
4. **M. Fawcett**, *Mary Wollstonecraft* (1891), pp. 22–3, quoted in **Constance Rover**, *Love, Morals and the Feminists*, Routledge and Kegan Paul, London, 1970, p. 53.
5. Quoted in J. A. and Olive Banks, *Feminism and Family Planning*, p. 93.
6. **Brian Harrison**, *Separate Spheres: The Opposition to Women's Suffrage in Britain*, Croom Helm, London, 1978, p. 56.
7. **Arabella Kenealy**, *Feminism and Sex Extinction*, T. Fisher Unwin, London, 1920, p. vi, p. vii, p. 74, p. 73.
8. Havelock Ellis, *The Task of Social Hygiene*, p. 75. Ellis was an enthusiastic defender of the work of the Swedish feminist Ellen Key, whose work he introduced into Britain, and who was an ardent advocate of new policies for motherhood; see **Ellen Key**, *The Century of the Child*, G. P. Putnam's Sons, London, 1909; and *Love and Marriage* (with a Critical and Biographical Introduction by Havelock Ellis), G. P. Putnam's Sons, London, 1911.
9. **Wilma Meikle**, *Towards a Sane Feminism*, Grant Richards, London, 1916, p. 83.
10. J. A. and O. Banks *op. cit.*, p. 92, and *passim*; Constance Rover, *Love, Morals and the Feminists*, Routledge and Kegan Paul, London, 1970, p. 98.
11. McLaren, *Birth Control in Nineteenth Century England*, p. 198, develops this argument with great cogency. I am also indebted to Martha McIntyre, whose paper on feminist attitudes to sexuality delivered at the Communist University of London 1977 I found very stimulating.
12. **Linda Gordon**, *Woman's Body, Woman's Right: A Social History of Birth Control in America*, Penguin, Harmondsworth, 1976, p. 110.
13. *Ibid.*, p. 113. It must be said, though, that many feminists, like Josephine Butler, recoiled from the full logic of repressive social purity.
14. **Edward F. Griffith**, *Sex and Citizenship*, Victor Gollancz, London, 1941, p. 148. It would be truer to point out that the female cycle is much less closely related to procreation than male ejaculation.
15. **Christabel Pankhurst**, *The Great Scourge*, E. Pankhurst, London, 1913,

p. vi. See also **Andrew Rosen**, *Rise Up, Women!*, Routledge and Kegan Paul, London, 1974, pp. 206–7.

16. See Chapter 6 above, and Weeks, *Coming Out*, Chs 7–9.
17. *The Freewoman*, 15 February 1912, p. 252; also 22 February 1912, p. 270.
18. Quoted in **David Mitchell**, *Queen Christabel: A Biography of Christabel Pankhurst*, Macdonald and Jane's, London, 1977, pp. 283–4. The article was published in the *Weekly Dispatch*, April 1921.
19. See **Lee Holcombe**, *Victorian Ladies at Work*, Archon, Hamden, Conn., 1973.
20. **Ruth Hall**, *Marie Stopes, A Biography*, Virago, London, 1978.
21. **A. R. Cunningham**, 'The "New Women" Fiction of the 1890's', *Victorian Studies*, Vol. XVII, No. 2, December 1973.
22. Quoted in *ibid.*, p. 183. Mona Caird saw the importance of neo-Malthusianism. 'If the new movement had no other effect than to rouse women to rebellion against the madness of large families, it would confer a priceless benefit on humanity.' Quoted in J. A. and O. Banks, *op. cit.*, p. 101.
23. For a general discussion of *The Freewoman* and its evolution, see **J. H. Lidderdale** and **M. Nicholson**, *Dear Miss Weaver*, Faber and Faber, London, 1970. Dora Marsden in the issue for 23 November 1911, p. 3, summed up the aims of the paper. 'Our interest is in the Freewoman herself, her psychology, philosophy, politics and economics.' I am grateful to Helen Rugen for information on this journal.
24. **Sheila Rowbotham**, *A New World for Women. Stella Browne: Socialist Feminist*, Pluto, London, 1977.
25. **F. W. Stella Browne**, *The Sexual Variety and Variability Among Women*, BSSP, London, 1916, p. 12. This has been reprinted in Rowbotham, *op. cit.*, pp. 91–105. It ends with a specific reference to the importance of eugenics.
26. For **Olive Schreiner**, see her *Woman and Labour*, Virago, London, 1978, Ch. V (first published by T. Fisher Unwin, 1911); and **Ruth First** and **Ann Scott**, *Olive Schreiner*, Andre Deutsch, London, 1980. See also **Catherine Gasquoine Hartley**, *The Truth About Women*, Eveleigh Nash, London, 1913. For brief description of other feminists who did take up the sex question, see Rowbotham and Weeks, *op. cit.*, p. 118; and J. Weeks, *Coming Out*, pp. 101–3. Other feminists involved in advanced discussions included Teresa Billington-Greig, founder of the Women's Freedom League, who broke away from the authoritarian WSPU; Edith How-Martyn; and Charlotte Despard. For earlier feminists with unconventional lives, see Walkowitz, *Prostitution and Victorian Society*, p. 123.
27. George Ives to Janet Ashbee, 15 February 1904: *Ashbee Journals*, King's College, Cambridge.
28. **Karl Marx** and **Friedrich Engels**, *On Religion*, Moscow, 1957, p. 329.
29. **Barbara Taylor**, 'The Men Are as Bad as Their Masters . . ., Socialism, Feminism and Sexual Antagonism in the London Tailoring Trades in the Early 1830's', *Feminist Studies*, Vol. 5, No. 1, Spring 1979, pp. 9, 10, 11.
30. *Ibid.*, p. 12; **Sheila Rowbotham**, *Hidden From History*, Pluto, London, 1973, pp. 45–6. See also **Gail Malmgreen**, *Neither Bread nor Roses: Utopian Feminists and the English Working Class 1800–1850*, John L. Noyce, Brighton, 1978.
31. **J. Beecher** and **R. Bienvenu** (eds), *The Utopian Vision of Charles Fourier: Selected Texts on Work, Love and Passionate Attraction*, Cape, London,

1972. See also **R. J. Evans**, *The Feminists*, Croom Helm, London, 1977, p. 155; Rowbotham, *Hidden from History*, pp. 41–2.

32. **Karl Marx**, *Economic and Philosophical Manuscripts of 1844*, Foreign Languages Publishing House, Moscow, n.d. p. 101.

33. **F. Engels**, *The Origin of the Family, Private Property and the State*, in **Marx** and **Engels**, *Select Works*, Vol. 2, Foreign Language Publishing House, Moscow, 1955, pp. 227–8, 234.

34. *Ibid.*, p. 239.

35. See Weeks, *Coming Out*, p. 145.

36. See **Yvonne Kapp**, *Eleanor Marx*, Vol. II, *The Crowded Years*, Virago, London, 1976. Both Vols I and II are illuminating on the values of Marx's immediate circle.

37. This is an important point made by McLaren, *op. cit.*, pp. 166–7.

38. **Stephen Winsten**, *Salt and His Circle*, Hutchinson, London, 1951, p. 64. On the SDF's general attitude to feminism and birth control, see McLaren, *op. cit.*, pp. 159 ff.

39. **Ernest Belfort Bax**, *Outspoken Essays: On Social Subjects*, William Reeves, London, 1897, pp. 5, 7, 8.

40. *Ibid.*, p. 14.

41. **E. Belfort Bax**, *The Ethics of Socialism*, Swan Sonnenschein, London, 1902, pp. 62, 126.

42. Based in turn largely on Fourierist ideas: see R. J. Evans, *op. cit.*, p. 155; Yvonne Kapp, *op. cit.*, pp. 83–4 ff; **August Bebel**, *Women in the Past, the Present and the Future*, Modern Press, London, 1885; and for a relevant series of texts see **Hal Draper** and **Anne G. Lipow**, 'Marxist Women versus Bourgeois Feminism', in **R. Miliband** and **J. Saville**, *Socialist Register*, Merlin, London, 1976.

43. See *Bernstein on Homosexuality*, Athol Books, Belfast, n.d. (consisting of two articles by Bernstein first published in *Die Neue Zeit* in 1895 and 1898).

44. *Ibid.*

45. See for instance his *Fraud of Feminism*, Grant Richards, London, 1913.

46. Robert Blatchford to Edward Carpenter, 11 January 1894, Ms 386–46. Edward Carpenter Collection, Sheffield City Library. For Blatchford's attitude to the family and women, very much in the Victorian tradition, see Rowbotham, *Hidden from History*, p. 73.

47. **Guy Aldred**, *The Religion and Economics of Sex Oppression*, in *Pamphlets for Proletarians*, Bakunin Press, London, 1908–11, p. 37. See also Aldred in *The Free Woman*, 18 July 1912; and McLaren, *op. cit.*, p. 161.

48. For a full discussion of his socialism and his views on sexuality see Rowbotham and Weeks, *op. cit.*; and J. Weeks, *Coming Out*, Ch. 6. His ethical socialist philosophy can be seen in his long Whitmanite poem, *Towards Democracy*, and in his essays gathered as *Civilisation: Its Cause and Cure* in 1889. In this he argued that 'civilisation' was not the culmination of human progress but a 'disease' which stunted human potentialities.

49. Carpenter to George Hukin, 31 July 1895, Ms 361–21, Edward Carpenter Collection, Sheffield City Library.

50. In 1902 he published *Iolaus: An Anthology of Friendship*, a collection of writings with homoerotic themes. *The Intermediate Sex* (1908) gathered together various essays on homosexuality written over the previous ten years. In 1914 he produced a volume on *Intermediate Types Amongst Primitive Folk*. He also published several essays on Whitman, including *Days with Walt Whitman* (1906), and *Some Friends of Walt Whitman: A*

Study in Sex Psychology (1924). And one of his last works was a study of the bisexual nature of the poet, Shelley. Though highly dated now, these works are still very revealing.

51. **Edward Carpenter**, *Love's Coming of Age*, National Labour Press, Manchester, 1896, pp. 68–9.
52. **Edward Carpenter**, *The Intermediate Sex*, 9th edn, Allen & Unwin, London, 1952, p. 17. Cf. **Otto Weininger**, *Sex and Character*, Heinemann, London, 1906.
53. Carpenter, *The Intermediate Sex*, pp. 93, 131.
54. See *The Adult*, February 1893; Ms 352 and Ms 354–31, Edward Carpenter Collection.
55. See Weeks, *Coming Out*, pp. 78 ff.
56. Rowbotham and Weeks, *op. cit.*, pp. 120 ff.
57. For which see **Stephen Yeo**, 'A New Life: The Religion of Socialism in Britain 1883–1896', *History Workshop Journal*, No. 4, Autumn 1977. See also R. Q. Gray's comments in *The Labour Aristocracy in Nineteenth Century Edinburgh*, pp. 178–9, speaking of Edinburgh socialists: 'Both for artisans, and for middle-class people to whom socialism made some appeal, the movement has to be seen in relation to a wider cultural rebellion. This included a self conscious rejection of such catchwords as "Respectability" which were seen by the socialists, in theory at least, as part of a system of oppressive and mystifying norms and values.'
58. **Sue Bruley**, 'Socialism and Feminism in the Communist Party of Great Britain', Unpublished Ph.D. thesis, London University, 1980.
59. See, for example, **M. Eden Paul**, *Chronos, or the Future of the Family*, Kegan Paul, Trench, Trubner & Co., London, 1930.
60. Rowbotham, *A New World for Women*.
61. **Alec Craig**, *Sex and Revolution*, Allen and Unwin, London, 1934. Craig was also author of *The Banned Books of England*, Allen and Unwin, London, 1937.
62. **Reuben Osborn**, *Freud and Marx*, Victor Gollancz, London, 1937; *The Psychology of Reaction*, Victor Gollancz, London, 1938.
63. Osborn, *The Psychology of Reaction*, pp. 278, 279–80. On Reich and Marcuse and their work, see **Paul A. Robinson**, *The Sex Radicals*, Paladin, London, 1972.

Chapter Ten

Sex psychology and birth control

Sex psychology

In the absence of any mass popular movement committed to radical transformation of sexual values, the reforming efforts of the more advanced feminists and socialists were concentrated in the single-issue campaigns that emerged at the turn of the century. They were, inevitably, constrained by their limited nature, and by the conservatism of their constituency. Socialists, of course, were in a difficult, almost contradictory position. As socialists they believed that sexual change could only truly come in the process of social transformation. But without work now, there would be no guarantee that social transformation would bring the sexual revolution. Later generations, from Wilhelm Reich onwards, were to attempt to argue that sexual repression was a key to general social reaction. None of the early sex radicals held to this position (at least in such an explicit form, though it is implicit in Carpenter) and in its absence, as good, humanistic reformers they naturally concentrated their efforts on what could be attained.

The nineteenth century, the great age of single-issue pressure groups, saw the development of a number of organisations committed to moral reformation, but until the latter years of the century none saw it as their task to advocate radical sex reform in any manner which would be recognisably modern, though an organisation like the Malthusian League was probably more successful as a challenge to respectable opinion than as an advocate of general birth control.

The Legitimation League, founded in 1897 to campaign for changing the bastardy laws and for reform of marriage and divorce legislation, was therefore an organisation of a new sort. It established *The Adult*, as a monthly journal for 'The Advancement of Freedom in Sexual Relationships', and in its first editorial offered to provide a forum for the discussion of sex questions ignored elsewhere:

We recognise the paramount right of the individual to self-realisation in all non-invasive directions. *The Adult* advocates the absolute freedom of two individuals of full age, to enter into and conclude at will, any mutual relationships whatever, where no third person's interests are concerned.[1]

George Bernard Shaw was typically scathing, complaining that they were 'extremely conventional, working for the legitimation of the illegitimate instead of the illegitimation of the legitimate, which is the true line of progress.'[2]

But other radicals, like Edward Carpenter and Havelock Ellis, offered their general support, Carpenter even contributing an article (on 'Evolution and Love'). But the League had a somewhat unsteady history, such issues as free love causing major fissures. And its most famous moment was one that illustrated all the conflicting motives that come into play when 'sex' becomes a public issue.

It started with Havelock Ellis's difficulties in finding a publisher for *Sexual Inversion*.[3] None of the orthodox medical publishers would take the book, and Ellis accepted the offer of one Roland de Villiers, apparently a liberal-minded independent publisher, to produce the English edition. De Villiers, it later become apparent, was a crook, wanted by the police of Europe and Britain.

The book was welcomed by the Legitimation League. *The Adult* was also published by de Villiers, and through him the society came to display the book in its offices. Unfortunately for Ellis, Scotland Yard was keeping a close watch on the League, convinced it was the haunt of anarchists, then currently the terror of respectable London. The police obviously felt that a book on 'sexual inversion', especially in the post-Wilde atmosphere, would provide a convenient hammer with which to crush the society; and any potential anarchists within.

The secretary of the Legitimation League, George Bedborough, was arrested and eventually brought to trial in October 1898 for selling 'a certain lewd, wicked, bawdy, scandalous libel', namely, Ellis's *Sexual Inversion*. Ellis himself was not charged, nor indeed was the book itself on trial as such. A Free Press Defence Committee was at once established to defend free speech and its membership read like a litany of political and literary liberalism, including amongst others, H. M. Hyndman, G. B. Shaw, Edward Carpenter, E. Belfort Bax, Grant Allen and George Moore. But its efforts were not needed. Bedborough, under strong police pressure, was persuaded to plead guilty and was bound over. This had the effect of preventing anyone giving evidence on the book's merits. Ellis himself was never called to the stand, and the book was labelled scandalous and obscene, completely undefended.

The police meanwhile had achieved a signal victory: they effectively banned *Sexual Inversion* without its being tried on its merits (and Ellis determined that future editions of his *Studies* would not be published in Britain); and they crushed that putative haunt of anarchists, the Legitimation League.

The next major attempt at a sex reform organisation was more solidly based. The British Society for the Study of Sex Psychology (BSSP)[4] was established in July 1914 with Edward Carpenter as a life member and first president. In an obituary address to the society after

Carpenter's death, the educationalist Cecil Reddie observed that, without Carpenter, the society would never have come into being: 'sex study was in England almost totally tabued (*sic*)'. And Reddie pointed out the special qualities Carpenter contributed: 'it required courage to start a society for sex study. More even than courage, it required extreme care and tact. Here Carpenter's inimitable gift for discussing problems moderately and persuasively yet firmly and frankly, was invaluable.'[5]

Such 'extreme care and tact' was already felt to be a little old-fashioned by younger elements. Laurence Housman, chairman of the society, felt that Carpenter was often too indirect and evasive for his pleading to hit home, and that he was too hedged in with appeals to extenuating circumstances.[6] But only Carpenter and Havelock Ellis, who was another, if characteristically elusive, early backer, could provide the necessary prestige to get a reform society off the ground.

Another important influence was Magnus Hirschfeld, a major stimulus for many British reformers, and the informal ties began to crystallise after 1912 when a British branch of the Scientific Humanitarian Committee, Hirschfeld's homosexual reform organisation, was first mooted. The crucial event seems to have been the Fourteenth International Medical Congress, held in London in 1913, at which Hirschfeld was one of the leading speakers.

The congress had been a revelation for many of the ordinary medical people who attended, especially on the subject of homosexuality. One of the complaints of the British doctors there, according to Housman, was that there was no 'informed public' in Britain to encourage research along the lines that Hirschfeld detailed. It was apparently in the minds of the founders of the British Society for the Study of Sex Psychology, encouraged by the contacts and these reactions, to help to develop the nucleus of such a public.

By 1914 the time seemed opportune to launch the Society publicly, the lead being taken by Housman, George Ives and Stella Browne (all convinced socialists and feminists). It was established, in the words of its 'Policy and Principles', 'for the consideration of problems and questions connected with sexual psychology, from their medical, juridical and sociological aspects'. The aim was to adopt a 'scientific' (that is, humane and rational) approach to the problems of sex. But inextricably linked with the research and investigation was the question of public sex education. The society's ambition was, through lectures and the issues of pamphlets, 'to organise understanding in the lay mind on a larger scale, to make people more receptive to scientific proof, and more conscious of their responsibility'. By laying the basis of a new informed awareness, the society hoped to pave the way to needed reforms.[7]

The focus of the work of the British Society for Sex Psychology was the attempt to create a sympathetic public. Talks were often given monthly in the 1920s, and open to a wider public, while many of the lectures and talks to members were later published as pamphlets. These covered a wide range of topics, from the first, *Policy and Principles* –

General Aims, which set out the outlines of the society's policy, to the seventeenth, *A Plain Talk on Sex Difficulties*, the substance of a lecture by F. B. Rockstro on 'Some Difficulties in the Technique of Conjugal Relationships' given before the society in March 1933.

Several of the pamphlets were relevant to feminist politics, such as Stella Browne's *Sexual Variety and Variability among Women* (No. 3) and Havelock Ellis's *The Erotic Rights of Women* (No. 5). Others raised more general issues on sexuality. Eden Paul published a pamphlet on *The Sexual Life of the Child* (No. 10), and Paul and Norman Haire jointly produced one on *Rejuvenation: Steinach's Researchers on Sex Glands* (No. 11), which discussed the function of the sex hormones in determining personal characteristics. All these touched on central questions in the exploration of sexuality: the nature of sexuality in the young and in women, the factors that determine sexuality, the significance of monogamy and the nuclear family.

The discussion of homosexuality was also basic to the society's work. There were, after all, other societies dealing with related aspects of the 'sex problem'. The long-established Malthusian (later New Generation) League and the Eugenics Education Society concerned themselves in differing ways with birth control, and after 1921 were joined by Marie Stopes's Society for Constructive Birth Control and Racial Progress and other birth-control groups. Stella Browne was active in many of these, while Ives maintained contact with the Divorce Law Reform Union and the Howard League for Penal Reform. The original contribution of the British Society for the Study of Sex Psychology could be in helping to shape the field of sex psychology as one of prime significance for social reformers, and in debating the particular topic of homosexuality. This is less surprising when we consider that most of the leading lights who dominated the society from Carpenter to Housman and Ives, were homosexual.

The Society's second pamphlet had indicated this involvement. It was an English digest of a famous German pamphlet by Hirschfeld, originally published in Germany in 1903 and into its nineteenth edition within four years. The English version, *The Social Problem of Sexual Inversion*, was published with suitable caution: 'Issued by the BSSP to members of the Educational, Medical and Legal Professions'. But as the Introduction noted: 'That any courage should be needed in a demand for facts to be recognised and scientifically investigated, is in itself a condemnation of the obscurantist attitude which prevails so largely among us in regard to this question.'[8] And despite its belief that changes in the law were not yet on the agenda, it called for the harmonising, as far as possible, of social and juridical practice with scientific investigations and conclusions. Certain other BSSP pamphlets were directly concerned with homosexuality, while a special sub-committee devoted itself to the study of homosexuality.

It is difficult to estimate what influence the society (which became in the 1920s the British Sexological Society) could have had. In 1920 there were under 250 members, and this was probably the median size. Up to forty or fifty people often attended its meetings and the pamphlets had a fairly wide circulation, but is is highly unlikely that it made any deep penetration into public consciousness, though the more sexually aware atmosphere of the 1920s meant that it had a wider constituency to influence. Its membership and support was wide among progressive intellectuals including George Bernard Shaw, E. M. Forster, Radclyffe Hall and Una Troubridge, Edward Westermarck, Bertrand Russell (whose *Marriage and Morals*, 1929 is a useful summary of progressive views) and Dora Russell. Abroad the society maintained important links; with Hirschfeld and his colleagues in Germany, with the birth-control pioneer, Margaret Sanger in the United States, and many others around the world.

It is doubtful, however, whether the society greatly extended its natural constituency, and it certainly could never claim to have revolutionised attitudes. Neither did it have any obvious influence on government policy. At the most it strengthened the self-awareness and sexual knowledge of a narrow stratum of people. But in its talks and publications, it did attempt to extend the pre-1914 concern with feminism and sex reform and its main achievement was probably to develop the belief that sexuality was an area worthy of conscious social intervention. Moreover, during the 1920s it was to become part of a wider current, with the development of the international sex-reform movement.

International movements

The immediate post-war years had indeed seemed to herald a new era of sex reform. In post-revolutionary Russia the Bolsheviks had legalised divorce and abortion, encouraged birth control and decriminalised homosexuality. In actuality, the effect of what Reich called the sexual revolution' was limited, given the immense backward nature of Soviet Russia, and it was to be followed by a massive retreat in the 1930s. But, for progressive opinion in the 1920s, Soviet Russia was an important model. Norman Haire, anything but a socialist revolutionary himself, saw the sexual code of the USSR as a 'fascinating experiment which we sexologists in other countries are watching with great interest'.[9] In Germany, too, during the 1920s there seemed to be the possibility of great advance. In 1919 Hirschfeld fulfilled a long ambition and opened the Institute for Sexual Science – 'A child of the (German) Revolution', as he called it – as a centre for sex research and the dissemination of scientific knowledge. It sponsored sex education, provided a pioneering marriage-counselling bureau and gave advice for sex variants. And in 1921 the first of a series of World Congresses on Sex Reform met under his auspices, which were to lead, in 1928, to the formal establishment of a World League for Sexual Reform.

According to Wilhelm Reich, the League in the 1920s 'comprised the most progressive sexologists and sex reformers in the world'.[10] It developed no single theoretical line or approach, nor did it have a single political line. It had representatives from the USSR (including Alexandra Kollontai, the great Bolshevik feminist) as well as from the Western capitalist countries, but its method was essentially reformist, interested primarily in putting forward a definitive programme – 'a sexual sociology', as Hirschfeld called it – which could be presented to the legislators of the world. The 1928 Congress appealed 'to the legislatures, the Press and the Peoples of all countries, to help to create a new legal and social attitude (based on the knowledge which has been acquired from scientific research in sexual biology, psychology and sociology) towards the sexual life of men and women'. This approach suggested implicit contradictions in its attitude to sexual politics from the first, but these did not come to a head until the mid 1930s. Up to 1932 at least, the League worked in a cautious way to build up a basis of sexual knowledge and awareness.

Its declared aim, in the tradition which Havelock Ellis and the British sex reformers had always espoused, was to harmonise social and judicial practice with the 'laws of nature'. Its specific planks included support for the political, economic and sexual equality of women and men; reform of marriage and divorce laws; improved sex education; the control of conception; reform of the abortion laws; the prevention of venereal disease and prostitution; the protection of unmarried mothers and the illegitimate child; and the development of rational attitudes towards sexual 'abnormality'. The basic principle was established in Point 9 of its aims which advocated that 'only those sexual acts were to be considered criminal which infringe the sex rights of another person'.

British reformers, members of the British Society for the Study of Sex Psychology and other organisations, were drawn into the work of the League from the start. Havelock Ellis was a joint Honorary (if rather passive) President, while a British section of the League was established in 1928. Norman Haire was chairman, while Dora Russell became its secretary.[11] In an ambience where most of the international sex reformers were socialists of one sort or another (Hirschfeld, for instance, was a supporter of the German Social Democratic Party), Haire, was, in his own words, 'an old fashioned Liberal . . . an opponent of egalitarianism'.[12] He was nonetheless a dedicated advocate of birth control and sex reform in the inter-war and immediate post-war years.

Dora Russell was quite a different sort of person, considerably further to the left than Haire, and had opposed the non-political stance of the World League for Sexual Reform. At one meeting of the British section, Robert Boothby, later a Conservative MP, and peer, stood up and accused her of dragging the class war into the organisation.[13] But there was no real danger of this while Haire remained in command; the section remained resolutely non-political in a formal party sense.

Boothby nevertheless touched on an issue which was eventually to split the League. The 1929 World Congress in London had been a major success in terms of the members attending, offering papers on topics from censorship to abortion and birth control, the major issues covered. But the methods for producing change were less energetically discussed. Dora Russell recalled that in the 1929 Congress: 'the contributions were nearly all designed to inform and influence public opinion rather than to organise political action for the ends which were thought desirable ... on the whole my learned colleagues contented themselves with describing the state of public knowledge and practice, exposing the inhumanity of the laws without envisaging any serious organisation to change them.'[14]

Dora Russell was later to come to believe that the wide gap between cultural opinion and political activity was one of the factors which contributed to the inroads of reaction. Indeed, the 1929 Congress was the high tide. Two further congresses were held, in Vienna in 1930 and in Brno in 1932, but in 1933 the world movement was deeply disrupted by the Nazi accession to power in Germany. Hirschfeld's Institute was amongst the first to suffer the impact of the Nazis. In May 1933 the premises were sacked. The archives and library containing irreplaceable material, and the records of the World League for Sexual Reform, were removed, and burnt later in a public ceremony. A bust of Hirschfeld was carried in a torchlight procession and was thrown on to the pyre (Hirschfeld was himself luckily abroad at the time). A year later, in the USSR, homosexuality again became a criminal offence, and the law on marriage and divorce was tightened up.

The fundamental premiss for the work of the World League for Sexual Reform was the possibility of convincing governments of the rationality of sex reform. Following the economic collapse of the World capitalist economy, the threat to the bourgeois democracies posed by fascism, and the reversals in the USSR, this hope seemed doomed.

After the death of Hirschfeld in exile in 1935, the two remaining Presidents, Dr J. Leunbach of Denmark and Norman Haire, split over the next step. Leunbach believed firmly that the League had failed because of its unwillingness to join the international workers' movement, to integrate the struggle for sex reform into the struggle against fascism and for socialism. Haire remained firmly apolitical. This split was basic, and in the ashes of the international movement could not be easily resolved. The two presidents consequently dissolved the World League for Sexual Reform, with the recommendation that national sections should remain in being where they could. In fact, by the late 1930s, only Haire's organisation in Britain, the Sex Education Society, survived, and that a tiny organisation.[15] (It continued on a small scale until the war, and was revived afterwards.) By the 1930s, radical sex reform seemed completely off the agenda. It was left to other single-issue campaigns, particularly those for birth control, to harvest what crops remained.

Parenthood and birth control

Sex reform is always constructed across the dialectic of social control on the one hand and individual freedom on the other, and this, as eugenics had pinpointed, was particularly the case with the issue of contraception. Subtle changes in terminology etch in potential differences of approach. 'Neo-Malthusianism,' the common nineteenth-century term, and 'family planning', the preferred term from the 1930s, suggest one tilt of the balance, evoking the social, organising and planning role of contraception policies. 'Voluntary motherhood' and 'birth control', the term introduced by Margaret Sanger and favoured amongst feminists, point to the element of individual choice. There was no absolute division between the two approaches. Marie Stopes, the most famous advocate of artificial contraception during the 1920s, was clearly within a fairly conservative, familial tradition (her organisation, founded in 1921, was known as the Society for Constructive Birth Control and *Racial* Progress) but her work helped thousands of women to exercise individual choice. Even the old Malthusian League found it necessary, under the pressure of new circumstances, and of an influx of feminist birth-controllers, to change its name to the New Generation League in 1922.[16] Stella Browne, on the other hand, though one of the most ardent exponents of 'a woman's right to choose' in the inter-war years, never entirely sloughed off a eugenic skin, despite her belief that the Eugenics Education Society displayed a 'class-bias, sex-bias', and ignored the positions of unmarried mothers or illegitimate children.[17]

These differences of approach, and their ambivalent interconnections, became more apparent in the inter-war years, as the question of artificial contraception became a major issue. The decline in the birthrate had been going on since at least the 1870s, and by the 1920s it was apparent that manual workers were also now restricting births on a parallel scale to non-manual workers. So although the population in the decade 1931–41 was two-thirds higher than in the period 1871–81, the number of births was 3 million fewer. A couple in mid-Victorian England could expect 5.5 to 6 live births – a couple 1925–9 would expect 2.2.[18] But despite clear evidence of restriction of births throughout all classes, it was also apparent that the majority of couples still used pre-industrial methods, and this was true even amongst professional people. A survey of mainly college graduates conducted by the Birth Rate Commission showed that 51.7 per cent of their sample who practised birth control did so by restraint, abstinence or the use of the 'safe period' rather than by mechanical or chemical contrivances.[19] The proportion would have been much higher amongst working-class respondents, where abortion was still a common form. (During the 1930s there was sufficient concern about abortion for an inter-departmental committee to be set up in 1937, under Lord Birkett, to investigate the question.)

Several factors combined in the 1910s and 1920s to make *artificial* birth control an important issue. The First World War undoubtedly helped to break up much official prejudice about contraception, largely because of the increased use of the condom as a preventive against venereal disease. In 1917 nearly 55,000 British soldiers were hospitalised by VD and this aroused a considerable medical debate. The sheath was an obvious safeguard against infection, though its use aroused fears that it would encourage immorality.[20] But the war and its aftermath did more than familiarise people with the use of prophylactics. It also brought to light again some of the conditions in which motherhood took place. The Women's Co-operative Guild's publication of its letters on *Maternity* in 1917 vividly illustrated the awful conditions of some mothers and the effects of medical indifference on the question, and the figures for maternal mortality remained appallingly high during the inter-war years.[21] The question of the quality of the population emerged again as a vitally important one, in the light both of the casualties of the war (it was estimated that the population loss was something like 7 million, including both casualties and loss of potential offspring)[22] and of the impact of inter-war economic problems and fear of absolute population decline. If women were restricting births anyway, by whatever means, it was clearly better that this be done by safe and healthy means. And by the 1920s technical advances did seem to open up the possibility of artificial control on a large scale.

There could be no doubt of the demand for information on fertility control from all sections of the population. As we have seen, this demand was already apparent in the vast response to thinly veiled advertisements for abortifacients in the late nineteenth century. During the 1920s it was also manifested in the public response given to birth-controllers. Stella Browne and similar feminist birth-controllers found themselves addressing overflowing meetings of working-class men and women on the topic in the 1920s.[23] Marie Stopes was even more graced by public interest. Her book *Married Love*, published in March 1918, sold over 2,000 copies in the first fortnight, and by the end of 1923, in 22 reprints, had sold over 400,000 copies. *Wise Parenthood*, published in November 1918, had sold over 300,000 copies by 1924. Her clinic, founded in 1921, had after a slow start (just over 500 visits in the first six months) advised 10,000 women by 1930.[24] Stopes, moreover, was deluged by thousands of letters from all sections of society, dealing not only with contraception problems but with a whole range of sexual questions. It was not only that there was a great demand for birth-control advice, but it also became obvious that ignorance was rife, even amongst the medical profession itself.[25] And the effects of such ignorance on married life – a major preoccupation of Marie Stopes – was apparent. As one wife wrote to Stopes: 'I am so afraid of conception that I cannot bear for my husband to even speak fondly to me or even put his hand on my shoulder for fear he wants his rights. . . . It is two months since I last allowed him intercourse.'[26]

These revelations of sexual misery had a major impact on a new generation of feminists in the inter-war years. With the achievement of a limited female suffrage in 1918, feminist energies were being dispersed into a variety of channels from campaigning for 'equal citizenship' to advocating family allowances and child welfare. The 'new feminism' that emerged showed much more public interest in fertility control than previously, though usually it was less in terms of sexual freedom than with reference to questions of health and poverty. Eleanor Rathbone, for instance, the chief advocate of family allowances, declared her anxiety that the poor should not proliferate. But often the two elements of health and sexual freedom combined.[27] Dora Russell has recorded her reaction to the demand for birth control at the Labour Women's Conference of 1923: 'I, like others present, had been astounded at the fury against child-bearing. . . . Here were women fiercely repudiating what has been preached at us as the noblest fulfilment of our womanhood.' Dora Russell now received what she called her 'true political education. Feminist indeed, I began to wonder if the feminist has not been running away from the central issue of woman's emancipation.'[28]

Marie Stopes would not have endorsed such a left-feminist position, despite (or perhaps because of) her impeccable suffragist background. But in an important way that made her role even more significant after she became a public figure from 1917 onwards, rather like Margaret Sanger in America (with whom she did not get on),[29] she was able to embody and represent a number of often contradictory strands. There was quite clearly a new mood even before she emerged. The Malthusian League had pointed to a new evaluation in 1913 when it took the decision to publicise its case amongst the working class of East London. A 'practical pamphlet' was produced on family limitation, though advocating 'every precaution against its being disseminated among young unmarried people'. Within a year 3,000 copies had been applied for, and by 1917, 21,000.[30] The League, moreover, proposed in September 1919 to set up in the East End the first British birth-control clinic – though this was not actually established (in Walworth) until 1922. Marie Stopes was to establish the first, in March 1921, in Holloway Road, North London, along with a society to support it.[31] It was she who most dramatically represented the new approach.

Two factors have to be taken into account in trying to assess Marie Stopes's influence: firstly, her personality and beliefs; and secondly, the social space she occupied. With regard to the first there can be no doubt that the major impulse behind her work was her experience of her first marriage, ironically to the eugenist Reginald Ruggles-Gates, which was never (at least on Stopes's account) consummated. As she wrote in the preface to *Married Love*, 'In my own marriage I paid such a terrible price for sex-ignorance that I feel knowledge gained at such a cost should be placed at the service of humanity.' The book, dedicated to 'young husbands and all those who are betrothed in love', is a rhapsodic treatise on the importance of sexual fulfilment in marriage ('The Glorious Unfolding', as the last chapter is called): 'When knowledge and love together go to the making of each marriage, the joy of that new unit, the pair will reach from the physical foundations of its bodies to the heavens where its head is crowned with stars.'[32] The hints on birth control which she dropped in this threnody were taken up more concretely in its sequel *Wise Parenthood* (a guide to contraceptive methods) the same year and its social consequences were revealed in *Radiant Motherhood* in 1920. The rather cosmic and elevated tones of Stopes's writings and public persona fed into a very important stress on conjugal love which was to have other powerful advocates during these years (van de Velde in particular, but owing a great deal, too, to Havelock Ellis).[33]

This leads us to the second important factor about Stopes: she occupies, in her preoccupations and concerns, a significant space in attitudes to social policy. She was able, for instance, to respond simultaneously to the new anxieties about the health of the mother *and* to wider racial questions. Whereas the propaganda of the Malthusian League had always been essentially negative, designed to prevent births, Stopes stressed the 'constructive' sides of fertility control. She emphasised three types of control. The first type was negative, control of conception, for women who should not have children (the congenitally diseased, the physically or mentally handicapped, those with previous difficult pregnancies). After 1928 the Society for Constructive Birth Control began to advocate sterilisation, but even this was interpreted in terms of its positive advantages. The second type was positive control – essentially the giving of advice to those who wanted, unsuccessfully, to have children, a side of her work that Stopes was proud of. The third type was optimum control or 'geroception', which implied the use of birth control to space children, which would enable the birth of healthy babies to healthy mothers. All could help the individual mother; but all, as well, addressed the concerns about the quantity and quality of the population.[34]

This was regarded by Stopes as an essential aspect of her work because she fully shared the eugenic world view. In 1920 in *Radiant Motherhood* she had written:

society allows the diseased, the racially negligent, the thriftless, the careless, the feeble-minded, the very lowest and worst members of the community, to produce innumerable tens of thousands of stunted warped and inferior infants. If they live, a large proportion of them are doomed from their very physical inheritance to be at the best but partly self-supporting, and thus to drain the resources of those classes above them which have a sense of responsibility.[35]

The better classes, freed of their responsibilities, would better be able to multiply their own superior stock. In 1922 Stopes sought bourgeois support precisely on this basis. She sent a circular to all prospective candidates in the General Election asking them to sign a declaration:

I agree that the present position of breeding chiefly from the C3 population and burdening and discouraging the A1 is nationally deplorable, and if I am elected to Parliament I will press the Ministry of Health to give such scientific information through the Ante-natal Clinics, Welfare Centres and other institutions in its control as will curtail the C3 and increase the A1.[36]

Marie Stopes directed her work in the first place at the middle class – with the quite conscious aim of making birth control respectable. But she evoked an immediate response amongst working-class women, though in fact they always remained a minority amongst the clients of her clinic. *A Letter to Working Mothers* from Stopes in 1919 attempted to disseminate contraceptive advice; unfortunately, health visitors were unable to distribute it, and her attempts to deliver it personally met with hostility. The first breakthrough came in February 1923, after her unsuccessful libel action, which enormously increased her correspondence. The same occurred after articles by her appeared in *John Bull* in 1926. Her replies to working-class respondents were generally compassionate, even when, as in the case of abortion (over 20,000 requests were received in the three months after the *John Bull* articles) her advice had to be negative.[37]

Stopes displayed nevertheless a deep ignorance of working-class life. She extolled, for instance, the virtues of the cap, which she wrote, 'could be fitted at any convenient time, preferably when dressing for dinner'. Her advice to new mothers in *Radiant Motherhood* that they should spend at least six weeks in bed recovering would have been equally laughable for most working-class women.[38] But the eugenic note was very important in shaping the influence of Stopes, for one of her major achievements was precisely to adapt eugenic arguments, which were traditionally hostile to birth control, to favour artificial contraception, and she could successfully link thereby her racial and sexual preoccupations with the more generally acceptable question of health.

What Stopes succeeded in doing, in short, was indeed to help make advocacy of birth control respectable. Her own mystical elevation of conjugal bliss, though not to everyone's literary taste, contrasted sharply with the traditional connection of birth control with free love. Stopes disapproved of such concepts, was unsympathetic to homosexuality and was ultra-cautious over abortion (despite the massive demand for it that her work uncovered, it was of course illegal).[39] Moreover, as a Christian, albeit of an esoteric sort, she broke clean away from the free-thinking traditions of the neo-Malthusians, from Bradlaugh onwards.

Stopes was careful to disavow any bonds with those less sturdily conservative than herself. In 1922 she withdrew her support from Nurse E. S. Daniels, a health worker in Edmonton, London, who had been dismissed from letting women at Maternity Clinics know where they could obtain contraceptive advice. More notoriously, she refused to support the socialists Guy Aldred (he of the earlier sexual restraint) and Rose Witcop, who were prosecuted for selling Margaret Sanger's pamphlet *Family Limitation: Handbook for Working Mothers* in 1923, just a few weeks before her own case of libel against Dr Halliday Sutherland came to court. Not only did she refuse support; she also took it upon herself to write to the Director of Public Prosecutions to say that the pamphlet was 'prurient' and 'both criminal and harmful'. Bertrand Russell resigned from the Society for Constructive Birth Control in consequence.[40]

Not everyone approved of the tone of her work. Norman Haire, himself a pioneering birth-control advocate, begged the medical profession in 1923 to study birth control properly: 'Only thus may it be rescued from the hands of quacks and charlatans and non-medical "doctors" who write erotic treatises on birth control conveying misleading information in a highly stimulating form.'[41] The *New Witness*, run by the Catholic G. K. Chesterton, expressed a similar (and more predictable) abhorrence: 'The peculiar horror of her book (*Wise Parenthood*) is that it is couched in pseudo-scientific terms, and is addressed to the married woman.'[42]

Stopes's endeavours had, however, the advantage of being morally conventional, despite their lyricism, romantically appealing and (*pace* Haire, and some controversial views on female physiology)[43] scientifically respectable. Stopes was a doctor, though not of medicine, and had before her entry into the world of birth control already established a high, if specialised reputation as a scientist specialising in the constituents of coal.[44] This background enabled her to bridge the gap between propaganda and the intellectual and moral prejudices of the traditional non-governmental bulwarks of opposition to birth control, medicine and the Church. A shift in these attitudes was crucial to further advance, and Stopes devoted a great deal of her considerable energy towards converting these.[45] The acceptance by both the British Medical Association and the Anglican Lambeth Conference of 1930 of limited birth control if the health of the (married) mother was threatened, was therefore a signal triumph for the sort of approach pursued by Stopes, and followed, indeed, by most of the other leading advocates of birth control during the 1920s.[46] It was in practice a small step forward, but compared to the previous hostility of both institutions it was an important breakthrough, pointing to further changes in the post-war world. It was, moreover, a breakthrough not won without considerable effort and continued hostility, particularly from the Roman Catholic Church, which issued the Papal encyclical *Casti Conubi* partly in response to the Lambeth decision, though partly also in favourable response to the new familial stress in fascist Italy. Its opposition remained adamantine into the 1970s.

Stopes therefore forged an approach which was much more practically effective than the negativism of the neo-Malthusians and the generalised propaganda of others. But it would be wrong to see her as working alone. She was part of a much wider movement in the 1920s, her society being one of several organisations working for general acceptance of birth control; and when in the 1930s she did plough an increasingly isolated path, it was by choice rather than by force of circumstances. Moreover, all the major organisations were agreed on their fundamental approach.[47] For what unified all the birth-control organisations in the 1920s was the conviction that it was absolutely necessary to persuade the government of the merits of artificial contraception. Independent clinics could be set up, but only the state had the facilities to provide birth control on a sufficient scale. The efforts to win over the conservative professions were therefore only a step towards the larger objective, which became the key goal during the 1920s. None of the major political parties showed any real enthusiasm: even those individuals in prominent positions such as Lloyd George, who favoured birth control, were reluctant to commit themselves too publicly. Of the major parties, only in the Labour Party and the Labour Movement generally was there any sustained effort to win over the leadership, but as a new potential party of government this was important.

The obvious demand for birth control by Labour women was beginning to break down the ancient prejudice against 'Malthusianism', and the dismissal of Nurse Daniels and the trial of Aldred and Witcop acted as a spur. The hostility displayed by the (Roman Catholic) Health Minister, John Wheatley in the first Labour Government in 1924 led to the foundation of a Worker's Birth Control Group by socialist women such as Stella Browne, Frida Laski and Mary Stocks, and they campaigned vigorously in the movement. A number of Labour councils passed resolutions (Brighton was the first in 1924) calling for the government to set up birth-control clinics and the Independent Labour Party adopted a similar policy in August 1924 though the Labour Party itself remained unsympathetic.[48] Women's organisations also took up the campaign. In June 1924 the National Union of Societies for Equal Citizenship (the former suffragist organisation) resolved that advice should be given in government Maternity and Child Welfare Clinics, while the New Generation League conducted a grass-roots campaign from 1925, distributing over one million leaflets urging people to write to the Minister supporting government action. This and similar pressure had some effect.

The return of a Labour Government in 1929 opened the way to a limited, but important change. By Memorandum 153/MCW, in July 1930, the Minister of Health permitted existing Maternity and Child Welfare centres to give contraceptive advice to married women, 'in cases where further pregnancy would be detrimental to health'. This was passed by Cabinet as a matter of routine business; there was no debate in Parliament; it was not sent out to local authorities as a matter of course: it had to be requested; nor was it publicised until Marie Stopes leaked its contents.[49] Moreover, gynaecology clinics could not be held in the same building as Maternity and Child Welfare clinics for fear of disrupting the work. But it was a crucial switch: for the first time the state had recognised the legitimacy of allowing birth-control facilities, if only on a very limited scale. The new policy's justification, it was clear, came not from any espousal of greater sexual freedom but from anxieties over health – precisely the grounds which had unified birth-controllers in the 1920s.

However, any further major advances were stymied by a renewed anxiety over the decline in the birthrate in the 1930s. In 1933 the net reproduction rate fell to 0.75; demographers believed that it had to be raised to 2 to ensure replacement of the population. Dr Enid Charles, in her book *The Twilight of Parenthood*,[50] offered three possible projections of population trends, the worst of which suggested that by the year 2033 the population of England and Wales would be less than that of the County of London in 1934. Neville Chamberlain, as Chancellor of the Exchequer, drew the moral in 1935 when announcing a marginal increase in income tax relief for children: 'I must say that I look upon the continued diminution of the birth rate in this country with considerable apprehension . . . the time may not be far distant . . . when . . . the countries of the British Empire will be crying out for more citizens of the right breed and when we in this country shall not be able to supply the demand.'[51] These themes were echoed in the first full-scale debate on the question in the House of Commons in February 1937, on a resolution which spoke of the 'danger to the maintenance of the British Empire' and the danger to the 'economic well-being of the nation'.[52] The economic effects of population decline produced a considerable debate amongst economists and sociologists (including William Beveridge, Carr-Saunders and Maynard Keynes) while others, even on the left, pushed for a more thorough-going population policy, with inducement to procreation such as family allowances.[53] The population policies of Nazi Germany or Soviet Russia held little appeal, except for the ardent, but many, like the social democratic Titmusses, favoured the Swedish policies sponsored by Gunner Myrdal in the 1930s, based on the goal of minimising the costs of necessary goods and services associated with childbearing and rearing by state intervention.[54] Richard Titmuss, like many others, worried about the potential imbalance between the races: 'the future of the white people now depends in the main not upon further reductions in mortality but upon the birth rate', and asked gloomily, 'Are the peoples of the West doomed to die out?' And with them the duties of the West to the 'teeming millions' of India and Africa?[55]

Such anxieties were representative but had little direct governmental response until after the war of 1939–45, when the continuing anxiety was reflected in the establishment of a Royal Commission on Population. The informal *ad hoc*, negative, population policies continued, reflecting the uncertainty amongst economists and policy makers alike of the import of providing incentives for working-class procreation.

Such further changes as took place in the 1930s were basically extensions of the 1930 Circular, concentrating on the centrality of health grounds. A Circular of 1934 extended the provisions to include women suffering from illnesses that would not necessarily be treated at either maternal and child welfare or gynaecology clinics, such as tuberculosis, heart disease and diabetes, while Circular No. 1622 (May 1937) permitted the giving of contraceptive advice to women at post-natal clinics.

Health provided a similar loophole with regard to abortion. The 1929 Infant Life Preservation Act had reaffirmed that termination of pregnancy was unlawful *except* when the abortion could be proved to have been done to preserve the life of the mother. A legal judgment, by Justice McNaughton in 1938, which passed into case law (R. *versus* Bourne) indicated that it was lawful for a doctor to terminate in order to safeguard the woman's health and to prevent her becoming a 'physical or mental wreck'. This left many loopholes and ambiguities, however, which were not to be tackled, and then only partially, until the 1960s.[56] In the meantime, the Abortion Law Reform Association (founded in 1936), though strongly supported by feminists like Stella Browne who believed abortion was a woman's right, followed the pattern laid down by the birth-control campaign of the 1920s in publicly arguing in favour of reform because of its role in reducing maternal deaths.[57] But even this made very little progress until the 1960s.

There was a subtle change in the role of the birth-control organisations after 1930. In that year all the major organisations including Stopes's had come together to form a National Birth Control Council, and in 1931 this became the National Birth Control Association (NBCA).[58] Stopes was soon to return to an independent role – she was ever a difficult colleague – but the Association, under the leadership of Sir Thomas (later Lord) Horder, was to assume a new importance. For Memorandum 153/MCW and subsequent circulars had provided local authorities and regional hospital boards with the power either to set up birth-control clinics themselves or to assist the Association in providing voluntary clinics. This latter policy was the one most frequently adopted. The voluntary movement possessed a virtual monopoly of contraceptive knowledge, and supporting them offered a more discreet way of coping with the situation than setting up official centres. The resulting increase in the number of clinics was not dramatic. In the decade 1931–41 some 60 were in operation (compared with less than 20 during 1921–31, and 140 in 1951). But what was significant was the close co-operation of the NBCA with local authorities: some two-thirds of their clinics were on regional hospital board or local authority premises, and over half received direct payments from the authorities.[59] So from being a fringe movement in the 1920s, birth control was on the road to being partially integrated into the official machinery by the late 1930s. There is one final indication of its changing role. In 1939 the National Birth Control Association became the Family Planning Association. Nothing better reflects the change from the feminist aspirations of many of the early birth-controllers to the social-planning emphases that were to become dominant from the 1940s.[60]

References

1. *The Adult*, Vol. 1, No. 1, 1897.
2. *The Adult*, Vol. 1, No. 2, 1897.
3. For a fuller account of this episode see **Arthur Calder Marshall**, *Lewd, Blasphemous and Obscene*, Hutchinson, London, 1972, pp. 193 ff.; and Vincent Brome, *Havelock Ellis, Philosopher of Sex*, pp. 101 ff.
4. A fuller account of the BSSP, on which this section is based, can be found in Weeks, *Coming Out*, Ch. 11.
5. **Cecil Reddie**, *Edward Carpenter*, British Sexological Society, London, 1932. See also **F. Stella Browne**, 'A New Psychological Society', *International Journal of Ethics*, Vol. XXVIII, Jan. 1918, pp. 266 ff.
6. Laurence Housman in **Gilbert Beith** (ed.), *Edward Carpenter: In Appreciation*, George Allen & Unwin, London, 1931, p. 110.
7. British Society for the Study of Sex Psychology, *Policy and Principles; General Aims*, London, 1915, pp. 3, 9.
8. *The Social Problem of Sexual Inversion*, BSSP, London, 1915, p. 3.
9. Haire is quoted in **Norman Haire** (ed.), *World League for Sexual Reform Proceedings 1929*, London, 1930, p. 110.
10. Quoted in **Robert Wood**, 'Sex Reform Movements', in **A. Ellis** and **A. Abarnel**, *The Encyclopaedia of Sexual Behaviour*, Vol. 11, Corsano, London, 1961, p. 961.
11. See **Dora Russell**, *The Tamarisk Tree. My Quest for Liberty and Love*, Elek, London, 1975, for details.
12. *Journal of Sex Education*, Vol. 3, No. 2, Oct.–Nov. 1950.
13. D. Russell, *op. cit.*, p. 206.
14. *Ibid.*, p. 218.
15. See *Journal of Sex Education*, Vol. 1, No. 1, August 1948, for an account of the break-up. For a discussion of the post war Sex Education Society, see Weeks, *Coming Out*, Ch. 13.
16. **J. Peel** and **R. E. Dowse**, 'The Politics of Birth Control', *Political Studies*, Vol. 13, 1965, p. 184.
17. Rowbotham, *A New World for Women*, p. 19.
18. J. A. Banks, *Prosperity and Parenthood*, p. 3; **A. H. Halsey**, *Trends in British Society since 1900*, Macmillan, London, 1972, pp. 51, 55. See below, Ch. 11 for details of class differentiation.
19. Searle, *Eugenics and Politics in Britain*, p. 101; see also McLaren, *Birth Control in Nineteenth Century England*, p. 135. For the general picture see **John Peel**, 'The Manufacture and Retailing of Contraceptives in England', *Population Studies*, Vol. 17, 1963, which gives details of methods used in 1920s and 1930s.
20. McLaren, *op. cit.*, p. 136.
21. Jane Lewis, *The Politics of Motherhood*.
22. Halsey, *op. cit.*, p. 24.
23. Rowbotham, *A New World for Women*, p. 30.
24. Ruth Hall, *Marie Stopes*, pp. 135, 190, 308.
25. Hall, *op. cit.*, p. 167; and below, p. 211.
26. Quoted in Hall, *op. cit.*, pp. 171–2.
27. See **Jane Lewis**, 'Beyond Suffrage: English Feminism during the 1920s', *The Maryland Historian*, Vol. VI, Spring 1975.
28. Dora Russell, *The Tamarisk Tree*, p. 175.
29. And for whom see Linda Gordon, *Woman's Body, Woman's Right*.

30. Peel and Dowse, *op. cit.*, p. 181; Gordon, *op. cit.*, p. 81.
31. Hall, *op. cit.*, p. 186.
32. **Dr Marie Stopes**, *Married Love: A New Contribution to the Solution of Sex Difficulties*, 24th edn, Putnam & Co., London, 1940, p. 156.
33. A number of American academics in 1935 listed *Married Love* as number 16 amongst the 25 most influential of the twentieth century: behind *Das Kapital, The Golden Bough* and *The Psychology of Sex*; ahead of Freud's *Interpretation of Dreams, Mein Kampf* and Keynes's *Economic Consequences of the Peace*: Hall, *op. cit.*, p. 128.
34. **Jane Lewis**, 'The Ideology and Politics of Birth Control in Inter-war England', *Women's Studies International Quarterly*, Vol. 2, 1979.
35. Marie Stopes, *Radiant Motherhood*, Putnam, London, 1920, p. 221.
36. Hall, *op. cit.*, p. 169.
37. Hall, *op. cit.*, p. 16. A selection of the *John Bull* letters was published as *Mother England: A Contemporary History self written by those who have had no historian*, John Bale, Sons and Davidsson, London, 1929. It was 'Dedicated to those who are expected to be the mothers of an imperial race'. The reference to the 20,000 requests for abortion occurs on p. 183.
38. See Hall, *op. cit.*, pp. 36, 178; also pp. 179, 183, 243, 244 for further examples.
39. *Ibid.*, pp. 123–4; and note 22 above.
40. *Ibid.*, p. 210. For details of the Aldred case see Rowbotham, *Hidden from History*, pp. 150–1; and **Guy Aldred**, *No Traitor's Gait!*, Strickland Press, Glasgow, 1956–63 (3 Vols).
41. Hall, *op. cit.*, p. 261. Haire and Stopes were rivals, but they also disagreed over methods. Stopes favoured the check pessary, which she called the 'Pro-race' cap (see Hall *op. cit.*, pp. 198–9, and p. 268 for the success rate) while Haire favoured the Dutch cap or diaphragm on the grounds that it was easier to insert. See **Norman Haire**, *The Comparative Value of Current Contraceptive Methods*, Cromer Health Centre, London, 1928 (pamphlet).
42. Hall, *op. cit.*, p. 150.
43. She shared with Havelock Ellis a belief in the physiological gains to be had from the mutual absorption of each partner's seminal and vaginal secretions during intercourse. She also stressed the cyclical nature of female sexual desire.
44. On the title page of her publications she carefully listed her qualifications: 'Doctor of Science, London; Doctor of Philosophy, Munich; Fellow of University College, London; Fellow of the Royal Society of Literature, and the Linnean and Geological Societies.'
45. Hall, *op. cit.*, pp. 155 ff. and 164 ff.
46. See **John Peel**, 'Contraception and the Medical Profession', *Population Studies*, Vol. 18, 1964. On the Lambeth Conference decision, see *The Times*, 19 August 1930.
47. Not only were there various British organisations; the birth-control movement was an international phenomenon. See, e.g., **R. Pierpont** (ed.), *Report of the Fifth International neo Malthusian and Birth Control Conference*, William Heinemann, London, 1922; and **M. Sanger** and **H. M. Stone**, *The Practice of Contraception: An International Symposium*, Baillière and Cox, London, 1931.
48. On the Labour Movement, see Peel and Dowse, *op. cit.*, pp. 184 ff.; Rowbotham, *A New World for Women*; S. Bruley, 'Socialism and Feminism'.

49. Jane Lewis, 'The Ideology and Politics of Birth Control in Interwar England'; and Ruth Hall, *op. cit.*

50. **Enid Charles**, *The Twilight of Parenthood*, Watts & Co, London, 1934.

51. Quoted in **Noreen Branson** and **Margot Heinemann**, *Britain in the Nineteen Thirties*, Panther Books, St Albans, 1973, p. 183.

52. *Ibid.*

53. Jane Lewis, 'The Ideology and Politics of Birth Control in Interwar England'.

54. **Richard** and **Kathleen Titmuss**, *Parent's Revolt: A Study of the Declining Birth Rate in Acquisitive Societies*, Secker and Warburg, London, 1942, p. 105.

55. **Richard Titmuss**, *Problems of Population*, Association for Education in Citizenship, London, 1942, pp. 8–9. Mrs Neville Rolfe commented on the absence of any conscious population policy in **Sir Hubert Llewellyn Smith**, *The New Survey of London Life and Labour*, Vol. IX, *Life and Leisure*, King & Son, London, 1935, p. 292: 'Higher standards of living, new knowledge of contraceptive measures, education, housing, and insurance schemes follow the demands of public opinion and economic conditions without conscious administrative interference.'

56. See **Victoria Greenwood** and **Jock Young**, *Abortion in Demand*, Pluto Press, London, 1976, p. 20.

57. Rowbotham, *A New World for Women*, p. 67.

58. The five major organisations included were: Society for the Provision of Birth Control Clinics; Workers Birth Control Group; The Birth Control Investigation Committee; The Society for Constructive Birth Control; and the Birth Control International Information Centre.

59. Peel and Dowse, *op. cit.*, pp. 194 ff.

60. On the significance of similar moves in the American context, see Linda Gordon, *Woman's Body, Woman's Right*.

Chapter Eleven

Beliefs and behaviour
1914–39

A 'glorious unfolding'?

The period from the outbreak of the First World War to the start of the
Second has no 'natural' or pre-given unity. It is clearly post-Victorian in
social mood, even though many of the tenets of nineteenth-century
morality survived into the inter-war years. It is just as clearly pre-
permissive, despite the moral panics about sexual promiscuity generated
during the First World War, the myths of the 'Roaring Twenties' or the
concerns with sexual delinquency of the 1930s. But to conceptualise the
whole period as transitional is to avoid a whole catalogue of difficult
problems – and to assume that automatic ascent towards sexual
liberalism which we have earlier rejected. The organisation of sexuality
during these years was clearly a product both of the inheritance of a
series of moral codes and practices, and of exposure to the felt needs of
the time. The result was a complexly changing situation which makes
any simple schematisation virtually impossible. For the general
historian, the period falls into three more or less distinct phases: the
Great War itself with its ruptures of the social fabric; the 1920s, with
the early apparent optimism, the massive industrial strife, and the appearance of the emancipated (middle-class) woman; and the 1930s,
where mass unemployment scarred the older industrial areas, while new
industries developed in more favoured parts of the country; but which
was dominated above all by the threat of fascism and war. Each of
these phases significantly nuanced the sexual regime, but there were also
strong elements of continuity throughout the period.

It has been tempting for some commentators to discover a 'sexual
revolution' in the 1910s and 1920s followed by a 'backlash', or what
Kate Millett has termed a 'counter-revolution' in the 1930s, dominated
as it was by a conservative political climate.[1] There is some evidence for
both. Certainly amongst certain strata of the population the 1920s saw a
relaxation of some sexual taboos: the new feminists spoke of sexual
pleasure, birth control was more openly advocated, progressive intellectuals espoused sex reforms, while homosexuality caused a certain
fashionable *frisson*. By the 1930s this was clearly changing. Dora
Russell has recalled how a new authoritarianism entered into personal

relationships in the 1930s. Her own, 'open' relationship with Bertrand Russell collapsed in bitterness and recrimination.[2] Though anecdotal, such evidence is indicative. Simultaneously the reform organisations went into decline, and hopes for radical changes faded as more immediate political and economic concerns dominated. And yet, of course, there were significant cross-currents. The greater freedom to talk about sex in the early part of the period can be grossly exaggerated. Compared with the Victorian scandal sheets, the papers of the 1920s were discreet in the extreme in reporting the contents of marriage break-ups.[3] Homosexuality could be hinted at but never openly talked about. The *Evening News* (12 November 1920) noted that 'There are certain forms of crime prosecutions which are never reported in the newspapers and of which most decent women are ignorant and would prefer to remain ignorant.' And there were many feminists who felt the limits to sexual freedom; it often meant little more than freedom for men to exploit a woman's greater vulnerability. Similarly, the 'backlash' of the 1930s can be misunderstood if we look only at the fate of radical individuals. For the period also saw the appearance of a new literature of sexual pleasure in marriage which significantly looks forward to the post–Second World War period. This provides a clue to one of the two most important developments of the inter-war years: the growing emphasis on the importance of sexuality in married love, an emphasis which has its roots in the nineteenth century and its real efflorescence in the 1950s, but which crystallised in the inter-war years. There was a two-way movement at work. On the one hand, there was undoubtedly a greater stress on sexuality as an aspect of the familial norm. On the other hand, we can detect the refinement of new forms of control on sexual behaviour outside the norms (and it is in this context that we can understand the radical retreats). If there is a simple unifying factor during these years it is in this movement that we can find it: Marie Stopes's 'glorious unfolding'.

Associated with this was a new stress on the need to scientifically understand sexuality – and this is the second major theme of the inter-war years. Amongst the radicals this involved an attack on traditional morality in the name of scientific knowledge. Amongst the more religious minded reformers – such as Marie Stopes and Edward Griffith – there was an attempt to combine Christianity with the new insights.[4] This was the thrust behind the new texts on married love that appeared during the 1920s and 1930s. This openness to scientific insights was not, it scarcely needs stating, uniform. John Bancroft has complained that 'In the 1920s and 1930s the mental hygiene movement again succeeded in confusing mental health and morality.'[5] But few morality campaigners could now ignore the insights of Ellis, Freud and others without losing all credibility.

This stress on science, it is worth noting, has its incidental advantages for the historian. For the period also saw, starting in America, the first systematic attempts to survey sexual attitudes in representative samples of the population.[6] No significant attempt to do this of the British population was attempted before the 1940s, but the age cohorts then used do allow the historian some insights into sexual behaviour during the 1930s, which supplement the well-established figures of birthrates, marriage rates, illegitimacy rates and so on. As a result this is the first period for which we can begin to find a welter of data (supplemented by oral-history techniques)[7] with which to try to understand sexual behaviour.

In this overall context, three problems in particular need illuminating. The first is the significance of changes in the hegemonic ideology of domesticity and family life. Secondly, there is the changing role of the institutions of social regulation, which helped sustain and cement the social order: the state, the churches, the morality campaigns. Thirdly, there is the question of regulation, both legal and ideological, of sexual unorthodoxy. These three problems provide the framework for the remainder of this chapter.

Domesticity and family life

The period inherited the nineteenth-century domestic and familial ideologies, and these remained the frameworks within which sexuality was organised. But there were significant changes within the forms of the ideologies, and there continued to be a differential assimilation of the various elements through the filters of class, generation and regional differences.

Marriage was now the firm entrance to adult sexual life. The remarkable fact about marriage rates was their stability. Between 1871 and 1947, of those who lived to 45–54, between 85 and 88 per cent were, or had been married. The excessive female–male population imbalance, accentuated by the war, led to a significant increase in the marriage rates of men as compared to women during the 1920s (an excess of some 20 per cent, 1916–30) but by the 1930s this had evened out.[8] The statutory age of marriage rose in 1927 to 16 for both sexes; previously it had been 12 for women, 14 for men. But this had little effect as the average age of marriage had always remained much higher: in 1930 it was 29 for men, 26½ for women. There were, however, significant class differences. Amongst industrial workers who by and large could still expect full pay at 21, the average age was 18–24; it was higher amongst clerks (on an incremental wage scale) and higher still amongst professional people. This was reflected in regional differences, so that, for example, whereas by 1930 the total percentage of women marrying under 21 was increasing nationally, it was falling in London, with its larger professional population and absence of agricultural labourers.[9]

But if marriage was firmly fixed as the social norm, there were important changes in the notions of family life to which matrimony was the gateway. The sharpest reflection of this was in the new ideal of the small family. It was during this period that the 'nuclear' family began to come into its own. The decline in the birthrate was the most dramatic index of the changing ideals. At the beginning of the century (1901–5) the average annual crude birthrate per 1,000 of the population was 28.2; by 1921–5 it was 19.9; and by 1931 it was down to 15.0. The average number of legitimate births per 1,000 married women dropped from 230.5 in 1901–5 to 156.7 in 1921, 115.2 in 1931–5, and to 105.4 during the Second World War. In other words, the fertility rate was more than halved in less than sixty years.[10]

As a consequence of this, the size of the average family declined dramatically. Between 1900–9 and 1930 the percentage of couples with five or more children fell from 27.5 to 10.4, whereas the numbers of those with one or two children rose from 33.5 to 51.1 per cent. The average number of live births of those married 1900–09 was 3.37; for those married 1920–4 it was 2.38; and for those entering matrimony 1925–29, the numbers were 2.19. The family size of those married 1925–9 is 60 per cent lower than the mid-Victorian average; and by 1930, 81 per cent of all families consisted of three or less children.[11]

This decline was a significantly cross-class phenomenon. In 1911, the least fertile section of the population had been professional people. By 1931 the lowest fertility was amongst clerical workers. As the Titmusses put it, 'the clerical class in England and Wales are among the most infertile social groups in the whole of the world.' But during the previous decade the most rapid decrease in birthrates had been amongst semi-skilled and agricultural workers, demonstrating, as again the Titmusses put it, a 'democratisation of fertility rates'.[12] The size of the families of manual workers still remained considerably higher than the size of non-manual families (2.49 children to 1.73 for those married 1925–9).[13] At the same time there were important variations between sections of the workforce: miners still retained a higher fertility than other industrial workers, though the difference was narrowing. But it was manifest that the planning of fertility and the ideal of a small family were no longer middle-class priorities alone.

Though the figures are unambiguous, the changes of behaviour and beliefs which they suggest are not. There was undoubtedly a growing awareness of the possibility of controlling fertility, and this coincided in the 1920s and 1930s with a growing degree of sophisticated knowledge, thanks to the various birth-control campaigns.[14] But this cannot provide a sufficient explanation: there was an even greater knowledge of birth-control techniques during the 1960s, but this did not stop an increase in the birthrate then. The work of Stopes and others was vitally important, but by the time of Circular 153/MCW there were still only some thirteen clinics in the country. From a sample survey of the Manchester and Salford clinic, 1928–33, it appears that a higher proportion of manual workers' wives obtained birth-control information from institutional sources than non-manual workers', but working-class wives were a minority of clients – and their numbers seem to have declined in the late 1930s.[15] Availability of facilities did not automatically dictate behaviour, although knowledge of technique and of the body was obviously essential if the decision to control births was to be taken. Nor can imbalance in age or sex ratios provide a useful explanation: the effects of the First World War on such ratios had effectively run their course by 1930. Although fertility was highest in agricultural areas, which might be affected by differential sex ratios and age structures, such factors were of minor significance in the overall decline of fertility.

Other factors were clearly at work, and these in the end must be related to changes in ideals and ideologies – which in turn were the effects of different class experiences within the context of the overall ideologies of family life. For what is striking is the resistance of the population at large to the blandishments of government and experts concerning the precipitous fall in the birthrate and the need to procreate. Various groups were reacting to their specific awareness of their situations and carrying forward these experiences into new domestic ideals. One major experience, of course, was that of unemployment. 1933, the year in which the birthrate reached its lowest point in peace time, was also the year of highest unemployment.[16] It would be tempting, therefore, to find a direct correspondence between economic distress and the new family norm. But the trend towards smaller families was more marked in the relatively prosperous south than in the north or Wales, where unemployment was highest. And small families were noticeably present, as they had been for half a century, amongst professional people little affected by unemployment. A more directly relevant factor was the question of class status and security, which was particularly marked amongst the 1½ million clerical workers during the 1930s, who generally had job security but were confronted by high overheads (home mortgages, cost of travel to work, educational costs). More important still was the relevance of these factors to the maintenance of their precarious status: not fully members of the great middle class, but sharply demarcating themselves from the mass of the working class. Desire for a smaller family obviously had an economic rationale but the pressure came not so much from direct fear of poverty as from a (presumably ideological) wish to maintain a desired standard of living and way of life.[17]

Independent (but equally) complex factors were at work in relationship to decision making amongst other social groups.[18] Recent studies of working-class communities have, as we have seen, demonstrated the close relationship between female work patterns and fertility rates: women working outside the house (as in the textile areas) tended to have more knowledge of contraception, be more equal with their husbands, and to have a positive desire for fewer children. Women without outside jobs tended to invest more significance in the home, be more emotionally involved with their children and to be less aware of birth control. But in turn the increased emotional investment in children could lead to a decision to restrict further births. A study of South Wales miners' wives indicates the intricate elements at work.[19] Up until 1911 the mining valleys (with a traditionally high birthrate) had been characterised by a heavy inflow of migrants from rural areas, the absence of settled community patterns and the privatisation (and probable sexual ignorance) of the wife. After 1911 this migration ceased, and this in turn probably contributed to a consolidation of community values and information networks, which might have resulted in a greater knowledge of the possibility of fertility control. Economic insecurity, the decline in infant mortality, the fact that children were less of an economic asset and more of a liability in the new situation: all in turn might have helped shape the meanings given to the home and led to a new family ideal. Unemployment, meaning that miners spent more time at home, may have led to a greater male awareness of domestic problems and contributed to an increased equality in marital relationships. This in turn may have reinforced the new family ideals and eventually led to decisions to limit family size. These speculations need further historical investigation, but they are suggestive. The point of an account like this is that it provides an alternative explanation to the assimilation model, which sees a gradual filtering downwards of middle-class family ideals. The evidence, on the contrary, indicates the significance of a distinct experience shaping family aspirations. The Mass Observation survey of Britain's population decline in the early 1940s looked at the changing aspirations of, amongst others, a Mrs Smith's family of 13. They found a variety of motives as the immediate cause of the decisions of the offspring to limit births – consciousness of household routine, economic factors, psychological friction. But the basic underlying factor was that none of the daughters wanted to have large families. This was the fundamental change.[20]

A number of important changes during the inter-war years helped to reinforce this desire. One such factor, clearly, was the decline in infant mortality which led to the fading away of the traditional anxiety about physical survival and an increased concern with social and emotional factors. The 1930s saw as a consequence a new literature of child care, foreshadowing the better-known theorisations of the 1940s and 1950s.[21] Another factor was the development of new leisure patterns, in part reflecting the possibility for many of going beyond the question of sheer survival and of developing fuller lives, in part shaping the new family ideal (so we see the growth of holidays in the 1930s for the 'whole family').[22]

Housing policy is another index of the changing nature of domestic ideologies. The emphasis on subsidised municipal housing which had been one of the products of post-war optimism was adversely affected by the slump, but by the 1920s building societies were making arrangements which allowed clerical workers and the better-paid manual workers to buy their own homes. In the 1930s there was a massive housing boom, both in council and private house building. And the homes that were built assumed the centrality of the nuclear family. The new housing estates, as D. V. Glass put it, were 'designed not to draw people together, but rather to divide them from each other'.[23]

But perhaps the most potent factor of all, again prefiguring the affluence of the 1950s and 1960s, was the turn towards consumerism. This had begun in the late nineteenth century with the expansion of factory food production and home furnishings. This accelerated (though in a highly uneven manner) in the inter-war years, particularly through the growth of the electrical industries. There was, moreover, a substantial rise in real incomes for those in work during the period. New domestic equipment and prepared foods, combined with the reduced burdens of child rearing, powerfully worked to create the space for new ideals of an intense family life.[24] And these myriad pinpoints of consumption were served by tendencies in the mass press, building on and helping to form the new consumer market. The 1930s was the period when the mass media began to take on their full modern appearance and social significance, and this development was reflected in the appearance of new magazines, with mass readerships, catering especially for middle-class and lower-middle-class women. *Woman's Own* was founded in 1932, *Women's Illustrated* in 1936, and, most successful of all, *Woman* in 1937, appearing in colour, and with sales by the outbreak of war of three-quarters of a million.[25] Their new emphasis on home services was accompanied by an intensification of domestic ideologies. 'Happy and lucky is the man', noted *Housewife*, launched in 1939, 'whose wife is houseproud . . . who likes to do things well, to make him proud of her and her children.'[26] The elevation of female housework into a craft gave it the status of a profession, but simultaneously created a new climate for the selling of household commodities. This symbiosis between the new domestic ideal and the new consumerism should not be read deterministically, as if the new move in the economy *caused* the ideology. But there can be little doubt that the new consumerist outlook worked to reinforce tendencies which were clearly there in society, though they were tendencies which were not to become dominant for another two decades, and whose main impact was still on the middle class and sections of the upper working class rather than on the mass of the population.[27]

It is in this context that we must attempt to understand the new emphasis on sexuality in conjugal relationships. It would be facile to see this as an *effect* of consumerism, but again it must be said that there was no incompatibility between the new sexual emphasis and economic restructuring. Some indication of the changing mood can again be seen in the women's magazines. The *Lady's Companion* had drawn attention to a new interest in sex as early as 1920, while *Good Housekeeping* had noted the importance of Freud in convincing women that they had sex drives. And by the late 1930s there were some signs of a new frankness, though it was always tempered by a fear of going too far. The advice was often tart as well as discreet, as a reply in *Home Chat* illustrated: 'I am sorry I cannot answer so intimate a question through these columns and I am rather amazed at your ignorance about the facts of life. Ask an older friend to tell you.'[28] But by the outbreak of the Second World War, advice columnists were prepared to recommend booklets on family planning and to deal with marital problems in articles. *Woman* published a series on the 'Psychology of Sex' and included a test for frigidity.

However, the context within which such advice was given was all important. When the first 'Evelyn Home' (generic name of the agony columnist of *Woman*) advised a married woman to spend a weekend with her lover, the copy was quickly censored, and the 'Evelyn Home' soon departed.[29] The key element in the new mood was a relaxation in the 1920s and 1930s of the discretion concerning conjugal sex – but no relenting on the question of extra-marital or non-heterosexual sex. There were more radical works in circulation. Bertrand Russell's *Marriage and Morals* (first published in 1929, and enjoying numerous reprintings thereafter) had argued, in many ways following Havelock Ellis, that 'Children, rather than sexual intercourse are the true purpose of marriage,' so that marriage only became necessary when children came along. Nor should marriage exclude other sexual relations. Ellis himself published a number of essays on 'the renovated family', while Judge Ben Lindsey and Wainwright Evans's advocacy of 'The Companionate Marriage' was published in Britain in the late 1920s.[30] These were influential works. A luminary of a more conservative morality, Gladys Mary Hall, could rather scathingly reject the 'new morality' they represented while arguing that they had useful results in clarifying the meaning of marriage: 'A new conception of marriage has come into being, in which the object is the real mating of two independent personalities.'[31] As this indicates, the advocacy of the spiritual and unifying force of sexual pleasure could easily be assimilated into a more traditional familial framework, as the writings of Marie Stopes, deeply influenced by both Ellis and Edward Carpenter, amply demonstrate. Ellis's caution about the overemphasis on sexual foreplay was the other side of Stopes's emphasis on the bliss of coitus, and the proper sexual roles of men and women. Stopes felt it was 'against the true ideals for a woman to advertise to her husband what she is wanting'.[32] What was at stake, then, was the notion of reciprocity in sexual pleasure, but not the obliteration of gender distinctions, or sexual libertarianism.

Similar emphases were characteristic of the work of Theodore Hendrik van de Velde (1873–1937), a Dutch gynaecologist whose most important work was a celebration of *Ideal Marriage*. This work had some 42 printings in Germany, 1926–32; the English translation, published in 1930, went through 43 printings. It offered a potent mixture. He addressed his audience, as Edward Brecher has put it, in a language which neither startled nor disturbed them, working all the time within a framework of marriage, and concentrating on sex standards which he regarded as normal. He was above all anxious to make marriage sexually fulfilling. Like Ellis and Stopes, he rejected the notion that sex could take care of itself. There was a need to learn techniques to achieve the desired mutual orgasm. He stressed mutuality and sharing in the couple, and wanted brides to be virgins and husbands experienced. But he disapproved of adultery, prostitution and other non-marital adventures and firmly stated his 'intention to keep the Hell-Gate of the Realm of Sexual Perversions firmly closed'.[33] This was a representative note, echoed in many handbooks, and was widely influential. By 1932 even the old social-purity White Cross League could publish a Christian manual, *Threshold of Marriage*, offering instructions on simultaneous orgasm which sold over half a million copies. Edward Griffith's *Modern Marriage* first published in 1935 offered a similar emphasis on conjugal love ('there is no longer any necessity for sex to be a quagmire of mental inhibitions') and went through 19 editions between 1935 and 1946.[34]

At the centre of this new emphasis on conjugal sexuality was a re-evaluation of female sexuality, especially in the middle class. This did not amount to a revolutionary change. Virginity remained a priceless possession. But there is evidence of relaxation in the forms of control. This was clearly indicated in the decline of chaperonage during the First World War, when more pressing demands were made on the time of middle-class ladies. The growing employment opportunities for young women, during the war and later in the new consumer industries, also increased the chances of female independence (at least before marriage and children). Moreover, changes in leisure patterns – the growth of dance halls, cinemas and so on – had their effect, reshaping the possibilities of courtship, with a wider range of places to meet and less direct parental control. Mrs Neville Rolfe, a stalwart of the purity campaigns, noted in the 1930s that 'it is no longer an indication of the absence of moral sense if an acquaintance made at a dance hall or cinema should ripen into friendship and the change must be regarded as the inevitable result of changed social conditions, even though such casual acquaintances may sometimes become partners in extra-marital sex relations.'[35]

Accompanying this relaxation in formal surveillance was the decline of prostitution and the rise, as it was commonly put, of 'the amateur'. The First World War appears to have accentuated a trend which was already present, to such an extent that prostitution ceased to be an integral and easily accepted feature of the social scene. Sir Ernley Blackwell in the later stages of the war estimated that up to 75 per cent of the venereal diseases amongst the troops was caused by 'amateurs', not prostitutes.[36] There is strong evidence for a decline in prostitution; certainly it attracted less attention from the authorities, and seems to have become less blatant. In the early 1930s Mrs Neville Rolfe speculated that there were no more than 3,000 prostitutes in London (though this was impressionistic and probably a considerable underestimate) and that the area of street solicitation was smaller, and the importuning more discreet, than in 1900. This was an indication both of a change in general street behaviour (less rowdyness and drunkenness) and of, as usual, a change in the form of prostitution, associated with the rise of better types of night clubs. But there probably was, as well, a real decline. Obviously, many factors contributed to this decline, amongst them the extension of women's employment opportunities, but undoubtedly changes in general concepts of female chastity played a major part. Mrs Neville Rolfe, scarcely a libertarian, indignantly distinguished casual sex from prostitution, because it was of a non-commercial character and therefore had some emotional content. She went on, 'Whether this relaxation of the pre-marital standards of sex behaviour on the part of women and girls has resulted in an increase or a decrease in the total volume of promiscuity is impossible to say with certainty, but it has certainly reduced prostitution.'[37] Sexual contacts with friends was obviously preferred to commerce with prostitutes, especially with the increased awareness of the risks of venereal disease.

But with the still general inefficiency of birth-control methods, and continuing widespread ignorance, pre-marital activity continued to carry penalties and stigma. During the early years of the war it was still possible for a moral panic to emerge and run its course over the prospect of 'war nymphomania' and 'war babies'. A letter in the *Morning Post* from Ronald McNeill, MP in April 1915, warning of the risks of unmarried girls becoming mothers where troops were quartered, started an immediate flurry of press anxiety.[38] In actuality, 1915 saw a low illegitimacy rate and a high marriage rate. And although illegitimacy rates did increase during the war (by 1919 they were 30 per cent up on pre-war figures), by the mid-1920s they had stabilised at a lower figure, at which it was to stay for the remainder of the inter-war years. Illegitimacy continued to carry a bad social connotation (despite the fact that the first Labour Prime Minister, J. Ramsay MacDonald, was illegitimate), though there was a new recognition that the child should not be punished for the behaviour of its parents. The National Council for the Unmarried Mother and Her Child was founded in 1918 to encourage mothers' responsibilities towards their offspring, and its work contributed to the passing of a Bastardy Act in 1923, and a Legitimacy Act in 1926 which allowed children to be legitimised by a subsequent marriage of the parents. But unmarried mothers remained on the outer fringes of respectability.[39]

It is virtually impossible to judge with any accuracy whether pre-marital sex did increase, though some indication of its widespread nature can be gauged by the Registrar-General's statement in his report for 1938–9 that 'One seventh of all the children now born in this country are products of extra-marital conceptions, or to go further, that nearly 30 per cent of all mothers today conceive their first-borns out of wedlock.'[40]

A report by Eustace Chesser on *The Sexual, Marital and Family*

Relationships of the English Woman, although published in 1956, throws some light on the question of female sexual behaviour in the 1920s and 1930s because he analysed some of his data on the basis of age cohorts. There is an obvious danger in relying on figures from a problematical sample, but they do indicate important trends, especially among middle-class women, which correspond with other forms of evidence.[41] He found a considerable increase, for instance, in the incidence of petting. Some 7 per cent of the married women born before 1904 had engaged in non-coital sex before marriage; for those born 1904–14 (that is reaching maturity in the inter-war years), the figure had risen to 22 per cent; for those born 1914–24, the figure was 29 per cent. The figures for single women showed a similar increase: 11 per cent of those born before 1904 had indulged in petting, compared with 17 per cent for those born 1904–14, and 22 per cent, 1914–24. The figures for pre-marital sexual intercourse are equally revealing. Some 19 per cent of married women in the sample, born before 1904, had engaged in pre-marital sex; this had risen to 36 per cent for those born 1904–14; and to 39 per cent for those born in the next decade. The proportion for single women rose from 18 per cent for those born before 1904 to 32 per cent, 1904–14; there was a slight fall to 30 per cent for the next decade.[42] Unfortunately, there is no breakdown of these figures on a class or regional basis, though the bias of the sample was towards middle-class women. If approximating at all to what actually happened, they offer striking proof of a gradual change of *mentalité* amongst large sections of the population, though the norm was still, as the figures make clear, very definitely a chaste one.

How these changes affected marital sexual relationships is more difficult to tease out. We have very little evidence, for instance, on the frequency of coitus. A small sample of 56 nurses, aged 20–47 in the late 1930s suggested that intercourse took place 1.2 times per week. Another survey, which is relevant to the later part of the period, Eliot Slater and Mona Woodside's examination of the *Patterns of Marriage* of 200 working-class ex-servicemen, found the nodal frequency of intercourse was twice per week, gradually lessening in frequency with age.[43] But the subjective feelings behind the sex act, and the meanings given to both marital and extra-marital sex, are less amenable to surveys – though such evidence as there is suggests little fundamental change amongst working-class women. Slater and Woodside found in their working-class sample that for the men conjugal sex was a habit, leading to a complacency which was only disturbed by anxiety over whether they were able to satisfy their wives. They found a continuing pattern of male dominance: 'Responsiveness in their wives was hardly expected, and there was some suggestion that where the wife was more sensually disposed than her husband, her "hot nature" was disapproved, and even feared.'[44] The women, on the whole, not surprisingly tended to be more puritanical, indifferent and bored on questions of sex. Half the women in the sample found some pleasure in the sex act; and for a minority it was a source of real pleasure. However, compared with the experience of the men, orgasm for women was uncertain; only one-third always experienced orgasm; one-quarter infrequently or insufficiently. It would be useful to test these working-class figures by reference to other social groups, but unfortunately later surveys do not provide a sufficient age or class breakdown to allow simple comparison to be made. Nevertheless, it was towards middle-class wives that the conjugal handbooks were directed, and it is likely that the major changes in consciousness occurred in this stratum.

Such evidence as we do have, suggests that the mild relaxation of sexual taboos also had quite different implications for men and women. Janet Chance observed in *The Cost of English Morals* that:

The subject of physical happiness in marriage raises a pathetically eager response in working women's meetings. . . . It is often news to them that they might at all share the sex enjoyment of their husbands . . . . Twenty thousand letters have been received by the Divorce Law Reform Union over a period of years, from couples wishing to end their marriage, and in the majority of these cases the reason for failure was the distaste of one of the partners for the physical marriage relationship.[45]

Sexual misery, far from being ended, was disruptively common. Moreover, the new ideological stress in the marriage handbooks on the blissful orgasm could add an extra strain, making sexual harmony a gauge for the success or failure of the marriage. Paradoxically, one possible effect of the extension of the grounds of divorce in 1923 to include adultery by the man could, by increasing the penalties for extra-marital sex, make sex more of a duty then before for the wife. Moreover, with the ideal of the smaller family, the space for meaningful extended relationships and ties, through older and younger generations, was being narrowed. The space could be filled by new leisure activities, home building, emotional investment in children; but it also made the sexual element increasingly the essential element in choice of partners. The strains of such an emphasis were not to become fully apparent for another generation, but they were clearly already present in the 1920s and 1930s.

The correspondence of Marie Stopes is an excellent index of the price of the moral codes. She received letters from all walks of life, in vast numbers (her son still has 65 boxes of material in his possession which complements the huge collection in the British Library), and, as we have seen, from doctors and clergymen as well as from the lay public. Many of the letters reveal a general embarassment and guilt at talking about sex. More women wrote than men (56 per cent to 44 per cent) and the majority of correspondents were upper and middle rather than working class (60.7 to 39.3 per cent). And there was an interesting difference in content of the letters. Whereas most of the working-class correspondents were concerned with factual questions concerning birth control, most of the middle-class correspondence was generally concerned with issues related to what can loosely be termed sexual 'repression'. A survey of the correspondence by Marie Stopes's grandson, Christopher Stopes-Roe, reveals that questions of basic sex education – frigidity, impotence, premature ejaculation, masturbation, first-night difficulties – were still the cause of widespread anxiety.[46]

Sexual ignorance was itself, of course, the consequence of a restrictive moral code and this was reflected in attitudes to sex education. The prosecuting counsel in the Stopes libel case in 1923, who seemed to think that any form of stimulation was equivalent to prostitution, revealed all the usual moral and class prejudices. He asked Stopes if she would leave *Married Love* 'to be read by your young servants, or indeed, give it to your own female relatives'.[47] That of course, was her implicit intention. It was unlikely that they could easily read much else on the topic. Formal sex education was still extremely limited, though there was some change during this period. Amongst the women in Eustace Chesser's sample whose childhood fell between 1900 and 1939, there was a marked increase in the proportion who obtained their sex education from doctors, teachers and other adults (rising from one-tenth to one-fifth). Books and pamphlets as a source of knowledge also showed a marked increase (from 2 per cent pre-1904 to 14 per cent 1914–24; and 17 per cent, 1924–34). This development accompanied a slight growth in willingness to talk about sex. The proportion of married women who received an impression from their parents that sex was something not to be talked about dropped from 76 per cent (pre-1914) to 58 per cent (1924–34); and the proportion who received an unfavourable impression decreased, with the most substantial change occurring for those whose childhoods fell in the 1930s.[48] But it would be wrong to exaggerate the change: even amongst those born in the 1930s, a third still did not feel able to talk about sex at home.

The inter-war years did see a sustained effort – though usually from moral conservatives – to provide a basic awareness of sexual hygiene. The British Social Hygiene Council (founded as the National Council for Combating Venereal Disease in 1916) made strenuous efforts to stimulate biology lessons in school, helped by leading biologists like J. A. Thomson and Julian Huxley. Up to 1931 it held 24,000 meetings, attended by some 5 million people (excluding soldiers); it sponsored 3,000 conferences and 700 courses of lectures for parents, youth leaders and teachers. The general campaign against venereal disease was exempt from restrictions on frankness in films. A series of films, with titles such as *Waste, The Flaw, The Girl Who Doesn't know, Damaged Goods*, played to large audiences. In 1934 *Damaged Lives* played to 4 million people in 327 towns.[49]

But at a national level there was little formal encouragement of sex education. The Board of Education had recommended sex education in schools in 1927, but this was discretionary. Most of the school text books ignored the subject. Furneux and Smart's *Human Physiology*, a leading school textbook (published as one of Longman's Elementary

Science Manuals) still did not deal with sex organs or reproduction in its 1930 edition.[50] Local authorities were similarly discreet. A London County Council Memorandum on the Curriculum for Science (July 1935) had suggested the study of the reproduction of flowering plants and the life history of frogs and birds but had concluded: 'It will generally be agreed that class instruction in senior schools should not include mammals.'[51] On the eve of the 1944 Education Act only about one-third of secondary schools made any provision for sex education – chiefly through special lectures. The state still relied on voluntary efforts. Formal sex education remained normative in tone, inculcating a general respect for the ethics of married life, and condemning extra-marital or deviant sex. The more radical alternatives recommended by the British Sexological Society (the later name of the British Society for the Study of Sex Psychology) made no impact. The two attempts to establish Sex Education and Consultation Centres (by Janet Chance in London in 1929, and by Edward Griffith in Aldershot) to provide a wider range of advice were small and negligible in comparison with their models in Germany, Austria, Scandinavia and Switzerland.[52] There were, however, some changes in context of sex instruction, reflecting an awareness of new theoretical trends. In 1921 the social-purity White Cross appointed a sub-committee to revise its literature and invited the Freudian Ernest Jones to contribute. As a result, the more heavily moralistic of its tracts with enticing titles such as *The Perils of Impurity* were withdrawn, and their replacements began to speak of 'understanding, warmth and affection' as the best responses to masturbation. In 1932 the Student Christian Movement concluded that 'masturbation does no physical or mental harm'.[53] The morality being inculcated in the revised texts was a conventional one, but there was a new awareness of the need to make it more palatable and less authoritarian.[54] Like the marriage manuals for adults, the impulse behind the recognition of the need for a more sophisticated sex education for children was the desire to harness sexuality to the cause of morality. The problem remained that for many (the unmarried, the maritally miserable, the homosexual) that morality was still the major source of anxiety and guilt.

What was becoming increasingly obvious in the inter-war years was the growing conflict between the two separate strands of the dominant moral ideology. The Christian view of the sanctity and permanence of marriage was by no means necessarily compatible with the increasing emphasis on sexual harmony. Moreover, it had been obvious for generations that marriages often were not permanent, and despite the difficulties of divorce, separation was very common. But attempts to reform the divorce laws made little progress. The 1857 law was clearly inequitable, as between men and women, rich and poor, and its unsatisfactory nature had led in 1909 to the establishment of a Royal Commission under the chairmanship of Lord Gorell.[55] The Majority Report wanted to keep the concept of a matrimonial offence, but sought to increase its range. So it proposed an extension of the grounds for divorce from adultery to include desertion, cruelty, insanity, drunkenness and imprisonment. But despite the obvious and growing demand (during the First World War the number of divorces made absolute increased three-fold, at a rate of 2,954 per annum),[56] there was little advance in implementing the proposals. Proceedings were expensive, and until the early 1920s all divorce cases had to be heard in London before the Divorce Court judges. After 1923 cases could be heard in certain assize courts while the grounds for divorce were relaxed a little to include adultery on the part of the male partner, but legal aid, which could have helped the poorer, made little progress. The Committee for Legal Aid for the Poor, 1928, noted that 'It is manifestly in the interests of the State that its citizens should be healthy, not that they should be litigious.'[57] And it was not until the experience of the Second World War, and the government's concern for the morale of the troops, that the state recognised the need to back a legal aid scheme (institutionalised in the Legal Aid and Advice Act, 1949).

The Matrimonial Causes Act of 1937 (sponsored by A. P. Herbert) was the first really major change of the grounds for divorce since 1857. They were extended for husbands and wives to cover adultery, desertion for three years, cruelty, insanity and confinement for five years; and for the wife on grounds of rape, bestiality or sodomy. The grounds of nullity were extended to cover non-consummation, being of unsound mind, epilepsy, VD and pregnancy by another man.[58]

Though representing an important extension of the grounds for divorce, (and hence evoking fear that it would diminish respect for marriage), the Herbert Act suggested no major reconceptualisation of marriage. The Act began sonorously and truly, 'Whereas it is expedient for the true support of marriage . . .'. Many in the churches recognised this point. One of its clerical supporters, the Archdeacon of Coventry, observed that the maintenance of adultery as the major ground had been itself an inducement to immorality. There was certainly an increase in the divorce figures, rising from an annual average of over 4,000 during 1920–30, to 7,500 during 1936–40; and the number of petitions per 10,000 married couples rose from 1.38 in 1911 to 6.34 in 1937, and 26.98 in 1950. But compared with later decades, the figures were negligible. The law eased the difficulties of divorce, but scarcely encouraged t_rmination of marriage; formidable barriers remained, particularly as divorce continued to depend on the concept of a 'Matrimonial offence'. And as McGregor writing in the 1950s suggested, far from divorce implying the break-up of the marriage system, the search for a formal ending of a partnership indicated its more deeply embedded nature: 'The formalities of marriage are nowadays more commonly observed than fifty years ago.'[59] Moreover, divorce continued to carry a heavy social stigma. It proved impossible for a king to marry a divorced woman in 1936; and for a princess to marry a divorced man in the 1950s. The re-marriage of a prominent politician, Anthony Eden, could still generate splenetic protests from some churchmen as late as the 1950s. Re-marriage in a church, moreover, was virtually impossible for an Anglican, and entirely impossible for a Catholic. Marriage, sustained by Churches, state and public opinion, remained the bulwark of the sexual order.[60]

Protecting purity

That marriage was so deeply ingrained in the social consciousness was the product of a century of ideological endeavour. Social purity ceased during these years to be a mass movement but its influence was firm, and there was a continuing close, and often symbiotic relationship between morality pressure groups, church and state. One of the outstanding features of the period is the continued dominance of formal standards of respectability. The mistresses of Lloyd George and the Prince of Wales were discreetly screened from public view, while a Liberal politician preferred suicide to the threat of public accusations of buggery. The 'Royal Family' remained the acme of moral leadership; the publications of the National Council of Public Morals carried a quotation from King George V as its motto: 'The foundations of National Glory are set in the homes of the people – they will only remain unshaken while the family life of our race . . . is strong, simple, and pure.' Purity, familialism, public decency remained the social norms which the apparatus of formal moral regulation sought to uphold. The areas of tension occurred not with the desired aim but over the boundaries between the public and private spheres.

The First World War illustrated vividly some of the problems of formal regulation. Social purity and women's organisations were alarmed from the first by the dislocations of family life and the fear of promiscuity, and the result was a series of scare stories, such as the 'war babies' panic of 1915. Part of the trouble was that voluntary social workers, often middle-class ladies whose only previous experience of lower life was in contact with their servants, were now directly confronting the different *mores* of working-class life and were shocked by the casual behaviour they observed.[61] A number of women's organisations initiated patrols to keep watch for loose behaviour in open spaces and near military camps. Towards the end of the war the London Public Morality Council prepared a report on the observed sexual activities of couples in various open spaces (such as Hampstead Heath, Clapham Common and Parliament Hill Fields) which conveys an irresistible picture of respectable ladies pursuing their moral passion to the point of prying. It occasioned a faintly ironic put-down from the Assistant Commissioner of Police, who noted that 'The Council does not always bear in mind that the conduct of which they complain only constitutes an offence against the law when committed within the view of the public.'[62] Amongst other achievements, the Public Morality Council finally succeeded during the war in closing a number of music-hall promenades and in driving prostitutes from many of their customary haunts on licensed premises.[63]

One of the direct results of this moral enthusiasm was the establishment of a women's police force. The Voluntary Women's Patrols, set up by the National Council of Women at the beginning of the war, had by 1918 become a section of the Metropolitan Police, and by 1923 had full powers of arrest. Amongst their duties was to advise young girls, to investigate sex offences and to do plain-clothes work. There was another consequence of the women's services in the war: for the first time they gave the government a direct responsibility for female morals.[64] Local vigilance committees also continued throughout these years to keep watch for the obscene and the indecent. In London the Public Morality Council employed (up to the 1950s) a patrolling officer whose duties were to observe public behaviour, especially prostitution and male homosexual importuning; the officer was usually a retired member of the police force, and his reports were regularly forwarded to the Metropolitan Police for action to be taken.

Direct surveillance was one matter; how far the community could go in regulating private behaviour was another, and the issue remained unresolved. Some of the problems came to the fore in the debate over venereal disease. The Royal Commission on Venereal Disease, set up in 1913, had quickly become a focus for social-purity endeavour, and by the time it reported in 1916 the issue had become even more explosive because of the rapid spread of venereal diseases amongst the troops. The Report revealed a widespread incidence of the disease: 'In a typical working class population of London at least 8 to 12 per cent of the adult males have acquired syphilis, and at least 3 to 7 per cent of the adult females.' The figures for gonorrhoea were higher still. The figures were probably overestimates, but they were predictably exaggerated further in the press as if they applied to the population as a whole. The Report also revealed the strong class differences in treatment. The rich could easily be treated for syphilis with salvarsan; the poor were often refused admission to hospitals and could be refused outdoor relief or lose entitlement to insurance benefits.[65] Some form of national policy was obviously necessary but the Commission and the government were intent on avoiding the accusation of condoning immorality; and there was a great outcry in 1918 when the government seemed willing to condone its soldiers' making use of *maisons tolerées* on the French Front. It was forced to place them out of bounds. The resistance to the state regulation of vice remained very strong.[66]

The government accepted and implemented the main recommendations of the Royal Commission. State-backed pathology laboratories were established; free supplies of salvarsan were given to doctors; and local authorities were encouraged to set up free special clinics in general hospitals, with a 75 per cent grant from the Exchequer. This neatly avoided the controversial issue of providing special (and potentially 'immoral') prophylaxis for the troops by providing free treatment for all. This was to have major long-term effects in controlling venereal disease.[67] But with regard to the disease amongst the troops the burden had to fall on the women. Regulation 40.D, D.O.R.A. promulgated in Easter 1918 in effect made it an offence for any infected woman to have intercourse with a member of the armed forces.[68] This was attacked by moralists and feminists, and was clearly also against common sense, as it made it an offence for a diseased wife to sleep with a soldier husband, even if he infected her in the first place. But it was a logical effect of the unwillingness of the state to be seen to condone immorality.

The issue was whether to provide proper prophylaxis, and risk immorality, or to urge moral restraint and risk disease. This was never satisfactorily resolved during the inter-war years (and flared up as an issue again during the Second World War).[69] A good example of the dilemma occurred in Manchester in the early 1920s. Manchester City Council set up two experimental ablution centres in 1920 in two cubicles of public lavatories. The idea was that those who thought they might have had contact with an infected person could go for an assisted wash. The National Council for Combating Venereal Disease (set up to support the family and encourage moral purity and racial advance) supported the idea. But most social-purity organisations and some feminists were horrified. An organised public opinion achieved the removal of advertisements and by 1922 forced the closure of the cubicles themselves. Some 18,000 men had by then visited the centres, the majority in the early hours; but mundane matters, such as the prevention of venereal disease, were obviated by the moral anxiety.[70] Despite the greater willingness to talk about venereal disease, and the provision of full facilities for cure, a strong stigma remained. Shortly before the Second World War the Ministry of Health prepared a series of outspoken advertisements against venereal disease. The copy committee of the Newspaper Proprietors' Association objected to the way in which they were written. The words 'pox' and 'clap' were omitted from the copy; so was 'sex organs' and the words 'Professional prostitutes are not the only source of infection'. But the *Daily Express* and the *Evening Standard* still refused to publish.[71]

Social purity remained a formidable force, particularly through the agencies of well-organised pressure groups, with friends in high places. There was still, inevitably, a mass base of enthusiasm on which it could draw. In 1923 White Cross spoke of a vast growth of the market for purity literature over the previous ten years, and between the wars the Alliance of Purity enrolled over 100,000 young men in branches in YMCAs, churches and youth clubs. The London Public Morality Council and the vigilance organisations could draw on a multitude of sympathisers to vet immorality on stage and screen, hunt out rubber-goods displays in shops, report on indiscreet behaviour in streets or lodging houses and provide financial backing for their intense lobbying activities.

But social purity had in a sense done its foundation building work so well in the first decades of the century that a mass movement was no longer necessary.[72] The authorities were very responsive to their demands. The recommendation of the Joint Committee on Stage Plays in 1912 to abolish the Lord Chamberlain's highly anachronistic theatre censorship was ignored (and continued to be ignored until the 1960s), and in 1926 the Lord Chamberlain gave the Public Morality Council the privilege of regular access. The film industry voluntarily censored itself, and achieved a very close relationship with prominent moralists. The Bishop of London (*ex officio* head of the PMC) revealed in 1936 that 'Dear old T. P. O'Connor (a former President of the British Board of Film Censors) used to come down and have lunch with me when he had a doubt about a film.'[73] A later chief censor, Lord Tyrrell, afterwards became President of the National Vigilance Association. These close, even cosy, informal links had their effect in transatlantic film commerce: in 1930 the Public Morality Council became the official source of reaction to American films for Will Hays, whose committee enforced moral standards on the American film industry.

The police and government also proved vigilant in pursuit of the obscene. The sexually explicit works of D. H. Lawrence, literary and visual, faced constant harassment, as did a number of other works, of varying artistic merit, especially those dealing with lesbianism. An incident in 1923 illustrates the often discreet measures taken. Copies of Victor Margueritte's *La Garçonne* (for publication of which its French author was expelled from the Legion of Honour) began to appear in England at the beginning of that year and the question arose as to how to prevent its circulation. The police were able to make fine distinctions concerning its nature. As a Detective Inspector Draper wrote: 'I think I should say that although the book is full of description of indecent and revolting scenes, it does not strike me as being of the type of what we find in Rubber shops, or in such works as those of D. H. Lawrence or Elinor Glyn.' But the Home Office was anxious to prevent its circulation. On the other hand, there was an awareness that a prosecution would advertise the work. So discreet police action was opted for. Chief constables were authorised to detain and open postal packets believed to have copies of the book.[74] Direct prosecution was often unnecessary where pressure could be put on by public officials. In 1939 the *Daily Mail* reviewer of the memoirs of a prostitute sent his pre-publication copy to the Public Morality Council, which in turn forwarded it to the Home Office. This led to a threat to the publishers and the withdrawal of the book before distribution.[75]

A similar sequence had occurred in 1928 with Radclyffe Hall's *The Well of Loneliness*, and the book was withdrawn. The subsequent prosecution was as a result of the distribution of the book from abroad. But this case illustrates another important factor: the responsiveness of all levels of authority (MPs, the civil service, ministers, judiciary) to moral pressure, and the complicity between them. There is quite clear evidence, for instance, that the Home Office Under-Secretary was in close consultation with the Chief Metropolitan Magistrate, Sir Chartres Biron *before* he tried the case of Hall's novel. The Under-Secretary reported that: 'necessarily in the course of my interview we touched upon *The Well of Loneliness* and there can be no doubt what opinion the Chief Magistrate holds upon that book'.[76] The debate was always over the parameters of public action. A successful prosecution of a dubious work might 'help to stem the tide of degeneracy which is so fraught with danger', as the Home Office Under-Secretary put it; but the failure of a prosecution might add to that tide.[77]

For long periods of the inter-war years social purity had friends in very high positions. The Solicitor-General at various times between 1922 and 1936, Sir Thomas Inskip, was an ardent evangelical. The Director of Public Prosecutions, Sir Archibald Bodkin, was formerly a member of the Council of the National Vigilance Association. Above all, the Home Secretary between 1924 and 1929 was the most notoriously puritanical of all, Sir William Joynson-Hicks ('Jix'). He held a very traditionalist view of the role of the state: 'The government has a general responsibility for the moral welfare of the community which is traceable partly perhaps to the peculiar relationship existing between the Church and the State, and partly also to the duty inherent in all governments of combatting such dangers as threaten the safety or well-being of the state.'[78] He quite clearly saw his duty (like one or two crusading Home Secretaries since) as the guidance of public morality – towards a high moral standard at that. The result was a series of often absurd moral interventions with regard to obscenity.

Though the law remained the mainstay of the moral order, there was no major extension of its formal role during the inter-war years. The great expansion of the criminal code on sexual matters was clearly coming to an end. At one point during the late 1910s there were three bills on sexual offences before Parliament.[79] But the 1922 Criminal Law Amendment Act, passed after much debate and effort, was the last major change in the laws regarding the protection of young girls from sexual danger, and its changes were limited. (They were not necessarily libertarian, however; previously an accused man had been able to claim the defence that he had reasonable cause to believe a girl was over 16; this defence was now lost. There were also increased penalties for brothel keepers.[80]) The Street Offences Committee which reported in 1928 accepted the tradition that 'the common law has never taken upon itself the prohibition by criminal sanctions of voluntary illicit intercourse between the sexes', and proposed no new extension of the law (despite some ardent advocacy from the Public Morality Council that immorality should be made illegal). It confined itself to the recommendation that all existing legislation on street offences should be repealed and replaced by a single enactment, making it an offence for any person to importune another of the opposite sex for immoral purposes in a street or public place. This was not followed through.[81]

But just as there was no major extension of the criminal law, so there was no decriminalisation. Heterosexual deviance therefore remained outside the sphere of the law; homosexual offences just as clearly remained within it. The classic position was summed up by Sir Norwood East, the leading expert on the psychological treatment of crime during the inter-war years.

English law regarding sexual offences does not inflict criminal penalties upon all those acts which ecclesiastical law prohibits and used to punish . . . but it selects for criminal prohibition only those in which there is also present some further element – whether of abnormality or violence or fraud or widespread combination – that provokes such a general popular disgust as will make it certain that prosecutors and witnesses and jurymen will be content to see the prohibition actually enforced.[82]

The Street Offences Committee reaffirmed this double standard. The majority recommended (in Clause 6) that 'no change be made in the existing law regarding solicitation between men'. They thus endorsed the anomalous position achieved by the Criminal Law Amendment Act of 1912, which had increased the maximum penalty to six months' imprisonment and removed the right to jury trial. A minority report (signed by Sir H. Fairfax Lucy, Margery Fry and Sir Joseph Priestly) had commented:

In our opinion this is not just. It creates a position for which there is no justification unless it is that any person who has the misfortune to be charged with the very grave offence whether innocent or guilty is to be treated differently to other offenders charged with other crimes. It seems to ignore the rule that every man charged is presumed to be innocent until proved guilty.

This minority report was not (it goes without saying) signed by Sir Chartres Biron, another member of the Committee, who elsewhere had stated that jury trial was 'the only method of criminal trial in a civilised community'.[83]

The existence of laws and proscriptions is not, of course, a guarantee of their punitive usage, and there is continuing evidence of both regional and chronological variations. Dr Hermann Mannheim noted at the end of the 1930s 'a considerable rise in sexual offences' since the end of the war (which he put down partly to changing definitions and treatment of sexual crime; partly to the role of statistics themselves in generating interest; and partly to increased 'mental instability' as an effect of the war.)[84] Within this general trend, however, there were important fluctuations. The most striking involved the prosecution of prostitution offences, which in the late 1920s plummeted in London. The number of convictions fell from 3,191 in 1927 to 695 in 1930. This was in part a result of the relaxing of police pressure after the arrest of the former MP Sir Leo Chiozza Money and a Miss Savage in Hyde Park in 1928 and the furore it caused. In part, of course, it also reflected the long-term decline in prostitution, and the changes in its form. In 1900 there were 66 brothel keepers in Holloway prison, by 1930 there were only 14; during the same years the overall number of women in prison for prostitution offences fell from 546 in 1900 to 85 in 1930. But during the 1930s there was a considerable rise again in the number of convictions, rising by 1938 to the 1927 level.[85]

These changes were clearly a result of varying police activity;[86] certainly in London and other major cities like Birmingham there was a considerable back-up from the morality organisations which continued their campaign against public indecency. But the major focus of concern seems to have changed. As the forms of female prostitution became more discreet, increasingly male homosexual offences came to the fore. This was often conceptualised in terms of an increase in the incidence of homosexuality, but almost certainly was actually a consequence of an increased anxiety. During the 1930s, particularly, homosexual offences became a particular preoccupation of the Public Morality Council. In the 1920s the number of prosecutions in the London area at least remained fairly steady (averaging 69 per annum for males importuning, 86 for unnatural offences),[87] but from the 1930s there began what was to become a major trend of increasing prosecutions on a national scale. It seems more than an accident that this coincided with the development of new sexual attitudes, and the implications of this will be explored below.

The impact of these factors on the homosexual subculture are less easy to tease out. Mrs Neville Rolfe, writing in the early 1930s, detected a greater tolerance with regard to homosexuality, which she attributed (in a rather unlikely explanation) to the increase of cheap continental travel, which brought large numbers of men under the influence of a laxer public opinion.[88] But tolerance is a relative concept. In certain strata (the ancient universities, literature, the higher echelons of the state) there was possibly a greater openness than previously; and for many homosexuals, reflecting in old age, the 1930s may have seemed a golden age. But for many other (especially working-class) homosexuals who lived through the inter-war years there was still the primary need for secrecy. A recent series of interviews with male homosexuals who reached adulthood between 1910 and 1940 revealed a deep sense of fear and anxiety combined with an ability to adjust to and live through difficult circumstances. Some preferred to live abroad rather than risk arrest in Britain; others sexual abstention to public obloquy. But still others managed to develop relationships and integration into the (largely secretive) subcultures. These were still fractured by class divisions, forms of casual male prostitution playing a major role.[89] And press and public opinion continued to be feared. John Van Druten, the playwright, complained in 1929 of the portrayal in the theatre of homosexuals as 'effeminate men, mincing and wilting' while serious discussion was tabooed.[90] Inevitably the consciousness that developed remained fragmentary and guilt-ridden. But there are interesting cross-currents, particularly evident in the development in the 1920s and 1930s of a much more coherent lesbian sense of self. Radclyffe Hall and Una

Troubridge are the best-known examples. By the late 1930s it was possible for a member of one of Mass Observation's panels to declare herself as a lesbian – in representatively gender-invert terms: 'I am in a half way position, being officially a woman, yet dressing and regarding personal appearance from a mainly masculine point of view.'[91] The permanent paradox remained that authoritarian moral codes in acting out their logic (as in the case of the prosecution of *The Well of Loneliness*) produce by an inevitable reflex, an enhanced sense of identity.

Psychology and sex delinquency

Although never dominant during the inter-war years, there is another important tendency which was becoming articulate in this period – and that was the growing acceptance of the medical model – and hence a new willingness to consider either decriminalisation or new methods of treatment. As early as 1921 the Association for Moral and Social Hygiene (the successor to Josephine Butler's campaign against the Contagious Diseases Acts) stated that private homosexual acts between consenting adults should be legalised,[92] and the influence of Freud and Ellis began to infiltrate the writings of the relevant organisations and individuals. This was an aspect of a much wider tendency which had two overlapping concerns: firstly, to redefine certain categories of behaviour in terms of 'delinquency' rather than vaguer and more all embracing concepts such as 'degeneracy'; and secondly, an attempt to define the 'psychological' causes of such behaviour, and therefore prescribe 'psychological treatment' rather than penal incarceration. At the centre of the conceptual switch was a belief that instead of relying on traditional moral categories, crime and 'anti-social behaviour' should be 'scientifically' studied. A very important element in this was an attempt to integrate the findings of psychology and especially psychoanalysis into understanding what in the 1960s was to be called 'deviance' (another significant reconceptualisation). The acceptance of the new approach was by no means general. The criminologist Edward Glover has recorded how his first address to magistrates on the importance of psychoanalysis in understanding crime, in 1922, fell completely flat.[93] But by the early 1930s there was sufficient interest for an Institute for the Study and Treatment of Delinquency to be established, whose main work during the 1930s was to support the work of a clinic which paid especial attention to sexual matters.[94] The approach gradually began to seep into official discourse, largely through the work of Norwood East, whose studies for the Home Office during the 1930s (expressed in his 1939 *Report on the Psychological Treatment of Crime*, written with W. H. de B. Hubert) amounted to a cautious endorsement of a psychological approach.[95] Sex offences were central to this new type of investigation.

Delinquency and crime were not of course identical. Mrs Neville

Rolfe used the term 'delinquency' to include: 'all forms of extra-marital sexual intercourse, from the crude practice of commercial prostitution, through various degrees of promiscuity to isolated cases of "sex adventure", or the anticipation of marriage relations.'[96] None of these were crimes as such. But within the category of sex crimes finer distinctions were being made. East offered twelve distinct groups of offences, from the unnatural, through indecency with males, rape, indirect assault, incest, procuration to indecent exposure.[97] Implicit in the new approach was that certain types of sex crimes might be decriminalised – to be treated in other ways. There was no clear consensus on this during the 1930s. East did not wish to medicalise all crimes. He agreed that imprisonment might often fail to check sexual deviations and stressed that, for example, homosexuality and heterosexuality were not unrelated. But he was too cautious to endorse decriminalisation: 'My own experience leads me to believe that a sentence of imprisonment does prevent at least some homosexuals from further delinquency.'[98]

The corollary of a psychological approach, whether or not certain categories were withdrawn from legal purview, was the offer of medical treatment in prison. Edward Glover, in a lecture given in 1945, argued (as he had done during the 1930s) that every sex offender 'without exception' should be psychologically examined and given the opportunity of psychological treatment. The 1948 Criminal Justice Act made some provisions for treatment as alternatives to prison, but by the early 1950s the actual numbers being treated were still small (25 in 1951, 27 in 1953).[99] There is some evidence that by the 1940s at least *psychiatric* treatment was being imposed on adult homosexual offenders as a condition of probation but it was not until the 1950s that this became a major issue in social policy. Amongst juvenile sex offenders, however, there are signs of an individualisation and personalisation of treatment, and of subtle distinctions being made. Mannheim quotes a medical officer, faced with a homosexual youth, arguing that:

It is essential that he should be given work congenial to him; it is hopeless to think of sending him to sea, for instance. Possibly tailoring would suit him, so that he might find an outlet for creative work eventually in dress designing . . . . I do not consider him vicious, and he is altogether in a different category from the male prostitute type of offender.[100]

Arguments like these do not, of course, challenge hegemonic values or undermine the basic concept of 'delinquency'. They represent new methods of dealing with it.

This process of the psychologising of delinquency and crime offered both the formal and informal agents of sexual regulation a potent new means of social control, promising a more refined method of regulation than the blunderbuss of the law. Vice and moral turpitude could be replaced by 'psychological disorders' as the explanatory mode. Moral norms need not be changed; indeed they could be reinforced by new conceptualisations. What was offered in short, was a new weapon for the control of sexuality – at the service of a more or less conventional morality. But in the 1930s this was still a tendency rather than a basis of policy.

It was indeed, the unofficial bodies rather than formal state organs which generally accepted the psychologising approach. Cyril Burt, in his study of the causes of sex delinquency in girls had in effect argued for a new role for voluntary bodies. He suggested that of all the factors making for sex-delinquency in girls an over-sexed constitution was the commonest and most direct. But this could be obviated by preventive agencies providing a strong background. The true function of such agencies, therefore, was to protect susceptible girls against the accidents likely to lead them astray, to widen their range of interests, and to provide for friendship.[101]

Already by the early 1930s there were some signs of major changes in voluntary preventive and rescue work, with the advent of the 'scientifically trained worker'. Mrs Neville Rolfe noted a significant change:

Reports of rescue work published at the end of the last century attributed all faults to moral obliquity. Every act of extra-marital sex intercourse was a serious 'sin', for which each individual was held equally responsible. Today the reports of those organisations with trained workers show a clear appreciation of the bearing on conduct of physical and mental characteristics and general social change.[102]

Science was coming to the rescue of morality. This was perhaps one of the most significant developments of the years after the First World War.

In *The Cost of English Morals* Janet Chance distinguished between the 'dogmatic' and the 'realist' approaches to moral matters. There are some signs that the 'dogmatic' (or authoritarian) approach was losing its force, but there was no triumph for the realist (or liberal) approach during this period. During the Stopes libel trial in 1923, the Lord Chief Justice addressed the jury thus: 'Upon you has fallen in this matter, so far as it can any longer be controlled, the guardianship of public morals.'[103] Implicit in this was the belief that the traditional organs of moral guidance could not indefinitely maintain their hegemony. But at the same time there was a strong conviction in the fundamental solidity and orthodoxy of British morality. There was much evidence to sustain this.

There was undoubtedly a decline of religious observance. The Roman Catholics perhaps held up best, and the Anglicans benefited from the Establishment. But the nonconformist conscience was losing its political force.[104] Organised religion still counted in questions of marriage and divorce, in decision making on birth control, even in rituals of courtship.[105] But apart from the occasional crusading government minister (like Inskip or Joynson-Hicks), or public officials, few in positions of political leadership would have felt able to rely on religious sanctions for their views. But on the other hand there was no ready acceptance of pluralistic sexual values; on the contrary, what was clearly present was a deeply ingrained acceptance of the leading tenets of 'Christian' sexual morality, especially its familialism, at the same time as its religious framework was being undermined. The debates over the divorce reform in an important way dramatised this process, for the more far-seeing of the religious leaders were fully aware of what was happening. As Cosmo Lang, the Archbishop of Canterbury put it, with reference to the Herbert Bill, 'I came to the conclusion that it was no longer possible to impose the full Christian standard by law on a largely non-Christian population . . . I could not as a citizen vote against the Bill, but I could not bring myself as a Churchman to vote for it; and I announced I would not vote.'[106]

That abstention more than anything else symbolises the changes which were already modifying (if, certainly, not radically transforming) the sexual codes, changes which over the next forty years were significantly to reorder the place of sexuality in social life.

References

1. **Kate Millett**, *Sexual Politics*, Rupert Hart-Davis, London, 1971.
2. Dora Russell, *The Tamarisk Tree*.
3. **A. J. P. Taylor**, *English History 1914–45*, Clarendon Press, Oxford, 1965, p. 170.
4. Edward Griffith, *Sex and Citizenship*, p. 9: the new moral code 'must be strengthened by a synthesis of scientific knowledge and religious principles'.
5. **John Bancroft**, *Deviant Sexual Behaviour*, Clarendon Press, Oxford, 1977, p. 16.
6. For studies of the progress of sex research see Alfred Kinsey *et al.*, *Sexual Behaviour in the Human Male*; E. M. Brecher, *The Sex Researchers* p. 109 ff.; **Eustace Chesser**, *The Sexual, Marital and Family Relationship of the English Woman*, Hutchinson's Medical Press, London, 1956: Appendix, 'A Brief History of Surveys on Marriage Relationships'; and Max Nordann, *History of Modern Morals*. Kinsey was the key figure but though he tended to believe that they were pre-scientific, there were various predecessors. Even Ellis, who rather distrusted statistics, occasionally made use of them (not least in his tabulation of his own nocturnal emissions). Kinsey himself identified 19 surveys, 1915–47 the earliest of which was conducted by Dr M. J. Exner for the YMCA in 1915. Probably the best-known sex surveyor was Katharine Bement Davis, author of *Factors in the Sex Life of 2,200 Women*. Most of these early surveys were, however, confined to limited samples, often of college students, and all were American. Most were, moreover, characterised by an extreme caution in broaching sexual matters. The first systematic British study of fairly wide scope was Eliot Slater and Moya Woodside's sample of 200 working-class soldiers who under stress of warfare had been hospitalised for neurotic and other illnesses during the Second World War. Their findings were published as *Patterns of Marriage: A Study of Marriage Relationships in the Urban Working Classes*, Cassell, London, 1951. This survey, and Chesser, *op.*

cit., do however provide valuable information on attitudes prior to the Second World War.

7. The use of oral-history methods for the investigation of attitudes towards sexuality is still in its infancy, but in various spheres (such as attitudes to family relations, birth control, sexual variations, etc.) promises to bear useful fruit. For references see below.

8. J. A. Banks, *Prosperity and Parenthood*, p. 3. **Diana Gittins**, 'The Decline of Family Size and Differential Fertility in the 1930s', unpublished MA thesis, Sociology Department, Essex University, 1974, p. 23; **E. Lewis-Faning**, *Report on an Enquiry into Family Limitation and its Influence on Human Fertility During the Past Fifty Years*, Papers of the Royal Commission on Population, London, Vol. 1, 1949, p. 21.

9. **Mrs Neville Rolfe**, 'Sexual Delinquency', in **H. Llewellyn-Smith**, *The New Survey of London Life and Labour*, Vol. IX, P.S. King & Sons, London, 1935, p. 291; *Registrar-General's Statistical Review*, 1930, pp. 112–13.

10. **A. H. Halsey** (ed.), *Trends in British Society since 1900*, Macmillan, London, 1972, p. 31; **John W. Innes**, *Class Fertility Trends in England and Wales, 1876–1934*, Princeton University Press, 1938, p. 11.

11. Halsey, *op. cit.*, p. 55; Gittins, *op. cit.*, p. 16.

12. Richard and Kathleen Titmuss, *Parents' Revolt*, p. 86.

13. See **D. V. Glass** and **E. Crebenik**, *The Trend and Pattern of Fertility in Great Britain. A Report on the Family Census of 1946*, Papers of the Royal Commission on Population, Vol. 6, HMSO, London, 1954.

14. There was some concern that the greater availability of birth-control information would encourage 'immoral' sexual intercourse. But it proved difficult to devise legal measures to prevent the advertising and sale of contraceptives to all but the married. A bill to do this passed the House of Lords in 1933 but made no further progress. Mrs Neville Rolfe, *op. cit.*, p. 293.

15. **Diana Gittins**, 'Women's Work and Family Size between the Wars', *Oral History*, Vol. 5, No. 2, pp. 90–1. Lewis Faning's enquiries showed that over 60 per cent of couples married during 1930–4 had by 1946 practised some kind of birth control. But only some 25 per cent of social class 3 (unskilled) had used mechanical appliances, compared with 40 per cent of social class 1 (professionals). Dr C. P. Blacker's survey of Family Planning Clinics from 1938 to 1947 had further revealed that though the total attendance had risen substantially, there had been an absolute decrease in the number of working-class women attending: Ruth Hall, *Marie Stopes: A Biography*, p. 315.

16. **Noreen Branson** and **Margot Heinemann**, *Britain in the Nineteen Thirties*, Panther Books, St Albans, 1973, p. 180.

17. J. A. Banks, *op. cit.*, makes the classic argument for this. Richard and Kathleen Titmuss, *op. cit.*, p. 99, enumerate a number of factors for lower-middle-class infertility, including the marriage ban in certain professions (e.g. teaching, where married women were prohibited) and restrictions against early marriage. They make the point that many black-coated workers 'do not earn sufficient until they are over 30 years of age to maintain the standard of life which is considered necessary in their occupations'.

18. Edward Griffith, *Sex and Citizenship*, p. 183, enumerates various economic reasons for the middle class to control fertility, including inability to afford expensive nursing homes and private nurses.

19. Diana Gittins, *op. cit.*, p. 99.

20. Mass Observation, *Britain and Her Birth Rate*, John Murray, London, 1945, p. 227; Ch. XX makes the general point.
21. On the influence of Dr Truby King on child-rearing methods, see **Anna Davin**, 'Imperialism and Motherhood', *History Workshop*, No. 5, Spring 1978, p. 47; on general trends, see **Denise Riley**, 'War in the Nursery', *Feminist Review*, No. 2, 1979; for the influence on family ideals, see Diana Gittins, 'The Decline of Family Size', p. 77.
22. See James Walvin, *Leisure and Society*.
23. **D. V. Glass**, *The Social Background of a Plan*, London, 1938, p. 12; quoted in **Catherine Hall**, 'Married Women at Home in Birmingham in the 1920s and 1930s', *Oral History*, Vol. 5, No. 2, p. 62 ff.
24. C. Hall, *op. cit.*, p. 68; **John Stevenson** and **Chris Cook**, *The Slump*, Quartet, London, 1979, Ch. 2.
25. Branson and Heinemann, *op. cit.*, p. 269 ff; **Cynthia L. White**, *Women's Magazines 1693–1968*, Michael Joseph, London, 1970, p. 93.
26. White, *op. cit.*, p. 100.
27. This was reflected in the different emphases of magazines for working-class women which were primarily vehicles for pulp fiction. See White, *op. cit.*; and **Richard Hoggart**, *The Uses of Literacy*, Penguin, Harmondsworth, 1958, p. 206 ff.
28. White, *op. cit.*, pp. 107, 111.
29. **Robin Kent**, *Aunt Agony Advises: Problem Pages through the Ages*, W. H. Allen, London, 1979. pp. 247, 27.
30. Bertrand Russell, *Marriage and Morals*, pp. 133, 114; **Havelock Ellis**, *More Essays of Love and Virtue*, Constable, London, 1931 (Ch. 11, 'The Renovation of the Family'); **Judge B. Lindsey** and **Wainwright Evans**, *The Companionate Marriage*, Brentano's, London, 1928 (with introduction by Dora Russell).
31. **Gladys Mary Hall**, *Prostitution: A Survey and a Challenge*, William and Norgate, London, 1933, pp. 174, 180.
32. Quoted in **Ruth Hall** (ed.), *Dear Dr Stopes. Sex in the 1920s*, Andre Deutsch, London, 1978, p. 86.
33. Brecher, *The Sex Researchers*, pp. 89–90.
34. Bristow, *Vice and Vigilance*, p. 147; **Edward Griffith**, *Modern Marriage*, 19th edn, Methuen and Co., London, 1946, p. 1. Griffith's book was first published as *Modern Marriage and Birth Control* (Victor Gollancz, 1935). Other works by him include *Voluntary Parenthood*, Heinemann, 1937; *Morals in the Melting Pot*, Victor Gollancz, 1938; *Sex in Everyday Life*, Allen and Unwin, 1938; *The Childless Family. Its Causes and Cure*, Kegan Paul, 1939. Other representative works in this *genre* include **M. J. Exner**, *The Sexual Side of Marriage*, George Allen and Unwin, London, 1939, which argued that the failure to reach orgasm on the part of the wife was the bane of a happy marriage; **Gwen St Aubyn**, *The Family Book*, Arthur Baker Ltd., London, with an introduction by Harold Nicolson which advocated a compromise between the 'advanced school' and Victorianiasm; **Sofie Lazarfeld**, *Rhythm of Life: A Guide to Sexual Harmony for Women*, George Routledge and Sons, London, 1934; and two articles by **Harry M. Grant** (Executive Director of the Family Relations Center, San Francisco) on 'The Possibilities of Modern Marriage', in *Marriage Hygiene*, Vol. 11, Nos 3 and 4, February and May 1936.
35. Mrs Neville Rolfe, *op. cit.*, p. 295. Her article is useful on the 'rise of the amateur'.

36. **H. R. E. Ware**, 'The Recruitment, Regulation and Role of Prostitution in Britain from the Middle of the Nineteenth Century to the Present Day', unpublished Ph.D. thesis, London University 1969, p. 501.
37. Mrs Neville Rolfe, *op. cit.*, p. 296.
38. *Morning Post*, 17 April 1915; *Daily Mail*, 17 April 1915; *Observer* 18 April 1915; **Arthur Marwick**, *The Deluge: British Society and the First World War*, Pelican, Harmondsworth, 1967, p. 114.
39. On attitudes to illegitimacy, see Mrs Neville Rolfe, *op. cit.*, p. 316; **M. I. Cole**, *Marriage, Past and Present*, J. M. Dent, London, 1938, p. 140. For statistics on illegitimacy, see Halsey, *op. cit.*, p. 51; and J. W. Innes, *op. cit.*, p. 11. For a contemporary comment on the social effects of the stigma against illegitimacy (e.g. the higher infant mortality), see **Geoffrey May**, *Social Control of Sexual Expression*, Allen and Unwin, London, 1930, p. 215.
40. Quoted in E. Slater and M. Woodside, *Patterns of Marriage*, p. 111.
41. Eustace Chesser, *The Sexual, Marital and Family Relationships of the English Woman*. He points out (p. 15, note 1) the bias in his sample towards higher-income groups and occupational strata; single women are overrepresented (p. 16); middle aged and elderly are underrepresented (p. 17); so while the sample was broadly representative in respect of religion, age at marriage, it is not in others (p. 21). But as an index of trends, especially in the middle class, I think we can make use of Chesser's figures.
42. Chesser, *op. cit.*, p. 313, 311.
43. **R. A. McCance**, *Journal of Hygiene*, 1937, pp. 571–611; Slater and Woodside, *op. cit.*, p. 164. Slater and Woodside point out the limitations of their sample on p. 18 ff. They conclude it is a 'fairly representative' sample of working-class and lower-middle-class married Londoners, aged 21–47, a number of whom were married during the 1930s.
44. *Ibid.*, p. 167.
45. **Janet Chance**, *The Cost of English Morals* (with an introduction by Sir Thomas Horder), Noel Douglas, London, 1931, p. 35.
46. Ruth Hall (ed.), *Dear Dr Stopes*, Statistical Appendix, p. 215 ff.
47. Ruth Hall, *Marie Stopes. A Biography*, p. 216, p. 219.
48. Chesser, *op. cit.*, p. 160, p. 163.
49. Bristow, *Vice and Vigilance*, p. 151.
50. Janet Chance, *op. cit.*, p. 89.
51. Max Hodann, *History of Modern Morals*, p. 240.
52. See **Janet Chance**, 'Six Years in a Sex Education Centre', *Marriage Hygiene*, Vol. 1, No. 4, May 1935, p. 412 ff. The centre started in Kensington in January 1929, to provide instruction in the facts of life; to offer a platform for the discussion of sexual ethics; to give guidance and expert help in individual cases. It also supplied lecturers and had a lending library, offered personal consultations and provided an information bureau. Chance found it useful for ventilating her idea that 'there are large numbers of people who require guidance in sexual matters, often of an unbelievably elementary nature, and who do not know where to turn to obtain it'. People who came (there were 217 consultations up to 1934; the average attendance at lectures was 35–40) were generally fairly unorthodox in views and sought advice on such issues as pre-marital sex, impotence, homosexuality, sex education, jealousy, incapacity of wife to achieve orgasm, etc. The centre was founded, as Chance put it, 'not on any claim to expert knowledge

but solely on a readiness to share honestly the results of experience'. It thus prefigures the radical self-help groups of the 1970s. See also Federation of Progressive Societies and Individuals, *Experiments in Sex Education*, London, 1935; Hodann, *op. cit.*, p. 165.

53. Bristow, *Vice and Vigilance*, p. 146. See also **A. S. Neill**, 'Masturbation in Childhood', *Marriage Hygiene*, Vol. 1, No. 1, August 1934, p. 47 ff. He advocates the end of repression partly, at least, because repression might lead to homosexuality.
54. **G. O. Barber**, *School Education in Hygiene and Sex*, W. Heffer and Sons, Cambridge, 1936, is a representative example of the modified approach. The book consists of the lectures given by a School Medical Officer to boys between 13 and 15. They are more concerned with hygiene than with sex as such. The first four lectures deal with the Digestive, Circulatory, Respiratory, and Skeletal nervous systems. He offers a bald recital of the facts about sex, and a brief description of the sex act, and refrains from moralisms on masturbation. The last lecture was on venereal disease, and was given to boys before they left school. It amounts to a recital of the dangers if pre-marital sex was indulged in. For a general statement on the normative function of sex education, see Hodges and Hussain, review article of Donzelot's 'La Police des Familles', *Ideology and Consciousness*, No. 5, p. 117.
55. O. R. McGregor, *Divorce in England*, p. 28.
56. *Ibid.*, p. 36; Marwick, *op. cit.*, p. 118.
57. McGregor, *op. cit.*, p. 33.
58. *Ibid.*, p. 30.
59. *Ibid.*, pp. 36, 37.
60. For comments on the hypocrisies surrounding the divorce laws, see M. I. Cole, *op. cit.*, pp. 126–7; for an observation on the solidity of marriage, see Mrs Neville Rolfe, *op. cit.*, pp. 339, 290.
61. Bristow, *Vice and Vigilance*, p. 146; Ware, *op. cit.*, p. 476; Association for Moral and Social Hygiene, Committee of Enquiry into Sexual Morality, London, 1918.
62. See the files in the Public Record Office: HO 45/10526/141896: 'Indecency on Hampstead Heath, 1906–1919'.
63. Bristow, *Vice and Vigilance*, pp. 214–16.
64. Mrs Neville Rolfe, *op. cit.*, p. 326; Ware, *op. cit.*, p. 505.
65. *Final Report of the Royal Commission on Venereal Diseases*, Cmd 8189, HMSO, 1916, Appendix XII, pp. 140, 62, 2, 43; Ware, *op. cit.*, p. 464; Marwick, *The Deluge*, p. 117; Bristow, *op. cit.*, p. 148.
66. Ware, *op. cit.*, p. 510; for the differences between the policies of Britain and the other powers on venereal disease, see **Magnus Hirschfeld**, *The Sexual History of the World War*, the Panurge Press, New York, 1934, pp. 93–4.
67. For the significance of the free provision of facilities for the treatment of venereal disease, see **David Barlow**, *Sexually Transmitted Diseases. The Facts*, Oxford University Press, 1974, pp. 10 ff. The provision of free facilities did not, of course, mean the end of moralistic service, or the demystification of the diseases. For the effects of the new policy in the inter-war years, see Mrs Neville Rolfe, *op. cit.*, p. 313; Gladys Mary Hall, *op. cit.*, p. 107 ff.
68. Ware, *op. cit.*, p. 494. See **Susan Buckley**, 'The Failure to Resolve the Problem of Venereal Disease Among the Troops in Britain during World War

One', in **B. Bond** and **I. Roy** (eds), *War and Society*, Vol. 2, Croom Helm, London, 1977.

69. Order 33B, 5 November 1942, made treatment of venereal disease compulsory. The Public Morality Council continued to oppose it on the grounds that this amounted to the state acceptance and regulation of vice; they remained committed to an abolitionist position. Greater London Record Office: Public Morality Council PPP sub-Committee, 11 November 1942, Ac 70, 36, Box 32.
70. Bristow, *Vice and Vigilance*, pp. 151–2.
71. **Peter Fryer**, *Mrs Grundy*, Dennis Dobson, London, 1963, p. 85.
72. Bristow, *op. cit.*, makes the point. See also **Brian Harrison**, 'For Church, Queen and Family: The Girls' Friendly Society 1874–1920', *Past and Present*, No. 61, November 1973, p. 138, which notes the long-term decline of the mass-based GFS.
73. Bristow, *op. cit.*, p. 223.
74. Public Record Office: HO 45/11446/451040.
75. Bristow, *op. cit.*, p. 225.
76. Public Record Office: HO 45/15727/528248; memorandum, 15 October 1928.
77. For a discussion of censorship, see Alec Craig, *The Banned Books of England*; Ellis comments on the issue in his essay on 'The Revaluation of Obscenity', in *More Essays of Love and Virtue*. Bertrand Russell offered trenchant comments on sex censorship (as did others) during the 1929 World Congress for Sex Reform: see **Norman Haire** (ed.), *World League for Sex Reform Proceedings*, London, 1930.
78. **H. A. Taylor**, *Jix – Viscount Brentford*, London, 1933, quoted in Ware, *op. cit.*, p. 596. Jix's exploits are entertainingly recounted in **Ronald Blythe**, *The Age of Illusion: England in the Twenties and Thirties*, Hamish Hamilton, London, 1963, Ch. 2. In fact, as Ellis, *op. cit.*, p. 134, pointed out, Jix came out for moral improvement rather than state policing as the best preventative of obscenity: 'The Censorship of Books', *Nineteenth Century and After*, April 1929.
79. A point made by **George Ives**, *The Continued Extension of the Criminal Law*, London, 1922, p. 13.
80. *Ibid.*; Ware, *op. cit.*, p. 548; Gladys Mary Hall, *op. cit.*, pp. 120–5. It is worth noting that an attempt to bring lesbianism within the scope of the Criminal Law by the 1922 Act failed. See above, pp. 105–6.
81. *Report of the Street Offences Committee, 1927–8*, Cmd 3231, Parl. Papers 1928–9, Vol. IX, para 8; see also Ware, *op. cit.*, p. 559; and Rolfe, *op. cit.*, p. 319. The absence of any new principle in the Criminal Law does not mean the state did not extend its range. For instance, under the Children and Young Persons Act, 1933, it was provided that children and young persons under the age of 17 could be removed from surroundings of 'moral danger' and where necessary provided with accommodation, education and maintenance in schools and other institutions approved by the Home Office. As a general point we suggest that state interest in the organisation of, and protection of people from, sexuality, can proceed apace even as the Criminal Law abdicates general responsibility: See Chapters 12 and 13.
82. **W. Norwood East**, *Sexual Offenders*, Delisle Edition, London, 1955, p. 11.
83. See *Howard Journal*, Vol. 11, No. 4, June 1929, p. 334.
84. **Hermann Mannheim**, *Social Aspects of Crime in England between the Wars*, George Allen and Unwin, London, 1939, pp. 121, 122.

85. For the statistical movement, see Ware, *op. cit.*, pp. 526, 535, 523; Rolfe, *op. cit.*, p. 321; Mannheim, *op. cit.*, pp. 121, 352; *Howard Journal*, Vol. 111, No. 1, September 1930, 'Reflections on the Criminal Statistics 1928'.
86. *Howard Journal*, Vol. 11, No. 3, October 1928, p. 18, noted the significance of police activity; *The Report of the Street Offences Committee* 1928, para 11, also commented on the importance of local variations.
87. The figures are from Mrs Neville Rolfe, *op. cit.*, p. 345. It is interesting that she tabulates the offences under the heading of 'Male Prostitution', whereas in fact the figures related to all men caught for homosexual offences in public, and not just for those in commercial transactions. This is a useful example of that continuing identification between prostitution and homosexuality which I have explored at greater length elsewhere: **Jeffrey Weeks**, *Journal of Homosexuality*, Vol. 6, Nos 1 and 2; and above p. 114. For the increasing trend in prosecutions from the 1930s to the 1950s (and beyond), see J. Weeks, *Coming Out*; and Chapter 12 below.
88. Mrs Neville Rolfe, *op. cit.*, p. 322.
89. The interviews were conducted as part of the research project on 'Homosexual Subcultures in England, 1880s–1940s: A Pilot Project', financed by the Social Science Research Council and based at the University of Essex. The researchers were Mary McIntosh and Jeffrey Weeks.
90. Quoted in Haire (ed.), *W. L. S. R. Proceedings*, p. 319.
91. 'Directives on Personal Appearance', April 1939, 1206. Tom Harrisson, Mass Observation Archive, University of Sussex; see also 'Directives on Clothes', May 1939. It was a common view that the First World War had encouraged homosexuality amongst women. (A view that Radclyffe Hall's *The Well of Loneliness* encouraged). See Magnus Hirschfeld, *The Sexual History of the World War*, p. 50; and for a representative vitriolic account, see 'The Vulgarity of Lesbianism', *New Statesman*, 25 August 1928: 'Now it is a comparatively widespread social phenomenon, having its original roots no doubt in the professional man-hating of the Pankhurst Suffragette movement, but owing very much to wider causes, arising out of the war and its *sequelae*'.
92. Ware, *op. cit.*, p. 547, note 2; Marie Stopes, in her inimitable way, expressed the central elements in this medicalising tendency in a long letter to Lord Alfred Douglas, 2 August 1939 (Ruth Hall (ed.), *Dear Dr Stopes* p. 211). Her basic argument was that the young should be protected, but otherwise rejected 'vindictive' treatment of adult homosexuals as pointless to prevent the 'social disease'. The *Howard Journal*, Vol. 111, No. 3, 1932, Editorial, p. 24, made a more coherent and judicious statement of the same argument: 'The attitude of the state to sexual offences requires radical revision. With the criminal law as it stands today, persons are sentenced to terms of imprisonment for sexual acts of which the modern state should take no cognisance or which should be matters for psychiatric investigation and treatment rather than punishment.' It therefore advocated a 'curative' rather than a punitive approach and a 'general application of psychological methods of treatment' (p. 25).
93. **Edmund Glover**, *The Roots of Crime*, Selected Papers on Psychoanalysis, Vol. 11, Imago Publishing Co., London, 1960, p. 35.
94. *Ibid.*, p. xii. The Association for the Scientific Treatment of Delinquency and Crime was launched in a letter in the *Manchester Guardian*, 25 June 1932, signed by Havelock Ellis, Freud, Glover, Adler, Jung and H. G. Wells.

95. **W. Norwood East** and **W. H. de B. Hubert,** *Report on the Psychological Treatment of Crime,* HMSO, London, 1939. See also **East,** *Medical Aspects of Crime,* J. and A. Churchill, London, 1936. East's work is discussed in L. S. Hearnshaw, *A Short History of British Psychology,* p. 291.
96. Mrs Neville Rolfe, *op. cit.,* p. 287.
97. Norwood East, *Sexual Offenders,* p. 15. The Mental Classification of Criminals scheme adopted by the Prison Commissioners had 6 types of criminal. 'Perverts' (homosexuals, exhibitionists, sado-masochists, fetishists, necrophiliacs) joined unstable adolescents, schizoids, paranoidal persons in category four, the 'Mentally inefficient': quoted in East and Hubert, *op. cit.,* pp. 4–5.
98. East, *Medical Aspects of Crime,* p. 323.
99. Edward Glover, *op. cit.,* p. 142; East, *Sexual Offenders* (Appendix I Statistical Findings) p. 99; Criminal Justice Act, 11 and 12 Geo. 6, 1948, para 4. For an example of hormone treatment in a case of homosexual offences in the early 1950s see **Andrew Hodges,** *The Enigma of Alan Turing,* Andre Deutsch, London 1981.
100. Mannheim, *op. cit.,* p. 332.
101. **Cyril Burt,** 'The causes of sex delinquency in girls', *British Journal of Social Hygiene,* 1926, pp. 251–71. It is noticeable that delinquency in women always refers to sexual delinquency. See also Mannheim, *op. cit.,* pp. 338–9.
102. Mrs Neville Rolfe, *op. cit.,* pp. 340, 336, 337.
103. Quoted in Ruth Hall, *Marie Stopes: A Biography,* p. 213.
104. A. J. P. Taylor, *English History,* pp. 188–9; **S. Koss,** *Nonconformity in Modern British Politics,* Batsford, London, 1975.
105. On birth control, see E. Chesser, *op. cit.,* pp. 268–9, where samples revealed (in the 1950s) that Roman Catholics used birth control least, Jews and 'other religions', most, while Nonconformists were the highest users amongst the Christian denominations. On courtship patterns, see **Derek Thompson,** 'Courtship and Marriage in Preston Between the Wars', *Oral History,* Vol. 3, No. 2, p. 42; he suggests that religious denomination was a potent factor in partner selection.
106. Quoted in O. R. McGregor, *op. cit.,* pp. 195–6.

Chapter Twelve

The state and sexuality

Population and family life

The Second World War, and the subsequent problems of post-war reconstruction, reshaped old preoccupations and produced a new mix of anxieties and concerns. The creation of a Welfare State in the 1940s, based, however tenuously, on an ideology of social (and even sexual) reconciliation, inevitably involved a major reassessment of the whole field of sexuality. For at the heart of welfarism was a clear concern with the conditions of 'reproduction' – both in its widest social sense, of producing a healthy workforce in the context of comprehensive social security and full employment; and in its narrow, biological sense, of improving the conditions of parenthood and childbirth. This ensured that the major sexual controversies over the next four decades were to be around the balance between social intervention and individual freedom, and this was reflected in the three major areas of debate – population policies, family life and sexual unorthodoxy.

In the 1940s, given the nationalistic concerns inevitably generated by war, reconstruction and the onset of the Cold War, there was a refocusing on the population question, which was propelled to the centre of public debate. The Beveridge Report of 1942, the foundation document of the Welfare State, expressed the basic fear, that 'with its present rate of reproduction the British race cannot continue,'[1] and this had its echo in a host of official, semi-official and private publications. Mass Observation, in its 1945 report on the question, which 'lined up with those who do not want the English people to disappear', raised the stakes still further by seeing the birthrate as 'the coming problem for Western Civilisation'; while the Royal Commission on population, set up in 1944 as an admission of governmental concern, quite clearly related these two preoccupations in its *Report* in 1949. For the Commissioners worried about the effects of a low or declining birthrate on both 'the security and influence of Great Britain' and the 'maintenance and extension of Western values'. The two were apparently inextricably linked.[2]

These concerns, and even their tone and language, had, of course, a long lineage. But what was new was the social and political context in which they were now expressed, for the creation in the 1940s and 1950s of a political consensus around the idea of a Welfare State did imply a more coherent interventionism in wide areas of social life than ever before. The problem here, as elsewhere in this study, is that of teasing out the intentionality and strategic thrust of the policies advocated and adopted. It is tempting to find coherent planning where none existed. To take an example, the introduction of family allowances (that is, financial grants for children) during the war was widely seen in the population at large as a 'bribe' to boost the birthrate – and a very inadequate one at that (it stood at five shillings a week). But though many advocates of population planning did see family allowances as a necessary aspect of the encouragement of a higher birthrate, their actual adoption seems to have been much more a result of a desire to manage the economy and to alleviate poverty than a straightforward population stimulus.[3] Similar examples of a proliferation, sometimes even a confusion, of motives can be traced in other, related areas. For instance, the closing down after the war of children's nurseries, which had enabled mothers to shed at least part of their duties in child rearing in order to participate more fully in essential war work, has often been seen as an aspect of a governmental policy to 'reconstruct the family' and discourage married women and mothers from working. But recent research has demonstrated both the policy differences between various government departments on the question of nurseries and the absence of any single, coherent strategy to send women back to the home – at least in the 1940s. Indeed, nurseries were seen by many as a necessary adjunct to any policies to encourage maternalism and stimulate the birthrate.[4] So the population debate has to be analysed not so much in terms of functional intentionality, but more as the focus of various intersecting themes and social practices.

After its historic low point in 1933, the birthrate had stabilised for the rest of the decade, and during the early years of the war had begun a rapid rise. Between 1943 and 1948 the average annual number of births was above the pre-war level.[5] But the rise was clearly a result largely of wartime conditions rather than a reversal of the long-term reduction in family size. The large family remained generally unpopular, despite blandishments from Church, state and propagandists. The Archbishop of Canterbury, addressing the Mothers' Union in 1952, voiced a widespread official view that 'One child deliberately willed as the limit is no family at all but something of a misfortune, for child and parents. Two children accepted as the ideal limit do not make a real family – a family only truly begins with three children.'[6] But such emotional attempts to suggest the pathology of the small family cut little ice. A Gallup poll for the *News Chronicle* in 1944 suggested that the ideal family size was three, but even this, as Mass Observation pointed out, was barely above replacement level. At the same time, commentators observed a widespread hostility towards propaganda for larger families.[7]

Deeply rooted eugenic beliefs in any event militated against an indiscriminate encouragement of large families, for this would help the inadequate as well as the adequate. Mass Observation, quoting Richard Titmuss on differential class fertility, intoned against the 'feckless, irresponsible poor'. For a eugenic future, 'something . . . is needed . . . which will make the thoughtful breed as much as the thoughtless . . . the well educated as well as those who left school at fourteen.' Eva Hubback, leader of the Family Endowment Society and a Fabian feminist, had similar concerns to discourage what she representatively called the 'social problem group': 'The future happiness and greatness of our people would not be assured if we were to continue to draw as large a proportion of our children as at present from parents less well endowed than are their fellows as regards health, ability and uprightness of character.'[8]

There was a widespread concern in other words, for 'quality' as much as 'quantity'. At the same time the advocates of population policies were anxious to distance themselves from any suggestion that their policies were in anyway analogous to fascist population plans. Direct policies of encouragement for both these reasons were not, therefore, generally favoured. What were sought for were indirect means which would both stimulate a new mood favouring larger families and provide more favourable circumstances for parenthood. As Mass Observation put it, 'We have to construct a social framework where the family of 4–6, deliberately conceived by intelligent citizens with modern outlooks and modern interests, makes some sort of sense.'[9] Such a Fabian approach suggested a host of policies falling well short of direction. An encouragement of education was one representative approach. Eva Hubback amongst others called for an education for citizenship, which would involve the development of a sense of social responsibility, loyalty to country, high standards in family life, sexual responsibility, and a realisation that 'having children, though primarily their own affair, is by no means *only* their affair . . .'.[10] Voluntary parenthood, and the provision of birth-control facilities, as advocated by the Family Planning Association, was another necessary approach – if understood as 'planning' and 'spacing', not simply limitation of births. The National Health Service Act of 1948 had indeed widened governmental support for birth-control activities, and the Royal Commission in 1949 advocated that birth control actually become part of the health service.[11]

But a more thoroughgoing approach demanded, it was argued, the general mitigation of the economic and social disadvantages of parenthood. The Royal Commission *Report* put forward two ways in which this could be done: by measures that would give parents financial assistance or relief, such as by family allowances or income-tax concessions; and by the development of services for the special benefit of children and the support of mothers.

Much of this was implicit in welfare legislation already; some such measures had been clearly anticipated in the Beveridge Report with its proposals for marriage allowances and for the care of children; what was lacking was coherence or central planning: an official population policy, in other words. Unfortunately for the planners, this was never fully achieved. Even the Commission's proposals on birth control, though enthusiastically received by its advocates, took twenty years to reach the statute book. By the time the Commission reported, the population scare was fading away and no formal policy as such was adopted; by the 1950s the focus was moving away from concern with population decline to worries about overpopulation. So the real significance of the population debates lies in the assumptions they embody about procreation and sexuality.

The characteristic approach was based on a balance between creating the proper climate for individuals and allowing freedom to choose (what policy makers had already decided were) the correct procreative decisions. It is the creation of strong normative standards that appears to us now as the most characteristic achievement of the population panic. Much more important, therefore, than the formal policies proposed semi-officially and unofficially were the actual practices and beliefs already embodied in the organisations of the Welfare State. For at the core of post-war welfarism were a series of fundamental and essentially traditional assumptions about the family and motherhood. Beveridge had expressed a dominant concern about the importance of a child being brought up in the proper domestic environment, and was anxious not in any way to encourage illegitimacy, or immorality. The Report was shot through with normative assumptions and proposals; separate allowances for deserted, separated or divorced wives, for instance, were only to be paid if the woman could prove she was the innocent party. And there was a pervasive concern in the document to reinforce and encourage marriage; amounting to an ideological reconstruction of marriage as a vital occupation and career, so that 'Every woman on marriage will become a new person.'[12] These values were to permeate the whole structure of the Welfare State, making benefits in large part dependent on certain standards of morality. The most notorious example of this was the 'cohabitation ruling' which denied benefits to women living with men who were not their legal spouses, and which demanded an army of official 'snoopers' for its enforcement.[13] But a whole series of practices in the 1950s and 1960s showed a similar preoccupation. The growth of 'social work' was explicitly related to the need to reinforce traditional forms of family life, which was curiously seen both as 'natural' and permanent and as fragile and threatened. 'Family life is perpetuated of itself and by no artificial teaching, and if it is to be kept alive this can only be done by deliberately fostering of its vitality.'[14] And an essential adjunct to the vast expansion of social work in the community was the use of family 'casework', overwhelmingly influenced by modified forms of psychoanalysis. Although this never took hold to the extent that it did in the USA (in the form of ego psychology, with its emphasis on adjusting to the social norms), a modified psychoanalysis became a dominant element in social work during the 1950s, producing various techniques for that adjustment to emotional normality. A book edited by Lily Pincus, *Social Casework in Marital Problems*, published in 1953, made the classic case. It provided a catalogue of success stories achieved through therapeutic casework, with women 'making astonishing moves towards femininity', learning to become competent mothers, and men overcoming homosexuality, achieving new status in work, and doubling their earning capacities.[15] The aim was quite clearly to reconcile perceived sexual and emotional needs with the institutions of monogamous marriage, and to use the new practices of welfarism, official and voluntary, to further this aim.

The continuing official concern with the future of the family was demonstrated in a series of major commissions and reports, including those of Beveridge in 1942, the Curtis Committee on children in care in 1946, the Population Commission in 1949, the Morton Commission on Divorce, 1955, the Wolfenden Committee on homosexuality and prostitution in 1957, the Ingleby Committee on Children and Young Persons in 1960, up to the Finer Report on one-parent families in 1975. The more generalised, unofficial concern can be traced in the work of a host of social commentators, investigating the decline of the working-class extended family, the impact of marital break-ups, the importance of marital child care, and so on.[16]

It would be misleading to see these concerns as a simple resurrection of old themes; many of them were transformed in the new circumstances of welfarism and a growing affluence. There was, for instance, a considerable shift away from early twentieth-century domestic ideology in its crudest form. Policy moulders had to take some account of the changing situation of women. The Royal Commission on Population came out against any governmental action designed to force women back into the home: 'Such a policy not only runs against the democratic conception of individual freedom, but in Great Britain it would be a rebuking of the tide'.[17] There was a widespread recognition of the fact and importance of women working outside the home (and this was to become even more important in the 1950s and 1960s) and many, like the Royal Commission, recognised a real conflict 'between career and motherhood'. But this did not lead to any widespread interest or support in socialising child care, nor to any fundamental questioning of sex roles, but on the contrary to renewed emphasis on motherhood. The Commission sought policies which would enable women to combine outside work with the care of the home and motherhood. Eva Hubback believed that domestic tasks would still absorb the 'main energies' of most women; while maternalism became the hallmark of most progressive as well as conservative thought during the 1950s, amounting to a reconstruction of the ideology of motherhood, and was best exemplified in the work on childhood and attachment of John Bowlby, later to become a critical focus of opposition in feminist discourse, but in the 1950s an influential liberal force.[18]

But though the familial stress was very strong, it was accompanied by the official burial of an ideology of the authoritarian, patriarchal family. As a vivid expression of the new social-democratic consensus, there was a general emphasis throughout on the marriage relationship as a partnership in which the man and the woman should have 'complementary', not dependent roles. And alongside this, the sexual component was increasingly seen as a vital element in marital harmony. The 1940s and 1950s saw, in fact, the generalisation across all classes of the ideal of mutual sexual pleasure, but very much within the context of a stable marital relationship. A strong ideological tendency linked those who eschewed marriage and motherhood with emotional and sexual abnormality. Motherhood, wrote John Newsom in 1948, is 'the essentially feminine function in society', and he went on to suggest that 'almost all intelligent women' agreed with this assumption. Those who did not were 'normally deficient in the quality of womanliness and the particular physical and mental attributes of their sex'.[19]

This emphasis carried a weight of assumptions about the different sexual needs of men and women, but by 1948 David Mace, a leading member of the Marriage Guidance movement, could argue that 'A good sex adjustment for husband and wife means satisfying orgasms for both – simultaneous orgasm is a desirable ideal.'[20]

A series of concerns underlined this more explicit emphasis on sex, the major one of which in the 1940s was an awareness of the effect of the war on married life. The widespread social disruptions had inevitably widened people's sexual experiences and had threatened the stability of many families. It was estimated that wives could stand a separation of two years, but in the subsequent years they often 'lapsed'.[21] The ending of the war caused almost equal problems of adjustment, as often complete strangers found themselves bound to one another for life. David Mace, in a series of BBC broadcasts specifically on this topic in 1945, emphasized that 'marriage is a tough job', and needed careful working out both on the level of material needs (housing, economic security) and on the emotional and sexual level.[22] Accompanying this was a recognition that sexual harmony was not a natural given but a technique to be learnt – and learnt by the man who, as Havelock Ellis might have put it, had to kiss the maiden into being a woman. The Marriage Guidance Council, in response to a wide demand from young married couples after the war, published as its first booklet *How to Treat a Young Wife*, which suggested that the man should develop the sexual potentialities of his wife. This booklet, later revised and published as *Sex in Marriage*, had sold over half a million copies by the late 1960s.

The marriage-guidance movement experienced an extraordinary growth in the 1940s and 1950s.[23] The Marriage Guidance Council itself had been founded in 1938 by the Social Hygiene Council, and had begun its counselling work in the early 1940s. By 1948 there were more than a hundred marriage-guidance centres, and following the Denning

Report on reconciliation procedures in 1947, which recommended official assistance for marriage-guidance work, the movement received government recognition and financial aid, and was widely imitated. The Family Welfare Association, released from its old direct charity casework, set up a Family Discussion Bureau, while the Roman Catholics established their own Marriage Advisory Council. Their dominant aim was the resolution of the problems of relationships within the context of marriage, and a vital part of the task was the harnessing of sexuality to this ambition. The title of a book by Kenneth Walker published in 1963 aptly summed up the basic aim: *Marriage, Sex and Happiness.*[24]

The stress on the importance of sexuality, alongside the continued celebration of the family, inevitably produced its contradictions. The curious obsession with 'petting' in the sex literature of the period underlines most strongly the ambivalence of attitudes. On the one hand, there was a widespread recognition of the need for some sort of sexual outlet. But on the other, there was a generalised fear of unmarrieds going 'too far'. As Helena Wright argued in her much reprinted *Sex: An outline for Young People*, 'no-one should be allowed to expect full expression of his sex desires'.[25] Progressives tended to recommend early marriage as an antidote for pre-marital sex, and that topic itself still aroused a considerable controversy throughout the 1950s. By the end of the decade, pre-marital sex was *the* subject of anxious debate for it touched on all the taboos about sex. Eustace Chesser, writing on *Unmarried Love* in the mid-1960s, admitted that in his works he had hitherto evaded the problem of 'the sexual difficulties of the unmarried' because of potential hostility. When Professor G. M. Carstairs mildly suggested in his 1962 Reith lectures that charity might be as important a virtue as chastity he raised, as he put it, 'a storm of protest'.[26] All the evidence in fact pointed to most pre-marital sex taking place with future spouses, and liberals tended to justify it solely in terms of its likely contribution to future sexual harmony in marriage. As Walker and Fletcher put it, 'We do not agree that a pre-marital affair necessarily jeopardises the safety of a future marriage. More often than not, it is an excellent preparation for it.'[27] But even such caution strayed dangerously close to the presumed fringes of radicalism. The stress on sexuality did not burst the bounds of the family; but rather was designed to cement it, and a general puritanism of attitudes remained.

The debates around the proper mode of sexual behaviour reflected a widespread apprehension of the effects of social change, but in the 1950s at least the concern was out of proportion to the changes that had actually taken place. A survey conducted by Mass Observation at the beginning of the 1950s found that only one-third of the sample thought a good sex life was essential to happiness, and resented it being made the 'be-all and end-all of life'.[28] Geoffrey Gorer, taking an anthropologist's view of English character in the early 1950s, noted the exceptional chastity and fidelity of the English when compared to other

peoples. Half of his sample of the married population had had no sexual relationships either before or after marriage with anyone but their
spouse, though the figures for pre-marital sex were higher for the working class than for the middle class.[29] A general respect for the marriage
institution was also widely noted, and this went across class lines. The
middle class might see it as a 'noble institution' but the working class
had a no less deeply rooted if more pragmatic view, 'It's all right with
the right sort of partner', a fish-and-chip shop proprietor told Mass
Observation, 'if not, it's rotten'. But despite the 'rottenness', even the
divorce figures, which had aroused grave fears of the imminent collapse of the family in the 1940s, slumped in the early 1950s.[30] Official
sexual morality was in a curious state of tension. A fear of decline of
standards had to confront a considerable degree of stability in actual
behaviour, while the perceived dangers were to be curiously resolved by
an ideology that encouraged sexuality to flourish, but strictly within the
confines of a monogamous marriage. It was as if the age had developed
a growing fear of the effects of sex unconfined, so the chrysalis had to
be kept firmly locked in its cocoon.

'Wolfenden' and sexual liberalism

Not surprisingly, the major moral preoccupations of the 1940s and
1950s permeate the period's most influential liberal statement, the
Report of the Wolfenden Committee on Homosexual Offences and
Prostitution published in 1957. The Report acknowledged and regretted, like many other contemporary documents, the 'general loosen-
ing of former moral standards', the disruptive effects of the war and
'the emotional insecurity, community instability and weakening of the
family' inherent in modern society. It deplored any potential damage
to 'what we regard as the basic unit of society', the family.[31] But simultaneously, the Report articulated principles which, though themselves
not new, were to provide the pragmatic basis for the limited, but symbolically significant, social reforms of the 1960s, and the framework for
all the major 'official' proposals on morality throughout the 1970s as
well.[32]

There was nothing surprising in prostitution and (male) homosexuality offences being seen as a common subject for investigation. Not
only had they been historically intertwined in legal practice but both
were seen as evidence of a common problem: a decline in moral standards. The most widely offered evidence for this was provided by the
figures for prosecutions. In the case of street offences these had risen
from around an annual average of 2,000 in the early years of the war to
over 10,000 by 1952, and to almost 12,000 by 1955. The number of indictable male homosexual offences increased five-fold in the same
period. In 1938 there were 134 cases of sodomy and bestiality known to
the police in England and Wales; in 1952, 670; and in 1954, 1,043. For

indecent assault the increase was from 822 cases in 1938 to 3,305 in 1953, while for 'gross indecency' (the Labouchère offence) the rise was from 316 in 1938 to 2,322 in 1955.[33] Despite the dramatic rises, however, the Wolfenden Committee found little evidence that the incidence of these offences was actually increasing, though there was possibly a greater visibility of prostitution.[34] The main factor involved was undoubtedly an increase of police zeal in hunting out offenders, and this was more evident in one or two metropolitan areas than throughout the country as a whole. The stepping up of the purge of homosexuals and prostitutes appears to have coincided with the appointment of Sir Theobald Mathew, an ardent Roman Catholic, as Director of Public Prosecutions in 1944. The prosecutions reached a new peak in London in late 1953 following the appointment of a new Metropolitan Police Commissioner, Sir John Nott-Bowes, under the aegis of a fervently anti-homosexual and moralistic Home Secretary, Sir David Maxwell-Fyffe.

The real change in the 1950s was the growth of official concern and public anxiety to which the police zeal was a response. This in turn cannot be divorced from the heightened post-war stress on the importance of monogamous heterosexual love, which threw into greater relief than ever before the 'deviant' nature of both prostitution and homosexuality (though the overwhelming emphasis was on *male* homosexuality). It is striking that the estimated prostitution population of London in the 1850s of 50,000 was accepted with much less horror than the 2,000–3,000 or so in London in the 1950s. By the 1950s there appears to have been a widespread worry that young men who went regularly with prostitutes might never learn the value of sex within marriage. A related concern was echoed in the Wolfenden Report itself in the debate over whether buggery should be maintained as a special offence; the argument in favour of retaining it was that it most nearly approximated to heterosexual coitus, and might therefore be a temptation away from it.

The tensions that underlay these new emphases were expressed in a series of moral panics about the public visibility of vice from the late 1940s onwards. The idea that the streets of London were a disgrace to an imperial capital was strongly expressed both at the time of the Festival of Britain in 1951 and in Coronation Year, 1953, particularly with reference to the influx of foreign visitors, and was the major justification for the Tory government's rushing into law the Wolfenden Committee's major proposal on prostitution in 1959. But other important elements came into the arena with regard to homosexuality, for it played on wider anxieties generated by the Cold War and the fear of the enemy within. In the early 1950s, homosexuals emerged as scapegoats in the new international climate. The US State Department under the influence of McCarthyism, had already conducted a purge on homosexuals in its own echelons, seeing them as 'security risks' by reason of their 'lack of emotional stability', the 'weakness of their moral fibre' and their susceptibility to blandishments and blackmail. Following the defection to Russia of the British spies Guy Burgess and Donald Maclean in 1950 there is evidence for American pressure on the British government to put its own house in order, and certainly an air of paranoia about homosexuality suffuses public debate in the early 1950s (and was to be reactivated by the Vassall spy scandal of the early 1960s and the revelation in 1979 that Anthony Blunt, former Keeper of the Queen's Paintings, was a one time Soviet agent).[35] This came to a head following the sensational trial for homosexual offences of Lord Montagu of Beaulieu and Peter Wildeblood, Diplomatic Correspondent of the *Daily Mail*, in 1954. The trial revealed all the usual sexual and class prejudice (particularly focusing on the cross-class sexual liaisons) but also demonstrated the confusions in the legal position of male homosexuals. There was no evidence of 'corruption'; no suggestion that the acts were anything but consensual and in private, and the only evidence against the accused was that provided by participants in the acts, who had turned Queen's evidence.[36] The situation was demonstrably more absurd because of the disparity throughout the country of rates of prosecution and police zeal. The choice the government and police faced was clearly either to enforce the existing law more rigorously and uniformly (as the Home Secretary urged) or to investigate alternative means of control. Maxwell-Fyffe had an obsessive belief that: 'Homosexuals, in general, are exhibitionists and proselytisers and a danger to others, especially the young . . . . I shall give no countenance to the view that they should not be prevented from being such a danger.'[37] But under political pressure he conceded the need for an enquiry. It was in this climate, in the immediate aftermath of the Montagu – Wildeblood trial, that the interdepartmental committee under Sir John Wolfenden was set up in 1954.

Prejudice against homosexuality was much more deeply rooted than against prostitution. The Mass Observation survey had found 'a more genuine feeling of disgust towards homosexuality . . . than towards any other subject tackled',[38] and the general hostility was not helped by a new interest in the popular press which to an extraordinary degree reinforced popular stereotypes. A series of articles in 1952 in the *Sunday Pictorial* was greeted by the paper's former editor, Hugh Cudlipp, as 'an end to the conspiracy of silence', but silence might have been more humane: the series was entitled 'Evil Men' and described its aim as 'a sincere attempt to get to the root of a spreading fungus.'[39]

But there were more important signs of change, characteristically reflected in the new psychologising literature. The most important debate was again over the nature of homosexuality, but the Wolfenden Report showed a readiness also to explore the 'psychological element' in prostitution. In part, a new climate in discussing sexuality had been generated by the Kinsey reports on *Sexual Behaviour in the Human Male*, published with much *eclat* in 1948, and *Sexual Behaviour in the Human Female*, published in 1953.[40]

The radical long-term effect of the work of Alfred Kinsey and his colleagues was to undermine the idea of a nature-given normality. Kinsey's stress on sexual 'outlet' as opposed to object choice, 'condition' or identity fundamentally demystified the sex act, as was clearly recognised by liberal critics such as Lionel Trilling at the time, and although Kinsey himself maintained a clearly familial and heterosexual emphasis, his work ultimately suggested that behaviour was more important than belief or morality.[41] But perhaps more relevant in the short term was his demonstration that 37 per cent of his male sample (admittedly of white, middle-American males) had experienced same-sex contact to orgasm. If homosexuality was a problem, it was not a tiny one and here, of course it fitted in with the army of statistics that was being marshalled elsewhere. But as important as Kinsey in the immediate context was the acceptance of a medical model of homosexuality relying largely on a sub-Freudian psychological explanation both in the medical profession and in the old-established public-morality bodies. The Public Morality Council was in the vanguard of those pressing for an enquiry into homosexuality in the late 1940s on these grounds, while the National Vigilance Association by 1951 believed that the time was ripe 'for new methods and a new approach to a problem which to a great extent might be regarded as much as a mental illness as a criminal act'.[42] Other hints of change came from the Church of England, whose Moral Welfare Council produced a report in 1954 on *The Problem of Homosexuality* which, while not denying its sinfulness, attempted to separate the ecclesiastical and legal aspects, and called for law reform. As the National Vigilance Association put it, 'the problem requires fullest investigation by experts in the light of the new knowledge now available'.[43]

The paradox at the heart of the Wolfenden Committee's work, its status both as an expression of 1950s moral anxieties and a blueprint for the 'permissive' legislation' of the 1960s, can be partly grasped if we see its roots in this search for a more effective regulation of sexual deviance. The problem the Committee was established to consider was not how to liberalise the law (though many outside and on the Committee had that question in mind), but whether the law was the most effective means of control. It is in its response to this question that the Wolfenden Committee offered an outline of a new moral economy, responsive to underlying shifts in post-war society.

The basic principle behind this was a selective re-interpretation of legal utilitarianism. Jeremy Bentham a century and a half earlier had classed homosexuality as an 'imaginary offence', dependent on changing concepts of taste and morality,[44] and the utilitarian tradition, best expressed in John Stuart Mill's *On Liberty*, had generally argued that the only justification for legal intervention in private life was to prevent harm to others. The Wolfenden Report, following on from this, argued that the purpose of the criminal law was to preserve public order and decency, and to protect the weak from exploitation. It was *not* to impose a particular pattern of moral behaviour on individuals. It followed that there were areas of life which were no concern of the criminal law, even though they might be of moral concern to individuals and society. What they proposed therefore was a partial retreat of the law from the regulation of individual behaviour. Just as prostitution as such was not illegal, so male homosexuality in private should be decriminalised. The Report recognised the argument that homosexuality might be a threat to the family, but so, it was suggested, were adultery and divorce, and these were not illegal. On one level, therefore, the Report was simply proposing an extension, to cover homosexuality, of the pragmatic rule which had guided legal attitudes to prostitution (and which had been endorsed by the Street Offences Committee in 1928).

But the logic of the distinction between private and public behaviour was that the legal penalties for *public* displays of sexuality could be strengthened at the same time as private behaviour was decriminalised. Thus, with regard to prostitution, the Committee proposed that the maximum penalties for 'street offences' be increased, and that other restrictions should be imposed on the prostitutes rather than on the clients: 'the simple fact is that prostitutes do parade themselves more habitually and openly then their prospective customers, and do by their continual presence affront the sense of decency of the ordinary citizen. In doing so they create a nuisance which, in our view, the law is entitled to recognise and deal with.'

The same logic was pursued regarding homosexuality. It should not be legitimised or even made fully lawful: 'It is important that the limited modification of the law which we propose should not be interpreted as an indication that the law can be indifferent to other forms of homosexual behaviour, or as a general licence to adult homosexuals to behave as they please.'[45] Hence the two central proposals of the Report: that with regard to prostitution the maximum penalties for street offences be increased and the law be generally tightened up; and with regard to homosexuality, that homosexual behaviour between consenting adults in private be no longer a criminal offence. By the application of a single principle the Report achieved an apparently contradictory series of effects: restrictive in one direction, liberal in the other. The unifying element was the belief that by ceasing to be the guardian of *private* morality, the law would more effectively become the protector of *public* decency and order.

The debate between the absolutist and the utilitarian views of the law was not of course a new one. Its terms of reference had been clearly laid down in the arguments betwen Mill and James Stephen in the nineteenth century and had been echoed by reformers in the inter-war years.[46] But it was in the 1950s and 1960s that they reached the heart of public policy. Lord Devlin in his Maccabean Lecture in 1959 firmly asserted the absolutist view that 'Society cannot live without morals', and that it was fundamental to society that laws be based on morals – or on 'those standards of conduct which the reasonable man approves'.[47] Devlin's views were powerful and began an important legal – and political – debate. But the utilitarian arguments provided a more effective starting point for reformers – and offered a more pragmatic way of approaching the question of moral regulation, one which by the 1960s was to become the dominant form.[48]

The key point is that privatisation did not necessarily involve a diminution of control. The Wolfenden Report rejected the idea that homosexuality was a disease, but as noted above, it did accept a psychologisation both of homosexuality and prostitution, so though agnostic about 'treatment' and 'cure', it did not reject them out of hand. On the contrary, the Committee urged further research into the topic. Hence their final two recommendations on homosexuality:

'(xvii) that prisoners desirous of having oestrogen treatment be permitted to do so . . .

(xviii) That research be instituted into the aetiology of homosexuality and the effects of various forms of treatment.'[49]

In part at least, the Committee was proposing no more than a shift of emphasis away from the law towards the social services as foci for social regulation. But even in terms of legal changes, the proposals were modest. It was estimated that 4 per cent of the male prison population were there for homosexual offences; the proposals would have reduced the numbers by half. And with regard to prostitution offences, criminal penalties were to be increased, and the regulation of the lives of prostitutes (not their clients) tightened up.

The immediate impact of the proposals, published in 1957, were, not surprisingly, paradoxical. The proposals relating to prostitution were rushed into law with an indecent haste, in the Street Offences Act of 1959, which drove prostitution off the streets by increasing fines and imprisonment. But simultaneously it led to a reorganisation of prostitution, contributing to a vast expansion of commercial prostitution agencies and call-girl rackets. By privatising prostitution, Wolfenden (who had recognised the danger but balanced it against the reduced public visibility) and the legislators had the effect of freeing prostitution for an increased rate of commercial exploitation.[50] But no official support came for the decriminalisation of male homosexuality. Though transparently a grave injustice, and a law that was unworkable, this had to wait on public opinion gradually changing. So it was the repressive rather than the liberal aspect of Wolfenden which triumphed in the first place. It had nevertheless set out a moral taxonomy for the next, 'permissive' phase of moral reform, and this was to be its major long-term historical significance.

References

1.   **William Beveridge**, *Social Insurance and Allied Services*, HMSO, London, 1942, p. 154; the report of an interdepartmental committee set up under the chairmanship of Beveridge in 1941.

2. Mass Observation, *Britain and her Birth Rate*, John Murray, London, 1945, p. 7; *Report of the Royal Commission on Population*, Cmd 7695, HMSO, London, 1949, p. 226. Other works expressing similar themes include **Mark Abrams**, *The Population of Great Britain*, George Allen & Unwin, London, 1945; **J. C. Flugel**, *Population, Psychology and Peace*, Watts & Co, London, 1947; **G. F. McCleary**, *The Menace of British Depopulation*, George Allen & Unwin, London, 1945; **Sir James Marchant** (ed.), *Rebuilding Family Life in the Post War World*, Odhams Press, London, 1945; **R. M. Titmuss**, *Birth, Poverty and Wealth*, Hamish Hamilton, London, 1943; **Grace Leybourne White** and **Kenneth White**, *Children for Britain*, Pilot Press, London, 1945; **R. F. Harrod**, *Britain's Future Population*, OUP, 1943; **Fabian Society**, *Population and the People*, George Allen & Unwin, London, 1945; **Eva M. Hubback**, *The Population of Britain*, Penguin, West Drayton, 1947.
3. Slater and Woodside, *Patterns of Marriage*, p. 189; Eva M. Hubback, *op. cit.*, p. 192; **Lucy Bland**, **Trisha McCabe** and **Frank Mort**, 'Sexuality and Reproduction: Three "Official" Instances', in **Michèl Barrett**, **Philip Corrigan**, **Annette Kuhn** and **Janet Wolff**, *Ideology and Cultural Production*, Croom Helm, London, 1979.
4. **Denise Riley**, 'War in the Nursery', *Feminist Review*, No. 2, 1979.
5. *Report of the Royal Commission*, p. 220.
6. Quoted in McGregor, *Divorce in England*, p. 124.
7. Mass Observation, *op. cit.*, p. 79: Slater and Woodside, *op. cit.*, p. 181 ff.
8. Mass Observation, *op. cit.*, p. 201; Hubback, *op. cit.*, p. 14.
9. Mass Observation, *op. cit.*, p. 227.
10. Hubback, *op. cit.*, pp. 158, 165 ff. She stresses the importance of sex education, not just in the family, where shyness inhibited useful information, but in the school. An Association for Education in Citizenship, supported by various Fabian Socialists, had been founded in the 1930s; it published *The Citizen*, 1936–40.
11. *Report of the Royal Commission*, Ch. 16. The NHS Act 1948 had authorised contributions to organisations providing clinics, such as FPA branches; authorised *per capita* payments for patients attending FPA clinics; and gave permission to the FPA to use local-authority premises at low rents.
12. Beveridge, *op. cit.*, pp. 135, 131; Lucy Bland *et al.*, *op. cit.*, pp. 89, 87.
13. **Elizabeth Wilson**, *Women and the Welfare State*, Tavistock, London, 1977, pp. 80–1. The ruling was justified on the grounds that as a married woman living with her husband could not claim supplementary benefits for herself, to allow a single women living with a man to do so would be to discourage marriage.
14. **J. Heywood**, *Children in Care*, Routledge and Kegan Paul, London, 1959, p. 139, quoted in Wilson, *op. cit.*, p. 84.
15. **Lily Pincus** (ed.), *Social Casework in Marital Problems*, Tavistock, London, 1953; Wilson, *op. cit.*, pp. 84–7; see also **Elizabeth Wilson**, *Only Half Way to Paradise*, Tavistock, London, 1980, and in particular her chapter on 'The Boundaries of Sexuality'. I am very grateful to Elizabeth Wilson for allowing me to read this chapter in typescript.
16. The most famous works on working-class families are **M. Young** and **P. Willmott**, *Family and Kinship in East London*, Routledge and Kegan Paul, London, 1957; **Richard Hoggart**, *The Uses of Literacy*, Chatto and Windus, London, 1957. The most influential work on child care and theories of maternal deprivation were John Bowlby's, heavily influenced by

Kleinian theories. See **J. Bowlby**, *Childcare and the Growth of Love*, Penguin, Harmondsworth, 1963. For the classic social-democratic statement on the family, see the 1945 Labour Party election manifesto, *Let Us Face the Future*.

17. *Report of the Royal Commission on Population*, p. 159.
18. Eva Hubback, *op. cit.*, p. 174; **Birmingham Feminist History Group**, 'Feminism as Femininity in the Nineteen Fifties?', *Feminist Review*, No. 3, 1979. See pp. 51–2 on ideologies of domesticity in schools during the 1950s.
19. **John Newsom**, *The Education of Girls*, Faber, London, 1948, p. 146.
20. **David R. Mace**, *Marriage Counselling: The First Full Account of the Remedial Work of the Marriage Guidance Council*, J. & A. Churchill, London, 1948, p. 123.
21. Slater and Woodside, *op. cit.*, p. 219 ff.
22. **David R. Mace**, *Coming Home: A Series of Five Broadcast Talks*, Staple Press, London, 1945.
23. See **J. H. Wallis** and **H. S. Booker**, *Marriage Counselling*, Routledge and Kegan Paul, London, 1958; and **J. H. Wallis**, *Marriage Guidance: A New Introduction*, Routledge and Kegan Paul, London, 1968. Elizabeth Wilson makes the point that the gradual move from the strict monogamous emphasis of Mace's book to the more relaxed liberalism of Wallis's is a good index of a changing sexual climate. Wilson, *Only Half Way to Paradise*.
24. **Kenneth Walker**, *Marriage, Sex and Happiness*, Odhams, London, 1963. Cf. also another typical title: **J. H. Wallis**, *Sexual Harmony in Marriage*, Routledge and Kegan Paul, London, 1964.
25. **Helena Wright**, *Sex: An Outline for Young People*, William and Norgate, London, 1956, p. 109 (3rd rev. edn; first published as *What is sex?* in 1932). For examples of the stress on petting, see **Alfred Kinsey**, **Wandell B. Pomeroy** and **Clyde E. Martin**, *Sexual Behaviour in the Human Male*, W. B. Saunders Co., Philadelphia and London, 1948; Eustace Chesser, *The Sexual, Marital and Family Relationships of the English Woman*; and **Michael Schofield**, *The Sexual Behaviour of Young People*, Longman, London, 1965.
26. **Eustace Chesser**, *Unmarried Love*, Jarrolds, London, 1965, p. 9; **G. M. Carstairs**, *This Island Now: The BBC Reith Lectures 1962*, The Hogarth Press, London, 1963.
27. **Kenneth Walker** and **Peter Fletcher**, *Sex and Society: A Psychological Study of Sexual Behaviour in a Competitive Culture*, Frederick Muller, London, 1955, p. 102; see also Chesser, *Unmarried Love*, p. 40.
28. **Leonard England**, 'A British Sex Survey', *The International Journal of Sexology*, Feb. 1950. See also **J. H. Wallis**, *Sexual Harmony in Marriage*, Routledge and Kegan Paul, London, 1964, p. 6, which cites evidence for the 1950s that although sexual problems were the main factor in marriage breakdown, this still only accounted for 17–18 per cent of the total.
29. **Geoffrey Gorer**, *Exploring English Character*, The Cresset Press, London, 1955, pp. 87, 97; England, 'A British Sex Survey', p. 151; cf. McGregor, *Divorce in England*, p. 157; Slater and Woodside, *op. cit.*, p. 117.
30. McGregor, *Divorce in England*.
31. *Report of the Committee on Homosexual Offences and Prostitution*, Cmd 247, HMSO, London, 1957, reprinted 1968 (hereafter referred to as the Wolfenden Report), para. 45, p. 20; para. 54, p. 22.
32. See for example the recommendations of the Criminal Law Revision

Commission, Policy Advisory Committee on *The Age of Consent*, HMSO, 1979; and the *Report of the Committee on Obscenity and Film Censorship* (chaired by Professor Bernard Williams), HMSO, 1979.

33. The figures are from the Wolfenden Report, Appendix 11, p. 143; Appendix 1, p. 130.

34. Cf. Helene Ware, 'The recruitment, regulation and role of prostitution in Britain', p. 616. On differing police attitudes see **Robert Fabian's** reactionary *London After Dark*, Hamilton and Co., London, 1958; and **C. R. Hewitt** (C. H. Rolph)'s arguments in favour of scrapping the whole system of laws in *New Statesman*, May 1947.

35. See J. Weeks, *Coming Out*, Ch. 14; **H. Montgomery Hyde**, *The Other Love: An Historical and Contemporary Survey of Homosexuality in Britain*, Granada Publishing, London, 1972, Ch. 6; **Peter Wildeblood**, *Against the Law*, Penguin, Harmondsworth, 1957; *The Times*, Nov. 1979, *passim*.

36. See Wildeblood, *op. cit.*

37. Montgomery Hyde, *The Other Love*, p. 240.

38. England, 'A British Sex Survey', p. 153.

39. See my discussion of this in *Coming Out*, pp. 162–3.

40. **A. Kinsey** *et al.*, *Sexual Behaviour in the Human Female*, W. B. Saunders Co., Philadelphia and London, 1953.

41. For further comments along these lines, see **Paul Robinson**, *The Modernization of Sex*, Elek, London, 1977; and Wilson, *Only Half Way to Paradise*. The classic liberal attack on Kinsey's stress on behaviour as opposed to values came from **Lionel Trilling**, and is republished in *The Liberal Imagination: Essays on Literature and Society*, Mercury Books, London, 1964, p. 223 ff.

42. *National Vigilance Association 64th Annual Report*, for the year ending 30 April 1951, p. 8. Mrs Neville Rolfe, still a doughty purity exponent, was in the vanguard of those pressing for a change of attitudes, and she convened a special subcommittee to look at the question. See its *Interim Report*, Public Morality Council, PPP Sub Committee, Box 1, Ac.70.31, Greater London Record Office. For a text which usefully embodies the contradictory attitudes, see **Gordon Westwood**, *Society and the Homosexual*, Victor Gollancz, London, 1952. This was a major liberal statement, written pseudonymously by Michael Schofield.

43. The characteristic approach distinguished 'inversion' from 'perversion', the former being 'natural', the latter a social crime. For a Christian exposition of this, see **D. S. Bailey**, *Homosexuality and the Western Christian Tradition*, Longman, Green and Co., London, 1955. Wolfenden actually rejected this distinction as having little value.

44. On Bentham's views, see **Louis Crompton** (ed.), 'Offences Against One's Self: Paederasty', Part I and Part II, *Journal of Homosexuality*, Vol. 3, No. 4, Summer 1978, and Vol. 4, No. 1, Fall 1978.

45. Wolfenden Report, pp. 87, 44.

46. **James Fitzjames Stephen**, *Liberty, Equality, Fraternity*, Smith, Elder and Co., London, 1873.

47. **Sir Patrick Devlin**, *The Enforcement of Morals: Maccabean Lecture in Jurisprudence*, OUP, London, 1959, p. 25.

48. The classic response to Devlin came from **H. L. A. Hart**, *Law, Liberty and Morality*, OUP, London, 1963; see also contributions to this debate, rejecting absolutist positions in the context of the divorce debate, from

O. R. McGregor, *Divorce in England*, p. 196; and **Barbara Wootton**, 'Holiness or Happiness', *Twentieth Century*, Nov. 1955, p. 407.

49. Wolfenden Report, p. 116; cf. recommendation xxv on prostitution, 'That researches be instituted into the aetiology of prostitution'.

50. See Elizabeth Wilson, *Women and the Welfare State*, p. 67; Lucy Bland *et al.*, *op. cit.*, pp. 108–9; Wolfenden Report, p. 69. There was a drastic decrease in conviction: 2,726 in 1960, 1,652 in 1970, compared with 19,536 in 1958. But the law became more punitive. In 1958, 0.8 per cent of prostitutes were imprisoned. In 1960, 16.3 per cent. And the percentage of those imprisoned for over 2 months rose from 1 per cent in 1958 to 69 per cent in 1961. See **Victoria Greenwood** and **Jock Young**, in **National Deviancy Conference**, *Permissiveness and Control: The Fate of Sixties Legislation*, Macmillan, London, 1980, pp. 160–1.

Chapter Thirteen

The permissive moment

'Permissiveness'

By the 1960s 'permissiveness' had become a political metaphor, marking a social and political divide. But it was a charged and emotive term, obscuring, in its ambivalence, more than it illuminated. Those who were supposedly chief advocates of the 'permissive society' would rarely have used the term; while for the defenders of 'traditional' (and largely authoritarian) values, 'permissiveness' became an almost scatological word of abuse, a phrase which welded together a number of complex, and not necessarily connected changes, into a potent symbolic unity. And by erecting that symbol of sexual relaxation, of loose moral standards, of disrespect for all that was traditional and 'good', it became easier in the 1970s to recreate a sense of crisis around social changes and the beginnings of a mass support for authoritarian moral solutions.

In a contemporary climate where the term has become a poisoned chalice, it is difficult to unthread the tangled elements, to distinguish the long-term trends from the conjunctural needs and the subjective hopes and ambitions. So if it is to have any meaning as a historical description we must use it carefully. From a political and juridical perspective the term has been used to describe a particular legislative moment, producing a complex body of legislation passed in the decade after 1958, including reforms of the laws governing gambling, suicide, obscenity and censorship, Sunday entertainment, the abolition of capital punishment for murder, as well as liberalisation of various statutes governing sexual behaviour.

But from a sociological point of view 'permissiveness' can be applied to describe a much wider series of changes, attendant upon the impact of the long post-war boom and the generalisation of economic affluence. In the quarter of a century after the Second World War the world capitalist economy experienced an unprecedented period of economic expansion. In Britain, this boom was much more hesitant than elsewhere, and by the early 1960s signs of economic instability were reappearing, alongside the 'rediscovery' of poverty and inequality. But however flimsily based, the British economy itself saw a growth unprecedented in its modern history, leading to the dawn of what was optimistically labelled the 'age of affluence'. Its impact was to reshape many areas of social life, from class relations to moral attitudes and family life, leading to the emergence of new social opportunities, new sub-classes, changed political alliances, significant modifications in the relations between the sexes, an explosion of youth cultures, the fragmentation of the moral consensus – and in the end, acute social tensions. But perhaps most significant of all was the completion of that re-orientation of the economy towards domestic consumption which had begun in the nineteenth century and had already become a significant economic factor by the 1930s. This had two major effects which are relevant to the history of sexual norms. In the first place, as Eric Hobsbawm has pointed out, a mass-consumption society is dominated by its biggest market, which in Britain was that of the working class.[1] As the consumer society penetrated this new market, increasingly commercialising all aspects of life, the pattern of autonomy and isolation which had marked working-class life began to dissolve; and to an unprecedented degree styles of life were 'democratised', even 'proletarianised'. This did not lead to the elimination of class distinction, which in very many areas of life remained rigid, nor to the ending of privilege and exploitation. But it did herald a greater 'flexibility' in social attitudes which was reflected in the gradual shifts in many traditional beliefs in the 1960s and 1970s.

The second effect is more speculative, and concerns the exact nature of the relationship between transformations in the economy and attitudes to sexual morality. There is no doubt that the prolonged boom depended in part upon a switch in moral attitudes away from traditional bourgeois virtues of self-denial and saving ('prudence') towards a compulsion to spend. And as we have seen, these general moral characteristics – 'saving', 'spending' – have for long held strong sexual connotations. This has led a number of cultural critics, deeply informed by a Marxist reading of Freud, to interpret the liberal changes that undoubtedly did take place in the 1950s and 1960s as no more than necessary adjustments by capitalism to its changing demands. So Wilhelm Reich could argue in the sad, exiled last years of his life that the relaxation of moral attitudes in post-war, McCarthyite America was no more than a corrupted utilisation of sexual libido. Herbert Marcuse and Erich Fromm, in their different ways, though both outcrops of the Frankfurt School, discussed the character structures that capitalism at its different stages demanded. So just as 'anal', retentive and ambitious qualities were necessary in the early stages of capitalist accumulation, late capitalism, with its new orientation towards maximised consumption demanded the privileging of 'oral' characteristics. In his *Eros and Civilisation*, published in the early 1950s, Marcuse argued for the necessary subordination of the pleasure principle to the achievement principle in early capitalism, and so the narrowing of the sexual drive – with the development of surplus repression. In his later work,

One Dimensional Man he developed his theory of 'repressive desublimation' which claimed to account for the eroticisation of social life within the controlling terms of capitalist need.

Such views were very influential in the 1960s, particularly amongst radicalised youth (see below, pp. 282 ff.) because they appeared to account for the partial and limiting changes that had taken place. By the 1960s there was undoubtedly an increasing eroticisation of many aspects of social life, from the increasing sexual explicitness of advertising, where sex became an obvious inducement to ever-extending and often useless consumption, to the growing squalor and exploitativeness of pornography in major cities, with Soho in London leading the way. But the obviously partial and often demeaning eroticisation of life that did take place cannot be explained simply as a response to the needs of capitalism. To justify such an explanation we would need both to show how the changes were implemented by a coherent 'policy' and the clear intentionality behind the work of reformers. No such unilinear links can be demonstrated. But this does not mean there were no connections between wider social changes and a relaxation of sexual codes. What is crucial for the historian are the mediations through which this took place. The work of the Frankfurt School was immensely significant in suggesting necessary connections – and perhaps even more important in its socialist critique of the forms of the liberalisation. But the task still remains to tease out the complex interactions which produced both the change in *mentalité* and the actual practical reforms (reforms, it should be noted, which were common to most of the leading capitalist countries in the 1960s, though the actual form they took varied considerably).

To take the actual reforms first: from a contemporary vantage point we can see clearly enough that the legislative reforms were in large part an attempt to come to grips with the problems posed by the long-term changes. But what is historically important is not so much the attempt at problem solving – which is, after all, a continuous part of governmental action – as the terms in which this took place. Some of the legislative reforms can be readily understood as a direct response to the new affluence and apparent economic and financial opportunities (the relaxation of controls over gambling is an obvious example). Others can apparently be read straightforwardly as long-overdue and humanising reforms of archaic laws, a necessary part of what was termed 'modernisation' in the 1960s (and here we can cite the removal of suicide from the list of criminal offences, the abolition of capital punishment, reform of the laws on divorce, homosexuality and abortion). But at the same time a number of these reforms have a wider significance. As Professor Hart put it with regard to the Suicide Act of 1961, which heralded the major reforms: 'It is the first Act of Parliament for at least a century to remove altogether the penalties of the criminal law from a practice both clearly condemned by conventional Christian morality and punishable by law.'[2] There was a move, in other words, towards the centrality of individual 'consent' in place of the imperatives of public morality. The separation of law and morality developed in Wolfenden becomes the hallmark of 'permissive' legislation and marks a crucial stage in shifting the balance of decision making from the public to the private sphere. But this often had a double thrust, for as the Street Offences Act underscored, reform could sustain and strengthen social control as easily as remove it. What needs to be understood in this period of legislative reform is the *balance* of liberalisation and control and the rationale for the changes. For what was taking place in the 1960s was not a simple reform of outdated laws, but a major legislative restructuring, marking an historic shift in the mode of regulation of civil society. And at the heart of these changes were the great series of reforms of the laws relating to sexual behaviour, amounting to the most significant package of legislative changes on morality for over half a century. These have to be understood both in the context of major shifts of social attitudes and behaviour (especially amongst the young and women), and in the political context in which they were enacted.

Youth

The problems of youth were dominating themes in the sexual debates of the 1960s. By the beginning of the decade their new social and economic position was manifest. There were a million more unmarried people in the age range 15–24 than ten years previously – a 20 per cent increase. And they wielded a new economic power. Average real wages increased by 25 per cent between 1938 and 1958, but those of adolescents by twice this. And though they disposed of only some 5 per cent of total consumer spending, they were the biggest purchasers of certain commodities – 42 per cent of record players, 29 per cent of cosmetics and toiletries, 28 per cent of cinema admissions, and so on. Here was a vast new consumer market, with an abundance of relatively free income.[3]

At the same time as their social weight increased, their dependence remained prolonged, particularly given the increase in the school-leaving age (15, then by the end of the 1960s, 16), and the increased numbers in further and higher education. The age of marriage continued to fall, from just over 27 for bachelors and 24.5 for spinsters, 1946–50, and just under 26 and 23.5, 1956–60, to 24.6 for men and 22.5 for women, 1966–70 (during the 1970s the figures rose again slightly).[4] But this was more than compensated for by earlier ages of maturity in both boys and girls – largely an effect of increased prosperity. By the early 1960s the average girl reached menarche by the age 13½, compared to 16–17 a century earlier, while boys reached full growth (and the peak of sexual potential) at the age of 17, compared to around 23 at the turn of the century.[5] So a large gap remained between economic independence and sexual maturity on the one hand and emotional independence and sanctioned sexual activity on the other. It was this gap that constituted the core of the perceived sexual crisis.

In fact, standards of sexual behaviour remained remarkably chaste. There was certainly an increase in illegitimacy, rising from 5 per cent of all births in 1955 to 8 per cent in 1967, but this partly reflected the increase in numbers of the age group likely to experience pregnancy, partly a greater freedom from the compulsion on a pregnant girl to marry during the 1960s.[6] As Alex Comfort suggested in his book *Sex in Society*, published in 1963, the 'biggest change in behaviour has been one of timing'[7], so that there was a movement of illegitimate births and pre-marital conceptions to a slightly younger age group; but this was chiefly the result of earlier maturity rather than a vastly increased 'immorality'.

We must treat the figures for venereal disease with similar caution. There was a substantial increase in overall infection from the mid-1950s, following a post-war dip, and this was part of a world-wide phenomenon. But the increase largely related to gonorrhoea, which through the advent of penicillin and other antibiotics (and despite the development of super-strains) was a relatively straightforward disease to deal with. The incidence of syphilis, a more potentially dangerous disease, fell dramatically, so that by the early 1970s infections were only about one-fifth of the 1951 figure, and in the words of a recent expert, had become 'a very rare disease', the only major area of increase being among male homosexuals.[8] And even the danger of this venereal disease had been dramatically diminished, through the introduction of effective drugs. The demystifiers were clearly able to show that the fear of the disease was grossly exaggerated, particularly amongst the young. Michael Schofield pointed out in 1965 that the chances of a girl aged 15–19 getting venereal disease were some 1,000 to 1. Moreover, in a period when venereal disease figures went up by 34 per cent, hospital admissions generally went up by 43 per cent so there was no vast disparity, and the increased attendance at VD clinics was in part an indication of a greater willingness to seek advice from the specialised service (especially from male homosexuals).[9] But during the 1960s a rational argument had to face an onslaught of fear, generated in large part by the youth problem. The British Medical Association produced a report on *Venereal Disease and Young People* in 1964 which hysterically suggested a vast increase in promiscuity among the young, and throughout the 1960s and 1970s the VD figures were treated as an index of immorality, or in the vivid phrase of a leading expert on the subject, were part of a syndrome of illegitimacy, violence, drug taking and homosexuality as evidence of 'social pathology'.[10]

What is most striking now, however, is not 'pathology' but the general conformity of British youth. The Latey Committee on *The Age of Majority* in 1967 found that most adolescents differed little in their social attitudes from their elders. Similarly, Michael Schofield in his study of *The Sexual Behaviour of Young People,* published in the mid-1960s, found a general conservatism about the purposes of life, marriage, homosexuality, and the purposes of sex. The vast majority wanted to marry, and expected faithfulness. Most boys felt that if they got a girl pregnant they should marry her; and although nearly half the boys in his sample were in favour of pre-marital sex (compared to a quarter of the girls), the majority still wanted to marry virgins. Moreover, despite alarmism, youthful promiscuity was not a major problem. Over two-thirds of the boys and three-quarters of the girls in Schofield's sample had experienced no sexual intercourse at all.[11]

Ten years later there were still few signs of general sexual libertarianism. In the early 1950s Geoffrey Gorer had suggested that 'Most English people's views on sexual morality are more rigid than their personal practice.' In the 1970s several commentators noted that while attitudes had relaxed considerably on a whole range of sexual issues, behaviour had altered little: their practice was now more rigid than their beliefs. By the beginning of the 1970s many, perhaps most, people under thirty regarded pre-marital chastity as unimportant, but not everyone did in fact have sex before marriage, either from choice or lack of opportunity. In a survey conducted by Geoffrey Gorer for *The Sunday Times* in the late 1960s, a quarter of the married male informants and nearly two-thirds of the women said they were virgins at marriage. There had indeed been a remarkable liberalisation, but it scarcely constituted a revolution.[12]

And yet throughout the 1960s and 1970s it was the sexuality of youth that provoked the fiercest debates, and the likeliest elements of backlash. Mrs Mary Whitehouse began her mission to 'clean-up' television and purify the nation in 1963 precisely because of her conviction that young people were sexually at risk.[13] What was clearly taking place was a displacement of the anxieties aroused by the nature of the social changes, especially expressed in the growing autonomous styles of the various youth cultures, on to the terrain of sexuality, where hidden fears and social anxieties could most easily be stirred. For though the standards of behaviour of young people overall changed relatively little compared to the pother aroused by them, where behavioural styles changed they changed dramatically, and in a way where social and economic power was married to an aggressive sexual challenge.

Rock n' Roll was the obvious example of this.[14] The term itself was originally a sexual synonym; and sexual outrage became an aspect of the music's sexual appeal. Rock music, and the rather more vapid forms of pop music it transformed, became the context for dating and courtship, the means of emotional expression, and a social cause for the newly enriched young. Amongst its most ardent advocates rock became a liberalising force, an expression of the new society in the offing. For the majority, pop music was the essential background to social life. And at the centre of the appeal of rock music and its derivatives was a potent sexual aggressiveness. Its most successful exponents were male, challenging other men, and constructing a powerful sexual imagery of dominance, boastfulness, prowess and control, and flirting, narcissistically and dangerously with women – 'under my thumb'.

Associated with the great pop personalities of the 1950s and 1960s was an outrageous style – sexually and socially (drugs, extravagant lifestyles) – which dramatised a social divide. But for other, less elevated, elements in the young population, there was a revolt into style no less potent or spectacular for its minority nature. For sections of working-class youth this was expressed in the emergence of a series of apparently exotic subcultures throughout the 1950s, 1960s and 1970s (teddy boys, mods and rockers, punks), ritualistic forms of resistance to the changes that were disrupting working-class life (the break-up of communities, the speed-up and alienation of factory work, the dreariness of 'new-town' social life).[15]

For the better-educated middle class, or newly de-proletarianised youth, the 1960s saw the birth of a counter-culture, less apolitical than the working-class culture, more challenging (at least in theory) of bourgeois hegemony. Music, clothes, style became the hallmark, the crack in the paintwork, of the traditional society that seemed to be vanishing for ever, and though in fact many of the youth subcultures were extremely puritanical, especially towards 'queers' and other obvious sexual 'deviants', violence, drugs, and sex, three major moral preoccupations of the 1960s and 1970s, blended symbolically in the image of youth in revolt.

Here then, was one area of social life that posed the question of control. For the liberal the way forward was relatively clear, involving greater help for young people; both formal, in the way of better, and more personally relevant sex education, access to birth-control facilities, information and advice on abortion, a sensible attitude to VD; and informal, stemming from a greater freedom in talking about sex, so there would be people the young could talk their sexual problems over with.[16] For the moral conservatives the answer was no less transparent, if less practical: the reaffirmation of the values of traditional family life. The Longford Report on Pornography in 1972 argued that a sound sex education could not come from the amoral instructions of the school but only from the familial framework; ignoring the fact, it should be said in passing, that opinion surveys demonstrated very clearly the general absence of parental sex advice for their offspring.[17]

It was inevitable that sex education would provide a conduit for the breezes of controversy – chiefly because of its transparent inadequacy. In 1943 the Board of Education published a pamphlet on *Sex Education in Schools and Youth Organisations*, noting the need for suitable instruction in schools, with parental backing, before strong emotions develop. Twenty years later, the Newsom Report on Secondary Education found it necessary to reaffirm the need (though within the firm context of monogamous heterosexuality).[18] In the meantime, relatively few teachers had carried out the 1943 recommendations, for a combination of reasons: general attitudes towards sex, and fear of promiscuity, the attitudes of parents and of teachers, and lack of definite leadership from local education authorities. In his survey of *The Sexual Behaviour of Young Adults* in 1973, Schofield found that only one in ten boys in his sample and one in five of the girls had 'adequate' sex education. And although the 1960s saw a boom in publishing sex-instruction manuals – so that no major publisher was without its sex-education textbook – most of these were either totally inadequate or endorsed a very conservative view of sex. Even the most liberal texts tended to endorse a 'stages' view of sexual development, which was either to be happily resolved in heterosexual monogamy or unhappily resolved in sadness and isolation. Homosexuals, as a 1967 textbook designed for teachers put it, must be regarded compassionately for many 'are suffering from psychological disturbance' and none of them 'can ever find the happiness of raising their own family'.[19] An examination of 42 books on sex education conducted for the National Secular Society in 1970 found most of them were obscure in style, inaccurate in content, and badly written. Nearly all of them were moralistic, particularly about non-marital sex; and some of them were positively dangerous. One text suggested that 'your eggs won't get fertilised until you are quite grown up and have a husband'. Another advised that it was morally and *legally* wrong to have sex before marriage.[20] But more radical approaches faced unpredictable hazards. Søren Hansen and Jasper Jensen in *The Little Red School Book* published (translated from the Danish) in 1971, with self-help and often sensible advice to school children about drugs, teachers, school work and sex, was legally suppressed. Contrary to the book's optimistic motto, some grown-ups proved not to be 'paper tigers'.[21] The question of youth, then, remained an unresolved battleground on which liberal, radical and conservative forces rehearsed their conflicts. It was an area which left many casualties, not least among the young, in the 1960s and 1970s.

Women

Youth may have constituted the major source of moral anxiety and panic, but it was women who experienced the most obvious sexualisation and who constituted the major focus of the legislative endeavour. Abortion and divorce reform, family-planning legislation, even reform of the obscenity law, had as their points of reference the changing social and sexual imagery and roles of women. Several long-term factors were unfolding, reshaping the region of female sexuality. There was, for instance, a growth in the percentage of women marrying (and therefore experiencing sexual relations), itself an effect of the number of men and women in the population (by 1966 there were more males than females for all age groups under 40). Whereas in 1911, 552 out of every 1,000 women between the ages of 21 and 39 were married, and in 1931, 572, by 1961 the number had reached 808. By the mid-1960s, 95 per cent of men and 96 per cent of women had married by the age of 45. And they were marrying at a younger age: whereas in 1921 the proportion of people married before the age of 21 was less than 5 per cent for husbands and 15 per cent for wives, by 1968 these figures had trebled – itself an effect of earlier puberty and greater affluence.[22] At the same time, following on from this, there was a growth in the proportion of women who became mothers, and a decline in the number of childless marriages. And because of the long-term decline in family size, improved conditions of childbirth and greater awareness of family planning, there was a compression of the years in which women bore children.

Marriage more than ever was 'an almost inevitable step in the transition to adult life', the essential gateway to independence, social status, sexual gratification and children, slotting people into their 'rightful places as adults in society'.[23] But the conditions of family life were changing significantly. Childbearing was more widely experienced but played a less central and dominating part than ever before; housework became less physically demanding. And all this complemented another significant shift: the mass movement of women into the workforce from the late 1940s, initially as the reserve army, alongside immigrants, but eventually as an essential contributor both to family prosperity and the workings of the economy as women's income became a vital element in the expansion of the consumer economy in the 1950s and 1960s, and central to the maintenance of financial stability in the economically more precarious 1970s.[24]

Given the limitation of the British boom to the sphere of private domestic consumption, particularly in the working class, women, both because of their income contribution and because of their traditional social responsibilities, became the key to the penetration of the family by the 'new capitalism'. As John Newsom put it in the 1940s, 'It is not an exaggeration to say that woman as purchaser holds the future standard of living in this country in her hands . . . . If she buys in ignorance then our national standards will degenerate.'[25] This seemed more and more true in the 1950s and 1960s.

But this major shift was only partly recognised at first in the range of discourses on femininity in the 1950s and early 1960s. Femaleness continued to be primarily defined in terms of motherhood and home building, and in fact there was probabaly an accentuation of this emphasis in the 1950s. The working mother was seen as a major factor in the causation of juvenile delinquency, as 'latch-key children' became a potent source of moral panic, while the working wife's contribution to family income was culturally diminished as 'pin money'.[26] By the 1960s a new ideal of the 'symmetrical family', based on a sharing of both work and domestic labour, was beginning to replace the 1940s ideal of the 'complementary family', but its reality was undermined by a continuing tradition that women were chiefly responsible for child rearing, and by a social-security system that was based on female dependence. The major legislative reforms of the late 1960s and 1970s (Equal Pay Act, Sex Discrimination Act) did little to fundamentally undermine this complex structure of female subordination[27] and the contradictions at the heart of femininity were, in turn, to give rise to a more militant women's movement by the turn of the decade.

Female sexuality lay at the centre of these contradictions. Women were necessarily wooed by the great consumer industries, but chiefly at first in their roles as controllers of the household purse. Their sexuality could be utilised, stimulated, reshaped as an adjunct to the demands of mass marketing, but it was a sexuality designed to capture the man – cosmetics, clothes, personal accoutrements were big business and essential parts of the reconstructed 'feminine mystique'. Sexuality was more explicitly than ever before playing over concepts of femininity, but the femininity that was being constructed in the process of sexualisation was that of the 'sex kitten', the 'sex bombshell', the Monroes and the Bardots replacing in popular iconography the more resiliently 'independent' female figures of the 1940s.

The popular female press expressed, and helped construct, the range of possible meanings in femininity. A well-established magazine like *Woman* was more sexually explicit in the 1960s than in the 1940s, but still found it difficult to handle sexual relations except on its problem page, or in relation to motherhood.[28] It represented a particular type of femininity, more relaxed than a generation earlier but still domestic in its setting. But more pleasure-oriented magazines were by the late 1960s offering alternative images.

The more sexually 'liberated' journals such as *Cosmopolitan* continued to take as their point of reference the norm of heterosexual partnership, even as they played on the range of possible sexual meanings. But as the decade advanced, the sexual imagery changed. What is striking about these later journals is the way in which, as Rosalind Coward put it, the female body is being constructed as 'sensitive and sexual, as capable of stimulation and excitation, and therefore demanding care and attention if women are to be sexual and sexually desirable to men'.[29] What was taking place was a redefinition of female sexuality in terms of its possibilities for pleasure, for enjoyment unbounded by the old exigencies of compulsory childbirth or endless domestic chores.

It was not a matter of consumerism penetrating a pre-existing market, to exploit an essential sexuality; it was partially constructing a female sexuality to accord with a series of major social developments. Amongst these we must place again the changing *mores* of the young. It was striking that while sex researchers found overall little change in attitudes to female sexuality in the population as a whole, amongst those born since 1945 the real change was significant.[30] Women were asserting their own perceived sexual needs, though largely within a heterosexual framework and in the terms allowed by commercialism.

A second development both complemented and contributed to the first: the growth of more effective means of birth control. Although the real breakthroughs occurred at the end of the 1950s, there had been steady progress in the provision of birth-control facilities throughout the previous ten years – partly stimulated by the Report of the Royal Commission on Population. In 1948 there were 65 clinics, with some 30,000 new users each year (compared with 61 clinics in 1938). But from the early 1950s clinics sprang up at the rate of one every two weeks. By 1963 there were 400, a six-fold increase over 15 years.[31] But still only a tiny minority had access to advice; it was estimated that even amongst those married in the 1950s, one in four or five were likely never to practise formal birth control, and the figure amongst manual workers was one in three. The methods recommended in family-planning clinics were in any case often inapplicable to working-class conditions. The abortion figures told a complementary story. By 1961 there were around 2,300 abortions a year on the National Health Service, rising to 9,700 in 1967. There were about 10,000 private abortions per annum; while the estimate for illegal, unofficial abortions ranged from 15–100,000.[32]

During the late 1950s, however, several factors combined to undermine resistance to birth control. In 1958 the Anglican Lambeth Conference finally gave a positive Church blessing to the use of contraception, declaring it was 'a right and important factor in Christian family life and should be the result of positive choice before God'. This nod towards greater respectability was given greater significance by the growing official fear during the 1960s of overpopulation, associated with a boom in the birthrate.[33] In long-term perspective this recovery in fertility proved short lived and by 1974 the birthrate reached its lowest ever figure. The rise appears to have been a result of a shift away from having one child or none at all, rather than any move towards large families, and it was amongst the younger-marrieds that the trend was most marked.[34] But during the 1960s there were widespread fears, accentuated particularly by the higher-than-average birthrate of the immigrant communities, and this helped undermine further resistance to birth control. As one index of official anxiety a Population Panel was established in the late 1960s, and during the 1970s there was even a revival of old eugenic arguments, with the Conservative ideologue Sir Keith Joseph warning that 'a high and rising proportion of children are being born to mothers least fitted to bring children into the world . . .'.[35] In this social context two traditional concerns of the right had to battle: the fear of encouraging promiscuity against the fear of a disproportionate birthrate among the lower orders, and in the new context it was likely that birth control would win (it was an anxiety over the birthrate that prompted the House of Lords to revolt against the government and ensure the final transference of the family-planning services to the Health Service in 1974).

What made the issue less decisively a question of social control than it was earlier, was the generalisation of birth control during the 1960s; and the major reason for this was the marketing from the late 1950s of the oral contraceptive pill. 'The Pill' did not, of itself, release women from the tyranny of boundless fertility. In fact, though widely employed, its incidence of use decreased down the social scale and in a movement from the south-east of England towards the north-west. It was likely to be the least promiscuous who used it, and despite the increased use of other female methods alongside the Pill during the 1960s (the coil especially), there remained a solid resistance amongst men, especially working-class men, to the abandonment of male methods of control.[36] Moreover, by the 1970s there was a widespread awareness amongst women of the possible danger to health in the use of the oral contraceptive. In 1977 over 500,000 women discontinued use of the Pill following a health report.[37] But what the introduction of the Pill did significantly do was begin an explosion of discussion in the context of which other methods were increasingly talked about and used. So one of the major effects was to increase the sales of all types of birth-control devices including one of the oldest of all, the sheath, which remained the most popular; and to stimulate improvements in other methods. By the end of the 1960s, amongst young married couples, birth control was almost universally used.

Many problems remained throughout the 1960s and 1970s. It was only slowly that the principle of giving contraceptive advice to unmarried girls was accepted. The Brook Advisory Centres supported by the Family Planning Association began giving such advice in 1964; after 1969 it could be given on the National Health Service.[38] But much depended on the social milieu in which the advice was sought. Doctors were far from being neutral servants of their patients. And it remained true that those most at risk – the young – were least likely to have adequate access to proper advice. Nevertheless the essential fact to be grasped was that the generalisation of birth control for the first time opened up the possibility for the vast majority of women to control their fertility in safety. The long-term implications of this were radical indeed. In the short term it had two practical effects. In the first place it undermined the moral compulsion towards female virginity at marriage. Indeed, as the veteran campaigner for birth control, Helena Wright suggested, sexual experience before marriage could now more safely enhance sex life in marriage.[39] Secondly, it opened up more decisively the possibility for the incorporation of the active, if male-defined, sexuality of women into the repertoire of public debate, including advertising and publishing. The eroticisation of modern culture could focus on the female body without most of the consequences which in earlier days had been feared and expected.

Ideologies

These long-term changes in the social structure tended to undermine the orthodox moral framework – and generate a sense of moral collapse.

As Professor Carstairs saw it in the early 1960s, expressing a general liberal viewpoint, 'Popular morality is now a waste land, littered with the debris of broken convictions . . . . The confusion is perhaps greatest over sexual morality.'[40]

A most significant factor was the breakdown of an absolutist position within the Christian Churches. A Prime Minister, Harold Macmillan, might say that it was the duty of bishops, not politicians, to give a moral lead, but the bishops no longer had a single standard to offer. The more progressive might experiment with radical departures, such as South Bank theology epitomised in John Robinson's *Honest to God*; a significant minority might stand by orthodox moral canons; but the majority of Christian leaders were increasingly adopting that abstentionism pioneered by Archbishop Lang in 1937. Given that Christianity had had the central role in articulating official moral ideologies for a millenium, a shift in its attitudes was central to any major change in official attitudes.[41] There was no single change: Anglicans remained divided; Roman Catholics remained firm on questions such as divorce, abortion and birth control (though this latter had only marginal effects on individual Catholics in Great Britain); most Nonconformists by and large maintained their puritanical stance. But the changes that did occur were highly significant and influential. Bodies within the Church of England began to re-explore sexual morality and to recommend more liberal stances: on homosexuality, sexual offenders, abortion and divorce. The more traditionally radical Quakers, in their *Towards a Quaker View of Sex* in 1963, set forth an immensely influential approach which placed 'love' at the heart of morality rather than tradition, authority or revelation. Moreover, there was a conviction that love, including homosexual love, 'can not be confined to a pattern'. This did not lead to an endorsement of 'promiscuity', and in certain regards its norm was excessively conservative. Lesbianism, for instance, was seen as an effect of the frustration of the maternal instinct and no attempt was made to question the centrality of the family. It was, nevertheless, a radical break with moral authoritarianism, and it was a representative document.[42]

The shift in certain sections of the Christian Churches reflected a wider shift in attitudes amongst certain strata of the population – particularly the new professional classes, young businessmen and sections of the governing class. It was indicative that, as Stuart Hall has pointed out, while the Churches closely connected with the state, the law and influential middle-class opinion changed their positions, those (largely fundamentalist groups) most closely associated with the low middle class and respectable working class remained conservative – and were to prove the chief reservoir of support and the organisational basis for the moral reaction typified by the National Viewers' and Listeners' Association (NVALA) and the Society for the Protection of the Unborn Child (SPUC).[43]

As religious ideologies declined there·was scope for the vacuum to be filled by more secular ideologies, of which perhaps the most potent were medical. Barbara Wootton deplored the tendency for notions of sickness to rush in to fill the gap vacated by the idea of moral failure, but in the 1960s she was a fairly lone voice.[44] However, no single socio-medical approach dominated. Kinsey's two great volumes with their naturalist's matter-of-factness about sexuality were a powerful subter-ranean influence challenging ego-psychology with its ambition of social adjustment. Elizabeth Wilson has recently argued that the popularity of a crude psychoanalytical approach – with its mechanistic emphasis on the stages of development and its assumption of the normality of a resolution into conventional morality – was in large part, indeed, a reaction to the radical implications of Kinsey.[45]

But a medical moralism suffused many official statements from the medical profession itself, particularly with regard to homosexuality, which received excessive attention. The British Medical Association's *Memorandum on Homosexuality and Prostitution* suggested that 'per-sonal discipline and unselfishness have little place' in the thoughts of homosexuals. Works such as early editions of D. J. West's *Homosex-uality* and Anthony Storr's *Sexual Deviations* sought after forms of analytical cures or adjustment.[46]

But the most ardent pursuers of 'adjustment' were the behaviour-ists, amongst whom, in the 1960s, there was as one defender of the approach has put it, an 'increase in therapeutic optimism.'[47] What mat-tered here was not so much notions of sickness as of 'maladjustment', and the most dramatic sign of what Thomas Szasz has called 'correc-tional zeal', appears in the development of methods of behaviour-modification theory for sexual deviants. During the 1950s and 1960s techniques of aversion therapy were perfected, designed to induce nausea when the subject was confronted with the objects of his desire. The technique had developed in the 1930s and 1940s to combat alcohol-ism. It was applied to fetishism in 1956, and the lead was followed for homosexuals and transvestites in the 1960s. Early methods had fa-voured chemical inducement to nausea but from 1963 electrical shock methods came in.[48] It never became a dominant approach and by the 1970s (largely as an effect of the rise of the gay movement) was rarely applied to homosexuals, nor did it become a compulsory alternative to prison for sex offenders, though such an approach had its advocates. But it placed a potentially powerful and dangerous weapon in the hands of the medical profession.[49] Behind the general approach was a strong assumption that only by conformity to existing norms could an individ-ual achieve satisfaction. In a period when the norms were being chal-lenged to an unprecedented degree, methods of behaviour modification were firmly seen by many liberals and radicals as little better than 'brainwashing'.

Though behaviour modification had its advocates, the social-delinquency approach remained a more dominant one amongst social scientists investigating (and hoping to 'solve') the problems of sexual variations. Valiant efforts were made to discover the aetiology of particular 'conditions', especially homosexuality. Weak fathers, overpowering mothers, absent mothers and dominant fathers, childhood traumas or gender confusion – all were wheeled forward, to little theoretical effect or enlightenment. Perhaps more constructive were the efforts to identify the characteristics of particular social 'problem groups', an effort at what has been termed 'social book keeping'.[50] The major influence here was again the work of Alfred Kinsey, though none of his British followers had access to his resources or range of informants; it was nonetheless an important contribution to demystification. Male homosexuals again received most attention. Michael Schofield produced several major studies, culminating in *Sociological Aspects of Homosexuality* in 1965, and there were many journalistic imitators. Schofield also explored the sexual problems of the young, the young adult and the 'promiscuous', while others, such as Eustace Chesser, charted the behaviour of English women, or like Geoffrey Gorer, attempted to use statistical cross-sections of the population to discover the range of sexual behaviour and norms.

During the 1970s there was a growing interest in less orthodox sexualities: the social exploration of lesbianism began, alongside the sociological charting of the characteristics of transvestites, transexuals and paedophiles.[51] Although many of these works started with a delinquency approach, the evidence they presented often undermined this, suggesting a range of behaviours, a continuum between 'normal' and 'abnormal' and the relative unimportance of essential characteristics when compared with the influence of social labelling. This was to have important effects in the development of radical deviancy studies in the 1970s, in which the 'normality' of the deviant subcultures for those participating in them was emphasised, in a strong current of moral relativism. But the short-term effect was to emphasise the existence of 'social problems' which could, given the will, and understanding be resolved by social and political intervention.

The political moment

It is this emphasis on the survival of, and need to resolve specific social problems that gives the reforming legislation of the 1960s its particular flavour and distinctive tone. There was no official endorsement of hedonism. There was in fact a strong element of negative utilitarianism in the legislation, more concerned with removing difficulties and minimising suffering than in positively enhancing happiness.[52] The Sexual Offences Act of 1967 attempted to redress the absurdity of the laws on male homosexuality, by carrying out in part the Wolfenden proposals, decriminalising private adult male activities. The Abortion Act of 1967 introduced the possibility of 'social' as well as medical grounds for a lawful termination of pregnancy because of the recognition of what was seen as the problem of a minority of (generally inadequate) women. Similarly, The National Health Service (Family Planning) Act attempted to regulate the situation regarding the unplanned spread of birth control by encouraging local authorities to provide facilities on social as well as more narrowly medical grounds. Reform of the divorce law in 1969 attempted to meet the challenge of increasing marriage breakdowns and the archaic nature of traditional grounds. Finally, the social regulation of what could be read or seen relaxed, partly to cope with an increasing tension between norms and behaviour. The Obscene Publications Act of 1959 (amended in 1964) responded to the contradictions between changing public standards of speech and taste (partly at least demonstrated in the vast growth of pornography) and antiquated obscenity laws by introducing the defence of literary merit. Other moves reflected a similar desire to do away with archaic survivals. The abolition of the Lord Chamberlain's censorship of the theatre in 1968 allowed a much more explicit portrayal of sexuality on the stage. Simultaneously, though without legislative fiat, cinema censorship was modified, leading to a new verbal and visual openness, particularly with regard to the sexualisation of the female body.

Shifts were at the same time taking place in the operation of the law, though we must not exaggerate the change. The legal victory of Penguin Books in its defence of the publication of D. H. Lawrence's *Lady Chatterley's Lover* in 1960, which heralded a more relaxed mood (and made the book a huge best-seller) was achieved by gathering a host of literary luminaries who attested to the book's literary merits and defence of the sacrament of sex. And there was no consistent movement towards liberalism. The early 1960s saw an important revival of legal moralism, with judges going out of their way to pronounce on sexual morality. In 1962 the House of Lords, in the case brought against the publisher of the *Ladies' Directory*, a prostitutes' contact sheet (Shaw *v.* DPP) revived the old common-law offence of conspiracy to corrupt public morals, which most thought had died out in the eighteenth century.[53] This was potentially a powerful weapon against sexual unorthodoxy. But despite many arbitrary actions as the 1960s and 1970s advanced, police and the prosecuting authorities became more reluctant to proceed and juries unwilling to convict in cases of obscenity.

All these reforms addressed themselves to elements in the family–procreation–sexuality nexus, and attempted to adjust the law to perceived changes. But though they appear in retrospect as a 'package' and have a cohesive approach, they must simultaneously be understood in their distinctiveness. They all had long pre-histories, and diverse roots. Agitation for the reform of the Lord Chamberlain's censorship had been going on for most of the century. The laws on male homosexuality had faced organised (if secretive) opponents since the 1890s. Fundamental divorce reforms had been discussed since the 1910s. Family planning had been a major issue since the 1920s, and abortion reform campaigned for since the 1930s. The contradictions in the workings of the existing laws had been further uncovered in a series of official enquiries (Royal Commissions, departmental committees, joint select committees) over the previous decade. And although their recommendations had varied from the ultra-conservative (Morton) to the liberal (Wolfenden) they had all demonstrated a widespread public anxiety about the moral health of the community.

Moreover, the reforms were preceded by a series of organised but separate campaigns designed to change influential opinion, and persuade the legislators. 'It is not so much public opinion as public officials that need educating', Oscar Wilde had written in 1898,[54] and the classic pressure-group tactic this indicated dominated the 1960s. The Abortion Law Reform Association, founded in 1936, had a new surge of energy; a Homosexual Law Reform Society was founded in 1958 to press for the Wolfenden reforms; and the Divorce Law Reform Union founded in 1906, joined with the Marriage Law Reform Society in the early 1960s to campaign more vigorously. Although their chief efforts were as auxiliaries to the Parliamentary reforms, they nevertheless did contribute to a shift in public opinion. By the mid-1960s most opinion polls were showing a majority for reform. In 1957, for instance, only 25 per cent of a sample were in favour of homosexual law reform; by 1965, the figure was 63 per cent, though 93 per cent now saw homosexuality as a form of illness requiring medical treatment.

So the ground was well prepared for reform by the 1960s, and it would be misleading to see the 'permissive legislation' as in any way an automatic response to social change. Nevertheless, it is possible to see elements of a political strategy at work, a strategy designed precisely to bring moral regulation into line with perceived social change as part of a wider political programme. And although the general approach crossed party lines, so that certain Tory Progressives can be associated with it as clearly as social democrats, it was amongst the 'revisionists' of the Labour Party, particularly associated with young theorists and politicians such as Anthony Crosland and Roy Jenkins, that moral reformism became central.[55] The key theoretical element in their approach was best expressed in Crosland's *The Future of Socialism*, a belief that because of welfarism and the emergence of managerial control of industry, the capitalist economy had essentially stabilised, making the old socialist shibboleths of nationalisation unnecessary and outdated. This did not mean that social problems had disappeared; on the contrary, during the 1960s Labour reformists were able to pinpoint a long list of necessary changes, effects of the 'candy-floss' economy. But these could no longer be conceived of as structural problems, they were residual problems that could be resolved by piecemeal social engineering. It was a short step from this to an identification of residual moral problems, that could equally well be resolved by localised reforms and moral engineering.

The second strategic element was political. For the revisionists the central task that the Labour Party faced after its election defeat in 1959 was to move away from its reliance on its old, and declining, manual working-class base, to achieve a new political alliance around other social forces. What this meant in practical terms was the wooing of the new social forces, especially young professionals, the new technocrats and the recently embourgeoisified. This was a much wider issue than simply the future of the Labour Party, for what was being sought for in the 1960s by the social democrats was a political strategy that would achieve social stability within the context of a reformed capitalism, and the task was increasingly central because of the transparent breakdown of the Conservative hegemony in the early 1960s. The strategy, therefore, was to build a political ruling alliance round the new social forces, and the social vision offered in the revisionists' case was precisely one designed to woo these forces, emphasising greater equality of opportunity, educational reform, social mobility, greater leisure possibilities, and liberalisation of attitudes. The various elements complemented one another, for economic success was the foundation of a richer private life, while a richer private life was even more necessary in an economy growing ever more bureaucratic, automated and alienating. Here we can see the place of the two key elements of moral reformism: its piecemeal nature, designed to eliminate the hangovers of an authoritarian society; and its stress on privatisation of choice, derived from wider moral arguments, but fitting neatly into the social distinctions that were being marked out. 'Revisionist' social democracy thus broke with traditional working-class moralism and with Fabian puritanism, to present a blueprint for a more 'civilised' and libertarian capitalism. 'Civilisation' was indeed Roy Jenkins's preferred synonym for the term 'permissiveness': 'the achievement of social reform without disruption . . . avoiding excessive social tensions'.[56]

There was, then, a fit, between a particular, influential, political approach, and the series of legislative reforms, and there is a certain historic aptness in the fact that the major social reforms, in education and morality, were presided over by the leading 'revisionists', Crosland (as Education Secretary) and Jenkins (as Home Secretary). But what cannot be detected is any careful strategy in the actual promulgation of the reforms. 'Revisionism', though immensely influential, never hegemonised the Labour Party, and the political bloc organised by the Wilson leadership to win the 1964 and 1966 elections had many of the same social elements but in a different mix, from the 'revisionist' model. The support of young professionals was won to the Labour cause not through visions of a 'civilised society' but through images of technological change. The pragmatic Wilson was less interested in moral change, and was rooted in that nonconformist morality which the revisionists rejected. Moreover despite a more or less favourably disposed Parliamentary majority following the Labour election victories in 1964 and 1966, all the reforms faced sharp opposition, including a great deal from more traditionalist Labour supporters, and in the case of abortion-law reform a nationally organised campaign supported by the full weight of the Roman Catholic Church. The cross-party reforming alliance was bitterly split on abortion. So a leading Labour 'revisionist' and Catholic, Shirley Williams, and a leading Labour individualist, Leo Abse (who had sponsored homosexual law reform) joined with a leading Tory Progressive, Norman St John Stevas (also a Catholic) in opposing abortion-law reform. Parliamentary majorities were never guaranteed, and despite the warm backing of Roy Jenkins as Home Secretary from 1965–67, which allowed government time to be used for the legislation, all of the reforming Acts began as private members' bills and were voted on as a matter of private conscience, not party loyalty.[57] The moral reforms were marginal to the central direction of the government, and were often seen as irrelevant by those who directed its strategy.

It is this range of circumstances, forming a complex political conjuncture, which in large part explains the contradictory nature of many of the reforms. They were the end results of a variety of different pressures: liberal reformist, pragmatic acceptance of the need for change, eccentric libertarianism, religious, especially Roman Catholic counter-pressure, and other sustained special interest agitation or opposition, channelled through Members of Parliament. Bearing this in mind we can try to unravel some otherwise puzzling features of the reforms.

The first was their self-contained nature. Each reform was argued for on its own merits and for each reform a separate constellation of support had to be constructed. The pressure-group tactics of the reform organisations reflected this. Their chief concern was to obtain a Parliamentary majority. They therefore carefully avoided any tactics which could alienate influential support, and their arguments were tempered by an acute caution, which by the 1970s was often seen as an incapacitating paralysis by their more radical followers. Their classic task was to identify a social problem area – the unfortunate woman who had got into trouble, and needed an abortion, the homosexual suffering from an unfortunate condition, and subject to blackmail and social ostracism – and press for isolated reforms which could alleviate the problem.

A second factor was the ultimately very limited nature of the reforms. Homosexual law reform did not legalise homosexuality as such; it narrowly decriminalised certain aspects of male adult behaviour in private, in England and Wales. After vigorous lobbying the merchant navy as well as the armed forces were excluded from its provisions. Moreover, despite the efforts of reform supporters, the threat of conspiracy charges continued to hang over homosexuals; and the prosecution for offences in public vastly increased over the next decade. Abortion law reform allowed social grounds for termination up to 28 weeks but fell far short of abortion on demand. Moreover, while the law took one step back, the medical profession took one forward; doctors became the crucial intermediaries in deciding on the access to abortion.[58] In a similar way, the divorce reform proved to be an uneasy compromise between the traditional concept of a 'matrimonial offence' and a new concept of the recognised breakdown of a marriage.

In attempting to meet real changes and real social problems caused by the challenge to an older moralism, the reforms of the 1960s produced very uneasy and sometimes unworkable compromises. Their chief effect lay not so much in what they achieved themselves, as in the spaces they created through which more radical pressures were able to emerge. Almost despite themselves, the reformers of the 1960s wrought more than they thought – and often more than they desired.

References

1. **E. J. Hobsbawm**, *Industry and Empire*, Penguin, Harmondsworth, 1969, Ch. 13.
2. H. L. A. Hart, *Law, Liberty and Morality*. Preface.
3. **Judith Ryder** and **Harold Silver**, *Modern English Society: History and Structure 1850–1970*, Methuen, London, 1970, p. 260; **Mark Abrams**, *Teenage Consumer Spending in 1959*, Press Exchange, London, 1961.
4. **Joan Busfield** and **Michael Paddon**, *Thinking About Children: Sociology and Fertility in Post-War England*, Cambridge University Press, 1977, p. 8. The figures for 1971 were 24.60 and 22.59; for 1972, 24.85 and 22.88; and for 1975, 24.86 and 22.72, reflecting probably a growing anxiety about economic prospects.
5. See **J. H. Tanner**, *Growth at Adolescence*, Blackwell, Oxford, 1962; and M. Schofield, *The Sexual Behaviour of Young People*, p. 10.
6. On illegitimacy trends see Ryder and Silver, *op. cit.*, p. 291; M. Schofield, *op. cit.*, pp. 11, 242, 251; **Virginia Wimperis**, *The Unmarried Mother and her Child*, George Allen and Unwin, London, 1960, Table 6; **S. F. Hartley**, 'The Amazing Rise of Illegitimacy in Great Britain', *Social Forces*, Vol. 44, No. 4, June 1966, pp. 533–45; **S. F. Hartley**, *Illegitimacy*, University of California Press, London, 1975; Busfield and Paddon, *op. cit.*, p. 121.
7. **Alex Comfort**, *Sex in Society*, Gerald Duckworth, London, 1963, p. 100.
8. David Barlow, *Sexually Transmitted Diseases*, p. 100; see also **Michael Schofield**, *The Sexual Behaviour of Young Adults*, Allen Lane, London, 1973, Ch. 3; and **R. S. Morton**, *Venereal Diseases*, 2nd edn, Penguin, Harmondsworth, 1972, who gives the figures for gonorrhoea infections, pp. 38–9, and for syphilis infections, pp. 40–1. By 1978 there were 96,600 patients with non-specific infection, 57,500 with gonorrhoea and 6,100 with syphilis. *Guardian*, 4 Feb. 1980.
9. Schofield, *The Sexual Behaviour of Young People, p. 242; and* **Schofield**, *Promiscuity*, Victor Gollancz, London, 1976, p. 29.
10. **British Medical Association**, *Venereal Disease and Young People*, BMA, London, 1964; **R. S. Morton**, *Sexual Freedom and Venereal Disease*, Peter Owen, London, 1971, preface.
11. M. Schofield, *The Sexual Behaviour of Young People*, pp. 119, 125, 128, 136, 248. Comparing his figures with other findings Schofield concludes (pp. 237–8) that the incidence of pre-marital sex was higher for boys in Denmark and the USA, but higher for girls in Britain than in Kinsey's figures.

12. Geoffrey Gorer, *Explaining English Character*, p. 94. **Gorer**, *Sex and Marriage in England Today. A Study of the Views and Experience of the under 45s*, Nelson, London, 1971, p. 31 and *passim*; Michael Schofield, *The Sexual Behaviour of Young Adults*, pp. 193, 14. Cf. **Jon P. Alston** and **Francis Tucker**, 'The Myth of Sexual Permissiveness', *Journal of Sex Research*, Vol. 9, No. 1, February 1973.
13. See below, pp. 277 ff.
14. There is little on the sexual content of pop music, but see **Simon Frith** and **Angela McRobbie**, 'Rock and Sexuality', *Screen Education*, No. 29, Winter 1978/79; and **Jenny Taylor** and **Dave Laing**, 'Disco-Pleasure-Discourse: On "Rock and Sexuality" ', *Screen Education*, No. 31, Summer 1979.
15. See **Stuart Hall** and **Tony Jefferson** (eds), *Resistance through Rituals. Youth Subcultures in post-war Britain*, Hutchinson, London, 1976; **Dick Hebdige**, *Subculture: The Meaning of Style*, Methuen, London, 1979; **Mike Brake**, *The Sociology of Youth Culture and Youth Subcultures*, Routledge and Kegan Paul, London, 1980.
16. See for example Schofield, *The Sexual Behaviour of Young Adults*,
17. p. 200.
17. **Longford Committee**, *Pornography: The Longford Report*, Coronet, London, 1972, pp. 334 ff.; Schofield, *op. cit.*, p. 35. For a representative confrontation of values and positions see the quotations from the transcript of a debate between Mrs Mary Whitehouse and Grapevine (a London group giving non-moralistic sex advice to young people, founded by the Family Planning Association in 1973) quoted in **Michael Tracey** and **David Morrison**, *Whitehouse*, Macmillan, London, 1979, pp. 127–130.
18. See **Albert G. Chantler**, *Sex Education in the Primary School*, Macmillan, London, 1966, for a summary of these developments; see also **Eustace Chesser** and **Zoe Dawe**, *The Practice of Sex Education: A Plain Guide for Parents and Teachers*, Medical Publications, London, 1945; and England, 'A British Sex Survey', p. 150.
19. Schofield, *op. cit.*, p. 25; and Schofield, *Promiscuity*, pp. 17 ff.; **Helene Wright**, *Sex and Society*, George Allen and Unwin, London, 1968, p. 134; **Julia Dawkins**, *A Textbook of Sex Education*, Basil Blackwell, Oxford, 1967, p. 76.
20. **Maurice Hill** and **Michael Lloyd-Jones**, *Sex Education: The Erroneous Zone*, National Secular Society, London, 1970, p. 6.
21. **Søren Hansen** and **Jesper Jensen**, *The Little Red School Book*, Stage 1, London, 1971. The publishers were convicted of obscenity in July 1971 following a legal case brought by Mrs Mary Whitehouse. See Tracey and Morrison, *Whitehouse*, pp. 135 ff.
22. Ryder and Silver, *op. cit.*, pp. 249–51; A. H. Halsey, *Trends in British Society*, p. 27; Busfield and Paddon, *op. cit.*, p. 132.
23. Busfield and Paddon, *op. cit.*, pp. 116, 118; see also **Diane Leonard Barker**, 'A Proper Wedding', in **Marie Corbin** (ed.), *The Couple*, Penguin, Harmondsworth, 1978, p. 57; and **Diana Leonard**, *Sex and Generation. A study of courtship and weddings*, Tavistock, London 1980.
24. For a discussion of aspects of these developments see **Irene Bruegel**, 'Women as a Reserve Army of Labour: A Note on Recent British Experience', *Feminist Review*, No. 3, 1979.
25. John Newsom, *Education for Girls*, p. 102.
26. These themes are discussed in **Birmingham Feminist History Group**,

'Feminism as Femininity in the Nineteen-Fifties?', *Feminist Review*, No. 3, 1979.

27. D. L. Barker, *op. cit.*, argues this point. On changes in family concepts, see M. Young and Peter Willmott, *The Symmetrical Family*, and Geoffrey Gorer, *Sex and Marriage in England Today*. On the 'dependent family', see **Mary McIntosh**, 'The State and the Oppression of Women', in **Annette Kuhn** and **Ann Marie Wolpe**, *Feminism and Materialism*, Routledge and Kegan Paul, London, Henley and Boston, 1979; and **McIntosh**, 'The Welfare State and the Needs of the Dependent Family', in **Sandra Burman** (ed.), *Fit Work for Women*, Croom Helm, London, 1979.

28. **Janice Winship**, 'A Woman's World. "Woman" – an ideology of femininity', Women's Study Group, *Women Take Issue. Aspects of Women's Subordination*, Hutchinson, London, 1978.

29. **Rosalind Coward**, 'Sexual Liberation and the Family', *M/F*, No. 1, 1978.

30. See Geoffrey Gorer, *Sex and Marriage in England Today*, p. 123.

31. See Family Planning Association, *Family Planning in the Sixties*. See also Slater and Woodside, *Patterns of Marriage*, pp. 194 ff.; *Report of the Royal Commission on Population*; E. Lewis Faning, *Report on an Enquiry into Family Limitation*; **Lella Secor Florence**, *Progress Report on Birth Control*, Heinemann, London, 1956.

32. Greenwood and Young, *Abortion in Demand*, p. 21; **Family Planning Association**, *Abortion in Britain: Proceedings of a Conference held by the Family Planning Association at the University of London Union on 22 April 1966*, Pitman, London, 1966; Schofield, *The Sexual Behaviour of Young Adults*, p. 156.

33. See Busfield and Paddon, *op. cit.*, pp. 4–5; Halsey, *Trends in British Society*, p. 28. The post-war bulge in the birthrate levelled off in the early 1950s to the rate of the 1930s (about 15.0 per 1,000 of the population). There were signs of an increase from 1956 reaching a peak of 18.7 per 1,000 in 1964, the highest level since 1947. Thereafter it declined steadily to about 13 in 1974 and to a low of 11.6 per 1,000 in 1977, followed by a slow recovery. By 1980 there was a reappearance of fears of an absolute decline. Birthrates in fourteen European countries, including Britain, were so low, one expert avowed, that the present generation of parents was not expected to replace itself: *Observer*, 13 January 1980, p. 7.

34. Busfield and Paddon, *op. cit.*, p. 11. For statements of concern at overpopulation, see **R. A. Piddington**, *The Limits of Mankind: A Philosophy of Population*, John Wright & Sons, Bristol, 1956; **Georg Borgstrom**, *The Hungry Planet. The Modern World at the Edge of Famine*, Collier Macmillan, London, New York, 1965; Michael Schofield, *The Sexual Behaviour of Young Adults*, pp. 214 ff.

35. Reported in *The Times* 21 October 1974. It is an index of changing attitudes that Joseph's rather frantic admonitions on this theme were widely seen as having cost him the leadership of the Conservative Party. On the work of official population experts, see *Report of the Population Panel*, Cmnd 9298, HMSO, London, 1973.

36. Gorer, *Sex and Marriage*, pp. 131 ff.; Schofield, *The Sexual Behaviour of Young Adults*, p. 99 ff.; *Promiscuity*, p. 23. Gorer (p. 142) found a remarkable cynicism and implicit racism about the Pill among his respondents, e.g., 'I think for under-developed countries and the world as a whole it is good, but I think there might be medical questions which need

answering before I would trust it.' and 'I never use the pill myself because it may be harmful, but it will be useful in India and places like that.'

37. *The Guardian*, 31 December 1979, p. 2.
38. On this see Elizabeth Wilson, *Only Half Way to Paradise*.
39. Helena Wright, *Sex and Society*, p. 74.
40. Carstairs, *This Island Now*, p. 55.
41. This point is made in **Stuart Hall**, 'Reformism and the Legislation of Consent', in **National Deviancy Conference**, *Permissiveness and Control*. Religious views on various aspects of moral debates are discussed in McGregor, *Divorce in England*, pp. 124–5; Gorer, *Sex and Marriage*, pp. 51, 153; Chesser, *The Sexual, Marital and Family Relations of the English Woman*, pp. 266–7.
42. **Alastair Heron (ed.)**, *Towards a Quaker View of Sex: An Essay by a Group of Friends*, Friends Home Services Committee, London, 1963. For an influential Anglican view, see **Derrick Sherwin Bailey**, *Sexual Offenders and Social Punishment*, Church of England Council for Social Work, London, 1956.
43. Hall, *op. cit.*
44. See **Barbara Wootton**, *Social Science and Social Pathology*, Routledge and Kegan Paul, London, 1959.
45. Elizabeth Wilson, *Only Half Way to Paradise*.
46. The BMA pamphlet is quoted in John Bancroft, *Deviant Sexual Behaviour*; see **D. J. West**, *Homosexuality* (first published by Duckworth, 1955, rev. edn Pelican Books, 1960; 2nd rev. edn, 1968); **Anthony Storr**, *Sexual Deviation*, Penguin, Harmondsworth, 1964.
47. Bancroft, *op. cit.*, p. 18.
48. *Ibid.*, pp. 21 ff., see also **H. J. Eysenck**, *Crime and Personality*, Routledge and Kegan Paul, London, 1964, p. 154, where he sees homosexuality as a conditioned response and describes aversion therapy.
49. On the recent use of chemical castration for sexual offences, see 'Sex Offenders and the Chemical "Cure"', *Evening Standard*, 7 February 1979, p. 3.
50. See Kenneth Plummer, *Sexual Stigma*.
51. See **Kenneth Plummer**, *Symbolic Interactionism and Sexual Differentiation: An Empirical Investigation*, Report to the Social Science Research Council, 1979. **Michael Schofield**, *Sociological Aspects of Homosexuality*, Longman, London, 1965; Chesser, *op. cit.*; Gorer, *op. cit.* Schofield, *The Sexual Behaviour of Young People*; and Gorer, *Sex and Marriage*, used opinion surveys, based on statistical cross-sections of the population, rather than the Kinsey method of interviews of volunteers.
52. **Christie Davies**, *Permissive Britain*, Sir Isaac Pitman, London, 1975, p. 3. He discusses the legislation of the 1960s, in terms derived from Weberian sociology, of a move from 'moralism' to 'causalism'. On the legislation generally, see **Peter G. Richards**, *Parliament and Conscience*, Allen and Unwin, London, 1970; and Stuart Hall, 'Reformism and the Legislation of Consent'. On homosexual law reform, see **Antony Grey**, 'Homosexual Law Reform', in **Brian Frost** (ed.), *The Tactics of Pressure*, Steiner and Bell, London, 1975; and Weeks, *Coming Out*, Ch. 15. On abortion law reform, see **K. Hindell** and **M. Simms**, *Abortion Law Reformed*, Peter Owen, London, 1971; and Greenwood and Young, *Abortion in Demand*. On censorship, see **Geoffrey Robertson**, *Obscenity*, Weidenfeld and Nicolson,

London, 1979; **Rajeev Dhavan** and **Christie Davies** (eds), *Censorship and Obscenity*, Martin Robertson, London, 1978. See also **W. H. G. Armytage, R. Chester, John Peel** (eds), *Changing Patterns of Sexual Behaviour*, Academic Press, London, New York, 1980, particularly the essays by Morrison and Tracey, and Christie Davies. Davies argues here that 'the moralist seeks justice, the causalist seeks welfare' (p. 14). So 'Causalism is the application of the ethos regulating bureaucracies to questions of individual morality' (p. 40).

53. See H. L. A. Hart, *Law, Liberty and Morality*, p. 7.
54. In a letter to George Ives quoted in Montgomery Hyde, *The Other Love*. On the role of pressure groups, see the discussion in **B. Pym**, *Pressure Groups and the Permissive Society*, David and Charles, Newton Abbott, 1974. For particular aspects of their work, see Weeks, *Coming Out*, Ch. 15; and Greenwood and Young, *Abortion in Demand*.
55. For a very suggestive discussion of this see Stuart Hall, 'Reformism and the Legislation of Consent', and in more general terms, **Stuart Hall** *et al.*, *Policing the Crisis: Mugging, the State and Law and Order*, Macmillan, London, 1978, Ch. 8. Relevant works include **C. R. A. Crosland**, *The Future of Socialism*, Jonathan Cape, London, 1956; and **Roy Jenkins**, *The Labour Case*, Penguin, Harmondsworth, 1959.
56. Jenkins quoted in Hall *et al.*, *Policing the Crisis*, p. 290.
57. See Peter Richards, *Parliament and Conscience*.
58. Under the terms of the Abortion Act which came into force in 1968, a person was deemed not guilty of an offence when a pregnancy was terminated by a registered medical practitioner, and if *two* registered doctors were of opinion that: (a) the continuance of a pregnancy would involve more risk to life, or cause injury to physical or mental health of pregnant woman, or any existing children than if a pregnancy continued; (b) there was a substantial risk that if the child were born it would be born with physical or mental handicaps. Environmental factors could be taken into account for health prospects. And the termination had to be carried out in a hospital or approved place.

Chapter Fourteen

Currents and counter-currents

The limits of permissiveness

At this stage we need to step back, to reflect on the achievements and failures of this 'liberal hour'. For in its contradictory course it revealed all the strengths and weaknesses of the liberal approach to sexuality. On its positive side were a series of important gains. Reform was achieved, through the pragmatic manoeuvres of the Parliamentary liberals and their extra-Parliamentary auxiliaries. There was an important shift towards privatisation of decision making, towards a legal acceptance of moral pluralism. But its weaknesses flowed from its strengths. Reforms were gained through a programme of necessary compromises; frequently they were piecemeal and often unsatisfactory in nature and implied no positive endorsement of radically different moral stances. Indeed, as Professor Richards has written, 'A feature of the Parliamentary debates on this subject is that the fundamental moral issue was consistently avoided.'[1] As a result they neither satisfied radicals nor appeased moral conservatives, and not surprisingly, morality became more than ever a battleground in the succeeding decade. Sexual liberals did not retreat from the front; on the contrary they produced an important series of documents advocating further reform – particularly on the 'age of consent' for women and male homosexuals, and on obscenity and film censorship.[2] But increasingly as the 1960s faded into oblivion and the harsher 1970s blew their cold winds, liberals lost their purchase on parliamentary reformers – and remember, the parliamentary moment is always the decisive one for the liberal approach to reform – and the initiative passed to more radical forces, relying to a much greater degree on the principles of self-help and popular mobilisation. On the left, the revival of the women's movement and the emergence of a gay liberation movement fundamentally challenged some of the sexual assumptions that were common to both liberalism and moral traditionalism; while on the right, the 1960s and 1970s saw a revival of an evangelical moralism, fired by an apprehension of basic changes, but made despairing by the legislative reforms. An anxious correspondent of Mary Whitehouse noted of the 1967 reforms: 'The last session of Parliament has subjected us to the progressive moral disarmament of the nation BY LAW and there's worse to come.'³ There was not – but the fear was real enough. The contradictory effects of some of the reforms provided fuel enough to the controversy, as a brief examination of three major reforms will underline: on divorce, on homosexuality and on abortion.

The 1969 Divorce Reform Act firmly asserted the institutional basis of marriage – its declared aim was to 'buttress the stability of marriage'. But by embracing a second aim – 'to enable the empty shell to be destroyed' – it effectively dismantled the apparatus of moral blame which attached to the concept of a 'matrimonial offence'. Once the partners had agreed that a marriage had broken down, a divorce was generally assured. The institutional framework of permanent monogamy was to that extent undermined. In a climate where the family appeared to be weakening as a unit as a result of long-term changes, economic and social, the rising divorce figures were inevitably seen by radicals as a sign of the family's instability and by conservatives as a sign of its breakdown. Both views were probably premature, though the increase in resort to divorce was dramatic. In 1911 the proportion of married who divorced was 0.2 per cent; by the mid-1950s it was 7 per cent; by the early 1970s it was 10 per cent and rising. Between 1970 and 1979 the divorce rate trebled for those under 25, and doubled for those over 25. In Britain, at the end of the 1970s, there was one divorce for every three marriages.⁴ Marriage was obviously no longer the sacred and permanent bond it was intended to be. But simultaneously, marriage remained as popular as ever, and nearly half of those who got divorced remarried within five years.⁵ Marriage, or at least coupledom, remained the social norm, though it was an alliance built increasingly along the lines of sexual attraction and emotional compatibility rather than an open-ended commitment for life.⁶

The tensions within the dominant ideology – between compulsory monogamy and pleasure, between enhanced individualism and familial responsibility – were thus transforming the nineteenth-century ideal. But what they implied for the future remained unclear. What they did not imply, however, was any collapse of the heterosexual norm. Reforms in other areas of sexual life were contained within this dominance, as the development of attitudes to homosexuality revealed. The Sexual Offences Act which liberalised the law on male homosexuality was never intended as a clarion call to sexual liberation. As Lord Arran, who piloted reform through the House of Lords, put it, 'I ask those who have, as it were, been in bondage and for whom the prison doors are now open to show their thanks by comporting themselves quietly and with dignity.'⁷ That appeal to discretion was echoed among many other erstwhile reformers, alarmed at what they saw as a rush towards openness. But even more than this cold shower, the new law itself imposed a series of drastic limitations. In the first place, homosexuality was never fully legalised, as a series of court decisions underlined. In June 1972 the House of Lords upheld the verdict against *IT (Interna-*

tional Times), which declared it unlawful to publish contact advertisements in which homosexuals indicated their wish to meet others.
Their lordships opined that the 1967 Act 'merely exempted from
criminal penalties' but did not make it 'lawful in the full sense'.[8] This
had important effects in the decisions of the police and the courts, but it
was compounded by a second factor deriving from the private
acts/public decency dichotomy of moral reformism. For one effect of
this was to define more clearly which activities (largely in the sphere of
'public decency', such as importuning in public lavatories and cruising
grounds) still remained offences, and the police in effect put this
clarification into practice. Between 1967 and 1976 the recorded incidence of indecency between males doubled, the number of prosecutions
trebled and the number of convictions quadrupled.[9] The prosecutions
caused less of a stir and perhaps had a less drastic impact on most individual's lives, as the stigma against homosexuality gradually changed;[10]
but the controlling effect of the law accentuated in certain areas, particularly as some crusading police chiefs sought to increase the 'privatisation' and moral 'segregation' of homosexuals.[11] But by an inevitable
reflex, the inadequacy of the law reform, and the continuing moral oppression, in turn provided some of the preconditions for the birth of the
gay liberation movement, concerned not with apologetics or liberal tolerance but with questioning the hegemony of the heterosexual norm.
Neither effect could have been intended by the reformers of the 1960s.

Similar contradictory results emerged from the Abortion Act, which
remained a much more controversial reform than any other. The number of recorded abortions went up significantly after 1968, rising from
35,000 per annum to 141,000 in 1975; or moving from a rate of 4 per
100 live births in 1968 to 17.6 in 1975.[12] By 1980 over a million legal
abortions had been carried out. Several factors accounted for this rise,
the major one being the move from 'backstreet abortions' to ones provided legally in the Health Service. But another important factor was a
probable increase in the resort to abortion, as publicity over it increased, as techniques improved, and as there was a growing acceptance
by women of abortion as an adjunct to birth control when that failed.
In other words, many women were seizing the opportunity provided by
the 1967 Act to deliberately control their own fertility. It was this area
of 'choice' which disturbed some former supporters of reform, and
during the 1970s they combined with the traditionalist opponents of
reform to try to amend the law in a more restrictive manner. There was
abundant evidence that the so-called 'abuse' of the law was minimal,[13]
and the actual elements of 'abortion on demand' in the 1967 Act were
limited, dependent as they were on the attitude of the medical profession. But by 1980 it was possible almost to succeed in amending the
law drastically in a restrictive manner, against a substantial mass of
medical and popular opinion.[14] What is striking about this is that
though the resolution necessarily came in Parliament, the battle had
been in large part fought out through propaganda and mass mobilisa-

tion on the terrain of public opinion. The Society for the Protecton of
the Unborn Child (SPUC) and similar bodies had been able to mobilise
considerable conservative, cross-class support from the late 1960s,
building largely on the organisational strength of the Roman Catholic
and evangelical churches. In response, the reforming initiative passed
from the Abortion Law Reform Society to the more militant groupings
within the Women's Movement, led by the National Abortion Campaign, which was able to mobilise mass feminist, libertarian and socialist support (culminating in a massive march sponsored by the Trades
Union Congress in October 1979) on a slogan of 'A Woman's Right to
Choose'. In arguing the positive merits of abortion, as a necessary
aspect of a woman's freedom to control her own body, the terms of the
debate were being altered. This was only one aspect of an important
shift in the debates on sexuality; the liberal moment was passing.

If we seek a single moment when the tide changed, we need look no
further than 1968. Towards the end of that year the Wootton Report on
Drug Dependency was published, advocating a more liberal attitude
towards 'soft' drugs.[15] The report was a classic exposition of liberal
reformist principles, which Baroness Wootton had long advocated, and
relied on the distinction between morality and law which was central to
the 1960s reforms. Its proposals were modest. But the social and
political climate had changed drastically. Symbolically, Roy Jenkins
had left the Home Office, to preside over the massive defensive actions
to shore up the British economy. He was replaced by James Callaghan,
the embodiment of labourist traditionalism. He rejected the Wootton
Report; and in so doing proclaimed that he was pleased to have contributed to 'a halt in the advancing tide of so called permissiveness'.[16]

But this was only one response to the more elusive undercurrents of
social life which were undermining the old liberal, social-democratic
consensus. For 1968 was the year of revolt and reaction through the
world, from the United States to Czechoslovakia, from Tokyo to Paris.
And the May Events in Paris above all demonstrated the fragility of the
post-war belief in effortless progress and prosperity, revealing sharply
the contradictions at the very heart of modernised capitalism, as one of
its major products – 'youth' – began to reject its values. The student
revolt, and the spark it provided for the French general strike, suggested
for the first time since the war that the old order could be overturned,
that 'anything was possible'.[17] The revolt was short-lived; the immediate effect a deeper political conservatism. But the intellectual and
moral ferment unlocked by the Paris events, and its echoes throughout
the world, posed fresh questions of both left and right. The deeply
unsettling problems left unresolved in 1968 set the agenda for social and
moral debates in the ensuing decade: the choice seemed to be between a
radical rupture or a deepening conservatism and a retreat to more
authoritarian positions. As Hall *et al.* have put it, 'The general social
and political polarisation which characterises the next decade began
from this point.'[18]

The effects, as ever, were more muted and fragmented in Britain than elsewhere, whether in terms of student radicalism or political conservatism. But as the Callaghan position indicates, it was still enough of a divide to take it as a symbolic starting point. For the eddies of the great events abroad deeply affected both the British counter-culture and the respectable, and one fed on the other.

The new moralism

Let us take, for a start, the 'respectable'. The student revolts, the first mass open-air pop concert, the continuing economic crisis, the panic over black immigration and the massive anti-Vietnam War demonstrations in Grosvenor Square: all apparently random events, but all connected in 1968 as signs of breakdown or transformation in the old order. What we can see, in response, from the late 1960s, is a growing sense of social crisis, which demanded general solutions. The series of moral panics over morality and manners which punctuate the 1950s and 1960s were giving way to a generalised social panic, and in this new climate, moral authoritarianism again came to the centre of the stage.[19]

Its archetypal exponent was a deeply religious, respectably middle-class lady, a former teacher whose ire had been stirred by the social changes of the 1950s and 1960s, and in particular their effects on children, and who from being a hesitant and reluctant campaigner in 1963 had by the late 1970s blossomed into an international figure, listened to by statesmen, commanding instant media attention, the model of a moral entrepreneur – Mrs Mary Whitehouse.[20] It will not do simply to personalise Mrs Whitehouse's campaigns. Far from being a crank, a latter day Mrs Grundy, she commanded wide, often cross-class support. And while she herself was rooted in a tradition of anti-communist Moral Re-armament, she was supported in her campaigns by old Roman Catholic social democrats like Lord Longford and by evangelical and Lawrentian humanists like David Holbrook, as well as by the more obviously disorientated 'respectable' middle class. But despite all provisos there was something deeply representative about Mrs Whitehouse and the campaigns she fostered. For in her profound religious conviction, in her desire for a new Christian-based moral order, in her yearning for a past that had gone (and perhaps had never been), in her sense of the damaging penetration of the privacy of the home and sacredness of sex by modern media, with its explicitness, agnosticism and ever-absorbing nature, she evoked that sense of collapse that underlay the move to the right in the 1970s, but had its origins in the changes of the 1950s and early 1960s. 'Significant social groups in society felt abandoned by the scramble of some for the affluent "progressive" middle ground and threatened by rising materialism below; amidst the "never had it so good society", they yearned for a firmer moral purpose. They provided the backbone for the entrepreneurs of moral indignation.'[21] A general sense of anxiety, generated by real (though often exaggerated) changes tended to find expression in resistance to changes which were actually marginal to the main thrust of social development, in morals and style. So Mrs Whitehouse's step in 1963, with one friend, and while still a teacher, to 'do something' about television explicitness, which led to the establishment of the Clean Up TV Campaign, immediately evoked a surprising but representative mass response. By the turn of the decade Mrs Whitehouse and the National Viewers and Listeners' Association (NVALA, successor to CUTVC) had become an influential social force, precisely because they expressed inchoate but basic fears.

Some attempt has been made by sociologists to explain the effectivity of the campaign (and similar ones with which it was closely associated, such as the evangelical Festival of Light) in terms of status loss amongst the threatened groups of the population. As Roy Wallis has put it, 'Economic and social changes have eroded the supports for formerly dominant values borne by a class of individualistic entrepreneurs . . . some social groups have proven resistant to new norms and values and their members are therefore mobilisable in the defence of the earlier standards of morality to which they adhere.'[22]

The problem with this approach is the rather mechanistic relationship it suggests between class position and moral values. It would no doubt be easy for an empiricist sociologist, exploring the membership of NVALA, to prove that it neither consisted entirely of threatened petit bourgeois, nor had any consistent class goals. As Tracey and Morrison have pointed out, a much more unifying factor for the new moral crusade was its opposition to the forms that 'secularisation' had taken and the general religious basis of its ideology.[23] What was sought after was a moral regeneration as a response to perceived moral decline and lack of moral leadership. But this in turn cannot be divorced from wider social and political currents. For just as the moral reforms of the 1960s were closely associated with a particular political approach, so the moral conservatism represented by Mrs Whitehouse, while eschewing overt political commitment, was fully complicit with a political approach which by the end of the 1970s had achieved a precarious hegemony. Sir Keith Joseph, representing the new conservatism, could, without any sense of incongruity, advise his supporters to 'take inspiration from that remarkable woman'[24], though in practice the new economic conservatism remained separate from moral conservatism (restrictions on abortion were not endorsed by the 1979 Conservative government). Nevertheless, the new moralism was indeed part of a general reaction against the social democratic ('Butskellite') consensus that had dominated the post-war world. As its underpinnings in post-war prosperity were undermined, and with a developing reaction to the 'socialism' and 'welfarism' that were seen as the roots of social decay, the restoration of moral standards and the stability of the family became one of the catchwords of the conservative repertoire, alongside law and order, and self-help. The religious absolutism of Mrs White-house and her supporters was merely one aspect of that wider social move. Its social bases *were* often the disgruntled middle class, the threatened professional, the small business ethos represented by Mrs Margaret Thatcher. But in the symbols it raised and the anxieties it articulated it was able to extend beyond to other, and perhaps unlikely, social supports.

For the liberal, throughout the twentieth century, sex has been seen, in the phrase endorsed by Havelock Ellis (almost the patron saint of 1960s reform) as the last refuge of individuality, the core of private life, the focus of social being. But just as, for the liberal, it was this area of life that most needed to be freed from religious constraints, for the moral conservative it was this area of privacy that had been most invaded, and desecrated by the post-war world. Sexual change therefore became the symbol of all the changes that had destroyed the stability of the pre-war moral order. As Mr Ernest Whitehouse (Mary's husband) put it, 'that has been the area in which the biggest breakdown in moral standards has occurred'.[25]

For Mary Whitehouse, as she said in a submission to the Annan Committee on Broadcasting, 'The essence of sex is that it is a private personal experience between two people'. She and her supporters were therefore gravely offended by the attempt to treat sex as something secular. 'To accept the biological imperative, to acknowledge the importance within human behaviour of gratification, to indulge in practices long forbidden, is to rid sex of its sacred connotations.'[26] Sex was clearly intended to be heterosexual and monogamous, the cement of marriage, not the focus for hedonism. And the shrine embodying this holy essence was the family. The strongest theme of the conservative moral ideology was now, as it had been for two hundred years, its familialism. It was the family that had been most undermined by the secularisation and demystification of sex. From this central commitment to the centrality and holiness of the family all the common concerns of the moral conservatives really flowed: with television, which penetrated the heart of this domestic setting, worming in its secular noises and visions; with pornography, making explicit and profane what should be privatised and sacred; and with blasphemy, which took in vain the name of the Father and Son, who gave meaning to the moral world, embodied in the family unit. The image and the word: these were the major foci for ardent moral endeavour. The elevation of Sir Hugh Greene, Director General of the BBC from 1960, to the pinnacle of the moralists' demonology (above even South Bank theologians and trendy sociologists) was no accident, for he embodied extremely well, and at its sharpest, the break with the Reithian moral principles that had guided British broadcasting – and indeed British life. As Director General of the BBC in 1948, Sir William Haley (later editor of *The Times*, itself equally moral) had affirmed the BBC's commitment to a Christian ethic. Greene, on the other hand, explicitly wanted to encourage, as he put it, the variety of British life, all that was new and adventurous – to express its pluralism of values. For his pains he, more than anyone, else, was blamed by Mrs Whitehouse for the decline of standards and the insidious weakening of morality.[27] Herein we see the epitome of the conspiracy theory of moral decay. It was not a result of social change but of the infiltration of godlessness that had entered into the heart of the body politic. If there is one characteristic that unifies the new conservatism it is the search for a single causative factor that would account for decay. It could be found in liberalism, permissiveness, socialism, spies within, or blacks. Mrs Whitehouse in addition found at least one seed of decay in the liberal figure of Sir Hugh Carleton Greene.

If broadcasting corrupted, pornography represented the final desecration and commercialisation of sex. Pornography (which *had* become more openly sold and explicit in the 1960s) became for the moralists of the 1960s and 1970s what prostitution had been for the social puritans of the 1880s and 1890s: a manifestation of decay,[28] a canker at the heart of respectability. But now the disease was terminal, unless a return to firm moral standards was orchestrated. For Mrs Whitehouse and most of her co-thinkers it was only religion which could provide the source for this renewed moral inspiration. Hence the growing concern with blasphemy. The most spectacular achievement of Mrs Whitehouse during the 1970s was the successful revival of the archaic blasphemy laws, which had long been thought to be in decent desuetude, in the case brought against *Gay News*. The publication by *Gay News* of a poem, 'The Love that dares to speak its name', in which a centurion expressed his homosexual fantasies about the crucified Christ, brought together all her major concerns, and determined her to make a once-and-for-all stand. For the lines of the poem were, in the words of Tracey and Morrison, 'not just offensive but constituted within themselves a radically different set of values and perspectives to those which the traditional Christian would accept as legitimate.'[29] Homosexuality was a potent symbol of this. Mrs Whitehouse might claim, as she did, that she loved the sinner while hating the sin, but the public and unashamed articulation of a homosexual consciousness perhaps as much as anything reflected the changes that had taken place. The success of her prosecution polarised opinion. For the liberal and radical it was a triumph of religious authoritarianism. For the conservative it was a victory for faith, a significant gain for the sanctity of Christian religion; and perhaps a protection that might be extended to all religions.

Though there is a consistency in the vision of the moralist as represented by Mrs Whitehouse, there is nevertheless a significant shift in tactics during the course of the 1960s which underlines the wider changes we have noted. Although there were various cross-currents, the purity organisations generally advocated a moral revival rather than a simple imposition of moral standards. NVALA as such rejected attempts to endorse a widespread moral censorship; what was necessary was a restored sense of 'responsibility'. The early emphasis was therefore on persuasion, especially of those in positions of power in broadcasting, to improve 'standards', particularly by removing 'corrupting influences'. Giving force to this attempt was a belief that public opinion was fundamentally behind the moralists. Over and over again the campaigners had recourse to the supposed weight of public support, as expressed in letters and petitions, as if the weight of signatures itself could move mountains. This populism reached its climax in 1972 with the launching of a Nationwide Petition for Public Decency following the quashing of the conviction against *Oz* magazine. There was a continuing appeal to the inarticulate to weigh in behind the moralists, to give them legitimacy. Inevitably this populism went with a sense of moral leadership. 'All history has been shaped by a tiny minority. The "misty millions" go where they are led.'[30]

But increasingly by the early 1970s, as the weight of the pen failed to move the establishment sufficiently, Mrs Whitehouse and her colleagues had recourse to the law – first, in the use of existing law, by the bringing of private prosecutions for obscenity (and blasphemy); second, by actually pressing for changes in the law. In the early 1970s there was a spate of prosecutions for obscenity, in many of which Mrs Whitehouse or her co-thinkers intervened; against *The Little Red Schoolbook*; against the School Kids' edition of *Oz* magazine; against the *International Times* for its contact advertisements, against the Swedish film, 'More About the Language of Love' and others, reversing the general official drift of the 1960s against prosecution. Not all were successful; the release of the *Oz* editors led to the launching of the National Petition. But it represented a new pursuit of the obscene through legal harassment, one sharpened by the emergence of well-placed police chiefs committed to evangelism and moral purity, as well as more traditional areas of 'law and order' within their purview; James Anderton of Manchester became the most representative figure of this type, but he was not alone.

This moral endeavour was supplemented as the 1970s wore on by ardent attempts in Parliament to change the law in a more restrictive fashion. The abortion law suffered a series of onslaughts, as we know. Less significant but equally indicative were the efforts to promote an Indecent Displays Bill, which would have limited the opportunities of shops to display any dubious published wares; and the panic passing of a Protection of Children Bill in 1978 which by seeking to control the use of children in pornography looked fair set to cause more problems than it resolved, because of its loose formulation and adoption of moralistic rather than utilitarian criteria.[31]

It was quite apparent that the morality campaigners tapped a vein of real unease, and the search for a new moral absolutism became the more ardent as the 1970s faded into the 1980s. Nor was this a localised phenomenon. Within the Christian world it was widely noted that Pope John Paul II was seeking to give a firmer moral leadership than his predecessors had found possible, a leadership based on very traditional standards with regard to birth control, abortion, marriage, divorce and homosexuality. While in the world of Islam a new fundamentalism burst over Iran and other nations, challenging the bitter fruits of inadequate 'modernisation' in the name of received truths – truths which led to the stoning or execution of adulterers and sodomites. In their search for moral revival, the British purity organisations were on a less fundamentalist and extreme plain. But many professed to see in Mrs Whitehouse and her colleagues a more domesticated but no less dangerous breed of *ayatollahs*. She and her co-thinkers had demarcated an important divide.

Alternatives

If 'liberalism' was seen as the cancer eating its way through British society by the new moralists, it was equally firmly seen as a 'fraud' by the libertarianism that exploded around the 'counter-culture' and radical fringe in the late 1960s and early 1970s. What were called the 'dialectics of liberation' detected in liberalism that 'repressive tolerance' that Herbert Marcuse in his moment of influence in the late 1960s had so eloquently described, and which in the area of sexuality allowed a controlled desublimation of libido in order to bind the individual ever more closely to the demands of consumer capitalism.[32]

The counter-culture itself was a curious, transient phenomenon. A rejection by largely middle-class youth of the values and avid consumerism of middle-class society, it was often largely parasitic on that parent culture. It was a mood and style, a network of interlocked cultural manifestations, which by its nature was unstable and ephemeral and which by 1972, in the context of a grimmer social and economic climate, and with the collapse of most of its 'alternative press', was effectively dead. But in its cultural and semi-political stance it raised many of the concerns that were central to the radical 'sexual politics' (a phrase of Wilhelm Reich that now came into general use) of the next decade: the questioning of the centrality of the family, the emphasis on 'sexual liberation', and the stress on the importance of the 'personal'.

The family, as the anthropologist Edmund Leach put it, 'with its narrow privacy and tawdry secrets, is the source of all our discontent'. It was, as Ronald Laing and David Cooper pointed out, in ever more metaphorical and opaque works, the cause of schizophrenia, the furnace through which individualism was turned into 'madness'. It was also, as the devotees of the rediscovered Wilhelm Reich upheld, the agency through which sexuality was controlled and contained to uphold the bourgeois order.[33] Against this, in an incoherent but potent fashion, were posed the merits of communal living,[34] the importance of personal expression ('letting it all hang out') and the healthiness and liberating quality of real sexual freedom: the eroticisation of the whole body, the acceptance of the pleasure principle as opposed to the bourgeois work ethic.³⁵ Of course, the 'liberation' expressed in the 1960s counter-culture had its limitations. Sex roles were rarely challenged, the new communes often having as rigid a division of labour over child care and domestic tasks as the old nuclear families. 'Sexual liberation' was confined to the heterosexual libido, and the belief in the release of the 'real' man and 'real' woman could have its bizarrely oppressive effects.³⁶

It was as much the contradictions of the counter-culture as its example which influenced the sexual liberation movements of the late 1960s and 1970s. But one stress above all was directly influential, for it broke with the rigid externalism of the traditional left groupings and parties: the emphasis on the relevance of personal experience. 'The personal is political' was, despite its ambiguities, a central slogan of the new sexual radicalism.

The sexual liberation movements that emerged in the late 1960s, at first in the United States, and then by the early 1970s in much of the Western world, had no single source or origin. Much of the rhetoric of the sexual radicals came from the counter-culture; their political prehistories were often in the civil-rights movements and student radicalism; their political commitments remained radical and frequently revolutionary, as sexual oppression came to be seen as an indispensable aspect of all social oppression. But the fundamental elements generating a sexual politics were the contradictions experienced in a culture which increasingly stressed the sexual but commercialised and trivialised the female body, denied the validity of homosexuality, and generally still subjected sexual autonomy and pleasure to the demands of heterosexual monogamy. As a consequence, the unifying force in a heterogeneous sexual politics was the emphasis on taking control over one's own life and body; and hence the characteristic slogan: 'Our bodies are our own.' It was from this that wider political consequences followed.

The rise of the Women's Movement was undoubtedly one of the most important political and cultural events of the 1960s and 1970s. Even though it was characteristically derided in its early days, as a social and political force it became a major influence which had to be coped with, either by rejection or adjustment.³⁷ Increasingly, the diversity of the movement appeared to triumph over its unity, as different types of analyses proliferated ('revolutionary feminist'/'socialist feminist'), as various campaigns were prioritised (the rights of working women, abortion, sexual autonomy) or as conflicting styles and modes of action flourished (the 'personal' versus the 'theoretical'). But in Britain at least, all feminists could agree on the importance of a basic series of demands which were set forth as a challenge to the traditional forms of female subordination: equal pay and the campaign for full legal independence, which would end the economic and social dependence of women on a male 'breadwinner'; free 24-hour nursery provisions, free access to birth control and abortion on demand which would end compulsory maternity; and the campaign for sexual autonomy and the ending of the oppression of lesbians which would break with compulsory heterosexuality. Together the demands constituted a powerful rejection of conventional female gender roles and sexual norms. But they did more than this, for the women's movement posed an equal challenge to the validity of all existing assumptions about the nature of gender and sexuality, for, as Beatrix Campbell has written, 'The potency of women's intervention in the sexual arena lies in the possibility of shedding the whole mythology of masculinity and femininity.'[38]

Inevitably, with regard to sex, it was the power of a 'denied' female sexuality that was at first stressed, and a series of sexological redefinitions in the post-war years were eagerly welded to the service of feminism. A number of sexual investigations, from Kinsey through to the sex therapists William Masters and Virginia Johnson, had perceived the 'orgasmic potential' of women and had questioned the stress on the vaginal orgasm so common amongst neo-Freudians.[39] Mary Jane Sherfey, in her book *The Nature and Evolution of Female Sexuality*, which relied on Masters and Johnson, denied the existence of the vaginal orgasm and stressed the potentiality for multiple orgasm of the clitoris. But this potential had been thwarted: 'The rise of modern civilisation . . . was contingent on the suppression of the inordinate cyclical sexual drive of women because (a) . . . women's uncurtailed hypersexuality would drastically interfere with maternal responsibilities; and (b) . . . large families of known parentage were mandatory and could not evolve until the inordinate sexual demands of women were curbed.'[40] This argument for the necessary frustration of female sexuality under patriarchy (the denial of female sexuality almost as a precondition for civilisation, in a curious transformation of Freud) was very influential. What it suggested was the 'sexual colonisation' of women by men: 'By robbing women of their sexuality, male society has created a certain kind of "female" personality . . . . When we reclaim our sexuality we will have reclaimed our belief in ourselves as women.'[41]

A powerful current of thought, however, rejected this notion of an essential, but denied femininity (a mirror image of the conventional view) and explored instead the multiple determinations and constructions of female sexuality and the category 'woman': from maternalist ideologies to advertising, from psychological structuring to pornography. Implicit in this was a recognition of the ways in which definitions of femininity had changed – but always within the framework of female subordination.

Of course things have changed over the years; we don't just endure sex any longer. It has been converted into a wonder of the world. We used to lie back and think of England. Now we lie back and think of the heavens . . . 'it's the most beautiful thing that can happen to you' said one of my teachers. Precisely, it happens to you. You don't do it, it's done to you.[42]

So the dichotomy which became central to feminist politics, was clearly marked. On the one hand was the perennial objectification of the woman in modern society, whether in visual representation or in personal relationships: 'the eternal feminine'. On the other was the privileging of a freedom of choice, which was the key to modern feminism. In the first place, this implied choice over the conditions of life: to work or not to work, to be a mother or not to be a mother. But increasingly it was seen also as a matter of choice of sexual orientation. The initial hostility in the women's movement towards lesbianism eventually gave rise to a recognition of its centrality as a test of female autonomy. By the close of the 1970s, indeed, the issue of lesbianism had become a focus of moral indignation for those opposing the women's movement, as lesbian mothers campaigned for custody rights. It reached a climax with a burst of anxiety about lesbians who, seeking to become mothers without conventional coupling, were using various techniques of artificial insemination.[43] The campaign for lesbian rights therefore became a vital current in the women's movement, not as a compulsory orientation but as an example of the range of possibilities of feminine sexuality that were occluded in conventional discourse.

Ultimately, the aims of the women's movement and the gay movement were similar: they both offered challenges, from separate starting points, to the rigid categorisation of masculinity and femininity, of heterosexuality and homosexuality, that dominate our sexual thinking. But the gay movement had its own specific roots. The gay liberation movement that exploded with vast energy in America in 1969, reaching Britain by the end of 1970, owed a great deal to the women's movement in rhetoric, terms of analysis ('sexism') and political style (small groups, 'consciousness raising'). But of course it was also located in a long history of homosexual self-definition within the terms of a morally and legally oppressive society. Since the 1950s in Britain there had, moreover, been a sustained, if politically mild, campaign to change the law, and its limited but important achievement in promoting such a change was a vital pre-condition for a more openly militant movement in the 1970s.[44] Already by the end of the 1960s there was a burgeoning of a more sophisticated homosexual subculture than the secretive and discreet clubs and pubs of the 1950s and earlier, and both male homosexuals and lesbians were beginning to create their own milieux. But the legacy of guilt and necessary timidity was still present, and a legal and social situation which was ambiguous at best provided no positive stimulus to a more enhanced sense of self. It was this essentially that the gay liberation movement provided. The Gay Liberation Front (GLF), which was founded in London in October 1970, offered three central principles: a sense of the absolute validity of homosexuality as a sexual orientation ('Gay is Good'); a belief in the vital importance of being open about one's homosexuality ('Coming Out'); and an emphasis on the importance of collective endeavour, self activity and self-help. 'Last time it was done by an elite, who did it by stealth . . . . This time it has to be done by us, brothers and sisters.'[45] This marked a decisive stage in the evolution of a new homosexual consciousness, and the appropriation of the word 'gay' is an important index of the change. What mattered was not the actual word itself but the fact that it was self-adopted. A term like 'queer' was a label from the oppressive culture; its use by homosexuals was a sign of oppression internalised. 'Gay' suggested a new defiance of moral norms and a new sense of pride in self. It was a public affirmation of the validity of homosexuality. The axioms of 'gay pride', 'coming out' and 'coming together' thus reinforced each other as necessary components of a new homosexual identity.

There was in this an apparent paradox. The analysis behind the concept of gay liberation suggested the arbitrary nature of sexual categories, the artificial limitation of a range of possible sexualities by restrictive moral norms.[46] But the gay movement in itself simultaneously represented a definite advance in the fixing of the category, in the achievement almost of an ethnic identity. For the first time historically, a homosexual identity became one that could be declared openly as a personal affirmation, and lived as a complete life career. This in turn gave rise to a new political consciousness. The gay movement itself waxed and waned (the GLF had collapsed in London by 1972) but in two ways it transformed the possibilities for being openly homosexual. In the first place, its encouragement of self-activity led to a vast increase in self-help organisations within the gay world, energising established organisations like the Campaign for Homosexual Equality which had descended from 1960s reformism, and inspiring a host of new organisations: telephone help-lines, community services, professional and trade union groups, gay theatre groups, gay cinema, gay newspapers and journals, all of which both expressed and shaped a new notion of a gay community. A growing public awareness of homosexuality, and a greater media interest in press and television, followed (though often with dubious results). In the second place, there was an even more spectacular expansion of the commercial subculture.[47] This was truer of major metropolitan centres than of the provinces; truer for the affluent middle-class male than for the working-class lesbian mother; but compared to what had existed before, it was a major transformation.

The emergence of the modern gay identity was uneven, an adjunct to existing homosexual ways of life rather than its supplanter. It was taking place, moreover, within a consumerist culture which shaped 'sexual liberation' to its own limited ends, so that choice became an adjunct to commercialised hedonism. Nor can homosexuals be said to have escaped from social oppression; prejudice lay deep, and indeed direct physical attacks and verbal abuse often increased as public knowledge of homosexuality grew. But what is true from the 1970s is that homosexuals have appeared as a distinct social grouping which has claims of its own on society at large. This was a major historical change.

Although still contained within hegemonic forms of sexual definition, homosexuals were now openly organising their own destinies within its confines.

But to return to our paradox: the gay movement did confirm the separateness of homosexuality, but it also set in motion the long-term disintegration of the category, for the very act of affirming a gay identity as a political act underlined its arbitrariness as a social description. One sign of this was the minute subcategorisation within the gay subculture that proceeded apace, particularly in America. The male and lesbian subcultures subdivided easily enough. But in the largely male subcultures a host of special types and tastes appeared, from traditional 'camp' to new 'macho', with bars and clubs as well as more personalised insignia, demarcating different tastes and attitudes.[48] Another sign was the emergence of new categorisations as those who had been loosely labelled with homosexuals began to develop their own subcultures and even political organisations: bisexuals; sado-masochists; transvestites; transexuals; paedophiles: all appeared as vocal sexual minorities in the 1970s.[49]

This proliferation of categorisations was one of the most paradoxical but probably most significant of developments. In the first place, it underlined a new stage in a long development which had made sexual characteristics a major organising element in our culture. Sexual orientation and behaviour had in many cases become the major focus of identity and of public reaction. This had been an implicit characteristic of the Western conceptualisation of sexuality from the eighteenth century. In the emergence of organised political and cultural groupings around sexuality in the late twentieth century, the long process of definition and self-definition may be said to have reached a qualitatively new level.

But in the second place, this form of organisation around sexuality also indicated a new stage in its demystification as an activity. The gay movement set in train a reversal of the historic tendency for sexual minorities to be defined and to define themselves, against an unquestioned norm of sexual behaviour. The characteristic tone of 1950s apologetics which excused homosexuals while rejecting aspects of their lifestyles (especially 'promiscuity' amongst males) was in the 1970s reversed by activists into a celebration of sexual pleasure for its own sake. But the implications of this were far-reaching, for they suggest both a focusing on sex and a devaluing of the importance culturally assigned to it. It is in this context that we may recall Michel Foucault's words,

I believe that the movements labelled 'sexual liberation' ought to be understood as movements of affirmation starting with sexuality. Which means two things: they are movements that start with sexuality, with the apparatus of sexuality in the midst of which we are caught, and which make it function to the limit; but, at the same time, they are in motion relative to it, disengaging themselves and surmounting it.[50]

The terms of that 'disengagement' and 'surmounting' are not transparent. What is clear, however, is that the movements which 'start with sexuality' but attempt to go beyond it pose ultimately fundamental questions of its nature.

By the 1980s the most striking feature is the absence of an agreed moral framework.[51] On the most basic level individuals cleaved to fundamental values, of love, honesty, faithfulness. But what these values meant in the real social world was far from clear. Did adherence to these values mean, for instance, that one had to adhere to the traditional values of family life? Or could they be realised in less formal, less binding, even less monogamous, frameworks? Did the new emphasis on sexual pleasure involve a commercialisation of sex, as the moralist believed? Or did it imply a healthy demystification of the sacredness of sex? Was sex being debased and trivialised, or was it being freed from the shackles of tradition and prejudice? For the historian the very posing of the questions is of major significance. It implies above all that the importance given to sexuality, and the individual and social meanings constructed from this process, are not eternal givens, are not simple products of objective forces outside human control, but are products of human endeavour in the context of given historical circumstances. It is this which in the end explains the great changes that have taken place in sexual definitions over the past two hundreds years. It is this which will account for the changes that will surely take place in the future.

References

1.   Peter G. Richards, *Parliament and Conscience*, p. 82.
2.   See for example: Sexual Law Reform Society, *Report of Working Party on the Law in Relation to Sexual Behaviour*, duplicated 1974; Policy Advisory Committee on Sexual Offences, *Working Paper on the Age of Consent in Relation to Sexual Offences*, HMSO, London, 1979; Joint Working Party on Pregnant Schoolgirls and Schoolgirl Mothers, *Pregnant at School*, National Council for One Parent Families, London, 1979. All these documents were concerned with the age of consent or minimum age for sexual activity; the first and third advocating a reduction of the 'age of consent' to 14, for homosexuals and females. The second was less liberal, suggesting, as a logical continuation of Wolfenden, a minimum age of 18, with a minority recommendation of 16. (It is worth noting that no male member of the Policy Advisory Committee signed the minority report). See also the *Report of the Committee on Obscenity and Film Censorship*, HMSO, London, 1979.
3.   Tracey and Morrison, *Whitehouse*, p. 67.
4.   Ryder and Silver, *Modern English Society*, p. 253; Office of Population Censuses and Surveys figures; *Guardian*, 19 December 1979; 24 September 1979.
5.   Which is not to say that signs of strain were not apparent. Between 1971 and 1976 the proportion of one-parent families rose from 8 to 11 per cent.

6. In some countries the logic of the development led to a decrease of legal marriage. In Sweden and Denmark during the 1970s the marriage rate halved, and cohabitation became common. One estimate suggested that only about 50 per cent of couples under the age of 30 who were living together were married. So between 65 and 75 per cent of all children born technically outside wedlock were born into marriage-like situations. Marriage might be declining but the ideal of the nuclear family was not. *New Society*, 6 December 1979. See also **Jan Trost**, 'The Choice not to Marry', in Marie Corbin (ed.), *The Couple.*
7. Quoted in Hyde, *The Other Love*, p. 303. For further details of the general exhortations to discretion see Weeks, *Coming Out*, pp. 176 ff.
8. 15 June 1972.
9. See **Roy Walmsley** and **Karen White**, *Sexual Offences, Consent and Sentencing*, Home Office Research Study No. 54, London, HMSO, 1979, and the commentary on it in *New Society*, 15 November 1979. For this reason many opposed reducing the age of consent to the new age of majority, 18, because it would only introduce a new threshold. For the working of this logic amongst gay activists in New Zealand, see **Lindsay Taylor**, 'Gay Politics in New Zealand', *Gay Left*, No. 9, 1979.
10. But see **Bob Cant**, 'Living with Indecency', *Gay Left*, No. 8, Summer 1979.
11. This was particularly true in Manchester under Chief Constable James Anderton; and also in certain police districts of London, e.g., around Earls Court.
12. See table in Greenwood and Young, *Abortion in Demand*, p. 70.
13. As was made clear in the *Report of the Lane Committee on the Working of the Abortion Act*, Vol. 1, Cmnd 5579; Vol. 2, Cmnd 5579 – I; Vol. 3, Cmnd 5579 – II, HMSO, London, 1974. The Committee was set up under pressure from backbench MPs.
14. See opinion-poll findings in *The Sunday Times*, 3 Feb. 1980, p. 3, in which only one-third of those questioned thought the law should be tightened up.
15. **Advisory Committee on Drug Dependence**, *Cannabis*, HMSO, London, 1968. For a discussion of the Report see **Jock Young**, *The Drug Takers: The Social Meaning of Drug Use*, Paladin, London, 1971.
16. Quoted in Hall *et al.*, *Policing the Crisis*, p. 250.
17. For documents on 1968, see **Vladimir Fisera** (ed.), *Writing on the Wall: May 1968: A Documentary Anthology*, Allison & Busby, London, 1978.
18. Hall *et al.*, *Policing the Crisis*, p. 242.
19. *Ibid.*, Ch. 8.
20. For **Mary Whitehouse**, see her own *Who does she think she is?*, New English Library, London, 1972; Tracey and Morrison, *Whitehouse*, which is based on papers and interviews with her and her colleagues in NVALA; and **David E. Morrison** and **Michael Tracey**, 'American Theory and British Practice: The Case of Mary Whitehouse and the National Viewers and Listeners Association', in Dhavan and Davies (eds), *Censorship and Obscenity.*
21. Hall *et al.*, *Policing the Crisis*, p. 234.
22. **R. Wallis**, 'Moral Indignation and the Media: An Analysis of N.V.A.L.A.', *Sociology*, Vol. 10, No. 2, May 1976.
23. In *Whitehouse* and in their article, *op. cit.*
24. Quoted in Hall *et al.*, *Policing the Crisis*, p. 314.
25. Quoted in Tracey and Morrison, *Whitehouse*, p. 177.
26. *Ibid.*, pp. 91, 185.

27. **William Haley**, *Moral Values in Broadcasting*, Address to the British Council of Churches, 1948; **Hugh Greene**, 'The Conscience of the Programme Director', Address to the International Catholic Association for Radio and Television, cited in Tracey and Morrison, 'American Theory and British Practice'.
28. The classic statement is *The Longford Report*, 1972; see Tracey and Morrison, *Whitehouse*, p. 181.
29. *Ibid.*, p. 91.
30. *Ibid.*, p. 142. There is a useful summary of the prosecution in *Uncensored: Journal of the Defence of Literature and the Arts Society*, No. 4, Winter 1979/1980.
31. The Protection of Children Act (July 1978) was designed, in the words of its preamble, 'to prevent the exploitation of children by making indecent photographs of them; and to penalise the distribution, showing and advertisement of such indecent photographs'.
32. **David G. Cooper** (ed.), *The Dialectics of Liberation*, Penguin, Harmondsworth, 1968; **Herbert Marcuse**, *One Dimensional Man*, Routledge and Kegan Paul, 1964. On Marcuse, see Paul Robinson, *The Sex Radicals*; and Martin Jay, *The Dialectical Imagination*. See also **Reimut Reiche**, *Sexuality and Class Struggle*, New Left Books, London, 1970.
33. Edmund Leach, in the 1967 Reith Lectures, quoted in Ryder and Silver, *op. cit.*, p. 267. See **R. D. Laing**, *The Divided Self*, Tavistock, London, 1960; **R. D. Laing** and **Aaron Esterson**, *Sanity, Madness, and the Family*, Penguin, Harmondsworth, 1970; **Laing**, *The Politics of the Family and Other Essays*, Tavistock, London, 1971.
34. See **Andrew Rigby**, *Alternative Realities: A Study of Communes and their Members*, Routledge & Kegan Paul, London, 1974; **Ross Speck** *et al.*, *The New Families*, Tavistock, London, 1972 (re USA); M. Schofield, *Promiscuity*, pp. 102–8; **Philip Abrahams** and **Andrew McCullough**, 'Men Women and Communes', in D. L. Barker and Sheila Allen, *Sexual Divisions and Society: Process and Change*.
35. Again best expressed by **Herbert Marcuse**, in *Eros and Civilisation*, Sphere Books, London, 1969 (1st edn 1955).
36. For example, see quotation in *7 Days*, No. 14, 2–8 February 1972, p. 22.
37. Characteristic early feminist texts include **Sheila Rowbotham**, *Women's Liberation and the New Politics*, Spokesman Pamphlet No. 17, Nottingham, 1971; and *Women's Consciousness, Man's World*, Penguin, Harmondsworth, 1973; **Germaine Greer**, *The Female Eunuch*, MacGibbon and Kee, London, 1970; **Juliet Mitchell**, *Women's Estate*, Penguin, Harmondsworth, 1971; see also **Michelene Wandor** (ed.), *The Body Politic: Writings from the Women's Liberation Movement in Britain 1969–1972*, Stage 1, London, 1972.
38. **Beatrix Campbell**, 'Sexuality and Submission', in **Sandra Allen, Lee Saunders** and **Jan Wallis** (eds), *Conditions of Illusion*, Feminist Books, Leeds, 1974, p. 109.
39. See **William Masters** and **Virginia Johnson**, *Human Sexual Response*, Churchill, London, 1966; and *Human Sexual Inadequacy*, Churchill, London, 1970; and the discussion of their work in Paul Robinson, *The Modernization of Sex*. Masters and Johnson became famous as the explorers of physiological response and the uses of marital therapy. Although conservative in the sense that (to a greater degree than Kinsey) they assumed the normality of a marital relationship, their physiological discoveries were

enormously influential. For later work on homosexuality, see their *Homosexuality in Perspective*, Little Brown & Co., Boston, 1979. An English exponent of sex therapy, to some extent in their mould, was Martin Cole. His sex-education film *Growing Up* caused a stir in the early 1970s, though it was heavily criticised by libertarians for its heterosexual assumptions. For his suggestion that young people who are unable to overcome strong sexual inhibitions can be helped by trained volunteers, see the *Guardian*, 5 May 1971.

40. **Mary Jane Sherfey**, *The Nature and Evolution of Female Sexuality*, Random House, New York, 1972, p. 144. She endorses Masters and Johnson's insights on the clitoral orgasm, pp. 142–3; the book is 'gratefully' dedicated to the sex therapists. M. Schofield, *Promiscuity*, pp. 201–2, 208, ff., discusses the impact of the clitoral-orgasm theory.

41. **Angela Hamblin**, 'The Suppressed Power of Female Sexuality', *Shrew*, 1972, republished in *Conditions of Illusion*, pp. 88, 95–6.

42. Campbell, *op. cit.*, p. 101. See also her article in *Feminist Review* No. 5, 1980.

43. See **Susan Hemmings**, 'Horrific Practices: How Lesbians were Presented in the Newspapers of 1978', in **Gay Left Collective** (ed.), *Homosexuality: Power and Politics*, Allison & Busby, London, 1980.

44. The fullest discussion of this is in Weeks, *Coming Out*, on which the following analysis is based.

45. Ray Gosling at a demonstration in Trafalgar Square, quoted in *Coming Out*, p. 185.

46. See for instance Guy Hocquenghem, *Homosexual Desire*.

47. This is discussed in its international context in **Dennis Altman**, 'What Changed in the Seventies', in Gay Left Collective (ed.), *op. cit.*

48. *Ibid.*

49. On bisexuality, see **Charlotte Wolff**, *Bisexuality: A Study*, Quartet, London, 1977. On the evolution of the categories of transvestism and transexuality, see Brian King in Kenneth Plummer (ed.), *The Making of the Modern Homosexual*; and for the political evolution of the category, see Weeks, *Coming Out*, pp. 224–5. On paedophilia, the most controversial of subjects by the late 1970s, see Schofield, *Sociological Aspects of Homosexuality*, which carefully distinguishes paedophilia from homosexuality; **Parker Rossman**, *Sexual Experience Between Men and Boys*, Maurice Temple Smith, London, 1979, which demarcates the category; **Kenneth Plummer**, 'The Paedophiles' Progress. A View from Below', in **B. Taylor**, *Perspectives on Paedophilia*, Batsford, London, 1980; and **Tom O'Carroll**, *Paedophilia: The Radical Case*, Peter Owen, London, 1980. For a general discussion of the theme see K. Plummer, *Symbolic Interaction and Sexual Differentiation, loc. cit.* On the evolution of discussion of heterosexual male sexuality as a response to the women's and gay movements, see **Andrew Tolson**, *The Limits of Masculinity*, Tavistock, London, 1978; and **Paul Hoch**, *White Hero, Black Beast*, Pluto, London, 1980.

50. **Michel Foucault**, 'Power and Sex: An Interview with Michel Foucault', *Telos*, Summer 1977, p. 155.

51. For evidence of a general liberalism in public opinion on sexual issues, despite a general drift to the economic right, see David Lipsey, 'Reforms People Want', *New Society*, 4 Oct. 1979. See also the critique of the conflation of moral and economic conservatism by E. Wilson in *New Left Review*, No. 122, July-Aug. 1980, p. 85.

Index

294   *Sex, Politics and Society*

Bernard, L. L., 143
Bernstein, Edward, 170
Besant, Annie, 46, 163
bestiality, 99, 239
betrothal, 60
Beveridge, Sir William; Beveridge
    Report, 137, 194, 232, 234, 236
Billing, Noel Pemberton, 116
bio-power, 8
biological sex, 2, 6, 11, 143–4, 155–6,
    173
biometrics, 131
Birkenhead, Earl of, 105, 117
Birkett, Sir Norman (Baron); Birkett
    Committee, 71, 117, 187
Birmingham, 72, 220
Biron, Sir Chartres, 117, 218, 219
birth control, *see* contraception
birth rate, 19, 45, 61, 63, 69–70, 122,
    123, 124, 125, 134, 162–3, 187–8,
    194, 201, 202, 233, 259, 270 n33
bisexuality, 102, 152, 155, 173, 287
Blackstone, Sir William, 99
Blackwell, Elizabeth, 41, 42, 44, 161
Blackwell, Sir Ernley, 207
blasphemy, 66, 280
Blatchford, Robert, 171
Blight of Respectability, The,
    (Gallichan), 86
Bloch, Iwan, 142
Bloomsbury, 174
Blunt, Anthony, 241
bodies, sexual potentialities of, 4, 7, 8,
    10, 11
Bodkin, Sir Archibald, 218
Bolsheviks, 167, 184
boom, post war economic, 249–50
Booth, Charles, 31, 60, 124
Boothby, Sir Robert (Baron), 185, 186
Boswell, James, 46
Boulton, Ernest, 101, 111
bourgeoisie, 26–30, 32, 45, 47, 74, 82,
    203
Bowdler, Thomas; bowdlerization, 19, 27
Bowes, Sir John Nott, 240
Bowlby, John, 236
Boy's Own Magazine, 49
Boy's Own Paper, 49
Boy's Penny Magazine, 49
Bradlaugh, Charles, 46, 163, 191
Brandt, Adolf, 172
Brecher, Edward, 206
Bright, Jacob, 41
British Board of Film Censors, 217
British Medical Association, 192, 253,
    262

British Medical Journal, 43, 44, 45, 142,
    253
British Social Hygiene Council, 211, 216,
    237
British Society for the Study of Sex
    Psychology (British Sexological
    Society), 114, 166, 174, 181–4, 212
Broadhurst, Henry, 68
Brook Advisory Centres, 260
Brooke, Emma Frances, 165
brothels, 87, 90, 92, 219
Browne, F. W. Stella, 136, 166, 167, 175,
    182, 183, 187, 188, 193, 195
buggery, *see* sodomy
bullies, 90, 92
bundling, 60
Burgess, Guy, 241
Burt, Sir Cyril, 223
Butler, Josephine, 24, 44, 88, 89, 160,
    161, 164, 221
Butskellism, 278

Caird, Mona, 165, 166
Callaghan, James, 276
camp, 111, 287
Campaign for Homosexual Equality, 286
Campbell, Lord Chancellor, 84
Campbell, Beatrix, 284
Cambridgeshire, 60
Cap, 191, 197 n41
capital punishment, 99, 100, 249, 251
capitalism, 3, 10, 21, 23, 25, 61–2, 82,
    133, 169, 174, 250–1, 266, 276
Carlile, Richard, 41, 46, 69
Carlyle, Thomas, 170
Caroline, Queen, 28
Carpenter, Edward, 19, 92, 104, 109,
    112, 161, 166, 167, 171–5, 180, 181,
    182, 206
Carrington, Charles, 142, 156 n5
Carstairs, Professor G. M., 238, 261
Casement, Sir Roger, 105, 110, 112
Casper, Dr, 104
castration complex, 3
categories, sexual, 5, 11, 285–7
celibacy, 13
censorship, 19, 21, 216, 217, 249, 264,
    280, 281
census, 123
Centuries of Childhood (Ariès), 48
Chaeronea, Order of, 114
Chamberlain, Lord, 217, 264
Chamberlain, Neville, 194
Chance, Janet, 210, 212, 223, 227 n52
Chant, Mrs Ormiston, 92